A PASSION FOR JUSTICE

J. Waties Waring and Civil Rights

Tinsley E. Yarbrough

New York   Oxford
OXFORD UNIVERSITY PRESS

Oxford University Press

Oxford New York
Athens Auckland Bangkok Bogotá Buenos Aires Cape Town
Chennai Dar es Salaam Delhi Florence Hong Kong Istanbul Karachi
Kolkata Kuala Lumpur Madrid Melbourne Mexico City Mumbai Nairobi
Paris São Paulo Singapore Taipei Tokyo Toronto Warsaw

and associated companies in
Berlin Ibadan

First published in 1987 by Oxford University Press, Inc.
Published by Oxford University Press, Inc
198 Madison Avenue, New York, New York 10016

First issued as an Oxford University Press paperback, 2001

Oxford is a registered trademark of Oxford University Press

Library of Congress Cataloging-in-Publication Data

Yarbrough, Tinsley E., 1941-
A passion for justice.
Bibliography: p.
Includes index.
1.Waring, Julius Waties, 1880-1968. 2. Judges—United States—Biography.
3.United States. District Court (South Carolina: Eastern District).
4. Civil rights—United States. I. Title.
KF373.W332Y37 1987 347.73'2234   87-1653
347.307234
ISBN 0-19-504188-7
ISBN 0-19-514715-4 (pbk.)

1 3 5 7 9 8 6 4 2

Printed in the United States of America
on acid-free paper

To
Henry Abraham

Preface

It was Monday, May 17, 1954. Earlier that day in Washington, D.C., the U.S. Supreme Court had held in *Brown* v. *Board of Education*[1] that state-prescribed racial segregation had no place in the field of public education. Amid the jubilation in the NAACP's New York offices that evening, James Hicks, a reporter and columnist for the Baltimore *Afro-American,* filed copy until he had no more to write. Later, Hicks would ask himself why that night, of all nights, he had not gone "celebrating up on Seventh Ave. in Harlem?" But on leaving the NAACP headquarters, he made his way to a small Fifth Avenue apartment overlooking Central Park, the residence "in exile" of Judge and Mrs. Julius Waties Waring.[2]

Hicks was not the only one to do so. Joining the Warings for a hastily arranged party that evening were many prominent figures in the civil rights movement, including NAACP executive director Walter White; board members John Hammond and Palmer Webber; the organization's publicity director Henry Moon; psychologist Kenneth Clark, who had provided controversial expert testimony for the plaintiffs in the school segregation cases; and Alan Paton, author of *Cry the Beloved Country,* an acclaimed account of South African race relations.[3]

They had joined the Warings to celebrate the Court's historic decision. But they had also come to honor their hosts. The rise of Waties Waring to the position of U.S. District Judge for the Eastern District of South Carolina, which he held from 1942 to 1952, had been relatively uneventful and essentially political.

An eighth-generation Charlestonian, with a prestigious Meeting Street address, impeccable social credentials and appropriate ties to such segregationist South Carolina senators as Ellison D. ("Cotton Ed") Smith and Burnet Rhett Maybank, Waring served as assistant U.S. attorney during the Wilson administration and as Charleston corporation counsel in the 1930s and early 1940s before finally obtaining the coveted judgeship. His judicial tenure, however, proved to be anything but uneventful. He ended racial designations on juror lists and other traditionally accepted discriminatory practices within his court; ruled in favor of equal pay for black and white public school teachers; and, in his most controversial rulings, struck down rules of the South Carolina Democratic party limiting membership and participation in the party's primaries to white voters only. He also encouraged Walter White, Thurgood Marshall, and other NAACP officials and counsel to make a direct assault on the "separate but equal" doctrine in the public schools. And when fellow jurists on a three-judge court upheld South Carolina's segregated school system in the first of the suits which eventually culminated in the *Brown* decision, Waring vigorously dissented, becoming the first judge in modern times to contend from the bench that *"Segregation is per se inequality."*[4]

Those gathered at the Waring apartment that evening praised the judge's significant record of service in behalf of civil rights. Walter White claimed, in fact, that it was Judge Waring who had first suggested to the NAACP that it face "the problem head-on" and admit that "there can be no equality as long as there is segregation."[5] Like the Warings, however, their guests could hardly escape a significant irony of that day's momentous events: Chief Justice Earl Warren's opinion for the unanimous *Brown* Court had made no mention whatever of Judge Waring's comments in South Carolina's *Brown* counterpart, which had anticipated the Warren Court's basic rationale. Judge Waring had contended in his dissenting opinion that "the mere fact of segregation, itself, had a deleterious and warping effect upon the minds of children," adding:

> the humiliation and disgrace of being set aside and segregated as unfit to associate with others of different color had an evil and ineradicable effect upon the mental processes of our young which would remain with them and deform their view on life until and throughout their maturity.[6]

The chief justice had quoted instead from the opinion of a Kansas court in the *Brown* case—a court that had reached the same conclusion in similar but milder language, and yet had ruled against the black plaintiffs. Nor was Chief Justice Warren alone in omitting reference to Waring's dissent. Apparently Justice William O. Douglas had rested his conference position in the school segregation cases on Judge Waring's opinion.[7] But the NAACP had not quoted the dissent in its briefs before the Court.

Robert McC. Figg, a Charleston attorney and later dean of the University of South Carolina law school, served as chief counsel for South Carolina through most of the school segregation litigation. He later attributed omission of reference to the Waring dissent to its tone. "If you read his dissent in that case," Figg asserted with vehemence more than thirty years after the *Brown* decision, "you probably were the last man to read it. Because it never was mentioned again. It was so intemperate it never was mentioned again in all the proceedings. The other side never quoted it; the Court never paid any attention to it."[8]

The Supreme Court's strategy in the school segregation cases was to avoid recrimination, attempting instead to appeal to the segregationists' sense of fairness.[9] The tone of the Waring dissent was incompatible with that strategy. In marked contrast to Chief Justice Warren's gentle appeal to the heart, Judge Waring had bluntly depicted segregation as a carryover from the "institution of human slavery"; ridiculed the practice's essential premises as "unreasonable, unscientific and based upon unadulterated prejudice"; and condemned the "sadistic insistence of the 'white supremacists' " on maintaining a segregated society. The immediate eradication of segregation, he concluded, was a "clear and important" necessity,

> particularly at this time when our national leaders are called upon to show to the world that our democracy means what it says and that it is a true democracy and that there is no under-cover suppression of the rights of any of our citizens because of the pigmentation of their skins.[10]

But it was probably not the tone of Waring's dissent alone that made the Supreme Court shrink away from its reference in *Brown*. Years before *Brown,* Judge Waring had become a detested figure among southern segregationists and was thus hardly a useful tool in the cautious approach to desegregation that the Court elected to pursue. Judge Waring had become a controversial figure in Charleston society, in fact, even before his involvement in racial litigation. In 1945, he had divorced his devoted wife of more than thirty years (in Florida—South Carolina then had no provision for divorce) and married Elizabeth Avery, a considerably younger Connecticut matron and Detroit native who had recently begun wintering in Charleston with her second husband. The divorce infuriated Charlestonian society; Waring's civil rights decisions aroused the entire state's white populace. Even more provocative than his decisions, however, were his numerous speeches, interviews, and statements from the bench attacking the "sickness" of southern society, scorning southern liberals who favored a "gradualist" approach to civil rights, and urging federal "force" as the only effective solution to the problem of racial discrimination. If anything, Elizabeth Waring was even more outspoken, condemning the "decadence" of white southerners, applauding the moral superiority of blacks, and advocating total integration, including interracial marriage. To most white Charlestonians, she was the "witch of Meeting Street."

Such harsh attacks raised serious questions of judicial propriety, but the targets of the Warings' scorn were particularly incensed. Except among Charleston blacks, whom, to the horror of neighbors, they began entertaining in their home, the Warings became pariahs in his native community and throughout South Carolina. A cross was burned on their lawn and they were subjected to a steady barrage of abusive mail and telephone calls. Mrs. Waring was jostled on the streets; a federally funded police guard became necessary. The Charleston newspapers dismissed the cross-burning and stoning incidents as probably the pranks of teenagers and insisted that regional ill will for the Warings stemmed more from the circumstances of the judge's divorce and their harsh attacks on white southerners than from opposition to his civil rights decisions. State congressmen and others demanded Waring's impeachment and the South Carolina House of Representatives voted to finance a federal impeachment inquiry and one-way tickets out of the state for the judge and his lady.

Among blacks across the nation, on the other hand, the Warings became heroic, revered figures. The national press depicted them as a courageous couple under seige in what Judge Waring termed a "savage" society, and widely circulated Waring's statement that, as a judge, he had gradually acquired a "passion for justice."[11] But his detractors saw a proud, often petty, aging jurist, dominated by his passion for a younger wife and bent on revenge against a society that refused to accept her.

In 1952, Judge Waring retired from the bench, and he and Mrs. Waring abandoned Charleston for New York, where they lived until their deaths within months of each other in 1968. But they would remain controversial figures in South Carolina long after they died. Following their burial in Charleston, Judge Waring's daughter planted a magnolia tree at the gravesite in their memory. Soon, however, the sapling was uprooted by vandals and had to be replaced.[12] In 1981, a bronze sculpture, presented in Judge Waring's honor by the Charleston chapter of the NAACP, was placed in the southwest corner of the city council chamber, overlooking the federal courthouse.

But, among some Charlestonians, feelings against Judge Waring remain high. Ruby Cornwell, a Charleston black who was perhaps the Warings' closest friend during their controversial last years in South Carolina, recently attended a reception given by the president of the Charleston art association. While talking with other guests, she encountered a lawyer who had been a neighbor of the Warings when they lived on Meeting Street. Assuming that time heals all wounds, she mentioned that she had been the Warings' friend. "This very objectionable little character," she recalls, then lashed out at Judge Waring, condemning his treatment of his first wife and attacks on white Charlestonians. "It was hard for me to believe," she added, "that after all those years, [someone] would still" harbor such feelings.[13]

Whatever the forces motivating Judge Waring, or the weight to be assigned his role in the history of the modern civil rights movement, his life is a fascinating chapter in that history. To date, however, he has been the subject of little extensive research and no published book, even though the enormous influence of lower court judges in a variety of fields is becoming increasingly obvious. What follows is an attempt to fill that void.

Greenville, North Carolina   T.E.Y.
May 1987

Acknowledgments

Whatever J. Waties Waring was, he was not uninteresting. In fact, as I hope this biography makes abundantly clear, Judge Waring was one of the most intriguing figures in the modern civil rights movement. Researching and writing this account of his fascinating and, in some ways, tragic life was hardly a chore; instead, it has been a thoroughly pleasurable experience—although at times also a disturbing one, given the complexities of my subject's personality.

I appreciate the assistance provided by a variety of individuals and organizations. Grants from the National Endowment for the Humanities, East Carolina University research committee, and Southern Regional Education Board provided critical financial support. I am also very grateful to the archival staffs of the College of Charleston, South Carolina Historical Society, Southern Historical Collection at the University of North Carolina at Chapel Hill, Duke University, South Caroliniana Collection at the University of South Carolina, South Carolina state archives, Library of Congress, U.S. Department of Justice, and particularly the Moorland-Spingarn Research Center of Howard University, repository for the expertly organized and indexed J. Waties Waring Papers. As important as the archival material I examined, however, was an extensive file developed on Judge Waring over many years by his nephew Thomas R. Waring, Jr., editor emeritus of the Charleston *News and Courier,* who graciously shared his collection with me. Extremely helpful, too, were recorded interviews with Tom Waring and other Waring contemporaries. I appreciate very much their willingness to discuss their recollections and impressions. In addition, Tom Waring, Eleanor Brown, Ann Mills Hyde, David Mills, and William Jennings Bryan Dorn provided valuable photographs, for which I am grateful.

I wish also to extend my sincere thanks to my colleague and friend Robert J. Thompson, who read the entire manuscript, offering excellent suggestions at each stage of its development; Julia Bloodworth, whose typing was flawless; Susan Rabiner of Oxford University Press, for critical early support; my first-rate Oxford editor Judy Mintz, for guidance throughout the project; Linda Grossman, for superb copyediting—and especially Mary Alice, Sarah, and Cole, whose love, affection, and patience are undeserved but cherished.

Finally, for his many years of encouragement, example, and friendship, my deep appreciation to Henry Abraham, to whom this book is respectfully dedicated.

Contents

A PASSION FOR JUSTICE

1

The S.O.B.'s

Waties Waring's ancestors were early arrivals in South Carolina. Charleston was founded in 1670 along a coastal peninsula between what are now the Ashley and Cooper rivers. Thirteen years later, the year of Charleston's incorporation, Benjamin Waring, the founder of Waties Waring's family in South Carolina, settled on 700 acres of land along the Ashley River and soon became a man of some prominence. In 1693 he was a member of the colonial assembly from Berkeley County; in 1703 and 1711 he served as commissioner of taxes for the north side of the Ashley. His sons Thomas, Benjamin, and Richard also held public offices. William Waties, the first of Waties Waring's maternal Welsh ancestors to migrate to South Carolina, settled on 250 acres of coastal land in 1694.[1]

The Civil War had had a devastating effect on the fortunes of many South Carolinians, including the Waring and Waties families. By the time of Waties' birth on July 27, 1880, however, Charleston's economic recovery was proceeding rapidly. The use of phosphate fertilizer had restored area agricultural production, and in 1882, the state agricultural society held a major exhibition in Charleston to advertise state progress in agriculture since the war. Earlier that year, the U.S. Electric Illumination Co. of Charleston began providing electric lighting for the city, though for a number of years the service would remain largely a novelty item. With a population of more than 52,000, Charleston was by far the state's largest city as well as its major port, rail, and trade center. Voluntary military companies, including such elite independent units as the Charleston Light Dragoons, were numerous and well-organized. Social organizations also thrived in this most socially conscious of southern cities. In 1883, by one count, residents supported more than fifty societies and clubs, not including the Masonic order and other secret organizations. But there was another side to the city's prosperity and social graces. The city's blacks lived a semislave existence. Although they constituted 54 percent of Charleston's population, they possessed less than 4 percent of the total wealth.[2]

The fortunes and social position of the Waring and Waties families had fluctuated widely after the arrival of Benjamin Waring and William Waties two centuries before Waties Waring's birth. Both of Waties' parents came from relatively modest backgrounds. Edward Perry Waring was born in 1848 into a large Charleston family. While a young cadet at the state military academy in Columbia in the last year of the Civil War, he entered the Confederate service. After the war, he married young Anna Thomasine Waties, who had been orphaned at a very early age. At the time of his parents' marriage, Waties Waring would later recall, they were "in pretty bad shape financially." Edward Waring acquired a clerical position with the South Carolina Railroad Co., however, and soon rose to a fairly prominent position with the firm. He remained with the company for twenty-two years. Then the company went into receivership, was swallowed up by the Southern Railway Co., and Waring lost his job and the economic security it had provided in the difficult postwar years. For a period thereafter, the family experienced difficult times. In 1904, however, Waring was elected county superintendent of education, a position he held until his death in 1916. Like his son later, he enjoyed a respected social position as a steward of the South Carolina Society and a member of Charleston's prestigious St. George Society.[3]

Waties Waring recollected his father as a rather handsome extrovert "thoroughly saturated with the Confederate cause. . . . He didn't read much. He read newspapers, current events, and was friendly with people, did his work, but wasn't what you'd call a literary man." His mother, on the other hand, read extensively and was, Waring recalled, "a person of rather independent thought." He enjoyed a close, but different, relationship with each parent.

> [Father] was very fond of children, cheerful, bright fellow that played with kids. He liked to carry on that way. We were awfully fond of father. I think that mother was more intellectual. I talked problems with her more, but I had fun with him.[4]

The differences in his parents' personalities extended to religious matters. Both parents were active Episcopalians, but Edward Waring accepted church doctrine less critically than his wife.

> My father wasn't a great questioner, and he followed along like most Episcopalians who are good churchmen and don't worry too much about doctrine. . . . I don't think religion upsets their mode of life, though I think that it helps their respectability and their ethics.

But his mother "revolted a little bit from strict church doctrine, I think, though she continued to be a member."[5]

Like his mother, Waties ultimately became a questioner. "In my early life, of course, I went to church. I went along, I had to go, but then the regime was relaxed . . . and I was left a good deal to my own devices so that by the time I got through high school and college I began to have a good many questions about the riddle of existence." He never really became antireligious or antichurch, and for a time as a judge he even entertained the notion that churches might lead the fight to eliminate segregation. But he did voice his religious opinions "freely and perhaps lightly." In fact, when he was being considered for a federal judgeship, an intimate friend urged him to avoid the topic. "Don't talk about the church!" Waring would later recall being told. "It'll hurt you. Don't make fun of it!"[6]

Waties had a sister, Margaret, and two brothers, Edward and Thomas Richard. He would remember Tom, nine years Waties' senior, as having perhaps the greatest influence on his life. After schooling in Charleston, Tom had attended an Episcopal college in New York. In their youth, Tom had told his younger brother of the classics and read to him from Greek mythology. When he returned to Charleston from college, he helped Waties with his schooling. Tom "was pretty advanced and liberal in his thoughts," Waties later recalled, "he had a good deal to do with [my] intellectual development, if I ever had any."[7]

Waties' own formal education was confined to Charleston. As a youth he attended the University School, a small private institution with about eighty students and a faculty of three. The school was located at a considerable distance from Waties' home, and he traveled by horsecar to and from school, finding it "quite an adventure" to "swing off without telling the driver to stop." The University School provided a classical curriculum—reading, writing, and arithmetic to begin; then geography, history, Latin, French, and Greek, though Waties escaped Greek.[8]

Academically, Waties gave the school mixed marks. But its headmaster, Walter McKenney, had a significant influence on his life. McKenney "was trained in the Southern tradition . . . a Virginia gentleman, highly educated and cultured," a very ethical man. He maintained an honor system and imbued his boys with its principles.

> If a boy lied, the boys afterwards would probably beat him up. They wouldn't stand for it. You couldn't lie to McKenney. You could do anything you wanted. You could talk, throw spit balls and that sort of thing, but if he said, "Did you do it?" you had to say, "Yes." If you said, "No," he accepted your word, and a new boy coming in that would half lie, McKenny would look at him and say, "I thought I saw you talking, but if you tell me you didn't, of course I'll accept it."
> The fellow would shrivel up and never lie again.
> That was a pretty fine school.

Later in life, Waring gave McKenney "great credit" for his own ethical standards, "if they are right and if I have them."[9]

When Waties was ready to begin college in 1896, his father's financial situation was "going from bad to worse," and Waties enrolled in the College of Charleston. Although a municipal school with only a fair endowment, the college, with several faculty members of excellent ability, provided Waring with a good classical, liberal arts education. He read extensively in the classics, including Virgil, Catallus, Horace, Livy, and Cicero. He became a member and officer in the college literary society, taking an active role in debates, readings, criticism, and orations. He also joined the campus chapter of the Alpha Tau Omega fraternity.

> [W]e were cliquish. We had a fraternity, and we just didn't let them in un-less they were strictly our kind. Fraternities are pretty good things in some respects but they can be awfully aristocratic. I can look back and think of some pretty good fellows who were friends of mine. We turned thumbs down on them just because they didn't quite measure up to what we wanted . . . it was cruel. It had a social implication. Boys that graduated and lived in Charleston and had full access to the highest social circles, if we didn't like them, they didn't come in our fraternity. . . . We liked it. The gov-erning group always likes it. The stricter the rules the better. . . . We were the elite. And unfair.[10]

In 1900 Waties graduated with honors, second in his class.

Near the end of his senior year, Waties decided on a career in law. His maternal great-grandfather, Thomas Waties, a delegate to the South Carolina convention that ratified the U.S. Constitution, had been chancellor of the state court of equity from 1811 until his death in 1828. Waties' maternal grandfather had also been a lawyer, but Waties had no immediate family connection with the law. There had been something of a family consensus, however, that he was to become a lawyer. His mother spoke of it often. His father jokingly referred to him as "Judge," asking often, "How's the Judge today?"[11]

Given the family's financial situation, law school seemed out of the ques-tion, and Waties prepared for the bar examination by reading law. On the day of his graduation from college, he went up to the family cottage in the mountains of North Carolina and read Blackstone's *Commentaries.* To get a flavor for law practice he also visited court in downtown Asheville. Then he returned to Charleston and read law, without fee, in the firm of his father's friend, J. P. Kennedy Bryan. Bryan, a brilliant trial attorney, had been a classmate of Woodrow Wilson at Princeton. Waties did odd jobs about Bryan's office, occasionally serving legal notices, delivering documents, or questioning potential witnesses. Mostly, however, he sat in the corner of the office, reading the state-prescribed course of texts, asking questions of Bryan and other attorneys, and absorbing what he could of his mentor's many years of experience. After two years with Bryan, he went to Columbia and took the bar examination. "At night we were told whether we had passed and went out and got a drink."[12]

Waties passed the bar examination and returned to Bryan's firm, where he was furnished office space and spillover cases from Bryan's practice. Like other young lawyers, he also did real estate title searches for established at-torneys. Eventually, he began to build his own clientele, handling mortgages, drawing contracts, representing indigent defendants, and trying cases in magistrate's court "where the fees weren't big enough for real lawyers to take." He took on the cases of a number of loan-shark victims, but otherwise no sense of the crusader motivated his development of a practice. His immediate career goal was simply a large clientele and a prestigious firm on Broad Street, the city's legal and financial center.[13] As the years passed, he moved steadily toward that goal.

Waring's social position in Charleston continued to rise as well. In 1913, he married Annie Gammell, a well-connected Charleston woman a year his senior. In 1915, they moved into a home Annie Waring had acquired at 61 Meeting Street. The house was a relatively small, two-story stucco, which once had served as the carriage house for a much larger adjacent home.[14] But the address was impeccable. Lying in the shadow of historic St. Michael's church, which the Warings attended, 61 Meeting was situated in the city's residential area south of Broad Street, wherein resided the elite of Charleston society, known to inhabitants and outsiders alike as the "S.O.B.'s."

Early on, Waties also became active in politics. He was not interested in seeking elective office himself, but he did recognize the professional contacts and opportunities political involvement could offer.

> You're delighted when you draw a jury and see some fellow there that you had seen around the polls and had worked with a few months before. Politics gives you a mixture with people and gets you known in the community. I went along taking small parts in the political setup.

Like virtually all Charlestonians and southerners, Waring was a Democrat. Over the years, that association would prove to be a rewarding one in many ways. Initially, it helped to provide him, in 1914, with an appointment as assistant U.S. attorney for South Carolina's eastern district, a position he would hold through the balance of the Wilson administration.

Francis H. Weston, the U.S. attorney under whom Waring served, was an older man, a resident of Columbia, who enjoyed the position and the publicity given his office, but was happy to give his younger assistant a free hand. Taking full advantage of the situation, Waring assigned himself the most interesting cases, handled the bulk of the district's appeals, and developed considerable expertise in federal litigation.[15]

In South Carolina, as elsewhere, there were several terms of federal court each year. A term ran for two weeks, six days a week, from ten o'clock in the morning to five-thirty or six o'clock in the evening, with an hour for lunch. On that schedule, Waring processed many cases each term. Grand juries posed few problems, rarely refusing to indict in cases Waring brought before them. "The truth of the matter," Waring later recalled, "is that I adopted somewhat a system [in which] I always took a lot of sure-fire cases and put them before the grand jury first so that they got confidence in me." His caseload ran the gamut—a celebrated shipboard murder; counterfeiting; mail fraud; land condemnation; wartime sabotage; and, under what Waring considered the "terrible" Volstead Act, a plethora of liquor violations. The latter "I used to try like they used to say about John L. Sullivan when he talked about training, 'All I need is a haircut and a shave.' Liquor cases I just tried by ear a good deal."[16]

Undoubtedly the most notorious case of Waring's tenure as assistant U.S.

attorney grew out of the outbreak of World War I. On August 4, 1914, the freight steamer *Liebenfels* arrived in Charleston harbor with a cargo of fertilizer. Germany and Britain had recently broken relations, and the ship's captain was fearful of venturing back to sea after unloading his cargo on the Charleston docks. Instead, the *Liebenfels* dropped anchor in the Cooper River. The ship's East Indian crew was eventually taken off the ship and returned to their homeland, but the German officers and crew remained aboard ship, living in Charleston harbor. Charleston had a large German population, and the ship's crew mixed extensively with the city's citizenry.[17]

As German-American relations deteriorated, however, the situation changed. In the early morning of February 1, 1917, the day fixed by the German government for the resumption of unrestricted submarine warfare, the *Liebenfels* was spotted partially sunk in the harbor. Two tug captains offered assistance, but the ship's captain refused aid. It was quickly determined that the *Liebenfels* posed no obstacle to entry at the Charleston Navy Yard but was a hazard to other navigation. On February 2, the port collector took possession of the ship and placed guards on board. Eventually, the *Liebefels* was raised, equipped, renamed the U.S.S. *Houston,* and put into the service of American forces.

Soon after its sinking, Waring, U.S. attorney Weston, and the port collector boarded the *Liebenfels* for an inspection. Their investigation revealed that much of the ship's equipment had been intentionally damaged, and they suspected that the captain and crew had sabotaged the vessel to prevent its falling into American hands. In mid-February, Waring secured an arrest warrant against the captain, J. R. Klattenhoff, and eight crewmen. In March, the crewmen were convicted in Florence, South Carolina, of sinking the *Liebenfels* but acquitted of conspiracy. In June, Klattenhoff, who had been ill when the crewmen were tried, pleaded guilty to sinking the *Liebenfels* but not guilty of conspiracy. In October, he was tried in Aiken, South Carolina, on the conspiracy count.

Tried along with Klattenhoff was Paul Wierse, an editorial writer and state news editor for the pro-German Charleston *American*. The government contended that Wierse had served as a go-between in the conspiracy for Klattenhoff and the German consul in Atlanta, who was believed to have fled the United States for Ecuador. The consul had received instructions regarding the *Liebenfels* from the German government, and Wierse allegedly had delivered messages from the consul to the captain.

The Aiken trial reflected the current divisions in Charleston politics almost as much as the legal issues the case had raised. Chief counsel for Wierse, as he had been for the *Liebenfels* crewmen, was John P. Grace, owner of the Charleston *American* and perhaps the most colorful and controversial of the city's politicians of that period. Grace had served as Charleston's mayor from 1911 to 1915 and would be elected for another term in 1919. Though at times a demagogue and not above occasional race-baiting, Grace was something of a progressive for his time—campaigning against "special privilege," monopoly, and the city's "bluebloods"; inaugurating numerous improvements in city services; even blasting that most venerable of Charleston social institutions, the St. Cecilia Society.[18]

Frank Weston made a closing argument, but Waties Waring had developed the government's case and had examined all witnesses. Squaring off in the courtroom, Waring and Grace seemed to personify the Charleston aristocracy and the challenge that Grace posed for much of that tradition. In fact, although repeatedly overruled by the presiding judge, Grace attempted to depict the case as a persecution of the *American* by the aristocratic owners of the leading Charleston papers, the *News and Courier* and *Evening Post.* The effort failed. Waring produced an incriminating letter and telegrams. Two of the convicted crewmen also testified for the government. Ironically, one of them, August Neuse, would settle in Charleston, marry, join the police force, and serve as a guard for Judge Waring when, over a quarter century after the *Liebenfels* affair, the judge himself became a threat to Charleston traditions. After less than an hour's deliberation, the jury returned guilty verdicts against both Wierse and Klattenhoff.

Had the Democrats retained control of the presidency in the election of 1920, Waring might have become U.S. attorney. Given the paucity of South Carolina Republicans, he might reasonably have been expected to keep his federal position even under a Republican administration. But Warren G. Harding was elected in 1920, and Waring did not like the "smell" of the Justice Department under the president's attorney general. While assistant U.S. attorney, moreover, he had been allowed to continue developing his private practice and naturally had also acquired substantial expertise in the field of federal trial litigation—skills of considerable value to other lawyers as well as clients.[19]

Waring decided, therefore, to leave his federal position and return to private practice. Before his appointment, he had a solo law practice, then briefly became a partner in the firm of von Kolnitz and Waring before returning to solo practice. Now he formed a Broad Street partnership with David A. Brockinton.

D. A. Brockinton was a decade younger than Waring. Reared on a plantation in Williamsburg County, he had worked his way through law school at the University of South Carolina. After a stint as a law clerk for a judge of the U.S. Court of Appeals for the Fourth Circuit in Richmond, he settled in Charleston, married a local woman, and joined the firm of Alfred Huger, a prominent admiralty attorney. Brockinton's wife was the daughter of Wilson G. Harvey, who later would serve as governor of South Carolina. A widower, Harvey had married Waties Waring's sister Margaret, and primarily through that relationship Waring and Brockinton became close friends. Wilson Harvey owned a bank specializing in commercial and farm loans, and he suggested that Waring and Brockinton form a partnership to handle the bank's legal business. In 1920, the firm was established.[20]

Waring and Brockinton thrived through the 1920s. Brockinton specialized in real estate and admiralty/maritime law. Waring's brother Tom was editor of the *Evening Post,* and the firm became counsel for the *Post* and the *News and Courier*. Not surprisingly given Waring's background, the firm also developed a large federal practice. During the 1920s and 1930s they acquired a substantial number of business clients, including insurance companies, the local S. H. Kress and Co. five-and-dime store, and the West Virginia Pulp and Paper's Co.'s Charleston area interests.[21]

The Depression came late to Charleston. By 1932, however, the city's economy was in grim shape. Banks were failing, businesses collapsing, unemployment rising. Like other firms, Waring and Brokinton fell on relatively difficult times.[22] But again, Waring's political connections, which he had continued to cultivate, would prove valuable.

In 1931, city alderman Burnet Rhett Maybank took office as Charleston's mayor. A handsome patrician in his early thirties, Maybank was a well-to-do cotton broker who later would serve as South Carolina governor (1939–41) and U.S. senator (1941–54). Maybank spoke a low country dialect with a very broad accent, generally fitting the stereotypical image of the aristocratic southern politician. The story is told that someone once asked who was sitting next to Maybank in the Senate chamber and was told, "Oh, don't you know, that's his interpreter." And when he died, a Senate colleague, in a funeral eulogy, is reported to have remarked: "We all knew Burnet. We all loved Burnet. We all wanted to do what Burnet wanted us to do—if we could just have understood what that was."[23]

Waring was Maybank's friend and political mentor and had worked actively in his bitter, hotly contested mayoralty campaign.[24] Maybank invited Waring to join his administration, and the city council elected him corporation counsel, or city attorney, a position he would hold until his appointment as district judge. Maybank's terms as governor and senator would be relatively undistinguished, but he forged an outstanding record as mayor in one of the most difficult periods in Charleston's history. By all accounts, Waring played perhaps the key advisory role in Maybank's administration.[25] Maybank's successor, Henry Lockwood, a rough-and-ready politician without Maybank's business and financial background, would be even more dependent on Waring's skills.[26]

During his administration, Maybank brought in a paper mill (which Waring and Brockinton represented) and built five public housing projects. He knew President Franklin D. Roosevelt and developed close ties with Washington, especially with Works Progress Administration head Harry Hopkins. With WPA backing, in 1937 Maybank's administration established Charleston's Dock Street Theater, a replica of eighteenth-century London theaters that would become a major addition to the city's cultural life. Maybank also backed creation of the Santee-Cooper project, which provided the area with cheap electric power.[27]

But Maybank's greatest triumph—and the one with which Waring was perhaps most closely associated—was the city's financial recovery from the Depression. Shortly after Maybank took office, People's Bank, the Broad Street concern in which all city revenues were deposited, failed. A lawsuit was brought against the bank to protect the city's interests, but Waring lost that battle; ultimately the city was treated as an ordinary depositor, recovering only about a quarter of its funds. Charleston also had what, for that period, was a heavy bonded indebtedness of over $3 million, which was then coming due; and many taxpayers had fallen woefully behind in their obligations to the city.[28]

Charleston's old-line financial interests were of little help. But with Waring providing the legal expertise—and cautioning his free-wheeling friend against courses bordering on the illegal—Maybank, who was something of a financial wizard, devised a number of effective measures for coping with the city's financial difficulties. To pay salaries of city employees and meet other current obligations in the face of the People's Bank failure, the city issued scrip, redeemable at 4 percent interest at the end of the year when city taxes came due. Merchants and others initially objected to the scrip arrangement, but it gradually won acceptance. To meet the bond obligations, Maybank persuaded bondholders to surrender the old bonds for new ones at a more favorable interest rate. A campaign was also begun to persuade citizens to pay their taxes, and discount incentives were offered for advance payment. With taxpayers who were chronically unable to meet their obligations, the city foreclosed and sold their property. Such measures were successful. At the end of the first year, the city met all its scrip obligations and even had a surplus. By the end of the second year, Charleston's administration had gained a sound financial footing.

While the city's financial problems occupied much of Waring's attention during his early years as corporation counsel, much of the work throughout his tenure was to be of the routine sort confronting any city administration. In 1934, he advised the council regarding a request from businesses along King Street to install sidewalk ventilators. Stringent provisions, he warned, were needed to assure the safety of pedestrians and the city's immunity from liability for accidents. In 1935, he drafted ordinances to regulate radio noise and garbage collection. Concerns requiring his attention in 1941 included barking dogs at a King Street residence and littering at a soda shop on Rutledge Avenue.[29]

On occasion, he cautioned the council against unduly extending its regulatory arm. In a letter to Mayor Lockwood, dated October 14, 1941, he opposed a proposal that the council become a judicial body to hear complaints against public nuisances:

> If the suggested plan were adopted the City officials would spend a large part of their time passing upon numerous minor complaints and would have to determine all disputes and disagreements between neighbors. The City would soon find itself in a position where it would bring a suit for A to enjoin B from burning bright lights upon the premises, and in a cross action represent B in preventing A from having barking dogs. I have always been of the opinion that the City where ever possible refrain from interfering in private quarrels. When it comes to places of business, such as beer parlors, amusements, bus depots or other places open to the use of the public, the police should be instructed to see that such places are run decently and

properly and that any objectionable, improper or immoral conduct is not tolerated. The police have plenty of access to these places and should in-vestigate and see that the law is obeyed.[30]

A year earlier, in a letter to August J. Tamsberg, clerk of the council, he assumed the same stance in reacting to the council's concerns about "profane language, disorderly conduct, noise, crowing of roosters and barking of dogs." He doubted the council would want to take the "drastic" step of banning chickens or dogs from the city and contended that it would be "practically impossible" to regulate the noise they create. Current ordinances, he added, were adequate to deal with the other sources of council concern. Waring prided himself on giving each issue, significant or trivial, the same methodical attention. Evidently, the council, Maybank, and Henry Lockwood were satisfied. Each year until his elevation to the federal bench, he was overwhelmingly reelected, often by a unanimous vote.[31]

Waring's handling of racial issues while corporation counsel was also entirely acceptable to the council as well as compatible with Charleston customs, offering little inkling of his later civil rights accord. In the environment in which Waring was raised, slavery had not ended with the Civil War. The master-slave relationship continued to exist; it simply lost its formal status. Those in Waring's class viewed it as essentially "a kindly, happy, understanding" arrangement. As a child, he had a black nurse, an ex-slave of the Warings named Hannah. Waring never knew whether she had a last name. Her husband, a powerfully built ex-slave named James, worked on the Charleston docks. Often he was jailed for public drunkenness, and Waring's father paid his fine, complaining mildly to Mrs. Waring: "why does he go off and get into trouble! It's going to cost me five or ten dollars again." Later, Waties Waring would come to recognize the inherent evils of this paternalism.

> [I]t's a pretty pleasant thing to be brought up in . . . if you're on the paternal side. It's like any kind of autocratic government. It's pretty nice if you're on the right side. I thought that the Russian Czarist government was a wonderful thing if you were a grand duke, but that it was hell if you weren't.

Through most of his life, however, Waring accepted southern racial mores without really questioning them.

> Most of the Negroes I knew were ex-slaves and you loved them, were good to them. We didn't give them any rights, but they never asked for any rights, and I didn't question it.[32]

Late in life, Brockinton would recall that his law partner seemed ill at ease around blacks and "really didn't understand the southern Negro." There were no black attorneys in Charleston, and the firm had many black clients. Waring generally preferred that Brockinton, who had been reared on a plantation, handle the cases their black clients brought to them. August Tamsberg, the clerk of the council during much of Waring's tenure as corporation counsel, remembered that Waring was respectful of blacks and, unlike Mayor

Maybank, did not address them by their first names in correspondence. In conversation, however, Tamsberg "never heard Waring refer to a black man or a black woman as 'Mr.' or 'Mrs.' It was always John or Sarah."[33]

Waring's defense of southern racial tradition while corporation counsel was revealed most clearly, perhaps, in city negotiations with the Army completed just forty-five days before his nomination to the federal bench. The issue in question arose over the lease of Charleston's Stoney Field to the Army as a recreational area. Paragraph 15 of the lease provided: "The use of the property shall be strictly limited to soldiers of the White or Caucasian Race." The area corps commander had no objection to this policy. In fact, his subordinate assured Charleston officials that the general would "never approve the use of the Charleston Recreational Area for any soldiers but those of the white or Caucasian race." The general simply believed that the more expedient course would be to handle the matter "administratively" rather than "as a part of an official document." As a substitute guarantee, the military offered a written statement, to be signed by appropriate officers and filed with the clerk of the city council, assuring that only whites would use Stoney Field.[34]

Waring found this suggestion "not entirely satisfactory." If the letter the general proposed be "in any way binding," Waring wrote the Army, "it would be an official document. If the letter is not an official document then it would not be binding." More important, he was concerned about the impression that might be created by deleting the whites-only clause from the proposed lease. "[T]o have this paragraph appear and be cancelled," he contended, "would practically be an affirmation of the use of the recreational area by troops other than white or caucasian." Waring suggested that if the Army continued to insist that the clause be deleted, an entirely new lease be drawn, omitting Paragraph 15. That course was followed and use of Stoney Field was limited to white soldiers.[35]

While corporation counsel, Waring continued to maintain close ties to Charleston and state politics. For years he was president of Ward One's Democratic club. He was also a member of the county party's platform committee, served as floor leader at county conventions, and filled the role of legal adviser to the county executive committee.[36] In 1938, service in that latter capacity further cemented his relationship with Burnet Maybank. That year Maybank made a bid for the Democratic gubernatorial nomination. He led seven other candidates in the first primary but failed to secure the majority needed to avoid a runoff campaign. Maybank's opponent in the second primary was Wyndham M. Manning, a farmer, ex-legislator, and son of a former South Carolina governor. In a particularly bitter campaign, Manning depicted Charleston as a veritable cesspool of corruption and charged Maybank with seeking to inject "machine politics" into state government; while Maybank, promising a "business-like" administration, cited his successes as mayor and as charman of the state agency then overseeing the $37 million WPA-financed Santee-Cooper power project.[37]

When the votes were counted, Manning led Maybank by about 6,000 votes elsewhere in the state. In Charleston County, however, Maybank won 21,864 to Manning's 1,374. An astonishing 95.5 percent of the Charleston electorate was reported to have voted.[38]

Manning cried fraud—not an unnatural reaction given Charleston's rather seamy election history. At his request, Governor Olin D. Johnston, a Manning supporter, ordered a national guard unit to enter Charleston's historic Hibernian Hall and maintain a vigil over the County's yellow tin ballot boxes until the state Democratic executive committee could hear Manning's challenge. When the former legislator announced that he might also protest the results of four other low country counties, the state party chairman ordered ballot boxes sealed there also.[39]

Maybank was Charleston County's representative on the state committee, but he obviously could not participate in its review of the Manning challenge. Consequently, he resigned his seat on the committee, and the local party elected Robert McC. Figg, then county solicitor and a Maybank partisan, as the mayor's replacement. Figg's selection assured another Maybank vote as well as a spokesman for the mayor's interests in the event that the committee went into executive session following a public hearing. Waties Waring was to be Maybank's chief counsel before the committee. With the help of assistant corporation counsel William Ehrhardt, Gus Tamsberg, and other Maybank stalwarts, Waring began collecting affidavits and developing a strategy for countering the Manning charges.[40]

One blunder by the Manning forces proved helpful to Waring's efforts. On the Sunday before the state committee's Tuesday session, the captain of the national guard unit, on orders from Governor Johnston, opened the ballot boxes and allowed a Manning lieutenant and four stenographers to inspect the voter rolls, though not the ballots. Henry Lockwood was then chairman of the county party organization. When he and other committee members protested the captain's action, they were escorted from the room where the ballots were under guard—at bayonet point, according to Lockwood's charges. The guard captain denied that bayonets were used and insisted that committee members could have remained in the room while the inspection continued. But Lockwood and other committee members complained to reporters that the committee could not be a party to illegal action, and a large crowd of angry Maybank partisans gathered outside the hall. The crowd eventually dispersed, and the Manning group left the city. But the Maybank forces could now claim that the Manning people had violated the sanctity of the ballot box.[41]

Armed with affidavits and backed by a delegation of twenty-five citizens, Maybank and Waring left Charleston September 19 for the executive committee hearing the following day in Columbia. At the hearing, Manning's counsel submitted eighteen affidavits claiming numerous election irregularities and petitioned the committee to void the Charleston returns. Among other allegations, they charged that the Charleston boxes had not been kept locked on primary day, that poll managers had allowed voting by persons not on the election rolls, that the managers had advised voters how to vote and wore

Maybank election buttons, that city police had attempted to influence voters and stuffed ballot boxes (Lockwood was then police commissioner), that "floaters" had voted at more than one polling place, that a number of tally sheets had been completed in advance of the counting of ballots, and that in some wards the number of votes cast exceeded the number of eligible voters! Of Maybank's remarkable 95.5 percent of the Charleston vote, a Manning spokesman drily observed: "the nearest I ever heard of this—I do not mean any reflection—was Hitler getting 98 percent. . . . To any reasonable person the whole thing was wrong and wrong throughout."[42]

Waring characterized Manning's affidavits as "false and slanderous" and presented affidavits designed to cast doubt about the credibility and general character of the Manning affiants. A member of the county party committee charged, for example, that a woman who supported Manning's charges had told him that she held Maybank responsible for a relative's discharge from a city job. It was learned that another Manning affiant had once stolen a cow. Given the assaults Manning had made on Charleston during the campaign, Waring added, Maybank's margin of victory there was not surprising. "The astonishing thing was not that Maybank received over 20,000 votes," Waring exclaimed, "but that Manning received more than 1,300."[43]

Assisting Waring, Donald Russell, a Spartanburg attorney who later would become a prominent figure in South Carolina politics, also challenged the Manning force's concern about the mayor's margin. "My friend talks about Hitler! Who used the bayonet . . . ? It was not Burnet Maybank." Capitalizing further on the Hitlerian allusion, Waring challenged the Manning force's "illegal" inspection of the Charleston rolls, asserting, "Are you going to decide" the issue "on the Democratic law or on the military law?" For his part, Bob Figg—perhaps reflecting on Charleston elections of the past—called the primary "the finest, cleanest, squarest election I have seen."[44]

Ultimately, however, simple arithmetic proved the decisive weapon in Waring's arsenal. Responding to a question from Edgar A. Brown, a powerful figure in South Carolina politics for decades, Waring reported that if all the boxes challenged by Manning were discarded, Maybank's Charleston majority would still be 11,850. A committee member pointed out that, under state law, an election permeated with fraud must be voided and a new one ordered. Others begged the committee to continue the inquiry. But Edgar Brown wondered aloud, to applause from other committee members, why the statements "of 18 persons" should "disenfranchise 20,000." And that attitude prevailed. With five members and Governor Johnston not voting, the committee decided 41–0 to reject Manning's challenge and declare Maybank the nominee. The member who moved dismissal of Manning's protest was "absolutely convinced," however, "that fraud permeated this election in Charleston from A to Z." The Manning supporter who made the motion declaring Maybank the primary victor agreed, warning: "Henceforth we call on the good, the honest and the decent people of Charleston to conduct their elections in such a way that we won't have to wash their dirty linen."[45]

Waring's political connections also led to an association with South Carolina's colorful senior senator Ellison DuRant ("Cotton Ed") Smith. Smith, first elected to the Senate in 1908, was born in 1864 on a 2,000-acre Lynchburg plantation that had been in his family since his English forebears settled there in 1690. He had earned his nickname as a leader of a movement to organize southern cotton growers early in the century, and he cherished the title. In his first Senate campaign, Smith, who was a spellbinding orator, proclaimed his devotion to "my sweetheart, Miss Cotton" while wearing a cotton boll in his lapel and perched atop two bales in a wagon drawn by mules plastered with lint.[46]

Despite deep ties to South Carolina's Bourbon aristocracy, and with an odd combination of progressive and conservative views, "Cotton Ed" waged a continuous battle against the tariff, Wall Street, big business, and other Populist enemies, while opposing federal child labor legislation and woman suffrage. "I don't know why women want any more power than they have already," he said on more than one occasion. "They run everything now."[47] But he was a reliable supporter of most of Woodrow Wilson's program and an early backer of Franklin D. Roosevelt. "Cotton Ed" played little role, however, in shaping New Deal farm policies, as he opposed crop controls, and had little enthusiasm for the WPA, the National Recovery Administration (NRA), and other agencies that threatened the South's social and economic structure. After 1935, he became more openly hostile to the Roosevelt administration; in 1938 he faced (and easily overcame) primary opposition endorsed by the White House.

Through much of his political career, Smith avoided race-baiting. In fact, Ku Klux Klan opposition and his support for the World Court almost cost him the election of 1926, when his opponent, Edgar Brown, claimed that the court's membership included three black judges. As he became more outspoken in his opposition to Roosevelt, however, "Cotton Ed" also became more demagogic, unleashing vitriolic Senate tirades against blacks and antilynching legislation. In his 1938 campaign, he regaled his audiences with the "Philadelphia Story"—his well-publicized walkout from the 1936 Democratic convention when a black appeared on the program.

Smith's racial diatribes became so dominant a part of the 1938 campaign that several of his advisers, apparently including Waties Waring, suggested that he devote more of his stump speeches to agriculture and foreign affairs. Smith took that advice, but only briefly. As he was explaining the refinements of national policy to one backwoods gathering, a one-gallused farmer stood up in the audience and got quickly to the point. "Aw, cut all that out, Ed," the farmer pleaded, "and tell us about Philadelphy." From that point on, the story ran, Smith followed the farmer's advice.[48]

Frank Weston, the U.S. attorney with whom Waring had previously served, was Smith's campaign manager for years, and Waring initially developed ties to "Cotton Ed" through Weston. Gradually, their association grew into a close and enduring relationship. Waring played an active role in Smith's campaigns, serving as his Charleston campaign manager and intimate political adviser. Waring's brother Tom, who had been editor of the *Evening*

Post, died in 1935. But Tom's son, Thomas R. Waring, Jr., had joined the *News and Courier* in 1927 and became its city editor in 1931. Whenever Smith was to visit Charleston, Waties Waring telephoned his nephew to arrange for an interview or some other publicity—an assignment Tom, Jr., often personally fulfilled.[49]

Waties Waring seemed genuinely fond of "Cotton Ed." In 1944, shortly after his defeat by Olin Johnston in yet another campaign to retain his Senate seat, Smith died. On learning of his friend's death, Waring gave the following statement to the press: "As an old friend and supporter of Senator Smith, I am shocked to hear of his sudden death. He had a long and honorable career and his passing will be mourned by the people of his state."[50] Even after his years on the federal bench, moreover, Waring would remember "Cotton Ed" affectionately.

> He was a good deal of a demagogue . . . his racial talks were to get the boys in the backwoods to vote for him, and they did. . . . I didn't have any admiration or particular respect for his opinions or the way he went on, but I had a kind of sneaking fondness for him. He was a nice old chap in a great many ways and very amusing and could make a wonderful speech to a half literate group of voters.[51]

Ultimately, both Senator Smith and Burnet Maybank would prove instrumental in Waring's elevation to the federal bench. In 1930, Waring had been a strong but unsuccessful candidate for U.S. attorney in his district, losing apparently largely because of his ties to the Charleston newspapers and their opposition to Prohibition. He was principally interested, however, in a federal judgeship. There were three district judgeships in South Carolina—one for the eastern district with a seat at Charleston, another for the western portion of the state, and a third "roving" judgeship sharing the caseload of the eastern and western districts. Waring had harbored an interest in the eastern district judgeship since his days as assistant U.S. attorney. In early 1934, Ernest F. Cochran, the presiding judge for the eastern district, committed suicide. Waring became a leading contender for the position, and his supporters bombarded the Justice Department with letters. Senator Smith offered his endorsement. A number of Charlestonians surveyed by the Justice Department in its investigation of his credentials focused on his "cold, aloof" personality. One indicated, for example, that Waring "might not forget an enemy, although he . . . did not believe that Waring would allow personal likes and dislikes to influence him in the decision of a case." Others claimed that he might prove to be a "dictator on the Bench," that defendants would be presumed guilty in his court, that he was "very smart, so much so that his smartness borders on insolence," and that he was "lacking in 'humanity.' " But each person interviewed praised his intellect, integrity, efficiency, and reputation; several suggested that his "impersonal disposition" was "a desirable quality for a Judge"; and his nomination seemed likely. To Waring's astonishment, however, the position went to Frank Kerchner Myers, a Charleston lawyer and equity master in the state chancery court. Myers' credentials were marginal at best. But he was a longtime friend of James F. Byrnes, South Carolina's junior senator; and while the two were working as young men for Mordecai and Gadsden, a prominent Charleston firm, Byrnes was supposed to have promised Myers a judgeship "when I became United States senator." Byrnes endorsed Myers. On this occasion, Burnet Maybank's political clout was of no help to Waring either. Maybank initially had indicated that he would support Waring for the position, but Frank Myers was Maybank's father-in-law.[52]

In 1939, when the judge then holding the "roving" judgeship died, Waring was again mentioned as a potential nominee. He quickly squelched that rumor, however, telling reporters that, though "personally flattered" to be considered, he was not a candidate. "It seems reasonable to suppose," he added, "that the third judge should be appointed from some section of the state other than Charleston. At any rate I have no thought of nor aspiration for this appointment; have made no effort to obtain it, and hope that none will be made in my behalf."[53]

In August 1940, after several years of declining health, Frank Myers died of cancer. Then, in the spring of 1941, another vacancy was created when Senator Byrnes assumed a position on the U.S. Supreme Court and Judge Alva M. Lumpkin resigned from the "roving" judgeship to assume Byrnes' Senate seat pending a special election. Waties Waring had maintained close ties with Senator Smith. Maybank, moreover, was now governor and a strong contender for the U.S. Senate seat vacated by Byrnes. At first blush, therefore, Waring's prospects for one of the vacant positions seemed excellent.

Eventually, Waring was to replace Judge Myers on the Charleston bench. For a number of reasons, however, the process would prove lengthy and complicated. For one thing, Waring's firm represented the *News and Courier,* perhaps the South's most vehemently anti-Roosevelt paper; his law partner, D. A. Brockinton, openly detested "Rooseveld." For another, "Cotton Ed" Smith's preferences hardly carried much weight with the administration, and apparently for a lengthy period he submitted no recommendations to the Roosevelt Justice Department.[54]

Most troublesome for Waring was the current status of his relationship with Burnet Maybank. For reasons now largely obscure, the two had drifted apart after Maybank became governor. On several occasions after Judge Myers' declining health had become apparent, Maybank had promised to support Waring as his father-in-law's replacement. But after Myers' death, Waring had heard nothing from his old political comrade. Instead, he had heard rumors of Maybank's promise to support others for the position. Then one day, as the governor was preparing to campaign for Byrnes' Senate seat, Maybank paid a surprise visit to Waring's office and asked Waring to manage his campaign in Charleston County.

> I said [Waring would later recall], "I don't know whether I can do that or not. You've put me in a very awkward position. The federal judgeship is open. You remember our former conversation." I reminded him that he had spoken to me about the judgeship two or three times. Perhaps condi-

tions changed. I told him that I was not repeating that in any way as a pledge, that he was entirely free. But that put me in a very awkward position because my friends were all asking me, "What does Maybank say about the judgeship?", and if I came out as his manager I would have to tell them that he had pledged to support me or that he hadn't and that I left it entirely to him. He said that he couldn't say anything about it at that time, that he couldn't commit himself. I said, "Neither can I. I'll vote for you but that's all."

Maybank left Waring's office "pretty disgruntled," and Waring "charged the judgeship off my mental calendar."[55]

For months, no action was taken on either vacancy. Several months before his appointment to the Supreme Court, Senator Byrnes had submitted to the Justice Department a list of thirteen names of lawyers that the senator thought "well qualified" for the eastern district seat. The list included Waring. The senator also named John Cosgrove, law partner of John P. Grace and corporation counsel during Grace's tenure as mayor of Charleston. Cosgrove was no friend of Waring's. When he later learned that he was no longer under consideration for the position, he and other members of the Charleston bar promoted Robert McC. Figg as an alternative to Waring. Figg did nothing to discourage their efforts, but his candidacy also made little progress.[56]

On October 1, 1941, after Maybank's election but before he had joined Senator Smith in Washington, Smith visited Attorney General Francis Biddle and presented him with a list of ten potential nominees. Christie Benet, a prominent Columbia lawyer, appeared first on the list; Waring's name appeared second. Smith declined to reveal the names on the list to reporters but said that all had his "hearty endorsement." "Cotton Ed" also complained to the press about the lengthy delay in the selection of nominees and warned that he must be reckoned with in the selection process.[57]

In early November, Attorney General Biddle wrote Maybank, seeking the new senator's impressions. A copy of Smith's list was attached to the Biddle letter. Maybank promptly responded, indicating that he would agree to any of Smith's choices, but adding:

> The first vacancy created was in the eastern district. The second man on the list recommended by Senator Smith is Mr. J. Waties Waring, of Charleston. I join in this recommendation by Senator Smith of Mr. Waring for judge of the eastern district.[58]

For the "roving" judgeship, however, Maybank suggested George Bell Timmerman, Lexington and Batesburg attorney, farmer, former legislator, former chairman of the state highway commission, and Democratic party leader, whose name did not appear on Smith's list. On the basis of Maybank's letter to Biddle, the senator's choice of Timmerman seemed solely a matter of geography.

> As to the appointment of a judge for the eastern and western districts [Maybank wrote Biddle], the headquarters of this judge are in Columbia. I rec-

ommend for the appointment Mr. George Bell Timmerman of Lexington, S.C. Lexington is approximately 15 miles from Columbia.[59]

One evening in mid-December Maybank telephoned Waring from Washington to report that the president was submitting his name and Timmerman's to the Senate the following day and to emphasize that the matter should be kept confidential pending a White House announcement. Waring was elated but shocked by the news, later recalling, "I almost fainted."[60] Although its contents differ in detail from Waring's recollection of a telephone call, Waring may have written the following, somewhat cryptic, undated handwritten note to Maybank during this same period.

> Received your wire and late yesterday after[noon] your letter. Shall keep same entirely confidential not even referring to its subject matter herein. Many *thanks*. Hope the entire matter will be cleared up soon and looking forward to seeing you when you come to Charleston. If other matters arise relative to appointments to which you hereto referred, call me either at office or house. Shall be out of town Tuesday or Wednesday but office can reach me. Many, many thanks.
>
> Waties[61]

Years later, Bob Figg contended that Senator Smith "couldn't have gotten the Apostle Paul appointed" to a federal position and inisted that Maybank actively campaigned for Waring, meeting at one point with the president at the White House to answer concerns about Waring's age and counter other objections to his nomination. Waring himself later speculated that, in the face of mounting political pressure from Timmerman's backers, Maybank had decided to endorse Waring in exchange for Smith's backing of Timmerman.[62]

There is some evidence to support Waring's thesis that Maybank and Smith struck a bargain. In his November letter to Biddle, Maybank conceded that Timmerman's name had not been on Smith's October list, but assured the attorney general that Timmerman was "a friend and political supporter of Senator Smith," adding: "I feel satisfied he will have no objection to him." According to the attorney general, moreover, Smith told a Biddle assistant on November 27 that Waring and Timmerman were acceptable and, at the assistant's request, wrote a letter to that effect. On the morning of December 4, Biddle himself called on Smith to advise him that the two were to be nominated; "Cotton Ed," according to the attorney general, again gave "full assurances" that he would raise no objection to either nomination, terming both "splendid selections."[63]

Any agreement that "Cotton Ed" may have struck with Burnet Maybank, however, clearly was not reflected in certain of his later actions or statements to the press. The Waring and Timmerman nominations were submitted to the Senate on December 18. On December 27, a subcommittee of the Senate Committee on the Judiciary convened a perfunctory hearing on the nominations. No witnesses appeared, but Senator Smith indicated that he wished to discuss the nominations before the full committee. On January 5, the committee postponed action on the nominations until Smith's return from a Christmas trip to South Carolina.[64]

Concerned that Smith might oppose the nominations, the committee chairman, Frederick Van Nuys (D-Calif.) apparently contacted Biddle. On January 9, the attorney general wrote Van Nuys, assuring him that "Cotton Ed" had indicated his support for both nominees before their names were submitted to the Senate. Several days later, however, Senator Smith complained to reporters that Biddle and Maybank had not had the "common decency" to "either consult or consider" him regarding the nominations. Instead, he said, they had called on him and "told me what was going to be done."

> The attorney general told me he wanted to consult me. I told him I thought he came to insult me. He didn't ask me which two candidates I personally favored. He told me who he was going to recommend to the White House.

Senator Maybank, he added, had taken the same approach. Waties Waring was Smith's "good friend and would make a fine judge." He "did not know Mr. Timmerman was being considered until about a week or two before the justice department recommended the two to the White House"; but Timmerman, too, "may be a competent man and if the people of South Carolina want him, it's O.K. with me." Smith simply objected to the manner in which the nominations had been handled.[65]

Whatever his status with the Roosevelt White House, Smith was then dean of the Senate, having served there longer than any of his colleagues. Had he formally objected to either nominee, the Senate very likely would have invoked the historic custom of "senatorial courtesy" and denied confirmation. On January 19, 1942, "Cotton Ed" appeared before the Judiciary Committee, discussed the manner in which federal appointments had recently been handled in his state, and voiced general disagreement with the administration's approach to a number of recent appointments. But Smith endorsed Waring and raised no objection to Timmerman.[66] On January 20, the Senate confirmed both nominations, without objection.

Many Charlestonians welcomed Waring's appointment. The Charleston bar honored the Warings with a testimonial dinner. The city council accepted Waring's gracious letter of resignation and voted to have the clerk send him a statement congratulating the district on the selection of "so able a jurist." The *Evening Post* praised him as "an excellent practitioner at the Charleston bar"; the *News and Courier* called him "an accomplished and industrious lawyer, of long and successful experience, a man of excellent character." Surprised but pleased that the hated Roosevelt "did not search for politicians already in office," the *News and Courier* termed the appointment "a happy ending to what, for inexplicable reasons, has been too long delayed."[67]

At noon on January 26, Judge C. C. Wyche, judge of the western district, administered the oath of office in the district courtroom of Charleston's post office at the corner of Broad and Meeting Streets. Waring's wife and their daughter Anne, now living in New York, attended the ceremony, as did Waring's sister Margaret; also at the swearing in was D. A. Brockinton, Tom Waring, Tom's brother Charles (who was replacing his uncle in the firm of Waring and Brockinton), Mayor Lockwood, and other close friends. Also attending were court functionaries and, the local papers reported, Corine Chisholm, the family's "colored servant for nineteen years."[68]

Judge Waring's acceptance speech was brief and unremarkable, largely tracking his oath of office. Viewed against his later civil rights decisions, however, his words take on considerable significance. "[T]his court," he said,

> belongs to the public. It belongs to the United States. And I am just the servant of the public in presiding in this court, attempting to do what I can to hold the scales of justice evenly, to see that those who come into the Court . . . get equal justice, irrespective of their rank or position, irrespective of wealth or poverty. And so help me God, I shall do that. . . . This court is one of the things that we are fighting for now. This court and all the other courts, because a free court is a court where a judge is at liberty to express his views and exercise his own discretion . . . without any coercion or pressure from anyone. That is liberty, and that is what America stands for.[69]

Waties Waring was sixty-one when he took the oath of office as a federal judge. He was entering what, for most men, would be the twilight years of life. They could have been comfortable, uneventful years. Waring was now perhaps the most prominent member of one of Charleston's leading families. He was a member of the city's prestigious St. George's and St. Cecilia societies, an officer in the Charleston Light Dragoons, and a member of the Charleston Club. He and his wife, Miss Annie, were at the center of the city's social life. They entertained often at their Meeting Street home and at their summer cottage on Sullivan's Island. An invitation to their annual New Year's party was considered a highlight of the social season. In 1937, their daughter had made her debut at the St. Cecilia Society. In the eyes of his Charleston contemporaries, Waties Waring "had everything." To their way of thinking, he was also soon to destroy his life. For others, he would soon give his life profound significance.

2

The Divorce

The small Charleston courtroom over which Judge Waring would preside—the same courtroom in which he had earlier argued cases for the government as assistant U.S. attorney—was located on the second floor of the city post office. A profile of southern progress, written for the *New York Times* in 1920, complained that the post office department had "committed a crime by erecting [the] nondescript granite building" at the corner of Meeting and Broad streets. In the graceful architecture of Charleston, the federal building was something of an eyesore. But it offered Judge Waring the advantage of convenience. Like St. Michael's church, situated across Meeting Street from the post office, Judge Waring's chambers were less than a block from his home.[1]

Waties Waring would serve ten years in the courtroom at the corner of Meeting and Broad. During his tenure, the higher courts would affirm his decisions forty-six times, reverse him on ten occasions, modify and affirm one decision, affirm and reverse in part in two cases, and dismiss two cases as prematurely decided—a reasonably good record for a federal judge. Waring held court primarily in Charleston, but sat a few days twice a year in Orangeburg to clear that division's generally sparse calendar; presided twice a year for several solid weeks of litigation in Florence, a busy rail point and center of the state's Pee Dee River agricultural area; and often went to Columbia to hear cases as well.[2]

To relieve congested caseloads—and later, to escape Charleston's hostile climate—Judge Waring frequently held court in other jurisdictions. As a Charleston attorney and as a corporation counsel, he had often visited New York before his appointment to the bench. He enjoyed the city's cosmopolitan atmosphere and welcomed opportunities to hear cases in federal court there. Initially, he held court four weeks each year in New York; later, he extended his annual visits to six weeks. During his tenure, he also held court in New Jersey, the middle and western districts of North Carolina, San Francisco, and Virginia, among other areas.[3]

As Judge Myers had been ill a lengthy period before his death, Judge Waring found a badly congested court calendar awaiting him when he as-

23

sumed the bench. At Waring's direction, Ernest Allen, the clerk of court, prepared a roster of untried cases. Allen's survey revealed a large number of cases dating back many years. Three, in fact, had been pending for fourteen years. Waring sent for the lawyers of record, refreshened their memories, gave them several months to prepare for hearings, and quickly cleared the most dated cases from the court's calendar. "I thought they owed me a debt of gratitude," he later recalled. "I suppose that they sent bills for their fees."[4]

Judge Waring took great pride in the efficient administration of his court and worked diligently to keep his calendar current. It was his view that the pace at which cases moved through the judicial mill was not solely the concern of the parties and counsel, but there was also a public interest in the prompt disposition of cases. If lawyers were not prepared to proceed in a timely fashion, he dismissed their cases with instructions to refile them when they were prepared. Since the lawyers generally wanted to avoid dismissals and the resulting awkward explanations to their clients, Waring's tactic usually worked. He frequently met, moreover, with Allen, the marshal, the U.S. attorney, probation officers, and other functionaries to discuss any delays in their operations and related administrative problems. For similar reasons, he pressed the Department of Justice to move more quickly in processing the compensation due property owners in land condemnation proceedings. In June 1946, he wrote Attorney General Tom Clark, urging prompt action. In October, he wrote Clark again, complaining that no action had yet been taken and that a number of compensation orders went back more than two years. "[P]rompt action" was needed, he asserted, in firing those responsible for the delays.[5]

On at least one occasion, Judge Waring's efficient administrative style attracted more than passing attention from the press. During one stint as visiting judge at the federal courthouse in Newark, New Jersey, he conducted fifteen trials over a twenty-nine-day period. He also instructed court personnel on the finer points of punctuality. On the day before he was to open court, he met with the clerk and U.S. attorney to discuss the upcoming docket of criminal cases. During the conversation, he asked when court opened in Newark, "and the clerk said, 'Oh, sometime after ten o'clock, ten-thirty or eleven, Judge, whichever is convenient.' " "Now listen," Waring quickly retorted, "I'll open at one and adjourn at two if you want. It doesn't make any difference to me when it is, but if you fix one o'clock, it's going to open at one. If it's ten, it's going to open at ten." Waring, a Newark *Evening News* journalist later reported, proved a stickler for court opening "on the tick of the hour scheduled. . . . While the resident judges generally adjourn no later than 4 p.m.," the reporter added, "Judge Waring frequently worked til near 5." And the court crier found himself setting his clock by Waring's arrival. The judge considered the profile "a rather nice compliment."[6]

Judge Waring's insistence on speed and efficiency extended to his opinion-writing habits and correspondence. He often issued orders from the bench immediately following a hearing. If a formal opinion was to be drafted, he dictated a statement of the facts as soon after the hearing as possible to assure accuracy, later filling in appropriate citations and details.[7] While rarely reflecting any literary flair, his opinions were concise and workmanlike. He was also unusually prompt in handling official and personal correspondence and expected similar dispatch from others.

While civil rights cases would make Judge Waring a controversial national figure, the bulk of his caseload usually involved other, more mundane issues. His criminal docket over the years included the trial of figures in an elaborate scheme to counterfeit American Express checks, a broad-ranging bank fraud scandal involving numerous prominent Virginians, bank robberies, and subordination of perjury charges against a San Francisco lawyer with ties to organized crime. Bootlegging cases also constituted a fair share of his South Carolina caseload. In 1946, for example, he sentenced a county policeman, a town marshal, and six others to two years in prison following conviction on federal liquor charges. His wartime criminal docket included many violations of Office of Price Administration (OPA) rationing regulations. In one such case, before Waring imposed a heavy sentence on a Florence black convicted by a jury, the defendant's counsel reminded the judge of "the thief on the cross," that it was "never too late to turn back." If that policy were adopted, Waring shot back, "we could tear down the courthouse, empty the jails and hire private guards to protect our homes."[8]

Judge Waring was a deeply patriotic man, and his harsh reaction to crimes threatening the war effort was not confined to rationing offenses. When four servicemen were convicted for dumping government food, blankets, and other supplies into Charleston harbor, he imposed stiff sentences and sought a congressional investigation into the pilfering of food by crews of government-owned ships. "People have got to wake up to the fact," he exclaimed from the bench, "that honesty is needed in the nation." In 1946, Waring gave a year's sentence to a medical officer at the Charleston Naval Base who pleaded guilty to pilfering two pieces of dental equipment. The officer was a lieutenant. Had he been an admiral, Waring asserted, "I would give him ten years. . . . When an officer of the United States Navy steps up here and admits he's a thief," he added, "he can be expected to be treated as a thief." The following day, he imposed stiff sentences on two white civilian employees charged with stealing food from a naval warehouse. Their action, he caustically remarked, was a "fine way" for them to conduct themselves while the nation was at war—and a "fine example" to the blacks employed with them.[9]

Most troublesome of the wartime cases for Waring were the conscientious objector claims of Jehovah's Witnesses. Congress had granted C.O. status to ministers, and under Witness doctrine, every male member of the sect was a minister. Judge Waring approved the Supreme Court's 1943 decision exempting Witness children from compulsory flag ceremonies in the public schools. ("If they [government officials] can make you salute the flag, they can make you do some other things that destroy your complete freedom of conscience and thought.") He was also generally sympathetic to religious liberty claims. But the Witnesses and their cases clearly bothered him, and he would have preferred that Congress eliminate all exemptions for ministers. He was outraged at the Witnesses' "lack of support for their government and their callousness" toward nonadherents.

> They get a blank look. They're fanatic, and they are right and everybody else is wrong. They have no respect or mercy for other people. All the rest of us are going to hell and are going to be actually put on a grill and burned forever. That's OK with them. That's the thing that annoyed me about them. They've got no feeling for the rest of us poor people.

He found their certitude particularly disturbing.

> I'm very flexible and very ignorant on the subject of the hereafter. I don't know and to have a man stand up and tell me that he doesn't think, *he knows*. I kind of gasp . . . not only at the incredulity but the effrontery of the thing. It shocks me.

And while he respected the talents of Hayden Covington, the New York attorney who argued the Witness cases before him, Waring suspected that Covington attempted to rush him and other judges into committing reversible errors.[10]

In protracted litigation involving one Louis Dabney Smith, a Jehovah's Witness minister, Waring's frustrations about the sect—and the darker, intolerant side of his personality—came bubbling to the surface. Smith was a former University of South Carolina student living in Columbia. He claimed to be a Witness minister, but the local draft board classified him 1-A. When his administrative appeal efforts failed, he was ordered to report for induction. He refused and was forcibly inducted, then held for trial before a military court-martial panel. Following a Supreme Court decision limiting military jurisdiction over such cases, he was released from military custody and indicted for violation of the Selective Service Act. After a jury trial in 1943, he was sentenced to three-and-a-half years in prison, but the U.S. Supreme Court reversed his conviction, holding that Smith was entitled to judicial review of his claim that his draft board did not have the authority to give him a 1-A classification.[11]

In a 1946 jury trial before Judge Waring, Smith was again convicted, the court rejecting his claim that he was entitled to C.O. status as a Witness minister. Before passing sentence, Waring probed Smith about his religious beliefs:

> THE COURT: As a boy, did you ever play baseball or marbles or pick a green apple, or did you spend all your time studying the Bible?
> MR. SMITH: I studied the Bible—I did play baseball.
> THE COURT: Did you have fun at it—take pleasure in it?
> MR. SMITH: Yes, sir.
> THE COURT: You think your father's damned to hell, don't you?
> MR. SMITH: No, sir.
> THE COURT: You think everybody else is?
> MR. SMITH: No, sir, I didn't make any statement like that—never.
> THE COURT: You think all are going excepting your sect?
> MR. SMITH: No, sir, that's not for me to judge.
> THE COURT: We haven't got much chance? . . . I'm dreadfully sorry

for you, not because I'm going to send you to jail, but I'm dreadfully sorry. It's the most depressing thing I've seen on earth. . . . Anything else you want to say?

MR. SMITH: Yes, sir, there is. The Bible records in many places where Christ Jesus served notice of great persecution for telling the truth to people, and foretold that in these last days—

THE COURT: Christ Jesus was a man who looked on the beauties of life—he taught a religion of love, of sweetness, of beauty, and kindness. . . . He didn't damn all people—he felt sorry for them.

MR. SMITH: He assailed the Scribes and Pharisees because they were teaching doctrines and traditions contrary to God's word.

THE COURT: Because they were narrow and hard and hypocrites.

MR. SMITH: Hypocrites—because they professed to be teachers of God's word, and they were actually teaching doctrines on traditions of men, which was a great reproach and blasphemy upon the name of Jehovah.

Then, Smith recited two verses from Jeremiah—verses, he said, "which would very firmly apply in this Court."

As for me, behold, I am in your hand: do with me as seemeth good and meet unto you. But know ye for certain that if ye put me to death, ye shall surely bring innocent blood upon yourselves, and upon this city, and upon the inhabitants thereof; for of a truth the Lord hath sent me unto you to speak all these words in your ears.

At least for the present, however, Judge Waring would have the last word.

THE COURT: Well perhaps I'm not as sorry for you as I first thought. Perhaps you are very fortunate since you put yourself in the place of Christ and Jeremiah.

The sentence of this Court is that you should serve three years and six months—the same sentence that was imposed before.[12]

Not all of Judge Waring's criminal litigation, of course, was as provoking for him as the Witness cases. One of the more amusing involved John Wesley Glasper, a black Mississippian charged with mail fraud. "Doctor" Glasper used amulets, "medicines," and other products to "cure" a host of ailments. The more curative "powers" he employed, the larger his fee. Judge Waring called him a "common swindler" and sentenced him to prison. Glasper took the judgment philosophically. He had not used his full "charms" to defend himself, he explained, because he wanted to give the court an even chance.[13]

Judge Waring's civil caseload was as varied as his criminal docket. In one case, a New York company was ordered to pay life insurance to a woman whose husband, a prominent Bennettsville merchant, had disappeared several years earlier, along with $20–30,000 in cash and a teenage neighbor. Another was a suit to nullify numerous fraudulent mortgages drawn up as part of a home construction scandal. While Waring could find no basis for assuming federal jurisdiction over the specific issues raised in the government's complaint, he was impressed with the nearly sixty affidavits filed in the case—affidavits alleging "a shocking state of affairs" in the federal housing administration.

If the statements are true, then it would seem that gross frauds have been perpetrated and that the government officials have been either gullible or corrupt. If the statements are not true, then it would seem that perjury has been committed by a large number of persons and fair reputations have been unjustly besmirched.

In an effort to stimulate an investigation and some sort of legal action, Waring forwarded copies of his order and the complaint to the attorney general of the United States and the federal housing administrator. To his disappointment, however, his materials simply "gather[ed] dust."[14]

One of Judge Waring's most tragic civil cases had roots going back, in a sense, to the Civil War. In the 1940s, Fort Johnson, a Civil War fort located on James Island, was being used by the federal government as a quarantine station. While portions of the facility were technically off-limits to the public, the grounds—which offered excellent views of Charleston harbor, the city, and historic Fort Sumter, among other area landmarks—were a favorite site for visitors. Dotting the grounds were several war relics, including a large Confederate cannon. One day in 1947, two Citadel cadets, one the son of a station employee, visited the grounds in search of powder for their homemade cannon and discovered a 200-pound shell wedged in the muzzle of the Civil War cannon. While the cadets were trying to pry powder from the shell, the station medical officer walked by, jokingly warned them that they could be arrested for theft or destruction of government property, told them to "be careful," and left them to their work.

When the cadets were unable to extract powder from the shell while it was wedged in the cannon's muzzle, they removed the shell and towed it across the grounds to a boat house, where they continued their efforts. At one point, a workman drilled a hole in the shell with an electric drill to give the cadets better access to the powder. While the cadets were collecting powder, two younger boys, fifteen and ten years of age, happened by and also began tampering with the shell. Suddenly there was a violent explosion. The older youngster was killed. The younger boy, William R. Beasley, son of the station's chief clerical administrative assistant, lost a leg and suffered other severe injuries.

The dead youth's anguished parents had no interest in pursuing a lawsuit, but William Beasley's parents filed a tort action against the government. After hearing the facts, Judge Waring awarded young Beasley $35,000, resting his decision primarily on an eighteenth-century English case in which the first person to throw a squib (or firecracker), in turn thrown by others, was held responsible for resulting injuries.

A train of circumstances was started right there in the presence of [the medical officer]. Almost any responsible individual would realize that when two youths attempt to defuse a shell it is reasonable to expect that you will soon have an explosion. . . . The resulting explosion was not at all an unexpected culmination of a series of dangerous acts. The officials, having allowed these boys to start on this dangerous mission, must be held responsible for the unfortunate results which they should have foreseen and prevented.

Waring refused to require the government, however, to pay the medical expenses Beasley's father had incurred for the care of his son. As an important official of the quarantine station, familiar with the dangers posed by the war relics there, Waring concluded, the father must share responsibility for the explosion that injured his son and killed his son's playmate.[15]

As a private attorney, Waring had handled admiralty litigation and regretted that such cases did not constitute a greater portion of his caseload on the federal bench. However, two of his more interesting civil cases did arise in the waters around Charleston. In one, a ship, the *Southport,* broke loose from its docking at a cotton storage and compressing firm, drifted down the Cooper River, and collided with a dry dock owned by the federal government and a shipyard company, causing over $60,000 in damages. Waring ordered the ship owners and the compress firm to share the damages. In the other case, which arose in 1948, a government cargo ship, the *Nicaragua Victory,* broke anchor and drifted into the John P. Grace Memorial Bridge, causing serious damage to the bridge and the drowning of a family of four whose automobile was knocked from the bridge by the collision. Several insurers and the state highway department brought a tort action against the United States. The evidence indicated that the vessel had been left in the hands of a retired seafarer who had been on duty forty-seven hours, without relief or sleep, when the collision occurred. Again, Waring found for the plaintiffs.[16]

Had his entire judicial career been devoted to such litigation, and his domestic life remained unchanged, Judge Waring might have spent the rest of his days as a respected member of the Charleston aristocracy. And the first three years of his tenure did proceed smoothly. In late March 1945, the College of Charleston awarded its distinguished graduate an honorary doctor of laws.[17] Even by that point, however, rumors were already circulating through Charleston that Waties and Annie Gammell Waring were on the verge of divorce.

In many ways, Waties and Miss Annie were a study in contrasts. "My recollection, and I don't want to be unkind to her," D. A. Brockinton, Jr., has remarked,

> is that Miss Annie wasn't on the same intellectual level as Waties. She was a nice person and a completely devoted wife, utterly devoted to Waties. . . .
> She worshipped the ground that Waties walked on, especially later when he became United States district judge. . . . But intellectually she didn't have the depth of Waties. And I always considered her to be a little bit on the frivolous or frothy side.[18]

Annie Gammell was raised in Charleston and attended Miss Peck's School in Philadelphia. While she was studying drama in New York, the great actress Sarah Bernhardt opened a two-week engagement there. The stagestruck Annie Gammell attended every performance, sent her idol flowers each matinee and evening, and carefully collected clippings for the scrapbook on Madame Sarah that she had been keeping for three years. She also had her French teacher help her compose a fan letter to the actress.[19]

Touched by Annie's devotion, Miss Bernhardt answered the young girl's letter promptly, inviting her to lunch. Beginning that year, Annie spent four winters in Paris, living near Miss Bernhardt, enjoying immediate access to the actress' dressing room between play acts or after performances, meeting the many famous artists who crowded into Miss Bernhardt's home, and virtually becoming a member of the Bernhardt household—a rather strange group consisting of the actress' illegitimate son, her niece, companion, secretary, and servants. Years later, Madame Sarah became godmother to the Warings' daughter Anne, and Miss Annie would show visitors her edition of Miss Bernhardt's memoirs and its cherished inscription: "To Annie Gammell, the most adored child that I know. A souvenir of the great affection of Sarah Bernhardt."

Some of the more "down-to-earth" members of the Waring family, Tom Waring recalls, were amused by Miss Annie's devotion to Sarah Bernhardt, and Waties' father once irritated Annie by asking, "How is Mum Sarah?" But the Waring family were genuinely fond of Annie, considering her a fine person and devoted wife and mother. For his part, Waties Waring, who was himself an inveterate theatergoer, probably found Miss Annie's devotion to Madame Sarah and the arts appealing. Whatever the attraction, they were married in 1913 in Bronxville, New York; by the time rumors of their divorce surfaced in 1945, their marriage had endured for nearly thirty-two years.[20]

Miss Annie was devoted to Waties and immensely proud of his position as a federal judge, as well as their prominent status in Charleston society. She particularly enjoyed their trips to circuit judicial conferences at the Grove Park Inn and other exclusive resorts in the North Carolina and Virginia mountains—and the attention given judges there by members of the bar. On one such occasion, D. A. Brockinton, Jr., recalls, the Warings and Brockinton's parents were standing in a hotel lobby when an attorney greeted both men as judges. Miss Annie was mildly shocked. "Why Brock," she said, *"you* aren't a judge."[21]

But while Charlestonians were obviously concerned by rumors of an impending divorce, many may have been surprised more by the fact of a divorce in the Waring social circle than by the revelation of strains in the Waring household. Waties genuinely liked the company of women. "He liked to talk with women," a friend of his daughter would later say, "to converse with them, whereas many men would be off in a corner, by themselves." In his bachelor days, moreover, Waties had a reputation as perhaps Charleston's foremost rake and "swordsman." His nickname was "Rex," and he was known as the "king" of the city's tenderloin district. There is evidence that he continued to enjoy that reputation long after his marriage to Miss Annie. D. A. Brockinton, Sr., would later recall that his only difficulties with his law partner had arisen over Waring's attentions to young secretaries in the firm. It was widely rumored, moreover, that Waring and a friend maintained a hideaway outside Charleston.[22]

Ultimately, in fact, Waring's reputation was to be immortalized, after a fashion, in the poetry composed by a colorful local figure. Through most of his adult life, Arthur Jervey Stoney, a Charleston insurance agent and local campaign manager for Wyndham Manning in the disputed 1938 primary, wrote clever, if often tasteless and at times cruel, doggerel about the personalities and life of Charleston. Judge Waring and the second Mrs. Waring were frequent targets of Stoney's pen. Following Waring's retirement from the bench and move to New York, the building that had housed Charleston's most venerable brothel was slated for destruction. Stoney wrote a plaintive appeal, urging his readers to "wire" a "noted lawyer" of the past to return and "save the glorious old Big Brick, Where he spent his happiest nights."

> He was King of the Tenderloin;
>   Big Brick was his Palace Hall;
> And the girls were wild with excitement,
>   When the lawyer was coming to call.
>
> The Madam's smile was wide for him,
>   He could charge up any amount.
> For he was one patron of the Brick,
>   Who enjoyed a charge account.
>
> The lawyer is old, his youth long past;
>   He can only dream and repine.
> But he was a master swordsman once,
>   And the Big Brick should be his shrine.

In an author's note, Stoney wrote: "Any resemblance to a lawyer living or practically dead is purely coincidental." He suspected that "the reader will find many an elderly member of the bar will give the impression that the above lines are inscribed to him." Charlestonians had no doubt, however, that Judge Waring was the subject of Stoney's wit.[23]

Waties Waring's lifestyle was hardly unusual for a man in his social class, and Miss Annie was apparently oblivious to his activities. But some sensed strains in their relationship. Gus Tamsberg, who served as clerk to the Charleston city council from 1935 to 1968, was not in the Warings' social circle, but he worked closely with Waring during his years as corporation counsel and credited Waring's prodding with his decision, later in life, to become a lawyer. During the Depression, the city instituted foreclosure proceedings on a Society Street house, which Miss Annie then acquired by payment of back taxes. Tamsberg handled some of the paperwork. When he approached Waring to discuss the transaction, the corporation counsel coldly responded that his wife's business was her own affair. Tamsberg gathered from that experience and others that Waring's relationship with Miss Annie was essentially aloof and formal. To their friends, however, the Warings appeared an ideal couple, thoroughly devoted to each other.[24]

Then, however, Waties Waring met Elizabeth Avery Mills Hoffman. Elizabeth Avery was born in Michigan in 1895. Her maternal grandparents were Connecticut natives, her grandfather an Episcopalian minister, and many of her other maternal ancestors were ministers, teachers, and lawyers. Her father, John Avery, was a direct descendant of John Alden of the Plymouth Colony. Her grandfather Avery had established a successful lumber business in Brewster, Maine, near Bangor, then extended the business to Michigan.[25] Elizabeth was reared in a life of privilege in the exclusive Detroit suburb of Grosse Pointe. She did not attend college but was a student at the Liggett School in Detroit, Sacred Heart School in Paris, and the Westover School in Connecticut. She also made debuts in Detroit and Chicago.[26]

Despite the affluent environment in which she was raised, Elizabeth had a troubled childhood. Her father was a charming, very attractive man and fine golfer whose daughter "never knew him working." John Avery was also an alcoholic—"a very pleasant one," Elizabeth's daughter recalls, but an alcoholic, nevertheless. He and Elizabeth's mother had a turbulent marriage, and their daughter was often called on to act as intermediary in their frequent quarrels.[27]

Elizabeth's first marriage, in 1915, was to Wilson Mills, whose father was New Mexico's last territorial governor and its first supreme court chief justice following statehood. A University of Michigan law graduate, Mills rose quickly to a leading position in the Detroit business community, becoming chief executive officer of the city's largest bank at a relatively young age. He was also a close adviser to Herbert Hoover and was offered the position of secretary of commerce, among other posts, in the Hoover administration. During the Depression, Mills left his bank position and returned to law practice, where he continued to enjoy a prominent community standing for the remainder of his career.[28]

Elizabeth and Mills had two sons and a daughter, and their marriage lasted twenty years. Elizabeth, who had studied voice and drama in New York, sang with Detroit opera groups, taught music at a home for crippled children, and otherwise lived the life of a well-to-do suburban matron. She was also an outstanding tennis player, winning the Michigan state women's open championship at age thirty-five, long after many players have retired from competition.[29]

While married to Mills, Elizabeth spent several winters in Ormond Beach, Florida. On one of these visits, she met Henry Hoffman, a wealthy Connecticut textile manufacturer and collector of antiques. At some time thereafter, she returned from a Florida visit to announce to her shocked and anguished daughter that she was going to Reno to divorce Mills so that she could marry Henry Hoffman, who was a generation her senior.[30]

News of the divorce shocked their children. "We occasionally heard our parents quarreling," their son David Mills remarked, "but we attributed that to mother's rather vitriolic personality" rather than to any basic problems in their parents' marriage. Elizabeth's sons sided with their father. One of her sons was killed in World War II. The other, David, eventually reestablished relations with his mother, but only after years of estrangement. Their daughter, Ann, at first lived briefly with her father following the divorce. Wilson Mills himself soon married again, however, and Ann's relationship with her stepmother proved strained at best. Under Michigan law, Ann could choose the parent with whom she would live once she reached age fourteen. When she came of age about a year after her parents' divorce, Ann went to live with her mother and broke off relations almost entirely with her father.[31]

Wilson Mills, however, remained the trusted confidant and attorney for Elizabeth's parents. They sided with him in the divorce, and Mills continued to manage his in-laws' financial affairs—including a trust established in 1929 for Elizabeth—after the divorce.[32]

Elizabeth was introduced to Charleston through her second husband. Charleston was a favorite wintering spot for wealthy Yankees, and Henry Hoffman owned one of the larger homes south of Broad Street. The connection was strengthened in 1942 when her daughter Ann married Simeon Hyde, a New Yorker whose parents had left Charleston in the Depression but still had relatives there. During the war years when Hyde was at sea in the Navy, Ann lived in Charleston with her mother and Hoffman. While living in Charleston during the war, Elizabeth did volunteer work for the Red Cross and local OPA office. Primarily, however, she enjoyed the city's active social life. "I was the toast of Charleston," she claimed to a journalist after her exclusion from that life. "They love rich Northerners. . . . and I was party material. They're not the least bit interested in your background or if you've a mind and can use it, or not."[33]

It is uncertain when Waties Waring and Elizabeth first met. D. A. Brockinton suggested that Waring often visited Simeon Hyde's parents on business trips to New York and met Elizabeth during one of these visits, but Ann Hyde believes that they did not meet until Elizabeth moved to Charleston with Henry Hoffman. Whatever the circumstances of their initial meeting, the Hoffmans were among the many wealthy Yankees in the Warings' social circle, and the two couples became frequent bridge partners. Soon, Elizabeth and Waties also became lovers.[34]

In the south of the 1940s, divorce was extremely rare, especially for a man in Judge Waring's position. In fact, except during Reconstruction, South Carolina had no provision for divorce. When an attempt to permit divorce under certain circumstances failed in 1883, the *News and Courier* approved the proposal's defeat with the headline, "The Divorce Bill Defeated—South Carolina Will Not Open the Door to Depravity." The "Old Lady of Broad Street," as the paper was known, neglected to mention that numerous houses of prostitution were then flourishing in Charleston or that, for the entire year, only one person, a black, had been convicted of maintaining a "disorderly house."[35] The mentality its headline reflected continued well into the next century.

Divorce, then, was serious business for South Carolinians. But Waties Waring had fallen hopelessly in love with Elizabeth Hoffman. One evening in late February 1945, he came home from his chambers, told Annie of his feelings, and said that he wanted a divorce. The widow of his brother Edward was then living in Jacksonville, Florida. Waties asked Annie to establish a residence there and obtain a Florida divorce.[36]

Annie was so devastated by this turn of events that she became ill and was placed under the care of two physicians. But she did as Waties asked, just as she had always followed his directions. When she arrived in Jacksonville on March 1, her sister-in-law was shocked at her appearance; during her stay in Florida, she lost twenty-five pounds.[37]

On March 17, Judge Waring wrote his sister-in-law, Rowena Taylor Waring, a letter intended to serve, no doubt, as evidence supporting Annie's claim to a divorce. It read:

Dear Rena;—

I think that you are entitled to hear from me in regard to Annie's determination to obtain a divorce. You probably think that I have acted brutally and cruelly to her. I cannot enter any denial and make [no] attempt to defend my actions. She has ample grounds for her application.

I shall state the matter to you baldly. I do not any longer love Annie as my wife and I do love someone else and desire to be free. I have told her this quite frankly and perhaps brutally. There is no use concealing it. In your eyes I assume, I have acted badly. I have chosen to be frank. We have ceased all marital relations for which I am solely responsible and to blame. I have told her that I have intended to separate and that she could stay in Charleston and if she did I would not live in the home longer with her or she might prefer to go away. She has chosen the latter course and taken up her residence in Florida not because she was seeking to separate but because I was. I have convinced her that my mind was definitely made up and I cannot deny that I have been the cause of breaking up our home since I have told her that I was unwilling that we should any longer share a home. Perhaps you will say that I have driven her out of the home. That is one way to put it.

Annie is entitled to demand financial aid and I shall not refuse that and have willingly agreed to provide to the best of my ability provided she makes a separate home.

Please understand that I do not accuse her of any wrong and make no complaint. I cannot because it is all caused [by] me and my feelings. I can only say that we have drifted apart because I have tired of our life together and I wish to get away from it and be free. I am sorry that this has happened but those are the facts.

Annie knows all. I realize that she has suffered and continues to suffer. And I frankly admit that I have been and am the cause of it; yes I agree with you that I have been cruel and brutal to treat her in this manner but nevertheless I have determined on my course and shall not change. Even should she be willing or offer to come back I should not agree. And if she did come back I would demand that she leave. I regret that I must speak so clearly and unkindly but you have asked for the truth and I give it to you. I am sorry to admit that I have treated her in so cruel a manner but there is no use in attempting to avoid or deny facts.

In early May, attorneys drew up a property settlement. No specific reference was made in this agreement to the Warings' Meeting Street home, which originally was acquired by Annie. Instead, it was provided that Waring would provide Annie $20,000 in cash, a $1,000 paid-up insurance policy on his life, a certificate of deposit for $2,048, and $250 each month for the balance of her life. Waring also agreed to will his entire estate to their daughter.

Florida had a ninety-day residency requirement. On June 6, a brief hearing was held in the circuit court for Duval County. Annie Waring testified that theirs had been an "ideal" marriage, that "we were considered the best and most completely happy couple in Charleston," that Waring had treated her "with kindness and consideration" always, that he had been "perfectly faithful to me all of those years," and that, though "very undemonstrative in public," he had shown her great affection in private. Her husband's revelation that he wanted to marry Elizabeth Hoffman "was such a shock" that she had "been ill ever since." Waring, she said, had "made life perfectly miserable for me. It was unbearable." Rowena Waring also testified briefly, and Judge Waring's letter to his sister-in-law was introduced in evidence. Counsel for Waring offered no defense. The formalities completed, on June 7 the presiding judge issued a decree dissolving the Warings' marriage.

In Charleston, Judge Waring telephoned his nephew Tom Waring and asked him to come by his chambers. He wanted Tom to publish a brief, unelaborated announcement of the divorce in the *News and Courier*. Tom had learned the details of the Warings' difficulties from his mother, who had gotten her information from Waties' sister Margaret. The divorce was also a hot item by then in the Charleston rumor mill. Tom speculated to his uncle, however, that the news was "surely going to rock Charleston." "Let her rock," Waring dryly retorted.[38]

A two-paragraph item on the divorce appeared in the June 9 issue of the *News and Courier*. While Annie Waring had been establishing a Florida residence, Elizabeth had gone to Reno to secure a Nevada divorce from Henry Hoffman, stopping en route in California, where Ann Hyde was then living, to tell her daughter the news. On June 18, the *News and Courier* published a brief announcement of Judge Waring's marriage to Elizabeth Hoffman, news Tom Waring had picked up from an issue of the New York *Herald Tribune,* on which he had once worked as a reporter. The announcement indicated that the couple had been married in the chambers of a Greenwich, Connecticut, municipal court judge on June 15, barely more than a week after the Warings' Florida divorce.[39]

As Tom Waring had predicted, news of the divorce and his uncle's marriage to Elizabeth Hoffman did "rock" Charleston. Local wits joked that Elizabeth must be *"some* bridge player," and at least one Charleston male suggested that a monument be erected in honor of the liberated Judge Waring. But many Charlestonians sympathized with Miss Annie. Apparently, as a part of the divorce settlement, Judge Waring acquired Miss Annie's Meeting Street home and returned there to live with his new bride following their marriage. Rumors circulated that Waring had stolen Annie's house and moved Elizabeth into Annie's home—and bed—even before the divorce was granted. Charleston matrons in the Warings' social circle were especially shocked and incensed.[40]

Elizabeth Waring's personality and background did nothing to assuage the situation. By most accounts, she was a very handsome, charming woman with considerable sex appeal; Waties' male friends could understand why he had fallen in love with her. "But," D. A. Brockinton, Jr., would recall years later, "she was also a Yankee, and she had those characteristics. Those women just don't seem to have the same manner southern women have. They are a little more aggressive, and they're a little bit more positive in their views. And they're probably a bit more flexible." Then, too, there was her previous marriage record. "By the time she got to Charleston," Tom Waring observed, "she had some experience with broken marriages. And that added to the accumulated ill will when she and Judge Waring became attached, and again a marriage was broken."[41]

Gradually Judge Waring and his bride became isolated from his traditional circle of friends and even from his relatives. Shortly after their marriage, Waties and Elizabeth had a large party. Few of those invited attended. The large number of invitations that Judge Waring had regularly received in the past quickly dwindled to a trickle. When they attended a party, the room soon emptied. Elizabeth complained to her husband of being snubbed by other wives at Ohlandt's, the neighborhood grocery that had served residents south of Broad Street for many years. One matron, "who wasn't too strong on judgment," Tom Waring recalls, greeted Elizabeth enthusiastically on her return to Charleston following the marriage—then, on learning that others were condemning the Warings' behavior, hastily withdrew her welcome. When Elizabeth asked another, "Aren't you glad to see me?" the matron coldly replied, "Indeed, I am not." Initially at least, many of Judge Warings' male friends sought to maintain cordial relations with him, but often excluded the couple from social engagements.[42]

When his later civil rights decisions and their attacks on southern racial mores began to attract national attention, the Warings claimed that white Charlestonians were ostracizing them because of their racial views and his rulings. Charleston whites would contend, on the other hand, that community hostility was rooted in the circumstances of Waring's divorce and the couple's verbal assaults on white southern society. In fact, a combination of all three factors appears to have been at work. There is evidence, moreover, to support the contention of several of his closest friends and relatives that Waring—hurt and angered at their refusal to accept Elizabeth with the enthusiasm he expected—initially cut himself off from them, and not the other way around.

Among the family, Waring's nephew Tom was the most persistent in pressing this interpretation of the Warings' exclusion from his closest Charleston associates. Although, as children, Tom Waring and his sister Rosamond had considered their uncle an aloof figure, "something of a cold fish," while Waties was serving as counsel to the *News and Courier,* Tom got to know, and like, his uncle better. They also served together on the board of the Charleston art association. "These contacts," Tom later recalled, "caused me to have a great deal of respect for his mind. He was a very precise and perceptive man. He caught the point . . . and could give a straight-forward opinion quickly."[43]

For several months after publishing announcements of Waring's divorce and remarriage in the *News and Courier,* Tom Waring had no contact with his uncle. Then, in early November, Judge Waring wrote his nephew a letter. The judge was a strong advocate of the United Nations. The previous March, in fact, he and five other Charlestonians, including the mayor and several labor union officials, had sent a letter and resolution to local and national organizations, urging support for the Dumbarton Oaks, Yalta, and San Francisco agreements. In his letter to Tom, Judge Waring enclosed a *New York Times* account of a recent speech James F. Byrnes had given in support of the United Nations concept, asking that his nephew also reprint Byrnes' speech. The letter was formal, its tone chilly. Largely because of Byrnes' ties with the Roosevelt-Truman administrations, the "Old Lady of Broad Street" and her colorful, reactionary chief editor William Watts Ball had grown increasingly critical of Byrnes. Waring closed the letter with a pointed reference to the newspaper's posture.

> Of course I realize the personal feelings of your chief against "Our Mr. James" and it may be for that reason it [the speech] would not be acceptable. However, I call it to your attention because I thought that irrespective of feelings or prejudices the public should get these views.[44]

In his reply, Tom Waring noted that the *News and Courier* had carried a wire service summary of Byrnes' speech but would also reprint most of it in an early issue, "in view of your suggestion." Tom took strong issue, however, with his uncle's characterization of the paper's attitude toward Byrnes. When Byrnes earlier had broken with the national administration, Tom Waring wrote, he

> had an opportunity to use his ability and influence to help bring back the traditional American system, which now seems to be on its deathbed. Instead, he gave up the opportunity and returned to the administration in which he has become a leader.
>
> The actions of the Roosevelt administration, and now apparently also the Truman regime, being opposed to our views of what is the best interest of the country, we naturally oppose the men who perform them, including one who happens to have come from Charleston. It would be prejudice on our part were we to refrain from criticism because he is a "hometown boy."[45]

In the winter of 1945–46, after his return to Charleston following a trip, Judge Waring visited the Dock Street Theater one evening and encountered his nephew and a mutual friend in the lobby. "I immediately realized from his manner," Tom Waring recalls,

> that he was cutting me, to use the old-fashioned expression. I made certain that it wasn't inadvertent by saying, in a rather loud voice, "Hello, Waties,

when did you get back to town?" And he turned on me, and he glared at
me, and he said, "I got back Tuesday." And he then greeted the man
standing by me rather effusively and said, "How glad I am to see you.
Please come and see us." And it made me realize that I had had it.

He later received the same sort of treatment from Elizabeth.

On the street she would cut me pretty dead. And I made a practice generally of just tipping my hat to make sure that she understood that I saw
her and recognized her and was not cutting her. But I got the frozen treatment from her, just as I got it from him.

From that point on, according to Tom Waring,

there was a series of incidents like this, in which Judge Waring was cutting
off members of his family and old friends. My brother and my sister made
efforts to maintain family relations with him, and eventually they got it,
too. All of us got it. . . . It sounds like trivial, smalltown gossip. But it's a
question of who ostracized whom.[46]

In November 1945, Judge Waring had turned over management of his
ailing sister Margaret's financial affairs to his nephew Charles, citing his
frequent absences from Charleston on judicial business. Since Margaret's
finances were hardly complicated, nor Waring's absences from the city a
new part of his judicial routine, his decision may have reflected growing
strains in his relations with family members. While Waring's treatment of
Annie Waring had saddened Margaret, however, she apparently remained
loyal to her brother until her death; and a June 1948, letter Charles Waring
wrote to her heirs indicates that Waties received a reasonable portion of her
estate. At the time of her death, moreover, he was providing his sister with
monthly financial support.[47]

Partly perhaps because he practiced before his uncle, Charles Waring
sought to maintain harmonious relations with Judge Waring and apparently
did so for several years following the divorce. In fact, the favorable treatment Judge Waring accorded one of his nephew's clients brought the judge
something approaching an official rebuke from a panel of the U.S. Court of
Appeals for the Fourth Circuit. In October of 1946, the federal Office of
Price Administration filed a suit in Judge Waring's court to recover damages
from the A. H. Fischer Co., a longtime Waring and Brockinton client. The
government charged Fischer with violating provisions of federal price control regulations. In its complaint, however, the government misnamed the
defendant the "A. H. Fischer Lumber Company." On Charles Waring's motion, his uncle denied the government an opportunity to amend its suit by
striking out the word "Lumber" and instead dismissed the action on this
narrowly technical ground. In January 1947, the government filed another
action, on this occasion against the "A. H. Fischer Company, Inc." Since
"Inc." was not a part of the company's formal name, Judge Waring again
granted his nephew's motion to dismiss.

Although Judge Waring relied for this technicality on a precedent of the court serving South Carolina's eastern and western districts, a three-judge Fourth Circuit panel was not impressed. "A suit at law is not a children's game," Judge John J. Parker caustically observed for a unanimous court in reversing Judge Waring, "but a serious effort on the part of adult human beings to administer justice."

> [T]he purpose of process is to bring parties into court. If it names them in such terms that every intelligent person understands who is meant, as is the case here, it has fulfilled its purpose; and courts should not put themselves in the position of failing to recognize what is apparent to everyone else.

"In order that there may be no further unnecessary delay in this matter," Judge Parker concluded, the panel's mandate was to "issue forthwith."[48]

Eventually, however, Charles Waring would complain that his uncle and Elizabeth were snubbing him and his wife too. When Charles first sensed his uncle's coolness toward him, he visited Waring's chambers on a peace mission, but to no avail. Over the years, Tom Waring would collect written summaries of incidents involving his uncle's treatment of close friends. A January 1949, entry involved Charles Waring.

> C. W. Waring called on business at the judge's office, and through an open door saw the judge dictating. Then the judge's attendant came out and told a colored man who was waiting that the judge would see him. The judge effusively greeted the colored visitor, then closed the door to the room where C. W. Waring was waiting. In a little while, the colored man left, the attendant said the judge would see Mr. Waring, and Mr. Waring was received with a cool nod.

Charles' wife Margaret was an independent, outspoken woman. One day Margaret paid a call on Elizabeth and was told by a maid that Mrs. Waring was ill. Margaret and Charles sent Elizabeth flowers. Later, they encountered the Warings at a judicial conference. "Elizabeth," said Margaret, "I never heard anything about the flowers we sent you." "Too little, too late," Elizabeth replied.[49]

Another of Tom Waring's entries involved Charles Baker. A Maryland native who had first moved to Charleston as a "timber cruiser" for lumber interests, then became collector of customs for the Charleston port, Baker had been Judge Waring's friend for forty years and credited Waring for his job with the city. Baker and his wife had continued a social relationship with the Warings after the divorce. One evening near Christmas in 1948, however, Mrs. Baker telephoned Elizabeth to arrange a game of bridge. Elizabeth indicated that she would need to consult with the judge, but that if Mrs. Baker heard nothing further from them, she should assume that the Warings would not be playing. Baker called on the judge in his chambers to seek an explanation. "Because you abandoned us," Waring responded, refusing to discuss the matter further.[50]

Judge Waring and his former law partner, D. A. Brockinton, never had a falling out, but eventually they too ceased contact. As law partners and friends before the divorce, Waties and Brockinton had been extremely close, almost like brothers. Their families visited each other often in their Charleston homes and Sullivan's Island cottages; Brockinton's son played frequently with the Waring's tomboyish daughter Anne. Following the divorce and Waring's marriage to Elizabeth, Mrs. Brockinton was "dead set" against continuing the relationship, but Brockinton insisted that they could not dictate their friend's private life. So the Brockintons paid the traditional call on the judge and his bride, first at their Meeting Street home, then in a Sunday afternoon visit to their beach cottage. Later, the Warings called on the Brockintons. After that, Brockinton would occasionally visit Waring in his chambers at the end of the day, but the families had no further social contact. When the Warings began entertaining blacks in their home, any social contact, in Brockinton's eyes, was out of the question. Further association at that point, he later remarked to his son, "would have opened us up to a lot of scandalous talk. We would have been a laughing stock." "I'm giving up on Waties," he finally told his family, "that woman has ruined him."[51]

In the eyes of Waring's detractors, the influence of "that woman" extended to his courtroom demeanor. Especially as Waring and Elizabeth became increasingly isolated from Charleston's social life, she spent a growing portion of her time in his courtroom, generally entering from his chambers and choosing a seat inside the bar, usually quite close to his bench. Waties Waring was always in complete control of his court, but while his demeanor was ordinarily formal and businesslike, he often relaxed and joked with counsel, especially when the lawyers gathered to arrange an upcoming docket of cases. When Elizabeth took her seat and gazed up admiringly at her husband, however, his demeanor changed, his critics claim, and the courtroom atmosphere became charged with tension. Joseph Young, a Charleston attorney whose family lived on Tradd Street near the Waring home, was a close friend of the judge's daughter Anne. His parents had been friends of Waties and Annie Waring; his Aunt Julia had married Henry Hoffman following Hoffman's divorce from Elizabeth. Young would become one of Judge Waring's most vehement critics. When Elizabeth entered the courtroom, Young recalls, "it was hell. It was no court. Nobody could do anything because he wasn't listening. He wasn't doing anything but paying attention to her."[52]

At times, counsel added to the tension. Once, Robert McC. Figg remembered, a lawyer commented that someone involved in a suit was not really someone else's wife. Judge Waring asked for an explanation. "Oh, he had one of these funny Florida divorces," counsel replied. "Your honor is familiar with that." "The bar," Figg added, "had a great, unanimous laugh." On another occasion, in his courtroom, Judge Waring asked former Charleston mayor Tom Stoney why he had missed a party the judge and Elizabeth had given shortly after their marriage. Stoney explained that he had not gotten his invitation. Waring replied that the incident would, of course, have no effect on their professional relationship. "Waties, you're damn right it won't," Stoney hotly retorted, "because I'll never appear before you again!"[53]

It is possible that later resentment toward Waring's racial views may have biased the recollections of his contemporaries. Clearly, however, the divorce was the initial catalyst for the Warings' isolation from his native community—an isolation that began at least two years before his civil rights decisions and their attacks on white southerners had made them national figures. In Charleston, his decisions and their provocative pronouncements simply aggravated an already strained relationship.

Annie Waring's pathetic life after the divorce was a continuing reminder of the roots of that strain. Following the divorce, Annie lived briefly in New York where their now married daughter had moved to live. Then, however, she returned to Charleston and rented a renovated kitchen house at 80 Tradd Street—within sight of, and no more than a hundred feet from, the rear of the Meeting Street home where her former husband now lived with his younger, attractive second wife. Charleston's converted carriage and kitchen houses were perfectly respectable residences. Although Waties Waring was not a wealthy man, the $250 he provided Miss Annie each month seemed small in comparison with the income of her former husband and his new wife. In his 1951 federal tax return, for example, he declared $16,250 in salary, $35.44 in interest income, and $1,639.66 in stock dividends. For a time, Elizabeth received allowances from her father's trust—funds administered, ironically, by her first husband who, at Elizabeth's insistence, transacted business related to the trust through Judge Waring. But the trust fund was relatively small. Nevertheless, seeing the respected Miss Annie reduced to a rented kitchen house while Waties and Elizabeth occupied *her* house, the house from which she had been *banished,* incensed many of Waties Waring's former friends. Miss Annie's lonely, often bedridden existence fueled their enmity.[54]

As a child, Tom Waring's daughter occasionally chatted with Miss Annie while playing with a friend who lived in the main house at 80 Tradd Street, and she wondered about the kindly elderly woman's connection with her family. Other members of the Waring family, however, apparently had little contact with Annie after the divorce. "Looking back on it," Tom Waring recalls, "I feel a certain amount of guilt at not having done anything much. I had never been very close, on social terms, with either of them. I felt personally distressed about how Annie Waring had been treated. But I'm afraid I did very little about it."[55]

At her death, however, the Warings closed ranks behind Miss Annie— and perhaps against her former husband. Annie Waring died in December 1954, several years after Judge Waring's retirement from the bench. She was buried in Charleston's Magnolia Cemetery at her parents' gravesite. At her funeral, all but one of her pallbearers were members of the Waring family.[56]

3

Rejoining the Union

By his own account, Waties Waring embraced southern racial traditions through most of his adult life. As Charleston corporation counsel, he had made certain that the Army use of Stoney Field would be limited to white soldiers. His other activities in behalf of the city apparently were also entirely compatible with southern customs. As an active member and officer of South Carolina's white Democratic party, he was closely associated with "Cotton Ed" Smith, the state's leading racist demagogue of the period; when Smith died, he praised the senator's "long and honorable" career. Against such a backdrop, it is hardly surprising that many white South Carolinians saw his civil rights decisions and attacks on the South as products of spite against a society unwilling to accept his second wife rather than as a reflection of principle.

Among certain of Judge Waring's contemporaries, however, there is doubt as to how deeply committed he was to the southern cause of white supremacism. "I don't think that Waties was a flaming liberal at any time in his life," D. A. Brockinton, Jr., has remarked; "but I don't think he was a super-Confederate either." Some of the evidence offered by white Charlestonians to establish his Confederate credentials, moreover, was ambiguous at best. Gus Tamsberg recalled, for example, that once, during a barbershop conversation following Waring's appointment to the bench, the discussion turned to a state trial then under way against taxi drivers accused of lynching a black charged with killing another driver. "Well, mark my word," Tamsberg remembered Waring observing, "if those men are acquitted, it's going to bring new federal law down on South Carolina." Tamsberg interpreted Waring's warning as a reflection of the judge's hostility to federal interference in southern racial affairs. It can just as easily be construed, however, as an expression of shock at the crime involved and hope that fear of federal intervention—if not a desire for justice—would prod the state into action.[1]

But even more revealing about Judge Waring's racial views prior to his divorce were the decisions he rendered in two significant cases involving dis-

42

crimination. Both involved racial inequities in the pay schedules of public school teachers. The first suit was filed in Charleston in November 1943. Black Charleston teachers, like those in the rest of the state, were paid substantially lower salaries than their white counterparts, and the local NAACP chapter had been considering legal action for years. The chapter persuaded one woman to become a party to a suit, but plans for litigation in her name had to be dropped when it was learned that she recently had been secretly married, violating a school rule forbidding married women teachers. The NAACP chapter then persuaded Viola Duvall to file a class action in behalf of Charleston's black teachers, and Thurgood Marshall came down from the NAACP's New York office to argue the case before Judge Waring. Joining Marshall was Harold R. Boulware, attorney for the state NAACP organization.[2]

The Duvall case was Thurgood Marshall's first encounter with Judge Waring. "When I took the teacher's salary case before him," Marshall recalled several years after the litigation, "I regarded him as just another southern jurist who would give me the usual legal head-whipping before I went along to the Circuit Court of Appeals." But Marshall was to be pleasantly surprised.

> [I]t turned out to be the only case I ever tried with my mouth hanging open half of the time. Judge Waring was so fair that I found my apprehension totally unwarranted. He made his position clear and told them that the 14th Amendment was still in the Constitution and that it still prevailed for all citizens in his court.[3]

The counsel for the Charleston school board quickly sensed the drift of the litigation also. At a hearing, Judge Waring heard the plaintiff's testimony and that of the school board's accountant. Then, the board's attorney asked that the proceedings be suspended and agreed to a consent decree obligating the school system to equalize salaries. Under the decree, filed on February 14, 1944, the school board conceded that Viola Duvall and all other black teachers and principals were paid lower salaries than whites "with like professional qualifications and experience and performing substantially the same duties." Judge Waring agreed to delay full equalization of salaries until September 1946. Beginning with the September 1944, school year, however, the salaries of black teachers and principals were to be increased by amounts equal to half the difference between their present salaries and those of whites with similar qualification, experience, and duties.[4]

Judge Waring's second, and more significant, teacher pay case arose in Columbia. On March 18, 1944, little more than a month after the *Duvall* decree was announced, the South Carolina general assembly established its own elaborate and time-consuming procedure by which public school teachers could challenge racially discriminatory pay schedules. The scheme provided for review of such complaints first by the county school board, then by the state board of education, next by a state court of common pleas, and finally by the state supreme court. In 1945, moreover, the state established a new teacher certification plan under which all teachers were to be graded, classified, and paid according to education, experience, and scores on an examination administered by the National Educational Board.[5]

Albert N. Thompson was a black teacher at Columbia's Booker T. Washington High School in the Richland County school system. In Richland County, the average salary was then $1,420 per year for white teachers, $1,026 for blacks. Following adoption of the state complaint procedure, Thompson petitioned the county school board, charging that his salary was lower than that of whites with comparable qualifications. When the board denied him relief, Thompson filed a complaint in federal court. Ordinarily, Judge Timmerman would have been expected to preside, but at Timmerman's request, Judge Waring agreed to hear Thompson's suit.[6]

Nine witnesses testified at a May 1945 hearing in the federal courthouse at Columbia. Counsel for Thompson easily established substantial differences in the salaries of white and black teachers. The inequities, they argued, were the product of discrimination rather than experience, training, or personal qualities. Thompson's attorneys also contended that the state certification plan would delay rather than promote equalization. "Instead of a speedy procedure," Edward Dudley of the NAACP's New York office complained, "we have a long and drawn-out 'remedy' which might take years." A school board member asserted that the inequities were largely a matter of supply and demand. There was little demand for black teachers in the north, he explained; "as a result, there are more teachers than jobs [in South Carolina] and negro teachers will work for less." Dr. Heyward Gibbes, a Columbia physician and school board chairman, agreed that racial as well as legitimate factors accounted for the disparities, but asserted that the board had begun to attack the problem in 1941 and asked the court for patience. "On the basis of equalification," he observed, "a discrepancy in white and negro teachers' salaries that has 200 years of social, educational and political background for a basis is being eliminated. . . . Nothing but a more or less violent action," he added, "can change it overnight." School superintendent A. G. Flora was even more candid. Flora testified that he was obliged to pay black teachers what the school board directed, readily conceded discrimination, and assured Judge Waring that he would be happy to comply with any equalization directive the court might issue.[7]

Counsel for the school board had raised two essentially jurisdictional objections to Thompson's suit. Since the plaintiff had initially petitioned the county school board, they argued, he should be required to pursue the entire state remedial scheme before being allowed to seek federal court relief. Through the recently enacted state certification plan, they further contended, South Carolina was already beginning to provide the relief Thompson was seeking. His suit thus raised no justiciable controversy.

In a ruling handed down on May 26, 1945, Judge Waring rejected both these contentions. Thompson's petition to the school board, he caustically observed, hardly constituted a waiver of his civil rights or a restriction on the jurisdiction of a federal court. "There is such ample authority to support this declaration," he added, "that I deem it unnecessary to quote a long line of decisions." Nor was the state's adoption of a certification plan of critical significance. That scheme, wrote Waring, quoting the statute at issue, was binding for only one fiscal year "and without committal for future years." Furthermore, the plan applied only to the distribution of state funds, while a substantial portion of teacher salaries was provided from county funds.[8]

Judge Waring then ruled in the plaintiff's favor. He recognized, he wrote, the complexities of the racial issue.

> The question of equality in rights and opportunities as between people of the white and negro races has been one of the great problems of the American people brought about . . . first by the enslavement and introduction into this country of people of alien and different race and color; and secondly by their sudden emancipation as a war measure, and theoretical immediate transition from complete slavery into complete equality.

He also appeared to embrace the view that the elimination of racial discrimination must be a gradual process, expressing views markedly more conservative than those of a few years later.

> The old cliché that Rome was not built in a day, is applicable to this situation. The idea that emancipation of a race long enslaved and without political rights, without political or any other kind of education, and without training to assume citizenship, would bring about a satisfactory situation over night could be held by only a few partisan, biased, persons motivated either by idealistic abstractions or by a spirit of political revenge and self-seeking aggrandizement. The emancipation proclamation of President Lincoln did not free the slaves in a day; and the enactment of constitutional amendments shortly thereafter and adopted for the purpose of giving equal rights to all the people of his country did not bring about that ideal condition merely because they were ratified. These things have to be lived through and arrived at after generations of experience, before men will accept them, understand them, agree with them and work for their effect and efficacy. Many years have elapsed without these constitutional amendments and the statutes passed under their authority, having their full force and effect. In fact, many doubt whether they are yet in full force and effect and point to the disparity in wages and salaries in South Carolina; the exclusion of negroes from railroad brotherhoods; and racial riots in New York's Harlem, as some of the proofs of this.

Finally, he was "greatly impressed by the intelligence, ability, interest and desire, to be just and fair to all parties, evinced" by Gibbes and Flora. They had simply inherited, he asserted, a racially discriminatory salary system which they were attempting to correct.[9]

Despite his faith in Columbia's school board chairman and superintendent, however, Judge Waring considered a remedial order necessary. There had been some reduction in salary inequities, he conceded, but "startling" disparities remained that could be explained only in terms of discrimination. Invariably, for example, white teachers were assigned beginning salaries several hundred dollars higher than those for black teachers. Nor was there any assurance that the school board would consistently back the commitment of its chairman and superintendent, or that county funds would be dispersed according to the racially neutral provisions of the state certification plan. The Richland County school system, he held, was to establish a salary schedule compatible with the state plan. The order was to go into effect in April 1946 and be retroactive for the entire 1945–46 school year.

The harmonious reception given Judge Waring's equal pay rulings by the defendants and other South Carolinians would stand in marked contrast to the hostility his later racial decisions aroused. Waring was especially confident of Flora's good faith, remarking years later that he found the superintendent a "capital man . . . clean-cut, decent, able, fine kind of chap, perfectly frank." Flora did not disappoint him. On March 6, 1946, he wrote the judge to report that the school system had completed its program of salary adjustments and paid all back salaries called for under Waring's order. In June of the previous year—on the same day, ironically, that the Warings were granted a Florida divorce—Dr. Gibbes had also written Waring. He had read the judge's ruling "with pleasure and complete approval," he wrote, adding:

> Your decision has not forced us into a new departure in school administration; it has rather tended to support us in a course which we had already determined upon. You may rest assured that the Columbia School Board is genuinely concerned with trying to solve their difficult problem. I think that there is a strong probability that they will succeed in carrying out a program that will prove satisfactory to reasonable people on both sides of the question.[10]

Judge Waring's opinions and off-the-bench statements on the equal pay cases did not contain the bite of his later pronouncements or reflect the aggressive civil rights posture he was soon to assume. In a June 6, 1945, letter, Edgar Brown, who was then serving as regional finance director of the Democratic National Committee and had sponsored the state certification plan in the general assembly, congratulated Waring on his "masterly understanding of the" issue. It was "comforting to have your Judicial Conclusion," Brown added, "that the program as written is free from the tinge of race prejudice." In his reply to Brown, Waring expressed his preference for a "moderate" approach to the issue. In his response to Dr. Gibbes, Waring was more direct. He conceded that South Carolinians of our state are "going to be hard to educate along these lines." But then he observed:

> I really believe that we liberal minded southerners may be able to eventually cure this situation, not by the radical methods of the Eleanor Roosevelt-Wendell Willkie School, nor by the reactionary methods of the old slave holders, but by moderate, gradual and understanding action.[11]

The equal pay cases can be considered, therefore, a midway point between Judge Waring's acceptance of the old order in southern race relations and the commitment to aggressive remedial action he was later to embrace.

White Charlestonians attributed that commitment to growing strains in his relations with them. Waring, however, cited the education in discrimination afforded him by the equal pay litigation and other early race cases.

Among other cases helping to mold his thinking, he would later claim, was a peonage suit that arose in 1947 in the Florence division. Waring had assumed that peonage was largely a practice of the past, even in South Carolina. "I had known that there was a lot of it in the early days," he later remarked, "but he felt that [while] in South Carolina we hadn't advanced a great deal in many respects . . . in some we had, and I thought that was pretty well over." He was astonished, then, when the Department of Justice instructed the local U.S. attorney to bring peonage and kidnapping charges against a prosperous Hartsville farmer, John Ellis Wilhelm, and his father, James Fred Wilhelm. A black youth, James DeWitt, agreeing to work on the younger Wilhelm's farm, had signed an agricultural contract and quickly became heavily indebted to his employer. When DeWitt decided to quit, Wilhelm had him arrested for violating the labor contract. A state magistrate's court held the contract illegal and ordered DeWit freed. Ten days later, however, Wilhelm and his father seized DeWitt outside a movie theater and forced him to work on the elder Wilhelm's Georgia farm at a wage of one dollar per day. With information supplied by local authorities, federal agents developed a case against the Wilhelms.[12]

Ordinarily, the Wilhelms could have been expected to plead innocent and be found not guilty by an obliging South Carolina jury. Since DeWitt had been carried across state lines, however, the defendants faced kidnapping as well as peonage charges. Kidnapping was a capital offense; while "juries in a Federal court in the deep South [would] usually acquit in a racial case," as Judge Waring later observed, there was "always the danger that some jury [might] make a mistake and convict." The Wilhelms decided not to take that risk. Their counsel had the case postponed a day or two, and the government attorney indicated to Waring that negotiations were under way. Ultimately, the kidnapping charges were dropped and the younger Wilhelm pleaded guilty to a violation of DeWitt's civil rights. Judge Waring sentenced him to a year and a day and a $500 fine.[13]

The *Wilhelm* case gave Judge Waring further insight into the dark side of the southern agricultural economy and the position of blacks within that system. A conversation with a prospective juror in the case also made a deep impression on Waring. The juror and other veniremen had discussed the case, he told Waring.

> [W]e all agreed that you were right in that case. That was an outrageous situation and that man ought to have been sent to jail and you were right in protecting that poor young fellow and punishing the man that treated him that way. But we also agreed that if we had had to pass upon it, we would not have found him guilty.

Waring found the juror's confession "an interesting and a very pathetic situation." The juror "was a first-class citizen—who knew the difference between right and wrong, but would not have been willing to do the right thing because of community pressure."[14]

A jury's reaction to a 1950–51 wage-and-hour case was equally revealing to the judge about the psychology of racism. Some time after the federal minimum wage was increased from fifty to seventy-five cents an hour, the United States brought criminal charges against three brothers who ran a sawmill near Florence. The defendants had indicated in their records that they were following the new wage schedule. But their workers, all of whom were black, had kept their pay envelopes; a comparison of the envelopes with company records demonstrated that the workers were being paid the old wage. Twenty black workers testified; the evidence seemed overwhelming. But the jury promptly acquitted the defendants. Judge Waring found the verdict "shocking," but understandable. "These fellows are guilty," he later speculated that the jurors had reasoned. "But we can't send white men to jail for violating a federal law. We'll have Negroes all over the state rising up and demanding their rights."[15]

The early case which apparently had the greatest influence on Judge Waring's growing commitment to civil rights, however, concerned Issac Woodward, Jr., a twenty-seven-year-old black whose wife was then living in Winnsboro. On February 12, 1946, Woodward was discharged from the Army at Camp Gordon, near Augusta, Georgia. That evening, he boarded a bus bound for his wife's Winnsboro home. At Batesburg, a sleepy village thirty miles from Columbia, he was taken off the bus by police and arrested. The next morning, he pleaded guilty to public drunkenness and disorderly conduct in the Batesburg mayor's court. Mayor H. E. Quarles imposed a $50 fine, but Woodward only had $44. Quarles collected that and suspended the rest of the fine. Woodward's eyes were red and swollen. Later that day, he was admitted to the veteran's hospital in Columbia. Three months later, he was released from the hospital—totally blind.[16]

Civil rights groups soon complained that Batesburg police chief Lynwood Shull had gouged the veteran's eyes with his blackjack, and by late summer, the Woodward case had become a national cause in the black press. Woodward's parents lived in the Bronx borough of New York City. In mid-August, 20,000 supporters, including a number of prominent entertainment figures, attended a benefit rally at a New York stadium sponsored by the *Amsterdam News* and the Issac Woodward Benefit Committee. In a speech read to the gathering in his absence, New York's Mayor O'Dwyer, honorary chairman of the benefit, condemned the "brutal treatment" to which Woodward had been subjected and announced that New York police had recently been issued a policy statement forbidding discrimination in the performance of their duties. In an interview with reporters the day before the benefit, Chief Shull readily confirmed that he had hit the veteran with his blackjack when he became "unruly." "I hit him across the front of the head after he attempted to take away my blackjack," Shull explained. "I grabbed it away from him and cracked him across the head."[17]

Through the NAACP, Woodward also told his story to the Department of Justice. Ordinarily, federal officials might have considered the incident a state matter, best left to the discretion of local authorities. But 1946 was a congressional election year. In late September, the Justice Department telephoned U.S. attorney Claude Sapp in Columbia, informing him that charges had been prepared against Shull and were being mailed to South Carolina for filing in the district court. Fearing that a grand jury would be unlikely to indict Batesburg's constable on felony charges, the Department had decided to bring misdemeanor charges against Shull under an information or affidavit of the U.S. attorney. On September 26, Sapp filed the information in the district court, charging Shull with a violation of Title 18, Section 52, of the U.S. Code.[18]

A remnant of the Reconstruction era, Section 52 made it a crime for persons acting "under color of any law, statute, ordinance, regulation, or custom" to interfere with rights "secured or protected" by the U.S. Constitution or federal law. Conviction carried a maximum punishment of one year, $1,000, or both. The information charged Shull with violating Woodward's

> right to be secure in his person and to be immune from illegal assault and battery; the right and privilege not to be beaten and tortured by persons exercising the authority to arrest; the right and privilege not to be beaten, tortured, and subjected to cruel and unusual punishment because of having committed any offense; the right and privilege not to be denied equal protection of the laws; and the right and privilege not to be subjected to different punishments, pains, and penalties by reason of his race or color.[19]

Following the filing of federal charges, South Carolinians closed ranks behind Chief Shull. In October, the state law enforcement association adopted a resolution protesting the "high-handed" interference of federal authorities in a "purely local matter," and a movement was begun to raise a defense fund in the constable's behalf. Three prominent Batesburg citizens, including Mayor Quarles and a former state highway commissioner, posted his bond. Civil rights groups continued to give the case extensive attention.[20]

Batesburg was Judge Timmerman's hometown, and he knew Shull and had no desire to try the case. As he had with the Columbia equal pay litigation, Timmerman asked Judge Waring to hear the case; Waring again agreed to preside. The trial was set for November 5, election day, in Columbia. Shortly before it was to begin, however, Claude Sapp visited Judge Waring's chambers and told the judge that he had been directed by the Justice Department to file the information against Shull, that the department had furnished him with no witnesses, and that the attorney general was now instructing Sapp to seek a continuance in the case.[21]

Judge Waring now suspected that the filing of charges had been a mere election-year ploy, and that, following the election, the charges would be quietly forgotten. He was shocked and furious. He told Sapp that he would deny any motion for a postponement of the trial. Instead, he would dismiss the charges against Shull and issue an order detailing his reasons.[22]

After Sapp left his chambers, Judge Waring prepared a rough draft of a memorandum order. Noting that the charges against Shull had been prepared in Washington and forwarded to South Carolina "for immediate filing," he asked: "Why this haste in [the] start of a prosecution and reticence in trying it?" Then, appearing to answer his own question, he observed:

> I am not unmindful of the fact that this matter has attained unpleasant and undesirable publicity. It is probable that agitators for prosecution and agitators against prosecution are not averse to the publicity which they themselves receive from the advocacy of these measures. I am also aware of the fact that a national election is impending.

Such factors, he asserted, should have no influence on the judicial process.

> I do not believe that a criminal prosecution in the courts of this country should be influenced one way or the other by the desire of any of such parties for publicity and the resultant benefit to seekers for public exhibitionism or for political preferment. I am of the opinion that justice in the courts should [be] administered irrespective of race or color and that judges and jurors must be color-blind in rendering justice. If this case is based upon facts and the defendant committed the acts as charged, he is guilty of a heinous offense and prompt trial should be had. If these charges cannot be sustained, then he is being subjected to grave injustice to allow the case to continue upon the calendar of the court. I am unwilling that a matter of this kind should be allowed to drag on and perhaps disappear after the national election. And I do not believe that this poor blinded creature should be a football in the contest between box office and ballot box. The case must be tried or dismissed and the government announcing that it is not ready for trial, accordingly it is ordered that the cause be dismissed for want of prosecution. The defendant is hereby discharged and his bail bond exonerated.[23]

It is not known whether Judge Waring shared his draft order with Claude Sapp. After conferring further with the Justice Department, however, the U.S. attorney reported to Waring that a department attorney and several witnesses would be available and that the case would go to trial on schedule.[24] On Monday, November 4, the first day of the term, Judge Waring disposed of nearly fifty cases, including nineteen revenue violations, three cases of automobile theft, and an embezzlement count. On Tuesday, a jury heard the Shull case.

Issac Woodward was the government's principal witness. Dressed in a brown suit and wearing sunglasses with green lenses, the slim black veteran testified that a few miles outside Augusta, when the bus made a stop to pick up passengers, he asked the driver to wait while he went to a restroom. The driver, he said, cursed him and told him to return to his seat. "[T]alk to me like I'm talking to you," Woodward said he retorted. "I'm a man just like you." Woodward then went to the restroom. When he returned, the driver said nothing. When the bus reached Batesburg, however, the driver summoned Woodward off the bus to meet "someone I want you to see." Once outside, Woodward encountered Chief Shull and another policeman. Woodward testified that when he attempted to explain his difficulty with the driver,

Shull told him to "shut up" and hit him on the head with his blackjack. Then he twisted Woodward's arm behind his back and led him up a street and around a corner, out of the view of the other bus passengers. Approximately a hundred feet beyond the corner, according to Woodward, Shull asked him whether he had been discharged from the Army. When Woodward indicated that he had, the police chief began beating him with his billy club and shouted, "You don't say 'yes' to me, say 'yes, sir!' " Woodward complied but then struggled with Shull, wresting the blackjack from the officer. Another policeman ran up at this point, Woodward testified, and threatened him with his pistol until Woodward dropped the blackjack. Woodward conceded that he had "a drink or two" but denied that he used profane or abusive language on the bus, or that any passenger had complained to the driver about his behavior. After his appearance in the Batesburg mayor's court, he added, he had been returned to his jail cell; no physician had examined him until his transfer to the veteran's hospital.

Two passengers on the bus, a University of South Carolina student and a white veteran, testified that they had not seen Woodward drinking, that he was simply the one among many Army dischargees "jollying around" on the bus who had been singled out for arrest. The testimony of most witnesses, however, differed markedly from Woodward's version of the events. Bus driver A. C. Blackwell of Columbia testified that Woodward was drinking on the bus and offered a drink to a white soldier. "He was drunk," Blackwell said, "he was pretty drunk," and had "caused commotions" at several points along the bus route. "Boy," Blackwell said he told Woodward at one stop, "I'm going to leave you somewhere." The black's language had been so profane, Blackwell added, that an offended white couple had asked that he be removed from the bus.

Lynwood Shull, dressed in a blue suit and appearing clean-cut, pleaded self-defense in the line of duty. Shull conceded that he may have "bumped" Woodward lightly with his nightstick at the bus station but insisted that he had hit the defendant only when Woodward attempted to seize his blackjack.

> I kept trying to hush him. . . . The next thing I knew he caught the loose end of my blackjack and pulled me right into him. I didn't have time to pick a spot. I'm sorry I hit him in the eyes and blinded him. I had no wish to blind anyone. I had no intention of hitting him in the eyes, but I had to hit him in self-defense because he was advancing on me.

Had Woodward "hushed up" his cursing, Shull said, he would not have arrested him. When Woodward first declined the police chief's offer to seek a physician following his court appearance the next day, moreover, the policeman had bathed the soldier's swollen eyes with warm water and a cloth.

Other witnesses backed Shull's position. Another policeman testified that he had not been present when the defendant and Woodward were struggling for the nightstick. But he agreed that the veteran had been cursing. Mayor Quarles reported that Woodward had admitted in his court to being drunk and disorderly. A Batesburg physician, who said that he had examined Woodward at the jail before his transfer to the veteran's hospital, testified that the injuries to both Woodward's eyes could have been caused by one blow, as Shull had testified. Under questioning from a government attorney, the doctor did concede that such a blow would have to be "perfectly timed." Three character witnesses, including the county sheriff and a black Methodist minister, declared that Shull was a man of fine character and reputation.

Throughout the trial, Judge Waring attempted to thwart the appeals to racism of Shull's counsel. In his charge to the all-white jury, moreover, he observed that the case's racial elements had attracted "unwanted and undesirable" publicity and urged the jurors to "put aside prejudice and give due justice. . . . You are trying only one police officer," he warned, not the South's racial customs or "black against white." In their summations to the jury, however, Shull's attorneys used a distinctly different approach. One claimed that Woodward belonged to "an inferior race" and that his "vulgar" talk was "not the talk of a sober South Carolina Negro. . . . If Lynwood Shull is convicted today," he warned, "you will be saying to the public officers of South Carolina that you no longer want your home, your wife, and your children protected." Another of Shull's counsel alluded heavily to the Confederacy and the Civil War. If delivering a verdict against the federal government "means that South Carolina'll have to secede again," he told the jurors, "then let's secede!"

Judge Waring doubted that the jury would deliberate more than a few minutes before returning to the courtroom with a verdict of acquittal, but he wanted to give the proceedings "a little more atmosphere of respectability." "I'm going out for a walk," he told the bailiff after discharging the jury, "and I'll be back in twenty minutes' time." "But Judge," the bailiff responded, "that jury ain't going to stay [out] for twenty minutes." "They're going to stay out twenty minutes," Waring countered, "because they can't come in until I come back, and I'm not going to be back here for twenty minutes." Judge Waring briefly walked the streets of Columbia, then returned to the courtroom. The bailiff met him at the door. "Judge, the jury's all ready; they're rapping on the door and say they want to come in." The case had gone to the jury at 6:30 P.M.; its verdict was delivered at 6:55. That verdict, as Judge Waring expected, was acquittal.[25]

Like other white-owned South Carolina newspapers, the Columbia *State* applauded the jury's decision. Evidence presented in the case, *The State* editorialized, established that "the Negro had caused trouble on the bus all along its route . . . that he was boisterous and caused offense by unseemly language," and that Shull had "struck the veteran in discharge of his duty and in self-defense."

A special prosecutor was sent to Columbia from Washington to try the case. This may have been an implied insinuation that the case would not receive fair and unbiased treatment in the South, but it also removes the possibility of any possible future implications of the sort. . . .
    Such intercession on the part of the central government in the affairs of the states can lead only to a renewal of argument over states' rights. It is

therefore an unwholesome influence against unity in the Union, and something to be studiously avoided whenever possible.[26]

While hardly agreeing with *The State's* assumption that justice had been served, Judge Waring had no quarrel with the Shull jury's verdict. "I made no comment," he later recalled.

> I have no comment or criticism of them now. I couldn't ask them to find [Shull] guilty on the slimness of that case, but I was shocked at the hypocrisy of my government and your government in submitting that disgraceful case before a jury. I was also hurt that I was made a party to it, because I had to be a party to it, however unwilling I was.[27]

Issac Woodward's plight, the racial appeals of Shull's counsel, and the Justice Department's failure to pursue the prosecution aggressively had a tremendous impact on Judge Waring. The case was also, he would later say, Elizabeth Waring's "baptism in racial prejudice." Partly to escape the increasingly chilly atmosphere of Charleston, Elizabeth often accompanied her husband when he heard cases in Columbia and other communities where they were still graciously received by the local bar. A March 1946 society column in the Columbia *State* noted, for example, "Mrs. J. Waties Waring, attractive wife of Judge Waring, lending a breath of spring to the federal courthouse yesterday with a lovely silk dress and charming straw hat." Elizabeth heard the Woodward case, then returned to their hotel room in tears. She told Judge Waring that she had "never heard such a terrible thing and had no idea how bad the situation was." When she confessed her shock to a Columbia matron, her acquaintance wearily responded, "Mrs. Waring, that sort of thing happens all the time. It's dreadful, but what are we going to do about it?"[28]

In her effort to do something "about it," Mrs. Waring began reading voraciously the history of southern race relations, including W. J. Cash's *Mind of the South,* Gunnar Myrdal's *An American Dilemma,* and other classic studies. According to one report, she also borrowed pamphlets from Samuel Fleming, a prosperous black Charleston shoemaker who counted many south of Broad Street residents among his clientele. In the evening, she read this material to her husband while he rested his eyes, and he, too, began to read on his own. Judge Waring found the works enlightening—and deeply disturbing. "I couldn't take it, at first. I used to say it wasn't true, it couldn't be. I'd put the books down, so troubled I couldn't look at them. We'd get in our car and drive through the night, miles and miles, just thinking and talking." Gradually, they absorbed a large body of the current literature, and in time Judge Waring, like Elizabeth, began to embrace what they read.[29]

Waring also moved to eliminate a number of discriminatory practices in his court. Previously, the juror lists were race-coded, with a "C" placed by the names of blacks. He ended that. By custom, black and white spectators were segregated in the courtroom. That practice was now eliminated. Waring noticed, too, that while the seating of racially mixed juries might initially be integrated, following recesses black jurors invariably filed back into the jury box last, taking seats on the end of the panel. Waring instructed the clerk to provide jurors with designated—and integrated—seating which they were to retain throughout the proceedings.[30]

Samuel Fleming alerted Judge Waring to another discriminatory feature of the court's routine. Once the black shoemaker was serving on a jury in Waring's court when the proceedings were recessed for lunch. The jurors were taken to a Charleston restaurant, where the white jurors and a deputy marshal were seated in the dining room, while Fleming and another black juror were relegated to the kitchen. Fleming resented this sort of treatment. He threatened to telephone Judge Waring, and the deputy grudgingly placed two extra chairs at the end of the table provided for the white jurors. When Waring learned of the incident, he instructed the chief marshal to see that the practice ceased. If whites complained, he added, the marshal could simply explain that the separation of jurors in a pending case was a violation of the law. The marshal followed the judge's instructions, and the restaurant proprietors complained that their white patrons were offended. "But nothing very much happened," Waring later recalled. "After all, you know, a judge has got a good deal of power. When he does these things, there isn't anybody can tell him he can't do it."[31]

Waring also attempted to cope with the shabby treatment generally accorded blacks in the courtroom. As he himself had done through most of his life, white attorneys addressed blacks by their first names. Often, too, blacks bore the brunt of crude courtroom humor. Waring addressed blacks by their titles, instructed courtroom personnel to do likewise, and made pointed remarks to lawyers in an effort to improve their treatment of black witnesses and parties—an effort only partially successful. In October 1948, he appointed Samuel Fleming's son John as court crier or bailiff, a move that, together with his civil rights rulings, assumed special significance in South Carolina's black community.[32]

Judge Waring realized that the elimination of segregated seating and other improvements in the treatment accorded blacks in his court were "little things." But he also knew that, in many ways, such reforms meant

> much . . . because when young people come along and serve on juries and they find they are segregated according to white and colored, that sinks in their minds, and they say, "Even in the precincts of the jury room we're separated, so it must be right. It's the law."
>
> If you break that down and they're accustomed to it, then they come out and they say, "Why, there was a colored fellow on there and he was a pretty good fellow." He had good ideas, or bad ideas, but at any rate he took part in it. I think those little things mean an enormous amount, and I tried to follow that up as much as I could, to sweep out of that court the idea that it was a non-American court. I tried to introduce what I call the American creed into a court, even sitting in segregated South Carolina.[33]

Whatever their ultimate significance, such reforms would not make much of a dent in South Carolina's segregated society and hardly made Judge Waring a controversial figure in his native state. Nor had his equal pay rulings seemed to affront southern tradition. Indeed, in 1942, Waring's nephew Tom, who in time was to become one of the staunchest defenders of the Confederate faith, had asserted editorially that "sooner or later South Carolina, along with many another Southern state, must face and solve the question of equal pay for negro teachers on the basis of equal training." The U.S. Supreme Court had recently ruled, he warned, that race could no longer be a determinant of teachers' salaries, and "[i]f the negroes decide to precipitate the matter, they can do so at any time by means of an injunction which would tie up the school system. . . . Sensibly enough,"

> their intelligent leadership has no such intention at this time. The leaders realize the state has not got the money to raise negro teachers' pay overnight; the alternative would be to reduce the white teachers' pay, or to close up many schools. Either step would only stir up racial hatred.

But if blacks did decide to act, Tom Waring added, "[t]hinking people admit there is no way to circumvent the supreme court ruling." Other South Carolinians shared Tom Waring's sentiments. Even before the Charleston equal pay suit was filed in Judge Waring's court, the state had begun making token increases in the salaries of black teachers, and a biracial committee was established to investigate the core problem of teacher certification.[34]

Around this time, Judge Waring's highly publicized 1947 trial of nine prominent Virginians on bank embezzlement charges enhanced his reputation as an effective, uncompromising jurist. Hugh N. Rakes was a wealthy Leesburg, Virginia, farmer and dairyman. To finance expansion of his various enterprises, Rakes allegedly entered into a far-flung "check-kiting" venture, establishing relatively modest bank accounts, then writing large checks on those accounts to create balances in other banks, which in turn were used to establish even larger accounts at other institutions. Ultimately, the scheme involved banks in Fredericksburg, Floyd, Purcellville, and other Virginia communities, and caused the collapse of Fredericksburg's Farmers and Merchants State Bank. After one of Rakes' co-conspirators was indicted by a state grand jury for misapplying nearly $500,000 of the Fredericksburg bank's funds, George R. Humrickhouse, a young assistant U.S. attorney for Virginia's eastern district, launched his own investigation of the scheme. With little assistance from other authorities, Humrickhouse persisted in his efforts, eventually securing indictments against Rakes, Rakes' wife, and seven prominent banking and real estate figures, including a member and a former member of the state general assembly, several bank presidents, and a former chief state banking examiner.[35]

Given the defendants' prominence, it was decided that a judge should be brought in from out of state to hear the case, and Judge Waring agreed to preside. Before it began, Waring agreed to postpone one defendant's trial for health reasons. The main trial began March 3, 1947, and lasted fifty-three days, becoming the longest in Virginia's eastern district since the 1807 treason trial of Aaron Burr. The proceedings produced a 1,300,000-word record, and over 1,400 exhibits were admitted into evidence. Character witnesses in-

cluded Virginia governor William Tuck and a justice of the state's highest
court. At one point, the defendants' attorneys would invite Waring to attend
a cocktail party, and the judge would decline the invitation. When John
Marshall was presiding in the Burr trial, he remembered, he had been sharply
criticized for attending a dinner at which Burr and his counsel were present.
"While I can never hope to reach the heights that Marshall attained," he
would later say, "I can avoid his depths." On April 25, 1947, following
seventy-one-and-a-half hours of deliberation, the jury returned guilty verdicts against all the defendants. Two hours later, Judge Waring assembled the
defendants for sentencing. Following the trial, a Virginia newspaper praised
the judge's patience in allowing the defense to exhaust several weeks presenting testimony which "a judge with . . . less determination for fairness might
have viewed . . . as superfluous and too time-consuming."[36] In sentencing
Rakes and his confederates, however, Judge Waring barely concealed his contempt for the defendants. An attorney for one reasoned that his client simply
had a blind loyalty to Rakes. "And also a profitable one according to the
evidence," Waring interjected. "I don't believe Rakes devised these banking
schemes," the judge added. "He had some cold-blooded bankers to do that."
"I hope you will not impose any prison sentence," the same attorney pleaded.
"I am, though," the judge replied. Another lawyer noted that he and his
clients were just simple "country" people. Waring was not moved. "Now
there's no jury here, Mr. Lee. You're an experienced lawyer . . . and you
know what you're doing. That might bring a sob from a jury but it won't help
before me." When yet another attorney sought leniency for his client, Waring
asserted: "I don't believe in sending a poor man to jail and letting a rich man
off with a fine. . . . The bigger they are," he added, "the harder they fall."
All but two minor figures in the scheme received jail sentences. With three
exceptions, the sentences Judge Waring imposed were stiffer than those the
government had recommended.

The day following sentencing, the Richmond *News Leader* praised Judge
Waring's conduct of the trial:

> Judge Waring presided with magnificent dignity and firmness and won the
> respect of all whom duty or curiosity brought into the courtroom. . . .
> Virginia must ask the privilege of thanking Judge Waring for the care with
> which he maintained the high tradition of the Federal bench.

The Roanoke *Times* echoed the *News Leader's* sentiments. Waring's "conduct of a difficult and involved trial," the *Times* asserted, "surely must have
served to enhance the public's respect for the Federal bench." Other Virginia
newspapers were equally complimentary, and the chief judge of Waring's circuit, John J. Parker, wrote him, "You have merely measured up to what I
expected of you."[37]

Even Waring's harshest South Carolina critics, however much they may
have disapproved of his handling of discrimination cases or of the scandal
surrounding his divorce, declared that he was an excellent jurist. It is thus
ironic that, while his overall conduct of the Richmond trial was praiseworthy,

his handling of one aspect of the proceedings won Rakes and the other defendants new trials. On April 20, two days before the jury began its delibera-
tions, one of the jurors was offered a bribe to deadlock the jury. The juror
promptly told his neighbor, a state circuit judge, of the incident, and at the
judge's suggestion, also contacted Judge Waring. Waring and prosecutor
Humrickhouse agreed that a thorough investigation should be conducted following the trial, and Waring instructed the juror to tell no one of the incident. But defense counsel were not informed.[38]

After Rakes and his co-defendants were convicted, a Richmond automobile salesman was found guilty of jury tampering in the case, and it was
learned that the juror approached had indeed discussed the bribery attempt
with several other jurors. Rakes and his co-defendants filed motions for a
new trial and asked that a different judge rule on the motions. Judge Waring, they asserted in affidavits filed with the court, had "a personal bias and
prejudice against [them] and in favor of the Government . . . because of
the" jury tampering incident.[39]

Judge Waring readily agreed to step aside, and following an October hearing, the resident district judge granted the defendants a new trial based on
information, he noted, not available to "the able judge who [first] tried the
case." In January 1948, the defendants were tried before a federal judge
brought in from North Carolina. As the Richmond *Times-Dispatch* later reported, the North Carolinian's "brand of justice stood in sharp relief" to
Judge Waring's. Two of the defendants were acquitted, outright; of the
others, only two were sentenced to prison terms.[40]

At the conclusion of the first trial, Judge Waring had been as complimentary of prosecutor Humrickhouse and the jury as he was contemptuous
of the defendants. "It may interest you if I do say," he told the jurors, that
"I happen to agree" with the verdict. He singled out Humrickhouse for particular praise. At times, he asserted, persons of the defendants' prominence
escape justice. "But where," he added,

> faithful public officials investigate over a period of years and an honest,
> intelligent and splendid young assistant United States attorney [has] the
> ability—and more than that—and the real courage in [the] face of discour-
> agements and perhaps not the thorough approval of all the public officials
> of this State to press this case to a conclusion over all the weeks that it has
> been tried—alone—I'm proud of him and you are, too.

Judge Waring's homage to the young Richmond prosecutor would soon
have special meaning for his own career. In less than three months, he was to
decide two important civil rights cases. His decision in one, like his equal pay
rulings, would have no far-reaching effect on South Carolina's segregated
society. The substance and tone of his ruling in the other, however, would
challenge a fundamental institution of white supremacy, make him a controversial national figure, and push him finally toward a complete break with the
South's—and his own—racist past.

The first of the cases turned on the law school aspirations of John H.

Wrighten, a black from Edisto Island, off South Carolina's coast. Wrighten was the eighth of nine children. His father had a small farm that Wrighten and his siblings tended while his father worked for wages as a day laborer. His family thus had a reasonably comfortable existence, and Wrighten was able to attend high school at Avery Institute, a Charleston school operated by the American Missionary Association.[41]

Following service in World War II, Wrighten completed his senior year at Avery and made plans to attend college. The failure of the state to prosecute the murderers of his brother-in-law, an independent black who refused to work for whites, had made Wrighten comparatively militant, at least by the standards of the coastal South Carolina blacks of the 1940s. So, too, had his experiences as a cabin boy at a tourist court used by white men for sexual encounters with black women. On graduating from Avery, where he had been a member of the NAACP youth chapter, he applied for admission to Judge Waring's alma mater, the all-white College of Charleston. After the academic year began, college officials informed him that a decision would be made on his application in October. Wrighten decided to enroll instead at the Colored Normal, Industrial, Agricultural, and Mechanical College of South Carolina, in Orangeburg.

After a year at State College, as the Orangeburg school was commonly known, Wrighten, along with thirty-two other blacks, again sought admission to the College of Charleston. It was now the early spring of 1944, and college officials announced that its board of trustees would meet in June and act on the applications. According to Wrighten, soon the president of the Charleston NAACP chapter and other local black leaders were pressuring the black students to withdraw their applications. Their efforts, they were told, were jeopardizing Avery Institute and race relations in Charleston.

Wrighten agreed to return to State College. But in June 1946, six months before his graduation, he again began to stir the waters of South Carolina's segregated academies. This time, he sought admission to the law school of the University of South Carolina in Columbia, an all-white institution. Wrighten's application was promptly denied on grounds of race. Wrighten then contacted Harold Boulware, and the state NAACP chapter agreed to file a suit in Wrighten's behalf. In *Missouri ex rel. Gaines* v. *Canada,* a 1938 decision, the U.S. Supreme Court had held that states must furnish "separate but equal" law schools for both races or admit blacks to all-white institutions. South Carolina had no law school for blacks. The NAACP counsel demanded that the state either admit Wrighten and other qualified blacks to the university or create a law school for members of their race.[42]

Judge Waring scheduled a hearing in the case for June 1947. Meanwhile, John Wrighten taught "Problems of Democracy" at Avery Institute, and South Carolina officials worked frantically to avert integration of the university. Article XI of the state constitution provided that "no child of either race shall ever be permitted to attend a school provided for children of the other race"; white South Carolinians were determined to maintain that tradition, even where the "children" at issue were would-be law students. During its

1946 session, the general assembly had appropriated $60,000 for the creation of a graduate and law school at State College. In an appropriation act adopted a month before the scheduled hearing on John Wrighten's petition, the legislature instructed State College officials to use as much of that fund "as is necessary to maintain and operate a law school during the coming fiscal year."[43]

At a pretrial conference in the case, it was agreed that the plaintiffs would challenge only the adequacy of facilities provided potential black law students, not the constitutionality of segregation itself. Atfer Judge Waring issued an order confirming the pretrial agreement, Robert L. Carter of the NAACP's New York office wrote the judge that he and his co-counsel would want the opportunity to challenge the "sufficiency and quality" of any segregated facility the state might provide and also to "go into the question of the sufficiency of any segregated facility to meet the requirements of the equal protection clause." In a letter to Carter, Waring observed:

> My understanding is that in this particular case the general question of segregation is not in issue. You were asked the question and answered it fully that you in no way waived that right and believed that segregation was illegal but that was not an issue in this particular case. Therefore, I think that this particular case will have to be tried as heretofore stated.

Except to assert in one of their briefs that the *Gaines* case had not gone "far enough," therefore, Wrighten's counsel raised no objection to the doctrine of segregation itself, either in briefs filed with the court or during the June hearing.[44]

At the hearing, attorneys for the defendants emphasized the state's plans to establish a black law school at Orangeburg and asserted that, to date, no blacks had sought a legal education there. Wrighten's counsel contended, on the other hand, that their client and other qualified blacks deserved immediate admission to the university since the proposed black school was not yet an accomplished fact. On July 12, 1947, Judge Waring rejected the NAACP's argument. Instead, he considered "it only fair and just, in view of all the circumstances" to give the state until September to open the Orangeburg school. "[I]f at that time," he asserted,

> the plaintiff and others who are qualified can and do obtain entrance to a law school at State College, satisfactorily staffed, equipped, and a going concern, and on a substantial parity in all respects with the services furnished at the University Law School, then the demands of the plaintiff will be adequately satisfied and no further action will be necessary by this Court. On the other hand, if that be not done completely and fully, then the plaintiff will be entitled to entrance at the Law School of the University.

"The third alternative," he added, "is that the State furnish no law school education to any persons of either white or negro race."[45]

In September, State College opened its law school with a dean and three faculty but no law building or library; John Wrighten refused to attend. In July 1948, following further proceedings, Judge Waring issued a second order in the case. By that point, the general assembly had appropriated $200,000 for a building and $30,000 for library acquisitions. But only eight students were enrolled in State College's law courses, and only four of those were law students. Judge Waring found it "almost impossible to intellectually compare" such a school with the university's law school, which had 342 students enrolled in the 1947–48 academic year. He professed mild bemusement, moreover, that the state would go to enormous expense for eight black students just "to prevent the meeting of whites and Negroes in classrooms." He agreed, however, that such policy judgments were for legislatures, not courts, and concluded that South Carolina had complied with his order and the dictates of the *Gaines* ruling.[46]

By the fall of 1949, a two-story law building had been constructed on the Orangeburg campus. Wrighten enrolled there in September and graduated in June 1952. After failing the state bar examination a third time, he wrote the University of South Carolina's law dean. Given his poor performance on the bar examination, Wrighten reasoned, South Carolina obviously had provided him with an inferior legal education at Orangeburg. Soon, he indicated, he would seek admission to the university's law or journalism school. In a few months, Wrighten was allowed to take the bar examination a fourth time. On this occasion, he passed.

Like the equal pay and Isaac Woodward cases, Wrighten's suit had originally been filed in the court of Judge Timmerman, who, as a trustee of the university, had asked Judge Waring to hear the case. Waring was not particularly interested in reviewing a routine "separate but equal" claim, but he found another case on Timmerman's docket, a challenge to South Carolina's all-white Democratic primary, very intriguing. "I liked it and I didn't like it," he later said.

> I liked it because I felt it was an opportunity, and I felt that somebody in the country ought to take a stand. . . . I felt that my state was backward, that it had been blind to decency and right, and that somebody had at last to face the issue. I thought it was a fine opportunity. I confess that I had some feelings the other way, some worries. I discussed it with my wife.

Waring told Elizabeth that they might have to pay a heavy penalty if he struck down South Carolina's white primary. His earlier racial reforms had been relatively noncontroversial; in Florence and Columbia, if not in Charleston, they were still invited to parties. A decision against the primary might mean their total isolation from white society. "She said, 'I think you ought to do it and I think you ought to do it right. . . . I'm with you, start to finish.' "[47]

Waring informed Judge Timmerman that he would be pleased to hear the *Wrighten* case, but suggested that he also take on *Elmore* v. *Rice,* the white primary challenge, since both suits involved racial discrimination claims. Timmerman readily agreed, delighted, apparently, to be rid of yet another distasteful civil rights dispute.[48]

The white primary had flourished for years as the most effective barrier to black participation in southern politics. Following the Civil War, the Democratic party had become the only viable political party in the South. The party's primary was thus tantamount to an election, and the exclusion of black voters from the primary effectively eliminated them from the southern election process—except, of course, as the campaign issue of demagogic politicians. In a number of rulings early in this century, the Supreme Court had declared the primary to be essentially a private affair, largely immune from constitutional obligations. However, in 1927 and 1932 the Court struck down Texas's all-white primary that was legislated by state law. But in *Grovey* v. *Townsend,* a 1935 case, it had upheld a Texas white primary scheme mandated only by party convention, and the primary's future seemed relatively secure.[49]

Grovey v. *Townsend* proved shortlived, however. In *United States* v. *Classic,* a 1941 Louisiana vote fraud case, the Supreme Court concluded that, "where the state law has made the primary an integral part of the procedure of choice, or where in fact the primary effectively controls the choice, the right of the elector to have his ballot counted at the primary is . . . included in the right protected" by the Constitution. In Texas, the primary was heavily regulated by state law; following the *Classic* ruling, a new challenge was mounted against the Texas scheme. In *Smith* v. *Allwright,* a 1944 ruling, the Supreme Court declared the Texas white primary unconstitutional. The state Democratic convention may have acted on its own in excluding blacks from its primaries, the Court reasoned, but in other respects the primary was an integral part of the state's election machinery and thus subject, under the *Classic* doctrine, to constitutional requirements.[50]

In the wake of the *Allwright* decision, South Carolina's political establishment moved quickly to preserve their state's version of the white primary. Within two weeks of the Supreme Court's pronouncement, Governor Olin D. Johnston called a special session of the general assembly. Perhaps assuming that the *Allwright* decision had been based on the state's regulation of the Texas primary, Johnston proposed repeal of all South Carolina primary laws. Prior to the session, he and the state attorney general assembled local prosecutors in Columbia to study the state statutes page by page, ferreting out all references to the primary. Few provisions were overlooked. In its April 14–20, 1944, special session, the general assembly repealed approximately 150 state laws. In November, South Carolina's voters approved an amendment erasing all mention of the primary from the state constitution. The state Democratic convention then incorporated virtually every one of the repealed provisions ino a set of regulations for the organization of Democratic "clubs" and conduct of primaries. Also adopted were qualifications for "club" membership and participation in the primaries. Of course, one of the most fundamental requirements was that a member be white.[51]

With all state regulations repealed, fraud in the conduct of the party's primaries was no longer a criminal offense, and the integrity of the primary was left entirely in the hands of party functionaries. *News and Courier* editor William Watts Ball, who favored resurrection of the convention method of nominating candidates to public office, was alarmed by the prospects. "Unless the chieftains, the candidates, the managers, the voters shall conduct primaries as gentlemen conduct elections in the colleges," the *Courier* editorialized, "the white man's party as a voluntary association similar to literary societies or congregations of churches, will be afflicted with internal combustion and blow up." But most white South Carolinians apparently shared Olin Johnston's priorities. "After these statutes are repealed," Johnston had told the general assembly,

> we will have done everything within our power to guarantee white supremacy in our primaries of our State insofar as legislation is concerned. Should this prove inadequate, we South Carolinians will use the necessary methods to retain white supremacy in our primaries and to safeguard the homes and happiness of our people.
>
> White supremacy will be maintained in our primaries. Let the chips fall where they may![52]

South Carolina blacks were equally determined to test the state's attempt to evade the *Allwright* ruling. When the Democratic party held its August 1946 primary, George Elmore, a black Columbia merchant, and other black voters attempted to vote at Richland County's Ward 9 precinct. When primary officials refused to allow them to cast a vote, Harold Boulware filed a class action against the county Democratic committee; Thurgood Marshall, Robert Carter, and Boulware began preparing Elmore's case.

The plaintiffs' brief relied heavily on the Supreme Court's conclusion in the *Classic* case that a primary is subject to the Constitution where "state law has made [it] an integral part of the procedure of choice, or where in fact [it] effectively controls the choice." "[T]he two tests set forth so clearly in the *Classic* case," the NAACP counsel argued, "are in the *alternative*. So that, under the *Classic* case, the plaintiff in this case is entitled to recover where either" condition was met. The South Carolina Democratic primary was no longer regulated by state law, but it obviously controlled the election choice in that one-party Democratic state. It thus violated the Fifteenth Amendment's ban on racial discrimination in voting.[53]

The language of the Supreme Court's *Classic* opinion clearly seemed to support the NAACP's interpretation. At one point, for example, the Court had declared:

> Here, *even apart from the circumstance* [emphasis mine] that the Louisiana primary is made by law an integral part of the procedure of choice, the right to choose a representative is in fact controlled by the primary because . . . the choice of candidates at the Democratic primary determines the choice of the elected representative.

In their motion to dismiss the complaint, however, the defendants urged Judge Waring to limit the Supreme Court's primary cases strictly to the fact of state regulation. In *Classic, Allwright,* and every other Supreme Court case subjecting the primary to constitutional or statutory requirements, the party's counsel argued, the primary at issue was regulated by state law. "[I]n all those cases the Democratic primary was by statute made an essential part of the statutory electoral process." Those rulings thus "must be held to sustain the proposition that where, as here, the primary is no part of the statutory process of election . . . there is no Constitutional right to vote in such primary."[54]

At a June 1947 hearing in the case, the defendants' lawyers continued to hammer away at this theme, equating affiliation with South Carolina's Democratic party with membership in a sewing circle, church, or country club. Elmore's counsel stressed, on the other hand, the Supreme Court's use of the disjunctive "or" in the *Classic* case, where it delineated the conditions under which a primary could be considered an election for constitutional purposes. Olin Johnston's call for a special session of the general assembly and candid summary of the repeal scheme's goals were also introduced into evidence. A number of witnesses were called, and the parties resolved a large number of factual issues by stipulation. For reasons now obscure, however, neither side chose to call William P. Baskin, chairman of the state Democratic party, to the witness stand. So Judge Waring called Baskin as the court's witness. "Baskin," Waring later said, "was a funny little fellow, rather absurd little creature—his feet hardly touched the floor when he sat [on] the witness stand—and he sat up there, quite important, and he liked it, I think. He was the big Democrat of South Carolina." Whatever Waring's general impression of Baskin, however, the judge found the party chairman a candid witness who made no attempt to conceal the state's obvious goal—the exclusion of blacks from all meaningful participation in South Carolina's elections.[55]

In May, a New Orleans attorney had sent Judge Waring an article defending Louisiana's white primary. In a letter of reply, Waring wrote that he had received the article—and a report of the president's committee on civil rights as well. He planned, he added, to read them "in conjunction and I know they will both throw light on a difficult and intensely interesting problem." Waring also collected a number of law review articles on the issue. One of them noted the doubts of some whether court decisions and congressional statutes could "ever achieve lasting results; they would emphasize instead the slower and less spectacular methods of education, moral suasion, and local action." Its author then observed, however, that

> [T]he practical effects to date of the Supreme Court's decision in *Smith* v. *Allwright* seem to indicate that the law can at least assist in hastening this social change. Ultimately the Negroes will exert a substantial influence in southern politics when the two-party system returns to the South. The election contests between rival candidates will then force the whites to compete for the Negro vote, as they now do in other regions of the country.[56]

On July 12, 1947, the same date that he issued his first order in the *Wrighten* case, Judge Waring sided with the NAACP's reading of the *Classic* decision—and perhaps the law review's prophesy. He was not unsympathetic to the post-Civil War efforts of southerners "to prevent a deluge of untrained, unlettered, and unprepared citizens from taking over control of the state government. That these efforts and the methods adopted were both born of necessity may be argued with show of reason." But the Constitution, he asserted, provided for universal suffrage free of racial discrimination, and South Carolina's Democratic primary could not be dismissed as a mere private club activity immune from constitutional dictates. The state's analogy of the current Democratic party to a ladies' sewing circle, he exclaimed from the bench, was "pure sophistry. . . . [P]rivate clubs and business organizations do not vote and elect a President of the United States, and the Senators and members of the House of Representatives of our national congress"; yet, since 1900, every South Carolina governor, state legislator, and congressman had been the nominee of the Democratic party. Certainly, he added, South Carolina's voters were aware of the primary's critical role in state politics: 290,223 voters had participated in the August 1946, primary from which George Elmore and other blacks were excluded; only 26,326 voted in the November general election that year. Other southern states had now abandoned the white primary. "I cannot see where the skies will fall," Waring asserted, "if South Carolina is put in the same class with these and other states."[57]

Two weeks before Judge Waring announced his decision in the *Elmore* case, President Truman had addressed the impact of the American racial dilemma on international relations. "Our case for democracy," the president had observed,

> should be as strong as we can make it. It should rest on practical evidence that we have been able to put our house in order.
>
> For these compelling reasons, we can no longer afford the luxury of a leisurely attack upon prejudice and discrimination. There is much that state and local governments can do in providing positive safeguards for civil rights. But we cannot, any longer, await the growth of a will to action in the slowest state or the most backward community.

In concluding his opinion in the primary case, Judge Waring quoted the president's remarks. Then he offered his native state some advice of his own. "It is time," he wrote, "for South Carolina to rejoin the Union. It is time to fall in step with the other states and to adopt the American way of conducting elections."[58]

His uncle's remarks infuriated Tom Waring. "When Judge Waring said that it's time for South Carolina to come back into the Union," Tom Waring remarked years later, "it galled me, because I knew that he was one of the fellows that kept South Carolina out of the Union." Had he and the judge been living during the Civil War, he asserted, "he and I would have both been in the trenches fighting for the Confederacy." But he added, "had Elizabeth turned up at that time, I don't know what would have happened."[59]

Tom Waring was not alone in his reaction. "It would have been edifying to citizens of his State," the Charleston *Evening Post* editorialized, "had Judge Waring informed them how long South Carolina has been out of the Union."

> Has it been since 1876, when the Democrats, led by Wade Hampton, crushed the carpetbaggers and scalawags and ended the Reconstruction orgy

of corruption, oppression, and plunder? The white Democratic party of today stemmed from the State's redemption in 1876.

And while Judge Waring was at it, wrote the *Post*'s editor, he might also have extended an invitation to the U.S. Supreme Court, which, after all, had upheld the Texas white primary as recently as 1935. Certain other southern newspapers followed the *Post*'s lead. But William Watts Ball declined a suggestion that the *News and Courier* publish a poll reflecting the hostility of South Carolinians to the judge's decision. In early August, while an appeal of the ruling was pending, Ball wrote Tom Waring from Caesar's Head.

> We must not, cannot, publish a poll as suggested by the gentlemen of Florence.
> It would be improper to take a poll in respect of a question pending before the courts. Courts are established to interpret the law.

Instead, he instructed, the *Courier* was to continue publishing letters and articles on the decision. "You did not answer with desirable emphasis your opinion," he added somewhat enigmatically, "whether my bodily presence is wished or required in Meeting Street."[60]

In late August, Judge Timmerman granted a temporary stay of Judge Waring's order, pending appeal of the case before a panel of the Court of Appeals for the Fourth Circuit. Whatever hope Timmerman's action may have given the defendants, however, soon evaporated. On December 30, the Fourth Circuit panel, speaking through Judge Parker, unanimously upheld Judge Waring. The Supreme Court refused to review the case.[61]

The *Elmore* decision won Waring the approval of blacks and the national press as well as the attention of the legal community. The *New York Times* termed his primary and law school rulings "a gain for fair play," and suggested, sympathetically if paternalistically, that "South Carolina may have to do what her neighbor Georgia shows a tendency to do—educate her Negro citizens and encourage in them a sense of civic responsibility." Benjamin Mays of Atlanta, the president of Morehouse College and a South Carolina native, wrote Judge Waring that he had "read no greater document in that field. . . . I saw in your statement more than a great mind interpreting the law of the Constitution honestly," Mays continued. "I saw a great soul, one who demonstrates in his person a democratic spirit. As one South Carolinian to another, I salute you." Other blacks, prominent and obscure, echoed Mays' tribute, while the Charleston chapter of the NAACP and a black minister's union adopted resolutions praising his primary decision, and law reviews sought advance copies of his opinion and gave the case extensive coverage.[62]

No South Carolina politician voiced public support for the decision. Letters critical of Judge Waring's stand were generally restrained, however, and to his surprise, he received a number of supportive letters from white South Carolinians. Stephen Nettles, a Greenville attorney whom Waring apparently first met at a judicial conference, wrote, for example: "So often in South Carolina an evil condition continues to exist simply because there is no leader with the mind and the courage to speak out and lead the way." Nettles praised Waring for refusing "to be a party to the perpetuation of a theory of government that is a disgrace to the state." Many of Nettles' clients were out-of-state insurance companies, and thus the young attorney was largely immune from economic reprisal for siding with Waring. But other white South Carolinians, including several Charlestonians residing south of Broad Street and a number of white ministers, also wrote congratulatory letters.[63]

Judge Waring and Elizabeth had expected virtually total repudiation of his decision by South Carolina whites. He knew, he wrote Steve Nettles,

> the unpopular and surprising thing it [would be] to the old line political element to be told that it was time to awaken and get out of their hide-bound prejudice. I also realize there has been a great storm of condemnation because one has dared to raise the iron curtain that has surrounded this state for so many years. Letting in a little light—even the little bit let in in this case, is not pleasant to those who like to live in the dark.

He and Elizabeth found special comfort, therefore, in the support he received from white South Carolinians. "It is very heartening and gratifying to know," he wrote one, "that I am not alone in this and there is a substantial stratum of sanity, decency, and liberality in our State." "When one is clear in his mind," he wrote another, "it is not hard to do a thing. . . . You and the others who think like us will eventually save our State from its backwardness."[64]

The *Elmore* decision and his invitation to South Carolina to rejoin the Union had put Judge Waring on an irreversible course of opposition to the deeply ingrained racism of his native state. The letters of support that he received from whites in the state indicated, however, that he and Elizabeth were not totally isolated from its white society. Partly for that reason, perhaps, Waring was not yet prepared to abandon the commitment to gradual racial reform characteristic of the southern liberal—the posture he had embraced in correspondence relating to the equal pay litigation and in other earlier incidents. In late December 1947, he wrote George F. Zook, president of the American Council on Education, regarding a recent council report on segregated schools. He did not believe, he wrote, that the Deep South would voluntarily abandon segregation. Nor did he favor immediate adoption of "coercive federal legislation" either. "Whatever is done," he asserted, "should be done slowly." He realized that eight decades had elapsed since the Civil War and that "little advancement" had been made in the interim. But even in South Carolina, he wrote, some progress had been made, and that progress should be nurtured "gradually."

> Too drastic measures may stifle it as it is not difficult for the agitators to stir up resistance against outside interference. In South Carolina, the spirit of secession is not dead and imitation halos of the Confederacy are still worn by our political candidates. . . . But there is a silent, thinking minority who are as yet little heard of. They must be encouraged gradually.

His preference for gradualism extended to the public schools.

The first step in educational institutions should be in those in a higher bracket. In my opinion it would be almost impossible to do anything in the primary, grammar or high school systems. Even in the colleges action will have to start first in the higher brackets of technical education such as law schools [and] medical schools.[65]

But the white primary litigation—and the metamorphosis of Judge Waring's racial views—was not yet complete. The equal pay cases and the plight of Isaac Woodward, John Wrighten, and George Elmore, like the teachings of Cash and Myrdal and Elizabeth Waring's counsel, were having their effect. Judge Waring had begun to rejoin the Union. Within a year his reconstruction would be total.

4

A Passion for Justice

Following college at Goucher, the Warings' daughter, Anne, had moved to New York and married Stanley Warren, an executive with the American Broadcasting Company. When her parents divorced, she wrote Judge Waring's cousin Dorothy Waring shortly after her father's death, her "sympathies were . . . overwhelmingly with" her mother. Annie Waring had lived in New York briefly after the divorce. Anne and Stanley saw her often there and admired her "quite . . . remarkable adjustment to a very difficult set of circumstances." They were saddened when she elected to return to Charleston and to the humiliating proximity of her ex-husband and rival, remaining there until her death in 1954. "We were sorry," Anne wrote Dorothy Waring,

> particularly as my father and stepmother still lived at 61 Meeting. I can understand that mother was lonely in New York, but I fear that the friendships she hoped to rediscover in Charleston were not as rewarding as she had hoped. To be cast in the symbolic role of martyr in order to nurture the discontent and disapproval of a society is indeed tragic.[1]

While her "first sympathy" lay with her mother, Anne had also sought to maintain cordial relations with her father and stepmother. "I did not feel I had the right to judge and automatically condemn my father, that my door should be open to him as well. I was also sympathetic to the judicial decisions he was making in the field of civil liberties." At least one of Waties Waring's Charleston critics remembered him as a stern, aloof father whose only child rarely measured up to his expectations; the correspondence of father and daughter over the years offers some support for that assessment. In November 1946, for example, when Anne was nearly thirty, her father wrote the Warrens regarding the theft of family silver from their New York apartment. "To be perfectly frank," he scolded, "I do not see how you could possibly let insurance lapse, particularly on borrowed property, and do not quite agree with your characterization that this is 'as is usual.'" Waring's sister Margaret had recently mentioned to her brother the possibility of turning over another set of flatware to Anne. "If Anne feels like it," Waring wrote, "she might drop her a note of suggestion. However, of course I would not like to suggest it and would prefer being left out of the picture."[2]

Usually, though, their correspondence was more cordial, reflecting especially Waring's love of the New York theater, motion pictures, baseball, and other sporting events. For example, after chastising his daughter for the loss of family silver in the November 1946 letter, Waring launched into a genial discussion of a performance of Shakespeare's *Henry V,* ball games he and Elizabeth planned to include in their next trip to New York, and "sucker class" spectators "silly enough to pay $100 a seat" for a recent Joe Louis boxing match. In a January 1948 letter, he wrote of his fondness for Greta Garbo's recently rereleased *Ninotchka.* "Have both of you seen it? If not, don't walk but run to the nearest entrance and see it *now.*" And of a risqué title then running at another New York theater: "Both Elizabeth and I think it is highly important that [Stanley] be taken vi et armis and without delay." When Judge Waring and his wife were in New York, moreover, they spent much of their time with his daughter and son-in-law. As Judge Waring began to acquire national attention, Anne, and especially Stanley, kept him and Elizabeth supplied with press clippings, broadcast and wire service tear sheets, and their assessments of press treatments given the judge and South Carolina's racial politics.[3]

The White Primary Battle: Phase Two

On April 20, 1948, Stanley wrote the Warings to congratulate them on the Supreme Court's refusal the previous day to hear South Carolina's challenge to the judge's ruling in *Elmore* v. *Rice.* "I can't wait," Warren joked, "to see what my pal Billy Ball has to say about it." A news item, he noted, indicated that South Carolina's Democrats had "decided to give in and accept the Supreme Court's order. Just what else could they have done?" Warren asked, "Secede?"[4]

South Carolinians were not yet prepared to secede. But they were not ready to accept Judge Waring's invitation to rejoin the Union either. The opinion Waring filed in the *Elmore* case had stipulated that blacks were to be admitted to the Democratic party and allowed to participate in its primaries, without regard to race or color. Technically, however, the ruling applied only to party officials in Richland County, and the judge's actual order in the case had referred only to primary participation, not party membership. At their May 1948 state convention, Democratic party functionaries adopted rules limiting party membership to "white" Democrats. Blacks were to be allowed to vote in the party's primaries, but only if they presented general election voter certificates not required of whites and took an oath supporting "states' rights" and "the social, religious and educational separation of the races," opposing "the proposed Federal so-called F.E.P.C. law," and swearing that they were "not a member of any other political party."[5]

Since few, if any, politically active blacks were likely to swear allegiance to segregation and South Carolina's interpretation of states' rights, much less disavow federal efforts to eliminate discriminatory employment practices, the oath's intent was patently obvious. Thurgood Marshall and Harold Boulware soon returned to Judge Waring's court with a suit against eighty-seven party officials, including state chairman Baskin, the members of the state executive committee, and the party chairman in every county but Richland, which was already covered by the *Elmore* order. As nominal plaintiff, the NAACP attorneys found David Brown a fifty-six-year-old Beaufort County service station operator. A coastal county with a large black population, Beaufort was composed largely of many small islands. During the Civil War, it was the first county in which black Union troops were enlisted; after Reconstruction it was the last to send black representatives to the general assembly. Following the *Elmore* decision, Brown and a number of other Beaufort blacks had been permitted to enroll in the county party. In the wake of the state convention's action, however, their names had been purged from the rolls.

The NAACP filed its suit in early July. Judge Waring issued a restraining order forbidding party officials to prevent blacks from enrolling and scheduled a hearing of the case for July 16. In the week preceding the hearing, southerners opposed to the civil rights plank in the national party's platform walked out of the Democratic national convention in Philadelphia. On the day following the hearing, dissident southern Democrats meeting in Birmingham nominated South Carolina governor Strom Thurmond for the presidency on the States' Rights, or Dixiecrat, ticket. "There are not enough troops in the army," Thurmond assured the faithful, "to force the South to give up segregation and admit the Negro race into our schools, our theaters, our swimming pools and our houses." The rhetoric of certain Dixiecrats was even more vitriolic. The party's central purpose, proclaimed a leaflet circulated on the streets of New Orleans by a Louisiana industrialist, was "to eliminate from the real Democratic party the alleged Negro LOVING, pink and red MONGRELS who FALSELY called themselves Democrats." W. P. Baskin and a number of other defendants were also delegates to the Philadelphia convention. Since the convention would still be in session when the hearing was scheduled to begin, Baskin wired Judge Waring to request a delay. Waring promptly denied Baskin's request. When the hearing convened on July 16, therefore, the atmosphere in his Charleston courtroom, like that throughout the deep South, was charged with tension. Obviously angered by the defendants' continued defiance, the judge would soon inflame feelings even more.[6]

While hardly liberal in their racial customs, the counties of South Carolina's northwestern piedmont had the state's smallest black populations, and their white citizenry had traditionally viewed the prospects of black voting with less alarm than their counterparts in South Carolina's coastal Black Belt. The Democratic chairmen in three upper piedmont counties—Greenville, Pickens, and Laurens—chose to ignore the directives of the state party convention and continued enrolling blacks. As the hearing began, Judge Waring dismissed them from the suit and praised their action, by implication condemning the other defendants. "I feel quite ashamed," he asserted from the bench, that there are only three counties in this state that recognize not only the meaning of the decision made by me, because there is no private opinion in this, but the decision made by the Circuit Court of Appeals and the Supreme Court of the United States, but much further the supreme law of the land as true Americans. I'm glad to see that the governing boards of three counties in this state are determined to run them, irrespective of any court action or any coercion or any proceedings or anybody telling them what to do—that they've got sense enough, they've got nerve enough, and they've got patriotism enough to make a true, fair and just decision. . . . I'm glad to see that some of our citizens realize that this country is an American country; that it is not a country of persecution; that it is not a country of minorities or parties, groups or religious creeds, races.

Although retaining jurisdiction over coastal Jasper County's Democratic organization, he also appeared to accept the Jasper chairman's assurances that the party there had taken a "perfectly fair position as far as race is concerned to date."[7]

Judge Waring then turned his attention to the other defendants and to the plaintiff's complaint. Thurgood Marshall spoke for David Brown; Sidney Tison of Bennettsville interrogated the NAACP's witnesses. But Robert McC. Figg—Charleston attorney, Waring ally in the disputed Maybank-Manning primary of 1938, contender for the judicial appointment Waring ultimately secured, an increasingly significant behind-the-scenes figure in the Dixiecrat movement, and chief architect, according to press reports, of South Carolina's efforts to maintain the white primary—also represented the defendants, though taking no part in interrogating the witnesses. "The case didn't take too long to argue," Judge Waring later remarked. "The position of the defendants was so hopelessly weak that it seemed to me almost ludicrous. The plaintiffs didn't argue to any great extent. They saw that I didn't want an argument on a thing that was so clear and apparent."[8]

Thurgood Marshall called only two witnesses, the plaintiff and state party chairman William P. Baskin. Marshall had David Brown briefly relate to the court the events leading to his enrollment in the Democratic party and his later purge from the party rolls. At a hearing on the issue before the county executive committee, Brown testified, Beaufort state senator W. B. Harvey had "talked a little, concerning . . . that they treats the colored race good, and they try to satisfy them." Shortly after Harvey spoke, Brown added, the names of all blacks "be purged off" the county rolls.[9]

In 1944, South Carolina blacks had formed the Progressive Democratic party with John H. McCray of Columbia, editor of a black paper, the *Lighthouse and Informer,* as its chairman and Charleston NAACP president Arthur Clement its executive secretary. In 1944 and 1948, the Progressive Democrats had sent delegations to the Democratic national convention, where they secured gallery tickets but no voting privileges. In 1944, the party ran a candidate against Olin Johnston in Johnston's successful U.S. Senate bid. State officials were now contending that Progressive Democrats had no right to membership in their party or to participate in its primaries. Thurgood Marshall questioned Brown closely on this point. No, the plaintiff testified, he was not a member of the Progressive Democratic party; no, he had no knowledge of Progressive delegations being sent to the Democratic national convention; yes, he had always voted a straight Democratic ticket in general elections.[10]

Under Sidney Tison's grilling, however, Brown began to modify his position. Just the day before the hearing, Tison asked, had Brown not admitted his membership in the Progressive party to a Beaufort County deputy sheriff? "I tell him I was a member of the club," Brown initially responded, "not the one he said." Pressed by Tison, Brown began to weaken. "I forget what I did tell him. I really forget, because he come up there and picked me up off base." Brown conceded finally that he had attended Progressive Democratic party meetings at a Beaufort church. "It wasn't even your church," Tison asserted. "You didn't go there for worship—you went there because the Progressive Democratic Party was having meetings? That's correct, isn't it?" "That's correct," Brown replied, "yes, sir." When asked by Tison whether he had contributed to the Progressive Democrats, Brown first testified, "I don't think so," then said he thought "just a little bit," and finally conceded making contributions.

Marshall next called William P. Baskin to the witness stand and had the party chairman describe the recent modifications in the party rules. Judge Waring had remained silent through most of David Brown's testimony, but he questioned Baskin closely. After the state Democratic convention had adopted the rules then at issue, Baskin and others on the state executive committee had made two revisions in the convention's language, dropping the word "religious" from the portion of the challenged voter oath requiring support for "the social, religious and educational separation of races," and eliminating "understand" from the requirement that blacks "understand, believe in and . . . support the principles" stated in the oath. The significance of their actions was unclear, but Waring found it very intriguing.

> THE COURT: You thought it would clarify the oath to strike out the word "understand," so that the voter would swear he would believe in something he didn't understand—was that the object?
> THE WITNESS: No, sir.
> THE COURT: Well, what was the object? Why did you strike out the word "understand"—a man swears to something he doesn't understand—it was objectionable to swear to something he understands?
> THE WITNESS: No, sir.
> THE COURT: Mr. Baskin, just tell me what it means. I'm interested in the mentality of these changes and of the committee—how did the committee figure out such a thing as that?
> THE WITNESS: Someone in the committee—I don't remember who it was—
> THE COURT: You don't remember who it was—it would be interesting?
> THE WITNESS: No, sir. Suggested that the word "understand" should be stricken—that it really was surplus, I think.

THE COURT: It was surplus for a person to understand what he swears to, is that your opinion, too?

THE WITNESS: No, sir. No, sir. . . .

THE COURT: You don't think it's material for a man to say whether he understands an oath or not? The understanding of an oath is not, to your mind, or the mind of your committee, a material thing? It's all right for a man to say "I believe" without understanding—you think that's a wholly immaterial matter, don't you?

THE WITNESS: Judge, I don't quite agree. . . .

THE COURT: But you are going to make people generally swear to what they believe without understanding?

THE WITNESS: No, sir, it was not that intention.

THE COURT: Well, leave it as it is. Proceed.

When counsel and Judge Waring were finished with Baskin, Marshall rested the plaintiff's case. Sidney Tison then told Waring that the defense would call no witnesses, and the judge pointedly invited Tison to argue the defendants' position.

THE COURT: . . . I'm very much at sea as to what issues you have raised . . . you've got a rule here that in my present state of mind, and apparently the state of mind of the other courts of the United States . . . is absolutely in conflict with the Constitution and laws of the United States. Now in the Elmore case there was a controversy, because there it was maintained that the Democratic Party of South Carolina was a private organization not bound by the general Constitutional provisions and laws of the United States, because it was purely a private, voluntary organization. And that was argued, very ably and very properly, and the decision of the District Court and of the appellate court did not sustain that point of view. Therefore, the party now is clothed with public functions, and you may argue if you wish, but really I can't see that there's an argument as to the party. . . . I would like very much, and it would interest me immensely, if the authors could explain to me the process by which they evolved [the current rules]. Of course I hoped there would be some witness who would go on the stand and tell me how their minds worked in evolving these things. If they don't care to do that, I'd be glad to hear argument—

MR. TISON: I don't think I could explain to your Honor satisfactorily.

THE COURT: No, sir; I don't think so.

At that point, Tison assured Waring that the defendants would obey any order the judge might issue, but urged him to draft one so clearly "worded that he who runs may read." Waring construed Tison's statement, correctly no doubt, as a disparaging reference to the judge's failure to ban specifically racial bars to party membership in his *Elmore* order, and his response to the attorney bristled with sarcasm. The *Elmore* opinion, he declared, had "distinctly" forbidden discrimination in both voting and party enrollment. The defendants were not bound technically by the *Elmore* order, which applied only to Richland County, he heatedly asserted. But "they should have considered themselves bound by the opinion, not as a matter of law but as a matter of common sense, to know what the courts would do in the future." Instead, party officials chose "to follow the order and not look into the opinion, the rationale or the spirit."

> This couldn't have been ignorance. If it was ignorance, it was ignorance so crass as to seem unbelievable in a body of several hundred men who are practiced politicians and have been running the Democratic party in this state for many years, many of whom are practicing lawyers who have practiced in all the courts of this country. It couldn't have been just immature, juvenile smartness, because I couldn't accuse them of that. And, therefore it must have been deliberate, and an attempt to evade the spirit of the opinion.

In the face of such defiance, Waring held, the court's only recourse was to issue an opinion and order so clear, "as you say . . . that he who runs may read it." The order would grant the plaintiff's request for a preliminary injunction. Under the injunction, enrollment in the party and participation in its primaries was to "be opened to all parties, irrespective of race, color, creed, or condition. I'd better put all those things there, though we are discussing only race here, because the next time they may exclude some of the Jews or Roman Catholics, or say somebody else can't come in."

> I'm going to say to the people of South Carolina that the time has come when racial discrimination in political affairs has got to stop. Neither this Court nor any court nor any government has any right to say anything about social or family contacts, that is none of my business and none of your business, but American citizens have got to be treated on equality [in voting].

The next primary was scheduled for August 10. The enrollment books, Judge Waring held, were to remain open through July 31. No person seeking to enroll in the party was to be required, moreover, to take any oath supporting particular "beliefs, tenets or opinions."

> Nobody knows what this oath means. Nobody knows to the extent they knowingly struck out the word "understand" . . . the oath said "I understand and believe in", and then that committee got together and said, "We'll take out the word 'understand', because these poor creatures have got to swear they believe in it without understanding." That just strikes me as the most absurd thing I ever heard of, and that's the Democratic Party of South Carolina that is trying to represent us in the nation.

Any violation of the order, he warned, would be punished as a contempt of court, violations would not be excused as clerical errors, and offenders would be jailed, not fined. "I say thank God for Pickens and Laurens and Greenville and Jasper," he concluded with vehemence,

> some men that put their feet on the ground and stood up in public and said, "We are Americans; we are going to obey the law." They ought to do it voluntarily; they ought to be glad to do it, and it's a disgrace and a shame you've got to come into court and ask one judge to tell you that you are

American citizens and going to obey the law. Now, gentlemen, you've put the burden on me, and I'm going to do it. It isn't a popular thing to do. [But] I don't care about popularity; I'm going to do my duty.

Judge Waring lost no time issuing a written opinion and order in the case. An order was filed on July 19, an opinion on the following day. Both documents essentially tracked his courtroom statements, albeit in more restrained language. Waring did not doubt the defendants' claim that David Brown was a Progressive Democrat, but he rejected their contention that Brown thus lacked standing to challenge the new Democratic party rules. The Progressive Democrats, he observed, were not "adverse" to the Democratic party; in fact, they had organized primarily because they were denied admission to the regular party and for the purpose of gaining entry to the party. "[E]ven if it were construed to be a separate and adverse organization," he added,

political history is full of many specific instances of persons changing from one party to the other, and there is no reason why one should be debarred from joining an organization because he had joined some other organization for the sole reason of attempting to get in the first-named one.[11]

One portion of the order prohibited the defendants from requiring any oath of prospective voters except that they swear that they met the qualifications set forth in the state constitution, were Democrats, and would "support the election of the nominees of the Democratic party at the ensuing general election." Critics of the ruling read that provision to mean all Democratic nominees, including the hated Truman, and thought that Waring's ruling required such an oath. Judge Waring considered the order "sufficiently clear and distinct for anyone to understand." But on July 22, he modified it, stipulating that any oath was optional with the defendants and that they could require the voter to "pledge himself to support the nominees of [the] primary," rather than all Democratic candidates.[12]

The modification did little, of course, to quell the furor Waring's ruling and remarks from the bench had aroused. Like the *Elmore* ruling, his decision in *Brown* v. *Baskin* attracted many supportive letters and comments, including several from white southerners. The praise of a black Elks lodge and a New Jersey Urban League official was to be expected, as were NAACP executive secretary Walter White's salute to an "uncompromising ruling," state NAACP head James Hinton's remarks in a similar vein, and the black-owned Pittsburgh *Courier*'s assessment of Waring as "one of a growing class of Southerners who live the broad ideas of the Nation more than they do the narrow selfishness of the white supremacists." But a white Virginia hardware dealer also sent his congratulations. "Thanks to men like Thurmond, Wright, Rankin, Bilbo, Long, Talmadge, and our own Harry Byrd," he wrote, "the South has become a stench in the nostrils of the civilized world." Waring had made him "a little less ashamed of having to live in it." A Montgomery matron echoed the Virginian's sentiments. You "make one less ashamed," she wrote, "of the behavior of Southerners as a whole . . . one feels encouraged that there are some of us who are a little above the lynch-mob spirit so blatantly expressed by our Rump Convention in Birmingham. We are indeed in a sorry plight." And the secretary of the South Carolina organization of Baptist student unions also commended the judge for his "courageous stand."[13]

Nor was the South Carolina press universally hostile to his action. The Greenville *News* saw his decision as "complete vindication of the course followed by Greenville and several other counties in defiance of state party primary rules." Even before the hearing, the Florence *News* had recommended educational qualifications for prospective voters of both races, finding it "rankly inconsistent to deny the most educated Negro the right of franchise and at the same time admit the most uneducated white person." On the day after the hearing, moreover, the *News* characterized the judge's order as "bitter medicine" for the state party, but "the kind of medicine asked for by [its state] committee through long series of actions antagonistic to, not to say defiant of, previous court decisions."

> Obviously, Judge Waring has had enough. At any rate, he made himself unmistakably clear not only in the order he handed down but also in his comments and conduct.
>
> It is a pity that the original decision could not have been accepted in both spirit and letter. Tension resulting from antagonism could have been avoided. It has been very plain from the beginning that the full effect of the decision could not have been indefinitely evaded. It would have been the part of far greater wisdom to have accepted it to begin with, with the time spent on fighting it having gone toward constructing a party framework designed to protect the best interests of an honest, democratic and efficient government.[14]

Within South Carolina, however, support for Judge Waring's action was dwarfed by a rising tide of intense resentment. The Warings' telephone began ringing incessantly, day and night. Some of the callers shouted epithets— "nigger lover" was the unimaginative favorite—into the phone. Others greeted the Warings' answer with silence or heavy breathing. The harassment came in such a steady stream that the Warings had difficulty making outside calls. Elizabeth tolerated the annoyance reasonably well, frequently attempting to engage the callers in conversation. "Do you ever go to church?" she would ask. "I hope you'll go Sunday and pray to God to forgive you for what you're doing." Judge Waring, on the other hand, found them a major irritant. Eventually, he had a second telephone installed with an unlisted number and began disconnecting the other phone at night. But annoying daytime calls would remain a regular occurrence for the rest of their years in Charleston. Passersby shunned them on Charleston's streets, and their circle of white Charleston friends continued to dwindle at an increasingly rapid pace.[15]

Judge Waring's relations with the Charleston newspapers he had once represented had deteriorated even before his ruling in *Brown* v. *Baskin.* Waring and his nephew Tom, managing editor of the *News and Courier,* were no longer on speaking terms. In early October 1947, moreover, Arthur Wilcox, a reporter for the *Evening Post,* had made a routine visit to Waring's chambers. Up till then, his relations with the judge had been cordial. On this occasion, however, Waring informed Wilcox that he would have no more to say to representatives of the paper his brother had served as editor and to which the judge had once contributed unsigned editorials. Pressed for an explanation, Waring cited a front-page editorial attack on his *Elmore* ruling which the paper had published the previous July. The following day, according to Wilcox, Waring sent his secretary to the *Post*'s offices with instructions to remove all photographs of the judge from the paper's files.[16]

But however the judge may, or may not, have exacerbated personal relations with those of the media, their editorial policies heaped vituperation on the civil rights philosophy Waring had lately come to espouse. The editorials of William Watts Ball are an example. *News and Courier* editor Ball was a southern aristocrat and political reactionary whose racial attitudes were entirely traditional. Tom Waring's own views were probably more moderate than Ball's. Tom had once urged him, for example, to require use of the courtesy title "Mrs." in articles on black school-crossing guards. After all, he would later recall telling the irascible editor, it "simply meant that a woman was married" and had no bearing on her social status. Ball had reluctantly acquiesced, though cautioning, "Don't go too far with it. No Misters." But Ball was Tom Waring's uncle by marriage, godfather, and mentor. And Waring, like Ball, found the judge's decisions almost as distasteful as his private life.[17]

Ball typed *Courier* editorials on spools of wire service tear sheets. When the typed copy stretched from his desk to his office door, he stopped and turned the fruits of the day's labors over to the printer.[18] In 1948, both the *Post* and *Courier* published numerous editorials, articles, and letters relative to Judge Waring's white primary rulings. But the *Courier* was especially prolific.

Ball's editorials fell into a number of categories. A large number favored elimination of the primary and its replacement with nominating conventions manned by propertied interests, or at least adoption of stringent educational and property qualifications for voters. "With laws and party rules what they are," he exclaimed on one occasion,

> we cannot have mixed primaries in South Carolina without unspeakable filth in them. "Popular government" can be so popular that it is idiotic. Too popular government implies the right to vote enjoyed by all negroes and all white persons, and democracy is a crazy conception.

"[W]hat have the white people to gain," he asked on another occasion, "by voting in primaries in which negroes, illiterate, ignorant, propertyless, who have not paid even a dollar poll tax, can vote?"[19]

Other editorials urged whites to abandon the Democratic party, praised the Dixiecrat movement, and ridiculed the current Democratic disarray. By breaking with the Truman Democrats, Ball reasoned, Governor Thurmond stood the risk of "never again" being elected to state office. "He has put interest of the state above personal interest. He is a leader." The Democratic party had fallen to such depths, on the other hand, "that any living organism which can be termed a human being, who has entered the first grade of school, or who can write his or her name, or who can make a legible 'X,' [should] be allowed to enroll."[20]

In spite of these sentiments, Ball had no use for the Ku Klux Klan and an occasional editorial repudiated its tactics. He also sought to convince his readers that the Dixiecrat movement was based on something other than racial bigotry. When Governor Thurmond rejected the support of the race-baiting American fascist Gerald L. K. Smith and his Christian Nationalist Party, Ball devoted an editorial to Thurmond's action. The "South opposes 'civil rights,'" he contended, "not because of hatred, but because of its belief that separation of races is best for both whites and negroes, and that constitutional guarantees concerning the sovereignty of states must not be abrogated by Congressional or judicial fiat." Even so, Ball frequently raised the spectre of black voters manipulated by "scalawags" in his attacks on Judge Waring's decisions. In a July 29 editorial, for example, he applauded a syndicated columnist's report on the national Democrats' "purchase" of the urban black vote. In most South Carolina counties, "if not all," he added,

> are white-skinned politicians, now lying low, who can and will form partnerships with negroes and gain their votes in primaries—if the federal court primaries shall continue to enroll and attract white people.
>
> The peril of South Carolina is not from the negroes. It is from scalawag material.
>
> If we shall have mixed primaries we shall have division of the offices in South Carolina. Not many years will pass before a negro federal judge will preside in the South and uphold the decisions of the federal courts that "Democrats" shall not refuse admission of negroes into "Democratic" primaries however the cost of conducting them be paid by white people.[21]

On the same day that he commended Thurmond for rejecting fascist support—and in the same week that Judge Waring issued his orders in David Brown's case—Ball wrote: "Today the negroes are coming into control of the Democratic party of the state, armed with the authority of the federal courts, encouraged by the promise that scalawags will ally with them to suck the substance of the whites." Two days earlier, he alerted readers to a *Reader's Digest* piece on "race war" in New York. And frequently he attacked the NAACP's "managers and masters." Other editorials, as well as letters from readers, moreover, reminded blacks of the fine treatment they currently enjoyed in the South and warned whites of the integrationists' ultimate goal. One of many such letters advised blacks that the "white people of the South are your only true friends," adding:

> Now come agitators from the North trying to create trouble between us and if they keep this up you may lose much of what you have gained. . . . I only hope that the Ku Klux Klan is not organizing as so many rumors suggest.

Another letter writer asserted, "It must be borne in mind that the negroes are firmly intent not only in political association with the White Democratic party, but also in their oft repeated assertions that they are working to an end of all segregation and demand full and complete association with the whites." Still other letters gave prominent display to the racial views of major figures in southern history and provided historical "evidence" of the obvious and inherent inferiority of blacks. One quoted Benjamin R. ("Pitchfork Ben") Tillman, South Carolina's leading redeemer of the post-Reconstruction era. "I tell 'em," Tillman had proclaimed, that "the white people are on top, and all the long-nosed Yankees between Cape Cod and hell's back gate can't keep us from it. . . . God almighty made me of better clay than the negro."[22]

Perhaps in part because of Tom Waring's association with the *Courier,* neither of the Charleston papers ever commented editorially on Judge Waring's divorce and remarriage. Editorials and articles regularly itemized, however, Waring's long association with South Carolina's white Democratic party and the benefits derived therefrom. Both papers also bemoaned the judge's "dictatorial" control of the party, suggested ways of evading compliance with the rulings, and at times came close to counseling outright defiance of his authority. At first, in one editorial, Ball called "on the people of both races, who have been dwelling in harmony these many years in South Carolina, to keep calm and not to let violence of any sort complicate the situation." After Judge Waring threatened to jail party officials who disobeyed his orders, however, the *Courier* concluded that the defendants' only refuges were "behind the iron curtain, or in the grave," complained that officials who opened their enrollment books to blacks were "submitting to forced labor on orders of the federal courts," and suggested that the party could withhold funds needed to pay enrollment clerks "without violating the court order." Ball conceded that party leaders faced prison if they defied Waring's mandates, but asserted, "Men have gone before to prison, and worse, in the cause of freedom." The *Courier,* he wrote, did not doubt the "good conscience" of federal judges. But "Courts, judges, may err. They cannot be clothed with infallibility though law arm them with power to enforce decrees." During Reconstruction, Ball reminded his readers, a Judge Bond had been "unrelenting toward the white citizenry of South Carolina."

> [H]e sent some of the people to prison, . . . drove others out of South Carolina and . . . supported with intellectual strength the political party of negroes and white men that misgoverned the state 10 long years.
>
> Judge Bond may have been faithful to his mind and conscience. Nothing to the contrary is the News and Courier saying.
>
> Men of South Carolina resisted him, obeyed their consciences and judgements and went to jail.
>
> Thank God for them.[23]

Like most newspapers, of course, the *Courier* did not speak with one voice. William D. Workman, Jr., of Columbia, who, along with Tom Waring, was to become a forceful spokesman for the southern cause in the clashes between civil rights advocates and white supremacists during the 1950s and 1960s, was the paper's most articulate correspondent of the period. Workman, like Ball, rejected the notion that South Carolinians should "[s]wallow pride, self-respect and tradition," and yield to Waring's "usurpation of party prerogatives." At the same time, he could not support continued legal challenges to Waring's assumption of authority. "Since this entails the risk of going to jail, and since there is an obvious reluctance on the part of leading Democrats to undergo imprisonment no matter what principles may be involved," Workman contended, "this course can be counted out." Nor, given the danger of "block voting" by blacks, did he favor Ball's proposal that the Democratic party be "relinquished . . . to the negroes and those whites who wish to travel with them," with white candidates selected in convention by a "White man's association." Instead, Workman favored the adoption of "rigid educational or property qualifications" for all would-be voters. If a grammar school education were the standard, such a requirement would initially favor whites over blacks, since 65 percent of the state's whites, but only 16 percent of its blacks, met that qualification.

> At the same time [he reasoned], imposition of such requirement would establish an objective, factual standard . . . [and] stimulate the desire for education. On the practical side, it would insure a transition period during which white men would be in political ascendancy, but in which negroes could move step by step toward participation more in keeping with their proportionate strength in numbers.[24]

While state papers put forth their views on Judge Waring's ruling, party officials and state politicians also reacted. William Baskin announced that the party would comply with the judge's order, but a number of low country Democrats were in a more defiant mood. At a meeting the night of Judge Waring's issuance of a written order in the case, the Charleston County executive committee rejected a motion calling for the state convention to reconvene, dismantle the primary, and adopt the convention approach to the nomination of candidates. "You are going to run right into this federal court order," a leading opponent of the motion cautioned. "I for one will not go along with that." But a number of committee members vehemently attacked Waring and his ruling. The judge had not yet modified the oath portion of the order, and his most vociferous critics at the meeting claimed that he was forcing all primary voters to swear allegiance to President Truman in the November election. "Maybe the time will come," one lamented, "when a man can vote with honor in the primary, but that condition does not exist as things are now. . . . New members have been thrust upon the party," he warned, "and they will vote as a bloc. I'm opposed to a primary as it now stands and I will not take any oath to support any man who doesn't stand for the things we believe in."[25]

In the ruling's wake, five low country candidates, including two from Charleston County, had withdrawn from the primary. The two Charleston candidates attended the county committee meeting, as did two others who had chosen not to withdraw from the race. The latter expressed doubt whether

Judge Waring was requiring any oath of primary voters, much less dictating support for Truman, and one suggested that a delegation be sent to the judge for a clarification. But the two dissident candidates did not want to settle issues that way. One of them, T. Allen Legare, an incumbent member of the state house of representatives, intoned, "[B]y fiat of a federal court . . . the walls of the [Democratic party] have been breached, and the way has been paved for every individual, of whatever traditions, of whatever political belief or persuasion, and of whatever political adherence, Republican, Communist or Progressive Democrat, to enroll and override the will of the real Democrats in South Carolina."

> If the ruling which has brought about this weird and ridiculous result is the law of the land, then we in America have truly reached the point when we need a new Magna Carta to defend and protect the liberties of American citizens.

Legare strongly endorsed Governor Thurmond's presidential candidacy and urged others to support the governor's fight "to save free constitutional government and to preserve our American way of life." The other dissident candidate was not to be outdone. "If we in South Carolina no longer have any rights as a sovereign state, then we are definitely on the road to totalitarianism and constitutional government as we have known it in these United States has been destroyed."[26]

The Judge as Campaign Issue

Judge Waring and his decisions on the white primary figured most prominently, however, as a political issue in the primary race for Burnet Maybank's Senate seat. Maybank faced four challengers in his reelection bid. During the county-to-county stump-speaking tour then traditional in South Carolina politics, all four attacked Waring and held Maybank responsible for the judge's appointment. But two of Senator Maybank's opponents—Congressman William Jennings Bryan Dorn of Greenwood and Alan Johnstone, a Newberry attorney—gave the Waring issue particularly extensive play. Johnstone was erect, white-haired, courtly, the scholar of the group, according to William Workman. "Possessed of a profound store of miscellaneous knowledge," Workman had written in a July profile of the candidates, Johnstone was "apt to interrupt himself at any time with a premeditated or impromptu dissertation on some aspect of history, government or politics. . . . [I]f mudslinging becomes the order of campaign business," the columnist added, "Alan Johnstone is equipped to fire with effect." Workman knew the candidate. At Saluda in late June, in a speech entitled "This State May Not Be Invaded," Johnstone proclaimed that constitutional amendments designed "to enfranchise the black man" were "dead letters" that would "remain so in spite of . . . the unwisdom of Judge Waring and the indiscretion of the senior senator from South Carolina" in securing his appointment. "We say to all of them . . . as Thomas Jefferson said to John Marshall," Johnstone asserted, with more feeling than accuracy, " 'You have made a law! See if you can enforce it!' "[27]

When Judge Waring convened the July 16 hearing on David Brown's complaint, Johnstone had attempted to address the courtroom, although not representing any of the defendants.

> MR. ALAN JOHNSTONE: If your Honor please, I wish to make an appearance here in this cause if this is an appropriate time—

Judge Waring knew Johnstone and his likely mission. He gave both short shrift.

> THE COURT: On whose behalf?
> MR. JOHNSTONE: My own.
> THE COURT: Are you a party?
> MR. JOHNSTONE: I'm a candidate for the United States Senate—
> THE COURT: This meeting is called for a judicial determination and not for campaign speeches. You are not admitted.
> MR. JOHNSTONE: But, your Honor, I'll not make a speech.
> THE COURT: Put the gentleman in his seat. If he creates any disorder, put him out. You've got your soap boxes on the street; not in the courtroom.[28]

Johnstone sat quietly through most of the remaining proceedings. But as the hearing was approaching a conclusion, Judge Waring asked the parties and counsel for suggestions regarding the order he was to issue.

> MR. ALAN JOHNSTONE: You asked for suggestions from—
> THE COURT: I asked in this cause. You are not in this cause. I don't care to sit here while you make a speech.
> MR. JOHNSTONE: I don't want to make a speech. Would you hear me for a moment? I don't wish to make a speech.
> THE COURT: You are not going to make a speech, so you're not going to talk. Put him out.
> MR. JOHNSTONE: I wish to file a paper here, if your Honor please.
> THE COURT: File your papers in the clerk's office. This man isn't a part of your organization?
> MR. TISON: No, sir; he is not.
> THE COURT: Has he any standing in your organization to speak for you?
> MR. TISON: Not that I know of. He has a paper he asked me to verify. I did it. That's a matter for the clerk.
> THE COURT: Let him go to the clerk's office or to the newspaper office or get the usual box.[29]

"The last time I saw Johnstone," Judge Waring remarked years later, "he was going out the courtroom door in Charleston backwards. And I never saw him again." After Waring retired from the bench and was living in New York, Johnstone applied for admission to the District of Columbia bar, and the District bar association wrote the judge about the incident in his courtroom that July years before. Waring replied that Johnstone "hadn't done anything really wrong; he made a fool of himself, but everybody had a right to make a fool of himself occasionally. So I hoped they'd admit him to practice; he was a decent person."[30]

The hearing may have been Waring's last personal contact with Alan Johnstone, but Johnstone was hardly through with him as a political issue. After being escorted gently but firmly from the judge's courtroom, and detained briefly in the marshal's office, Johnstone showed up later in the day at a stump gathering for local candidates in North Charleston. To the applause of spectators, he charged, "In that temple where we are accustomed to expect justice we have a judge who had pre-judged the issue. . . . Such a condition has not existed," he asserted, "since this section was invaded by the Union army." At Lancaster several days later, he delivered his sharpest attack to date. "That man who calls himself a judge," he indignantly exclaimed, "ordered his bailiffs to put their hands on me and push me bodily through a wall of negro flesh."

> [H]is order which commands enrollment and voting by a man simply because he is black is unlawful.
>
> His order which commands enrollment and voting in the Democratic primary by Republicans and members of other parties is unlawful.
>
> His language of abuse and his threats of arrest and imprisonment is offensive.
>
> His references to religion are wicked.
>
> His courtroom friends are carpetbaggers.
>
> His judicial conduct is tyrannical.
>
> He invites race suicide.

"There is no jail in South Carolina," Johnstone concluded, "strong enough to hold a free man who is right." For the balance of the campaign, Johnstone repeatedly hammered away at variations on these themes and at blaming Senator Maybank for Waring's selection.[31]

Congressman Dorn also spoke at Lancaster, terming the Waring appointment Senator Maybank's payment for political debts, referring to the judge as "that man down . . . at Charleston whom I did not appoint." Then only thirty-two, Dorn had risen rapidly in South Carolina politics. He was elected to the state House of Representatives at twenty-two. Two years later, he was seated in the state Senate by a unanimous vote of the body even though he was not yet the minimum age for the position mandated by the state constitution. After service in World War II, he won election to Congress. A populist from the South Carolina piedmont, Dorn devoted much of his senatorial campaign to attacks on the postwar relief programs, charging that the government was enriching corporations and "pouring money into rat holes all over the world while Russia [was] building an army." Years later, Dorn would remark that Judge Waring's divorce and remarriage had offended him. "That was one of the major bones of contention I had with him. I'm a Baptist and from the Bible Belt, the real Bible Belt. And South Carolina was at that time the only state in the Union that prohibited divorce. So that was part of our way of life." But he and his supporters also saw political value in the growing furor over Waring's civil rights decisions and in the judge's ties to Senator Maybank.[32]

In an April letter, Dorn had written potential supporters, "I am not going to sling mud. I am going to make a clean, vigorous campaign." But apparently he did not regard attacks against Waring's appointment as in that category. The next day a major low country supporter wrote to suggest that the congressman

> find out whether or not Maybank pushed Judge . . . Waring for the appointment as Federal Judge . . . and if you find that he did push him, I wish you would get some friend of yours, who is a Member of Congress, to wire me setting forth that fact. I believe that it would have more effect from some other member of Congress than from you. What do you think about that? These people down here and all over the State . . . are plenty mad about his decisions in the negro cases, and I think it can be used. What about getting it circulated in every county in the State.

Dorn found the tactic appealing. "I will do my best to find out about Judge Waring," he wrote in response.

> I understand Maybank did push his appointment but I will endeavor to find out for sure, and if he did, I will try to get someone else to wire you to that effect. Yes, I agree it ought to be circulated in every county in the state and also the kind of man old Waring really is.

By that point, however, the Waring-Maybank connection was already being aired by others; when another supporter pointed out the value of such revelations to Dorn's candidacy, the congressman replied: "It will help me politically because the people will resent it but I still regret that the story became public . . . it leaked out unknown to me and I would have given anything to stop [it]. I also like Senator Maybank personally and think he is a fine gentleman."[33]

While developing a file on the Waring issue, Dorn also recalled vaguely that Virginia governor William Tuck, a friend of long standing, had recently made some unkind remarks about the judge. Dorn telephoned Tuck at his Virginia Beach summer home and learned that the governor had appeared as a character witness in the well-publicized "check-kiting" trial that Judge Waring had heard in Richmond the previous year. The governor's impressions of Waring's conduct at the trial contrasted starkly with the praise given the judge in the Virginia papers. On the day he was to testify, Tuck had asked to appear earlier than scheduled, citing another engagement. Waring had denied his request, and the governor was still bristling with indignation over the judge's insolence—as well as his treatment of the prominent defendants on trial in the case, at least one of whom was Tuck's close friend.[34]

William Jennings Bryan Dorn, William Workman had written, had not only the name but also the "flair for rhetoric of the 'Boy Orator of the Platte.' . . . Neatly dressed and well-groomed, he manages to insinuate his entire body into frequent gestures." Armed with the additional ammunition

Governor Tuck had supplied, Dorn, like Johnstone, took to the stump, condemning Waring's divorce (" 'Wife of thirty-two years!' That's the way we used to put it on the platform"), his "arrogance and insolence" during the Richmond trial, and his "dictatorial" judicial orders (" 'just like Hitler,' we'd say"). "We gave him down the county," he recalled years later.[35]

As a member of the body with power to impeach federal judges, Congressman Dorn also enjoyed a platform not available to Senator Maybank's other opponents. On July 27, he introduced in the House of Representatives H. Res. 704, a resolution to authorize "a full and complete investigation and study of [Judge Waring's] conduct in office." Ordinarily, the House Committee on the Judiciary would have conducted such an investigation. But Dorn asked that the inquiry be undertaken by the Committee on Expenditures in the Executive Department, a committee on which he served. The resolution was referred to the House Rules Committee for scheduling, where it was quietly buried. When asked about it years later, Dorn could not recall ever having introduced H. Res. 704. At the time, however, it garnered him considerable press coverage.[36]

In addition to introducing the resolution, Dorn also prepared a lengthy House speech condemning Judge Waring and his conduct on the bench, which, although he didn't read before the House, he had inserted in the *Congressional Record*. "I regret to tell you," it stated,

> that in my good State of South Carolina, there is a Federal judge, who bears the name of J. Waties Waring, who is trying to force the members of the Democratic Party of South Carolina to forego the great principles of that party on important matters, entirely set apart for political consideration, and he is trying to force these South Carolina Democrats to accept what he thinks should be the political principles of their party, or perhaps, it is more correct to say that he is trying to tell the Democratic Party of South Carolina, "You cannot have any political principles at all."

To assure that blacks would have ample opportunity to enroll in the party and vote in its primary, Judge Waring had ordered enrollment books kept open at least from nine o'clock to one and three to six each day. Turning Waring's order on its head, Dorn accused the judge of denying the "working people of South Carolina" the right to enroll "in the nighttime or early in the morning before they went to work." He also claimed that copies of Waring's orders were delivered to many of the defendants "in the dead hours of the night," an "unheard-of procedure" in South Carolina. Such tactics, he charged, were the methods of "Hitler and Mussolini and today . . . Stalin."[37]

Then there was the matter of Waring's general fitness for office. Asserting that the judge was qualified by neither "ability" nor "temperament" to sit on the federal bench, Dorn scorned Waring as a "tyrannical" jurist whose decisions were designed

> to traduce the Democrats of South Carolina, and especially to humiliate the people of Charleston, his old friends, neighbors, and relatives, some of the finest people of that city, who, because of his ungentlemanly conduct in

many respects in the past, have refused to associate with him, and even now treat him with silent contempt.

"The people of that State would like to know," he added, noting that South Carolina had no provision for divorce, "how Judge Waring [could] obtain a separation from a lady to whom he had been married for approximately 30 years, remarry, and serve on the Federal bench in that great State." Although Dorn made no direct reference to Senator Maybank, in closing, he urged "the Department of Justice and the Senators and all those who are so much responsible for these appointments [to] forget any reward for political services and seek the services only of men of the highest character, excellent learning, and . . . judicial temperament."[38]

Dorn's remarks were clearly intended more for the folks back home than for his congressional colleagues. The evening following introduction of H. Res. 704, the congressman gave a statewide radio address orginating in a Charleston station. In it, he detailed his House action of the previous day and quoted extensively from his remarks in the *Record*. He also strongly implied that Senator Maybank was fully responsible for Judge Waring's appointment and flatly contradicted Maybank's assertion, then circulating in the press, that both he and "Cotton Ed" Smith had recommended Waring's selection. At a stump meeting earlier in the day, Dorn had sounded the same themes, while Alan Johnstone charged that the congressman was "not so much interested in Judge Waring's conduct as in a political fishing trip with himself at the head." Johnstone then accused the judge of spending the "early part of his life berating negroes, and the latter part giving them the kiss of death."[39]

Burnet Maybank was hardly an effective platform speaker. As William Workman reported early in the campaign, the senator's speeches made for "dull listening regardless of the merits or demerits of [his] record," and he spoke "more often in phrases than in sentences, [varying] the pitch of his voice not so much in accord with the text of his speech as with a regular pattern of rising and falling inflection." But the senator fully appreciated the political implications of his long association with Charleston's now thoroughly detested judge, and he pursued a cautious, deliberate campaign course designed both to blunt the impact of his opponents' attacks and to bolster his own credentials as a staunch defender of the South's racial traditions.[40]

Although Maybank's relations with Waties Waring had cooled considerably after his election as governor, the two had remained relatively close after Waring's appointment and, politically at least, even after the judge's divorce and remarriage. While Waring's nomination was pending in the Senate, the two had seen each other in Charleston, and Maybank had invited Waring to stop off for a visit in Washington on a forthcoming business trip to New York. Waring had been unable to accept the invitation, but he wrote Maybank after returning to Charleston that "it would have been very nice to have had an opportunity to talk over things" and offered his condolences on the recent death of the senator's father. "If there is anything I can do here," he added, "do not hesitate to call on me." In September 1945, three months after the divorce, Waring wrote Maybank an inconsequential letter from New York where he was then sitting as a visiting judge. "I am going to be up here until the 23rd," he noted in closing, "when I return to Charleston and expect to be there all winter . . . hope to see you in Charleston." Maybank's response was cordial enough, but suggested no social contacts with the judge or the new Mrs. Waring. As recently as early 1947, however, Maybank and Waring had exchanged letters and wires regarding an appointment of a U.S. attorney for the eastern district and a prospective nominee's abrupt withdrawal from consideration. "What is behind it all and what is the matter with the fellow?" Waring wrote the senator. "He certainly put everybody in an awkward fix and the whole affair has not been too pleasant."[41]

Maybank had also clearly backed Waring's appointment to the bench. Waring had been ranked second, it will be recalled, on the list of prospective nominees "Cotton Ed" Smith had given Attorney General Biddle before Maybank took his seat in the Senate; when Biddle sought Maybank's impressions of Smith's suggestions, Maybank had passed over Christie Benet, the Columbia attorney whose name appeared first on Senator Smith's list, and recommended Smith's second choice, Waring, for the post. But "Cotton Ed" had been the first to bring up Waring's name, so Maybank could now tell voters that he had merely "joined with Senator Smith in recommending" his former corporation counsel for the judgeship. Maybank also argued that neither he nor Smith should be blamed for Waring's current aberrations. In a statement issued the day after Judge Waring's written opinion in David Brown's case appeared, Maybank reminded voters that Waring had been "a strong supporter" of Smith when the late senator "was campaigning on a platform of white supremacy after having walked out of the Philadelphia convention in 1936." At the time of Waring's appointment, he added, the judge

> was conceded to be a staunch and loyal Democrat of the Jeffersonian school. I am not responsible for his conduct on or off the bench. I had every reason to believe that his actions would be entirely in keeping with those of the gentlemanly and scholarly lawyer we knew him to be at the time of his appointment.

Maybank reminded voters, too, that he had been the first South Carolina officeholder "to publicly state his opposition to [Waring's] actions." In Washington and on the stump, moreover, he became a particularly vocal critic of President Truman's civil rights program. As the primary date neared, he led a filibuster against an administration proposal to abolish the poll tax and vowed to "fight any so-called civil rights bill to the end." The South, he charged, had "been a political prisoner of war since 1865," and it was time that southerners "repatriated [their] displaced sovereign rights without the ill-advised aid of vote-conscious meddlers."[42]

Maybank's protestations had little effect on his opponents. Although Alan Johnstone attacked Congressman Dorn for merely investigating Judge Waring's conduct rather than instituting full-dress impeachment proceedings, the two candidates reserved their harshest attacks for Maybank and Waring. Emphasizing Senator Smith's well-known disfavor with the Roosevelt administration, Dorn and Johnstone continued to assert that Maybank alone was responsible for Waring's appointment. Then, in late July, Johnstone sent Maybank a telegram urging the senator to

> Impeach Judge Waring in the Senate. These orders by which he makes war on South Carolina, white and black, and in which he has gone berserk and dishonors the memory of Woodrow Wilson, Senator Smith, and yourself. This setting aside of our best traditions of a good life together, fair play, and a fair hearing. For it is not the good conduct which the Constitution demands of a judge with life tenure. All our people, including Negro citizens, deserve better conduct than this and can no longer risk the prejudice it stirs up.

Maybank dashed off a brief and pointed response to the Newberry attorney: "Yours. You are a lawyer and should know that impeachment proceedings must be brought in the House of Representatives." Then he obtained consent from the Senate to have Johnstone's wire, and his reply, placed in the record; reiterated his criticisms of Judge Waring; and assured "the people of South Carolina . . . that such action as has been requested of me can originate only in the House of Representatives."[43]

But Johnstone and Dorn were not about to see the issue die, and they soon acquired a potentially valuable ally. At one stump gathering, Dorn indicated that he had recently spoken to the late Senator Smith's son and daughter and that they were "shocked and amazed" at Senator Maybank's version of the Waring appointment. On August 2, Smith's son, Farley, a candidate for a seat in the South Carolina House of Representatives, released a statement to the press. "There were only two people," Smith declared, "who could have made the recommendation: my father and Senator Maybank, and it wasn't my father." President Roosevelt, Smith said, "told my father in the presence of witnesses that he would never get to name anybody to another federal job. After that, my father couldn't have had a post office clerk appointed."

> Waring was not my father's first, second, third, fourth or fifth choice. If Waring's name had gone down as one on my father's list he never would have been appointed.[44]

On August 5, Burnet Maybank again rose to defend himself on the Senate floor. Like other South Carolina newspapers, the *News and Courier* had given Farley Smith's charges prominent play. Maybank obtained unanimous consent to insert the *Courier*'s account in the Senate record. At one point, the *Courier* had cited Congressman Dorn's reference "to a previous statement by Senator Maybank that Judge Waring was appointed on the recommendation of Senator Smith." Maybank disputed that claim, asserting that he had said only that he had "joined" Senator Smith in supporting Waring and that Smith had first recommended Waring "to be judge before I was ever a United States Senator." Maybank then produced correspondence with Attorney General Biddle and the chairman of the Senate Judiciary Committee to support his account of the appointment and Waring's status as Senator Smith's second choice for the judgeship. He also claimed that he had endorsed his former corporation counsel only after Christie Benet, Senator Smith's first choice, had urged him to support Waring. Ernest W. McFarland (D-Ariz.), chairman of the Judiciary subcommittee that reviewed Waring's nomination, spoke, too, in Maybank's defense. On August 3, McFarland had written Maybank a letter summarizing the subcommittee's action on the appointment. On the Senate floor, McFarland asserted that Senator Smith had appeared before the full Judiciary Committee and endorsed Waring's appointment. "It is my opinion," he added, "that the nomination of Judge Waring would not have been confirmed had Senator Smith not approved it. I say that because of the high esteem in which Senator Smith was held by the members of the Judiciary Committee and the Senate."[45]

Farley Smith was not convinced. Three days before the primary, he issued another statement. Christie Benet, the Columbia attorney who was placed first on Senator Smith's list, had represented the defendants in the *Elmore* case. Ignoring the fact that Waties Waring was second on the list, Farley Smith now expressed pleasure that Senator Maybank had finally conceded "that the great defender of states' rights and the Southern democratic white primary, the honorable Christie Benet, was my father's choice." Benet was not appointed, Smith reasoned, "because he was my father's choice." His father had not supported Waring because in 1938 Waring had written Senator Smith a "rude and discourteous letter . . . charging that the family of Senator Smith was not wholeheartedly supporting Senator Maybank for governor. . . . If my father were alive," Smith concluded,

> Senator Maybank would not dare to pin the appointment of Waties Waring on him. All that my father's friends ask and all that his family asks is, now that he has gone, in the name of justice let him rest in peace.[46]

Congressman Dorn and Alan Johnstone also continued to attack the Waring-Maybank connection. But the most vicious assault on Judge Waring would come not from Maybank's opponents, but from Charleston's U.S. congressman. L. Mendel Rivers and Judge Waring had been frequent political allies before Waring's appointment to the bench. Even after Waring's divorce, they had continued to correspond cordially on a variety of matters. In the spring of 1946, for example, they exchanged several letters regarding an investigation that Waring had requested into the dumping of Naval food and supplies into Charleston harbor. "I am in thorough agreement with you," Rivers had written on one occasion, "that the parties responsible are guilty of a contemptible and unpardonable act in this time of world-wide famine and shortages." In the summer of that year, moreover, Rivers asked Waring to write a letter supporting the congressman's choice for a position with the federal Alcohol Tax Unit in South Carolina—a request the judge promptly honored.[47]

But Waring's rhetoric, if not his rulings, had undoubtedly angered Rivers. The congressman obviously realized, too, that his constituents expected action—or at least a speech. On August 4, Rivers requested one minute of time on the House floor to speak on the Waring issue. Up till that time, he said, he had fought "an almost irresistible impulse" to speak out for fear that any statement he made might be misconstrued as support for one of the senatorial candidates. Now that the matter had been "brought into the open," he could break his silence on Judge Waring's "highhanded, unjudicial, ungentlemanly, outrageous and deplorable conduct." The judge, he exclaimed, was

> as cold as a dead Eskimo in an abandoned igloo. Lemon juice flows in his frigid and calculating veins. By means of the FBI and the United States marshals, he has lampooned, lambasted, and vilified with unparalleled vituperation the comfort and ease of the outstanding members of the bar of South Carolina. At times he has literally banished some of them from his court by force. He should be removed by the force of a boot, if necessary, from office, because he is a disgrace to the Federal judiciary of South Carolina.
>
> Every lawyer in South Carolina lives in mortal fear of this monster and everyone who reads this speech will thank God that I made it because I am speaking for the vast majority of the bar of South Carolina.
>
> Vast numbers of lawyers have abandoned practice in the Federal Court because of this individual.[48]

Rivers assured his House colleagues that he had no complaints about Judge Waring's decisions regarding the all-white primary. Naturally, he opposed voting by "illiterates, white or black," and he had long favored educational requirements for suffrage. Even so, he was certain that there were "thousands of qualified Negroes in South Carolina who should be permitted to vote in our primaries." What concerned Rivers, he said, was the judge's temperament.

> [I]n the interpretation of what a judge considers to be law, whether he is right or wrong, he does not have to go through a metamorphosis and become a monster. The law should be interpreted so that people will have a respect for law. Judge Waring's miserable conduct in issuing orders has been nothing short of a star-chamber procedure . . . his clumsy handling of a delicate situation has hurt the case of the Negro in South Carolina. This is unfortunate and I trust will not long obtain. Unless he is removed, there will be bloodshed. I prophesy bloodshed because he is now in the process of exacting a pound of flesh from the white people of South Carolina because through his own actions he has been ostracized from their society.

Rivers next claimed that Judge Waring's decisions were "political," that he was simply seeking a court of appeals position "if by some curious twist Lightweight Harry Truman should slip into the White House for another term." "Who appointed this judge?" a colleague then asked. "Do not ask me that," Rivers, a Dixiecrat and member of the party's speakers' bureau, replied. "I will answer in this way, however: We have an organization now and we do not have to follow the screwballs who stole the Democratic Party."[49]

Following his remarks on the House floor, Congressman Rivers announced plans to introduce a resolution calling for an impeachment inquiry. He also conferred with attorneys familiar with the law of impeachment, who advised him that his resolution should state more specifically than its original version the grounds on which the judge's impeachment was sought. Rivers said, too, that he was beginning an investigation into Waring's conduct during the 1947 Richmond bank trial. These efforts quickly died. But Rivers apparently did not limit his assault on Waring entirely to the House. Chief Justice Fred M. Vinson was the member of the Supreme Court with supervisory powers over Waring and other judges of the fourth federal judicial circuit. In a signed article published the day after Rivers' House speech, the Charleston *Evening Post* reported that the congressman had contacted the chief justice shortly before his floor speech and asked Vinson to launch an investigation into Waring's conduct. Vinson, according to the paper, had "flatly refused" to look into Waring's conduct "on or off the bench," telling Rivers that any inquiry would be the responsibility of the Congress, not the courts. Rivers declined to confirm or deny the report but did say, "My speech yesterday was not born of a sudden impulse. I made it because I couldn't get action in other quarters."[50]

Even the *Post* termed Rivers' attack "on his fellow townsman . . . vitriolic." It was thus hardly surprising that civil rights leaders reacted harshly to the attacks on Judge Waring. Walter White of the NAACP was then writing a syndicated column that appeared in a number of major national papers as well as the black press. In one column, White heaped scorn on Rivers and Congressman Dorn, terming their assaults "tirades of incredible vitriol," delivered in "language more suited to the gutter than to Congress. . . . Such is the treatment meted out to a Judge of integrity and character," he caustically added, "who dared rule against open and unashamed violation of the federal Constitution." The remedy for such outbursts, White recommended, was elimination of the immunity enjoyed by congressmen against suits for libel and slander—an immunity which, in the hands of a Rivers or Dorn, had become a "national scandal." South Carolina NAACP president James M. Hinton wrote Rivers a scathing letter and provided reporters with copies. Hinton condemned the congressman's prophecy of bloodshed as "unwarranted, unfounded and equally untrue."

> You and others need have no fear of trouble from negroes in the coming primary. Negroes will not provoke any incident. We request from you and others cessation of unwise public statements which are beneath the dignity of your position.

The "only persons stirring up race hatred and inviting trouble," wrote Hinton, were "office-holders and office-seekers."[51]

Through all the turmoil, Judge Waring maintained an uncharacteristic silence. After Rivers' speech, Judge John J. Parker telephoned his colleague to offer encouragement. On August 5, Waring wrote the chief judge of his circuit a lengthy letter detailing his experiences. Enclosed with the letter were "miserable articles" from the Charleston papers giving Rivers' remarks extensive coverage. "As you have well said," Waring wrote,

> it is pretty lonely here for Mrs. Waring and myself. Instead of getting better, things have gotten worse and are coming to a head by reason of the bitter campaign that is being fought for the Senate.

Waring could offer no explanation for Rivers' attack except that "he is publicity minded to an extreme degree and undoubtedly wants to make use of this campaign of vilification." Waring assured Parker, however, that he had "refused to be drawn into any controversy" and realized "that when one has a duty to perform he has to have with it a strong stomach to stand poison of this kind."[52]

Judge Parker immediately answered his normally outspoken colleague's letter, praising Waring's restraint and encouraging him to continue that posture. Parker had read Rivers' remarks in the *Congressional Record*. "It is most unfortunate," he wrote,

> that a member of Congress should so far forget himself as to make this sort of attack on a member of the Judiciary. You are wise, of course, not to enter into the controversy.
>
>   It is hard for a man to restrain himself from utterance when this sort of attack is made upon him; but that is the only thing to do. The people realize that a judge cannot enter into a name calling contest, and the very violence of Rivers' attack will discredit what he says. Every brave man resents an attack on one who is not in position to strike back.

Judge Waring heeded Parker's advice. When pressed by reporters about Rivers' remarks, he could not resist observing, "It should be unnecessary to comment on these silly, childish ravings." Otherwise, he declined to comment on the charges of Rivers and his fellow sympathizers.[53]

Even without the stimulus of a venomous campaign, South Carolina whites were generally unhappy with Judge Waring and his orders. Some took the judge's intervention in good, if barbed, humor. In a letter to the *News and Courier,* one reminded "party bigwigs" of Waring's warning "that South Carolina jails are not air-conditioned and do not have room service or ice water"; lamented the passing of oaths and the "time-honored" requirement that "a hopeful voter of color . . . interpret such simple legal phrases as corpus delecti"; and expressed relief that "the judge cannot hear some of the oaths being used or our jails might be too full of politicians to take care of the ordinary rascals we have." Others were deadly serious. A Timmonsville subscriber berated the *Courier* for refusing to report details of Waring's private life. "Judge Waring did not stop at declaring the action of his fellow-citizens illegal," he reminded the paper's staff. "He went further, and gratuitously denounced the ethics of their attitude and the basic morality of their acts." Under such circumstances, asked the letter writer, were the people

> not justified in openly inquiring into his qualifications to act as their critic? Can they be blamed for asking out loud, whether this self-appointed mentor

is able to "come into court with clean hands." Is it improper to discuss the effect of his private actions upon his public decisions?

No man should ever be allowed to feel that he has grown too big for the copybook maxim: "People who live in glass houses should never throw stones."[54]

Despite such sentiments and the vehemence of the candidates, however, the primary proved anticlimactic. By the primary date, 35,000 blacks had been enrolled. Many voted, virtually without incident. On the date of the primary, Judge Waring and Elizabeth drove about Charleston, stopping at a number of polling places with large black enrollments. They observed no efforts to interfere with black voting. After a two-hour conference with the judge two days after the primary, Thurgood Marshall and Harold Boulware told reporters that no substantive violations of the order had been discovered. In letters to Judge Parker and to Elizabeth's son-in-law, Simeon Hyde, Jr., written on August 11, Waring agreed with the NAACP attorneys' assessment. But Waring entertained no hope of white sympathy. "You would suppose," he wrote Hyde, "that the decent people here would resent the personal attacks on me. But they do not, and in fact I believe they like it and either talk about me behind my back or preserve a stony silence." He was pleased, however, with the way in which the primary had been conducted. "[T]hey didn't shoot me," he wrote Parker. "The blacks behaved themselves beautifully and the whites did too. Though I am a little afraid the latter were moved mostly by fear of the Federal Court." "Things went off smoothly and beautifully," he informed Hyde. "So far as Charleston is concerned there was not the slightest disorder and a considerable number of Negroes went to the polls, voted quietly and went away."[55]

Of course, the 35,000 enrolled blacks were a small percentage of the more than 800,000 enrolled voters, and the array of senatorial candidates offered black voters no real choice. Senator Maybank, in fact, ultimately may have been the chief immediate beneficiary of the Waring issue and the judge's addition of blacks to the primary rolls. According to at least one report, Maybank told potential supporters in South Carolina's piedmont that Judge Waring had ordered blacks added to the rolls as part of a plot to defeat the senator's reelection bid. Whatever the impact of such tactics, Maybank easily won the primary, garnering over 175,000 votes against a combined total of 165,000 for his opponents. As the New York *Herald Tribune* observed in an editorial tribute to Judge Waring, however, the participation of blacks in the August 10 primary signaled an end to the state's "hocus-pocus theory that the Democratic party was a private political country club." And the man responsible had been "a Southerner of Southerners, speaking to his own people in the sternest terms."[56]

The Judge as National Figure

In the evening following his conference with Thurgood Marshall and Harold Boulware, the Warings left Charleston by train for a brief visit to New York.

They next journeyed to California, staying several weeks in Santa Barbara, then went back to New York and, in mid-October, returned to Charleston. During their extended absence from South Carolina, Waring remained a subject of continuing press interest—an interest now no longer confined to the state media. An article by veteran Charleston and Savannah newspaperwoman Rowena W. Tobias appeared in the August 14 issue of the *Nation* magazine. It described "the South's last-ditch abortivve battle to preserve a one-party, one-color political system." Later in the month, *Time* profiled "The Man They Love to Hate." The *Time* article reported that the judge and his bride had been "instantly ostracized" after his divorce and remarriage, duly recorded the complaints of Charleston lawyers that he had grown more "vituperative and irascible month by month," and cited the whispers of "one-time friends" that he was "out to get his revenge." *Time* also apparently gave the first national exposure to a Waring story then circulating in Charleston. When lightning struck a house next to Waring's summer cottage on Sullivan's Island, the magazine noted, his neighbor had nailed up a sign: "Dear God. He lives next door."[57]

The following week, a humorous article on Elizabeth Waring and the couple's difficulties in Charleston, "the mint-julep headquarters," appeared in a publication of considerably more modest circulation, the New Britain, Connecticut, *Sunday Herald*. Its author, Ethel Bickwick, spared no one. Elizabeth and Henry Hoffman had lived in Litchfield, Connecticut, when they were not wintering in Charleston. Bickwick compared Elizabeth to another Litchfield product, Harriet Beecher Stowe. Stowe's *Uncle Tom's Cabin* had incensed southerners. "The awful thing Mrs. Waring did, if you ask anybody in Charleston today," Bickwick wrote, "is this: 'She put those nawthun notions in her husband's head. . . . ' " Elizabeth was "one of the not-too-staid set who invaded the solid front of Litchfield purity some years ago." In Litchfield, she enjoyed "the reputation of the well-tempered matron." But when she met Judge Waring, who "must have fallen like the well-known ton," it was "springtime for Henry. . . . This invasion from Litchfield," Bickwick explained, "did not sit too well. . . . The judge and his wife noticed that the purple pajama set were going by their house. They got no invitations to cocktail parties." Waring was normally "a quiet fellow."

> but one who can throw a brilliant stroke when he wants to, [and he] got the pitch. . . . One day . . . he walked to his office and with one stroke of his pen threw Ca' lina's white and blue supremacy into catfits. Merely this: he forced the state party to open its enrollment list to negroes and to permit them—ah, the dawg—"full participation in party affairs." . . . Waring was jeered, but he "done it."[58]

The Warings resented any suggestion that the judge's civil rights rulings were the product of spite. Although few read Ethel Bickwick's article, the *Time* profile was a different matter. The Warings apparently shared their irritation with Anne and Stanley Warren. In a letter of response, Stanley reported that a *Time* editorial assistant—"a very prissy, stuffy young lady of the type that thinks Time Magazine is more important than the Bill of Rights or the Magna Carta"—had telephoned him while the profile was being compiled, asking that Stanley come to the magazine's offices to answer some questions. Warren had corrected a number of errors, but the editorial assistant— "as childish as an eight-year-old with a big secret"—refused to allow him to examine the entire file and offer other corrections. When Warren told the staffer that Elizabeth was not a "Connecticut woman," as the profile would report, she acted as if he were "trying to deny the fact." She was also unaware that Judge Waring had decided the equal pay cases before his divorce. The final product, Warren agreed, "seemed to read like a smear from Charleston toned down by Time's editors." He assured the Warings, however, that "[a]ll our friends and acquaintances who have read the piece think it makes the Judge out to be a great man. Really, they do. . . . If anybody has to hang their head in shame," he added, "it is the people of Charleston."[59]

Whatever their disappointment with the *Time* profile, the Warings were pleased with the national publicity given South Carolina's racial situation, and they were now seeking greater press attention for their cause. Like Anne and Stanley Warren, Elizabeth's daughter and son-in-law admired the judge's decisions. On the day his ruling in the *Elmore* case was issued, Ann Hyde had written the judge, praising his "splendid stand . . . [T]he Negroes will bless you and all decent white people will respect and admire you," she wrote, adding, "I can understand the Southerners' dislike of Northern interference—but what a disgraceful case that was." In the aftermath of the 1948 white primary ruling, Simeon Hyde had written Judge Waring a similar letter and cited the need for a major magazine article on the situation in Charleston. Judge Waring readily agreed and proposed that Hyde, then teaching in a Massachusetts prep school, write such a piece. The judge was "not sure" that even Hyde could "realize the intense introversion of the people here." But he hoped that a national magazine or newspaper would agree to send Elizabeth's son-in-law to Charleston and urged Hyde to undertake the project.[60]

Hyde never wrote the article Judge Waring had envisioned, and, in the Warings' eyes, the *Time* profile, with its allusion to a revenge motive for his civil rights decisions, was hardly satisfactory. But on their trip to New York and California following South Carolina's August 10 primary, Judge Waring had several opportunities to expose the status of civil rights in his native state—and further damage his image among white South Carolinians. In Santa Barbara, a local newspaper interviewed him and published a lengthy, flattering profile summarizing his rulings, outlining the controversy his decisions had generated at home, quoting extensively his impressions of southern race relations, and depicting him as a "judge of great courage, who held that even in South Carolina a man might not be deprived of his rights because of the color of his skin." In the interview, Waring had agreed that "social acceptance" of blacks by whites was a "personal matter," but contended that "the denial of a man's rights [was] another thing. . . . The sad part" of the South Carolina situation, he observed, was that the people "did not permit Negroes to vote because they wanted that, but because a judge told them that they had to." Most of the letters he had received from South Carolinians had praised his position, he added, but many of these had been marked "confidential." "There you have an indication of the situation," he concluded. "Many men in the South feel that the Negro should be given his rights— but are unwilling to say so in public."[61]

On returning to New York from California, Judge Waring was soon provided another platform. On October 11, he spoke at a luncheon given in his honor by the New York chapter of the National Lawyers Guild. "My people have one outstanding fault," he told his audience,

> the terrible fault of prejudice. They have been born and educated to feel that a Negro is some kind of an animal that ought to be well-treated and given kindness, but as a matter of favor, not right. That's not the kind of conception that we should show to the world.

He agreed that improvement in southern race relations was possible, but asserted that "the windows [would not] be opened voluntarily." Instead, gains in recent years had been forced by the federal courts and other outside agencies, and that trend, he declared, must be continued. Thurgood Marshall, a member of the Guild's executive board, was seated near Waring. The danger of Georgia governor Ellis Arnall and other southern liberals, Waring asserted, his eyes on Marshall, was "that they say: 'Let us alone and we'll do it ourselves.' Well, no Negro would have voted in South Carolina if you hadn't brought a case." In closing, he urged Guild members to continue their work in behalf of civil rights.

> [G]o forward with your work, but . . . be careful of your methods. A reformer who cowers to the South and says the whole civilization there is wrong is making a mistake. On the other hand, don't stay away. We have got to teach many people to want to improve. The situation has got to be handled gently but firmly.[62]

Judge Waring was now appearing to abandon the gradual, moderate approach to racial reform he had seemed to espouse less than a year before. And he was doing it off the bench and before members of the National Lawyers Guild, a group considered little more than a Communist front by many of the nation's conservatives. The Charleston *Evening Post* had reprinted the Santa Barbara newspaper profile without comment, but the *News and Courier* could not resist an editorial response to Judge Waring's New York speech. A news article in the *Courier's* October 14 issue carried a balanced report of the event. On the editorial page, however, William Watts Ball observed:

> It is the exceptional judge, state or federal, who delivers addresses advising public policy or criticizing political actions and tendencies of the republic, the states and communities. Nearly all judges scrupulously refrain from utterances interpretable as political save when they are directly relevant to and inseparable from a case in court and they are presiding. The separation

of the judicial from the legislative and executive branches of government is a principle fundamental in the United States. Departure from it by judges is occasional. Generally the judiciary practices withdrawal from political activity and expression and in that way commands and preserves the confidence of the people in its aloofness, its independence, its freedom from bias, from prejudice.

C. Rexford Raymond, minister of Charleston's historic Circular Congregational Church, was equally indignant. "My long experience in the South," Raymond asserted in a letter to the *Courier,* "make me object to the idea that racial prejudice is entirely prevalent there, though, of course, it is often found both in the North and the South. . . . For more than 50 years," he wrote, "I have had southern friends who have opposed the idea that negroes are not full American citizens." As evidence, Raymond cited the founding of Berea College in 1833 by antislave Kentuckians and the college's maintenance of an integrated student body until segregation was required by Kentucky law of private as well as public institutions. Berea's history, he contended, was proof, "[i]n the words of Lord Macaulay, [that] 'You cannot indict a whole people.' "[63]

The defendants in the white primary litigation also found Judge Waring's remarks of more than passing interest. The judge's intemperate remarks from the bench had themselves been of questionable propriety. But now Waring was traveling about the nation, discussing pending litigation and condemning the racial bigotry of white southerners—among whom, obviously, were the defendants in the trial concerning South Carolina's white primary. The previous July, Waring had issued only a preliminary or temporary order in David Brown's case; a hearing on the plaintiff's motion for a permanent injunction was yet to be conducted. On October 20, John C. Stansfield, state Democratic committeeman from Aiken County and one of the defendants in the case, filed an affidavit in the judge's court, charging that his "personal bias and prejudice" in favor of blacks was interfering with his obligation to render an impartial judgment. Stansfield quoted extensively from Waring's harsh attacks on the defendants at the July hearing and from his speech to the Lawyers Guild. Following the July hearing, the party committeeman stated, he had "preferred to assume" that the case still might be impartially decided. After reading a *New York Times* account of Waring's Guild speech, however, he had concluded that the judge had "a personal bias against [the defendants] because they are white people of the South with one outstanding fault—the terrible fault of prejudice—whom we have got to teach . . . to want to improve and who have the feeling, the sentiment, the creed that a negro is not an American citizen."[64]

In his original suit, David Brown had sought $5,000 in damages as well as an injunction. Motions for injunctions are traditionally heard by a judge, but defendants in federal damage suits are entitled to a jury trial, and Bob Figg and other attorneys representing South Carolina's Democratic officials were now claiming that their clients were entitled to have all issues heard by a jury of their peers. To avoid such a turn of events, Thurgood Marshall and

Harold Boulware had filed a motion to eliminate Brown's damage claim from their client's complaint.[65]

The Warings returned to Charleston in mid-October for a hearing on Marshall's motion. At an October 22 hearing, Judge Waring granted the motion and set November 23 as the date for a nonjury hearing on the motion for a permanent injunction. He also gave brief attention to John Stansfield's motion that he withdraw from the case.

> COURT: I have read the petition and statements and will hear from you on the matter if you care to discuss it.
>
> MR. TISON: We do not care to argue the motion your Honor.
>
> COURT: There are two parts to it. The first complains of my decision. Well, I am of the opinion that the decision was right. It is in conformity with the opinions in other cases, which have been affirmed. It is the plain law of the land and certainly it is the law in this case as this case hasn't been appealed from. The second one seems to be on the ground that I spoke in New York at a Lawyers meeting, which I did, based on some newspaper reports, which are mostly correct, and the address was to the effect that I was in favor of enforcing the law. I assume that if I had made a speech that I believed in enforcing the law against murder, I would have to disqualify myself from trying a murder case on this theory. I suppose that if I had said I was in favor of enforcing the revenue laws, I couldn't try any of the numerous illicit distilling violations. There is nothing to the motion. Petition dismissed.[66]

When he returned to his chambers following the hearing, Judge Waring found a letter bearing a Columbia postmark that had arrived in the morning mail. "We, in the name of the white citizens of South Carolina," it began, "do beg that you give due consideration in your decision that is to be rendered concerning the rights of negroes to participate in the matters of the white democratic party which will tend to break all segregation laws and customs in our State." Similar rulings during the Reconstruction era, the letter reminded the judge as "a white citizen of South Carolina," had produced "fearful conditions. . . . You must realize," it added, "the fearful racial hatred that will follow any adverse decision that you may render . . . against the white people of your own State." A "favorable decision for the white people," on the other hand, would "in the end do more justice to the negroes themselves than the past decisions that you have been making." The letter was signed, in red type, "Knights of the Ku Klux Klan Members."[67]

The letter's tone was respectful, and it contained no semblance of a threat. At that point, moreover, the Klan was largely moribund in South Carolina, though a number of meetings had recently been staged in the Columbia area. But the Warings considered the letter a form of intimidation—and an opportunity for additional publicity. After reading it, Waring turned it over to the FBI. He also attempted to reach Stanley Warren by telephone in New York and, failing that, mailed his son-in-law a copy of the Klan letter for ABC, Drew Pearson, and other columnists with whom Warren was acquainted. "The main reason for giving this publicity," he wrote Warren, "is to try and show the people of this nation how bad the situation is when a Judge is threatened with a communication of this kind."[68]

That evening, Judge Waring telephoned another possible press channel. Tom Peck was a reporter for the *News and Courier*. But he was also Charleston representative for the Associated Press and the son of a New York *Herald Tribune* reporter. Waring told Peck that he had received the Klan letter and asked whether the reporter would have it published. Peck replied that he would have to see it first and arranged to visit Waring's home later in the evening.[69]

When Peck arrived, he found Judge Waring's secretary in the living room typing copies of the letter. While Peck and the judge were talking, Mrs. Waring came downstairs and joined them. After examining the letter, Peck told the Warings that he would take a copy to Tom Waring and assumed that the paper would publish it. Did Peck think, Elizabeth asked, that his "people at the office" would attempt to prevent publication? Peck assured her that the letter was a legitimate news item but suggested that a statement from Judge Waring indicating that he thought it had come from the Klan would better justify its publication. Mrs. Waring replied that the letter could only have come from the Klan. At that point, Judge Waring interrupted, explaining that, legally, it was an anonymous letter. "After all, Elizabeth," Peck would later recall the judge saying, "we don't know whether it *is* from the Klan, or if someone is just trying to throw a scare into us." "If it were from anyone else," Mrs. Waring "very briskly" replied, "it would have been much more vindictive. You can imagine what would have been in it if Mr. Ball had written it, for example."

After a lengthy silence, Judge Waring conceded that the letter had been written very carefully—"cagily," Mrs. Waring interjected—by an intelligent man and that ordinarily a Klan letter would have been nasty and vindictive. But he agreed with Elizabeth that it had come from the Klan. He was simply uncertain, he said, about the sort of statement he should issue to the press. Mrs. Waring then proposed, according to Peck's later account of the conversation, that her husband "ought to say something about his not being afraid and that the public should be told that this organization had dared to threaten a federal judge." Judge Waring pondered his wife's suggestion, then began dictating a statement to his secretary.

While a statement was being prepared, Mrs. Waring asked Peck about his father's connections with the *Herald Tribune* and urged him to telephone his father with the story. When Peck declined, Elizabeth asserted, "You don't realize how important this thing is. I think it may stamp out the whole Klan business in the South." Peck then told her that his father was not responsible for that sort of news. "He could tell it to someone else," Elizabeth persisted. Mrs. Waring next inquired whether Peck would give the story to the Associated Press. He replied that he would but could not guarantee that the wire service would use it. "Of course, they will," Mrs. Waring responded. "All the big papers will eat this up. It's good political stuff just before the election."

While his secretary was typing the statement, Judge Waring returned to the conversation and "lectured" Peck on the history of the Klan in South Carolina. Many men prominent in the state's politics were members, he told Peck, including Senator Maybank and Tom Stoney. "Somewhere during the conversation," Peck later reported to Tom Waring, the judge also told the reporter that "he was not afraid of being killed, but whether he meant that in the heroic sense or that he didn't attach much danger to the 'threat' I cannot now decide."

The FBI never traced the letter's source, but the judge would receive no more correspondence bearing the Klan's name for the near term. His statement to the press largely tracked his wife's suggestions, though, as Tom Peck put it, "in a slightly more judicial tone." "Of course," Waring had observed, the letter "had had and would have no effect on any decision of mine on matters coming before me, but I believe the people of this country should be made aware of this attempt to threaten and influence a United States judge in his judicial decisions." The *News and Courier* carried the story, as did other papers and national radio commentators, including Cecil Brown of the Mutual Network. But it probably did not attract the extensive national attention Elizabeth Waring had anticipated.[70]

The *Courier*'s article, under the heading, " 'Ku Klux' Letter Called Threat By Waring," quoted the letter's timid request for "cooperation in a favorable decision for the white people" in the lead paragraph, and basically followed the judge's account; presumably the Warings were satisfied. But Judge Waring faced other problems from the paper he had once represented. Waring had picked October 22, the day of the hearing on the Stansfield affidavit and David Brown's motion, to announce his appointment of John Fleming as court crier. The *Courier*'s October 23 issue carried a brief item on the appointment, indicating that the last "member of the negro race" to hold the position had been selected by Ernest F. Cochran, "a Republican appointee." A black had last served in the eastern district during Judge Cochran's tenure. But the article did not mention that blacks were serving as bailiffs in the courts of Judges Timmerman and Wyche at the time of Fleming's appointment.[71]

On the morning that the story appeared, J. V. Nielsen, Jr., of the *Courier* staff, was called to the judge's chambers. When Nielsen arrived, Waring's clerk, Ernest Allen, dictated a statement correcting errors in the article. The judge, Allen said, wanted the corrections published. That evening, according to a memorandum Nielsen prepared for Tom Waring, the judge demanded to know whether the *Courier* planned to run a correction. The story the paper had intended to publish had indicated the source of the corrections. When Nielsen read it to the Warings, the judge demanded that the article omit any reference to him or his clerk and threatened otherwise to take legal action or "tell it to the New York papers. . . . They'll eat up that kind of stuff. I have lots of friends there who would see that it got publicity." On October 24, the *Courier* ran a correction, without reference to its source. "It is not at all unusual for the court to name negro bailiffs or for them to cry the court," the article concluded. "Any inference that there is anything unusual about the appointment of John Fleming to such a position is not justified." Two days later, the paper editorialized that "The position of court crier is not of any political or official authority or significance, and the appointment of a negro is in no sense objectionable to southern white people."[72]

On November 2, shortly after the Warings' return to Charleston, a profile drawn from an interview Judge Waring had given journalist Henry Beckett appeared in the *New York Post*. Some of the profile was of the Sunday-supplement sort. The "six-footer of 68 years," Beckett reported, considered himself "sedentary" and golf "silly"; enjoyed travel, the theater, and bridge; wished he shared his wife's enthusiasm for "the best music"; "drinks a little and used to smoke some, but not now." When in Charleston, he walked to court from his home "on that storybook thoroughfare, Meeting Street"; when hearing cases in New York, "he takes the B.M.T. from Central Park downtown to Foley Sq." Beckett naturally focused, however, on Judge Waring's decisions and the couple's treatment by white Charlestonians. He compared the judge to Franklin Roosevelt, whom "[p]lenty of Harvard men and Social Register people called . . . a 'traitor to his class' because he tried to pass prosperity around." Judge Waring, he wrote, now had "a similar status in Charleston," where a former friend might concede the legal soundness of his decisions, yet consider them "conduct unbecoming a Southern gentleman." "Old friends still speak to me on the street," Beckett quoted the judge, "but grudgingly, and nobody has defended me in public." In Waring's judgment the South's treatment of blacks was hurting the country internationally and "helping the Communists. . . . That is why you of the North," he told Beckett, "must interfere. Only do it with tact. Deal with wrong in the concrete. Don't condemn the South as a whole."[73]

"How is it, Judge," Waring had been asked, "that in your attitude as to the rights of a Negro in this country you differ so markedly from the majority of people in the South, people of the same background and grown up in the same tradition?" In responding, Waring rejected the thesis that his second wife was the critical factor, or that it was

> because he was fond of his "Dah," which is the Charleston word for "Mammy," that he feels as he does. The memory of his devoted Negro nurse is dear to many a Southerner who won't dine with Negroes.

Instead, the judge attributed his current stance to his experiences on the federal bench, where, he claimed, he had developed "a passion for justice."

> My full realization of the right and wrong of it has come to me since I have been on the bench. A lawyer, always taking one side, may have narrow views, but on the bench, where one has to administer justice according to law, a man must come to grips with the facts and reach a decision.
> I rather shrink from saying it for quotation, but it does seem to me that by being a judge I have gradually acquired a passion for justice. Especially in the Federal Courts, where a judge has a great deal of power, the bench

must guide the course of litigation according to law and must assist the jury to understand the evidence in the light of the law.[74]

Waring's observations to Beckett were mild compared with his vehement remarks from the bench the previous July to South Carolina's Democratic officialdom. At one point, in fact, he agreed that "There were fine, decent slaveholders, considerate and fine, and the loyalty of black slaves to such white masters was an appealing fact," though he immediately added that "even where the relationship was pleasant, it wasn't right and therefore could not be tolerated." But Waring's sympathy for South Carolina whites now seemed reserved almost entirely for James L. Petigru, the Charleston lawyer who had been a strong Unionist during the Civil War, and Justice William Johnston, the Charlestonian who had become the Supreme Court's first great dissenter. His advice that northerners use tact in challenging southern racial conditions, moreover, may have smacked as much of paternalism to the Charleston *Evening Post*'s editorial staff as the treatment accorded slaves by "fine, decent" masters had to abolitionists. Nor was the paper impressed with the judge's suggestion that his full awareness of racial conditions was a revelation of recent date. Judge Waring had ceased communication with the *Post*'s staff, of course, the previous year; and while the *News and Courier* had exercised restraint in attacking his decisions, the *Post*'s editorials had become increasingly sarcastic. On November 26, 1948, Judge Waring issued a permanent injunction in the primary case. In a December 2 editorial entitled, "Just Be Nice About It," the *Post* cited the Beckett profile and ridiculed Waring's advice to "Northern reformers who, having solved all of their own section's racial and political problems, want to save the South from perdition." Waring had found the South "backward and benighted," southerners "semi-barbarians," but the region's situation "not altogether hopeless," the *Post* reported. Critics following the judge's admonition must "pounce upon our many un-American failings, expose our many shortcomings, and insist upon our reforming ourselves in accordance with New York specification. . . . In that way it may be possible to make Americans out of us and, in South Carolina's case, to prompt the State to rejoin the Union." But, the paper cautioned, northern reformers

should strive to conduct their crusade in a nice way. Denounce the South, slander the South, be as ignorant and malicious as they will about the South, call the South names, reconstruct the South—but be tactful about it. If not, who knows but what His Honor may issue an order requiring them to be gentle as well as firm? He may, somewhere in the law of the land, find tactlessness unconstitutional. More remarkable things than that have been dug out of the Constitution.[75]

On December 4, the *Post* addressed "what to so many Northerners was one of the mysteries of the age"—the transformation of Judge Waring's racial views. "[H]is conversion," the paper reported, "came about automatically with his appointment to the judgeship." And therein lay the answer to South Carolina's racial problems.

The lesson is plain. The National Association for the Advancement of Colored People and all the other groups which seek to reform the South should press for passage of a law making all white South Carolina Democrats federal judges. It would not only insure lifetime posts at $15,000 a year for them, but would at one stroke end all injustice. The majority of us are handicapped by the fact that we are not on the bench and therefore have narrow views and can take only one side. If we were all appointed judges, we, too, would surely see the light, and South Carolina would overnight be rejoining the Union.[76]

Whatever the sentiments of the Charleston papers, Judge Waring's national image as a courageous reformer continued to grow through that fall and winter. In the November elections, Strom Thurmond carried only South Carolina and three other Deep South states where the Dixiecrats had won control of the regular Democratic party apparatus. Nationally, President Truman weathered the Thurmond threat and the Henry Wallace Progressives within his own party, as well as Thomas E. Dewey's Republican bid. On December 2, Judge Waring had an audience with Truman at the White House. Two days later, he had a lengthy meeting with Chief Justice Vinson. Waring had been disappointed with the Supreme Court's decision to deny review in *Elmore* v. *Rice*—an action that left the judge's decision, and the Fourth Circuit affirmance, to stand alone against South Carolina's continued efforts to impose the all-white primary. Vinson told Waring that another justice had also recently lamented the Court's action.[77]

After his meeting with President Truman, Waring termed the poll tax "stupid," reiterated to reporters his belief that "Negroes should be treated as American citizens," and urged federal intervention in southern racial affairs. The next day a *New York Times* editorial applauded Waring's racial stance, adding: "When Judge Waring's point of view is generally accepted in the South there will be less need for federal interference. Indeed, the road to the preservation of states' rights lies through the protection by the states of individual rights within the states." At its annual convention in February, moreover, the National Lawyers Guild conferred on Waring its Franklin Delano Roosevelt Award for 1948, lauding him as an "uncompromising executor of the constitutional mandate for racial and political equality among all our people" and a "vigorous advocate of social programs and of the rights of the common man and woman."[78]

Perhaps the most moving tribute came, however, from a fellow white southerner. Clifford Durr was a product of one of Alabama's more prominent Black Belt families. He was proud of his southern origins and made no apology for his "sectionalism." But he and his Alabama-born wife, Virginia Foster, like her brother-in-law Justice Hugo L. Black, embraced goals uncommon to their region. Mrs. Dorr had been active in the Southern Conference for Human Welfare and other groups seeking to abolish the poll tax and improve conditions for blacks. Her husband had served on the Reconstruction Finance Corporation and Federal Communication Commission under President Roosevelt. But he opposed the loyalty programs instituted by the Truman administration during the Red hysteria of the postwar years; probably for this reason, in 1948, he refused reappointment to the FCC.[79]

Durr was one of the speakers at the Lawyers Guild ceremony honoring Judge Waring. He applauded the courage of the military battlefield, but reminded his audience that soldiers "draw courage from each other. . . . A courage of a greater and rarer kind," he asserted,

> is required to face the disapproval of society in defense of a basic democratic principle. It hurts to be shut off from one's own people. It hurts even more when they are good people—friendly, basically decent and kindly, and the only barrier is an idea. Loneliness can be more painful than the wounds of battle, and few are willing to risk it. It takes real courage for a judge, in opposition to the deepseated folkways of those with whom he lives and will continue to live to say, "This is the law. It is my duty to enforce it and I will do my duty." It takes far more courage to say, "This law which you so strongly oppose is not only the law but it is morally right, it is elementary democracy."

Judge Waring's "only source of courage," said Durr, "has been his own conscience—and I suspect, not from knowledge, but from personal experience, his wife." But it was the sort of courage that represented "the best of the spirit which [had] come out of the South in the past," and that, Durr added, "[was] coming out of it again."[80]

Durr's remarks poignantly reflected the Warings' growing isolation within the judge's native city. Charleston's few outspoken blacks, of course, now regularly praised Judge Waring and his rulings. In a letter to the *News and Courier* published the day before the August 10 primary, for example, members of the Athenian Club commended his "steadfastness and ability to distinguish right from wrong." A number of Charleston whites opposed his judicial stance but silently admired his resolve. Privately, too, as Judge Waring had told reporters, a few supported his stand. Shortly after the August primary, Lewis West, a member of the Charleston staff of the federal Alcohol Tax Unit, wrote the judge that of those he had "heard express themselves on the subject privately, all but a few of the uninformed felt that you did no more than was your duty under the circumstances." West assured Waring that members of the Tax Unit "admired" his stance, then added that Senator Maybank's victory "was vindication of the judgment of the electorate in seeing through political demagogism."[81]

As noted earlier, such private expressions of white support were not confined to Charleston's contingent of federal employees, some of whom were dependent on Judge Waring for their tenure. In at least one instance, moreover, the support was public. Joseph Fromberg was a Charleston attorney; he had been a member of the South Carolina bar since 1911. Over his long career, Fromberg had served in the state House of Representatives, as a special federal prosecutor, and as a police court judge. "By race and religion," he once wrote, he was "a Jew, and proud thereof." But Fromberg was also a "native American," a "native Southerner," and lifelong Democrat. While attempting to develop a case against Judge Waring, congressmen Dorn and Rivers had written Fromberg and other South Carolina lawyers, seeking grist for their investigation. Fromberg might not have "agree[d] with the reasoning" Waring had resorted to in the primary litigation. But he had backed Waring's appointment to the bench, and unlike Senator Maybank and other former Waring partisans, he was entertaining no second thoughts about his choice. On the day of the August primary, Fromberg wrote Dorn and Rivers scorching letters, repudiating their "petty and demagogic" attempt to destroy a "highly capable, honest and fearless" judge, and advising them "to desist" from their "foolish, puerile and useless course." Fromberg did not stop at private correspondence. On the day of the primary, the New York *Herald Tribune* had published an editorial applauding Waring's stance. Fromberg sent the *News and Courier* a copy, asking that it be reprinted, and adding: "You are at perfect liberty to publish the fact of this request under my name and as being at my request." The *Courier* published the editorial—and Fromberg's cover letter—in its August 12 issue.[82]

The appearance of the editorial and its source hardly improved Fromberg's community standing. When Judge Waring wrote from New York to thank him for his support, the lawyer replied that, while he had not yet had a response from "that moronic statesman Mendel Rivers," Congressman Dorn's reply had been "calm and quite dispassionate." Local reaction was a different matter. "[A] few of the bigoted reactionaries," Fromberg wrote Waring, "have been bitterly critical and insulting."[83]

The vast majority of white South Carolinians were probably hostile to Waring and his rulings, and such feelings may have extended to the state's other federal jurists as well. When Judge Waring was preparing to leave Charleston following the August primary, he asked Judge Parker to designate another judge to hear a criminal docket scheduled during his absence. Parker suggested that Waring approach Judge Wyche and Judge Timmerman. "I believe that it would please them," Parker wrote, "for you to make the request of them and would pave the way to greater cooperation." Waring promptly replied that he had recently written Judge Wyche, proposing "that we should swap around occasionally and in view of his having taken a tax case for me in the Spring when I was in New York, I would be glad to come to Greenville or some other place for him at any time." To date, Wyche had not responded. "Under these circumstances," Waring wrote, "I think it would be perhaps better for you to make the designation some time later in the year." Parker agreed, advising his colleague to "[f]orget about all the troubles that you been through . . . and have a good time."[84]

In Charleston, Tom Waring continued to record incidents indicating that his uncle's isolation from his former friends and family was largely of his own choosing. In a December 8, 1948, entry, he wrote:

> Bonnie Huff says that he had Judge Waring's name as a prospect to contribute to the Community Chest. The previous year he had solicited him and he responded generously. This year he wrote a letter; and the judge

wrote in reply that he had decided not to contribute this year. Fearing he had given offense, Huff went to Judge Waring personally; the judge assured him the letter gave no offense, but that it appeared to him the community wanted none of him, and he wanted none of the community. Therefore he was withdrawing support and membership in all community affairs, including the chamber of commerce. Mr. Huff said he thought the judge was making a mistake; that whatever opposition there [was] had been to his judicial opinions, there was always a higher court to which people could appeal; and he hoped the judge would reconsider. The judge said he did not expect to change, and they parted pleasantly.

Although partially a self-imposed isolation, the Warings were now cut off almost totally from the white community. Since the St. Cecilia Society barred divorced persons and Elizabeth Waring was thus ineligible for membership, Judge Waring had resigned his membership in the society. In November, he also resigned from the Charleston Club and the South Carolina Society. When the latter's members were read his letter of resignation, one told Tom Waring, "there was applause."[85]

5

The False God of Gradualism

The Lawyers Guild's Roosevelt Award was only one of many conferred on Judge Waring in the wake of his white primary rulings. Not surprisingly, black organizations were especially appreciative of his efforts. In 1949 alone, the black-owned *Chicago Defender* named him, along with Eleanor Roosevelt and President Truman, to its 1948 "honor roll of democracy"; the Negro Newspaper Publishers Association cited his "impressive contributions to the advancement of Negroes"; *Color* magazine named him to its 1948 "Jury of Democracy"; and in the spring, the North and South Carolina chapters of Omega Psi Phi, a black fraternity, honored him at a mass public meeting in Charleston's Morris Street Baptist Church. In late January, moreover, eight civil rights groups, including the Anti-Defamation League, NAACP, and Freedom House, presented him with an award of merit for "important contributions to civil rights" in a ceremony at Carnegie Hall.[1]

Judge Waring was unable to attend the Carnegie Hall ceremonies, and Anne Warren accepted her father's award in his behalf. At the affair, Anne and Stanley were mildly irritated to discover that the judge was the only truly prominent figure, in their eyes, being honored, with other awards going to the Yale and Harvard football teams for electing a black captain and manager, an Amherst fraternity that had initiated a black member, a clergyman whose parish children had sent trees to Israel, and even the writers on the "Superman" radio show for humanitarian plot themes. "Why in hell," Anne wrote her father, quoting a friend, "should a bunch of kids get a citation because they decided to elect a Negro they liked to their club?"[2]

Whatever their varying degrees of significance, however, such awards reflected Judge Waring's growing status as a national civil rights figure. In press treatments of the issue, his name was now invariably linked with Mrs. Roosevelt's and others long active in humanitarian causes. With this increased prominence came opportunities for the Warings to establish what frequently were to become enduring friendships with such figures. In the spring of 1949, for example, they joined Mrs. Roosevelt and others at the Gramercy Park home of Benjamin Sonnenberg, wealthy head of one of New York's leading public relations firms, to discuss ways of promoting civil rights in the South. "I have always felt," Mrs. Roosevelt later wrote in her syndicated newspaper column, "that we, as Northerners, could do more harm than good by interfering in the South, and I am not convinced even now that there is much we can do beyond giving our money. But when people such as Judge Waring . . . urge some of us to come down and speak, it impresses me."[3]

The Warings were heroes to the average black citizen; redcaps vied for the privilege of carrying the Warings' luggage. They also formed extensive contacts with prominent black leaders, including Dr. Ralph Bunche, Thurgood Marshall, Walter White, Dr. Benjamin Mays, and Hubert T. Delany, a New York domestic relations court judge and NAACP vice president, as well as with prominent black journalists such as Ted Poston of the *New York Post* and Carl Rowan of the Minneapolis *Tribune*. The Marshalls and the Warings saw each other socially during the judge's frequent court sessions in New York. Waring and the NAACP's chief counsel often corresponded as well, and on topics going beyond the immediate concerns of cases then pending in the judge's court. Marshall kept Waring abreast of developments in NAACP-sponsored litigation, provided him with copies of association legal briefs, and assessed black organizations that approached Waring about speaking engagements. Waring, in turn, attempted to prod Marshall into an aggressive attack on the doctrine of segregation and alerted him to South Carolina racial developments. On one occasion, for example, Waring sought Marshall's impressions of a Harlem interracial group that had invited the judge to speak; when Marshall's response proved lukewarm, Waring decided to decline the invitation "and be busily engaged elsewhere." On another occasion, Marshall mailed Waring a copy of a brief the association had filed with the Supreme Court in a case challenging segregation on railroad cars. "The best thing about it," Waring promptly responded, "is that it boldly goes to the heart of the whole question and advances the sound theory that segregation is un-American and in conflict with the principles of our form of government."[4]

Marshall took some pains to maintain a good relationship with the Charleston jurist. When the *Lighthouse and Informer* published a lengthy editorial accusing NAACP attorneys of charging their clients unreasonable fees, Marshall wrote editor John McCray a detailed rebuttal, with a copy to Judge Waring. When Waring reacted angrily, moreover, to a letter John Wrighten had written Mrs. Waring, Marshall moved quickly to denounce his client's "extremely bad taste." While awaiting the opening of a black law school at Orangeburg, Wrighten had sought to enlist Mrs. Waring's help in securing financial aid. Judge Waring mailed Marshall a copy of Wrighten's letter, and Marshall wrote his client a scorching rebuke. "I cannot imagine the motive behind your letter," the obviously embarrassed attorney observed, "but I am certain that it should never have been written."

> If you are truly interested in obtaining a legal education, then there are hundreds of ways for you to do it. In the first place, you should . . . apply to a reputable law school and see whether or not your record is sufficient for you to be admitted. If it is possible for you to be admitted to a recog-

nized law school, then you can seek scholarship aid from recognized agencies in that field. Last but not least and certainly not unimportant you should be able to earn enough money yourself to attend the average law school with a little hope. Most of the lawyers I know of as well as judges earned their way through law school by working.[5]

"[O]n several occasions" in the past, Marshall added, "I have had to tell you that you should not take any steps . . . without consulting with your attorneys. . . . I hope that you will not do anything similar to this in the future."

Among national black leaders, the Warings' closest social contacts were initially with NAACP executive secretary Walter White and his handsome, white, South African-born wife, Poppy Cannon. For the Warings, White seemed too much the political realist, too willing to compromise his broader principles in the interest of expedient, short-term goals. But they admired his dedication, and the two couples may have found a common bond as well in the circumstances surrounding their controversial marriages. Like Judge Waring, White had divorced his first wife to marry, in 1949, his second. And many of the NAACP director's associates, white and black, were probably no more enthusiastic about his interracial marriage than Charlestonians had been with the circumstances of Judge Waring's divorce.

When the Warings visited New York, they and the Whites were frequent dinner companions. They also regularly praised and defended each other. White applauded Waring's civil rights stance in his syndicated newspaper column, and Poppy Cannon, in an article for *Negro Digest,* paid tribute to Elizabeth Waring's "fire and dedication," lamenting the "Golgotha of social ostracism" the Warings were forced to endure in Charleston. On at least two occasions, moreover, Elizabeth Waring rose to the Whites' defense. Beginning in 1947, the Warings had made annual summer visits to California. While there, they were guests at Santa Barbara's El Encanto Hotel. In 1949, Walter White was given a reservation at the El Encanto, then told that the hotel would be unable to accommodate him. When the Warings learned of the incident, Elizabeth wrote the hotel's manager to complain of its "unfair" and "inhuman" treatment. If the hotel objected to White's race, she asked, why did it accept Jews, "most of [whom were] very nice? . . . We would not expect you to take a LOW CLASS Negro," she added, but White was "a gentleman . . . of rare distinction and culture . . . the intimate friend . . . [of] those of America's highest social class. . . . He would honor and grace the El Encanto Hotel by staying with you."[6]

Mrs. Waring next took on the wives of NAACP officials. In the wake of his controversial marriage to Poppy Cannon, Walter White had taken a leave of absence from the association. In the interim, Roy Wilkins became NAACP executive secretary, and in the spring of 1950, Mrs. Wilkins and other women arranged a tea in New York to honor Mrs. Waring. Walter White's first wife was invited; Poppy Cannon was not. The Warings considered the omission an "insult," and Mrs. Waring refused to attend. The tea was given on schedule, with several matrons complaining, according to a newspaper's account, that only "a Harlemite [had] the right to set herself up as a 'social dictator' " for the city's black community. But Mrs. Waring stood her ground, and Poppy Cannon told a reporter that she and her husband were proud that the Warings "honor us with their friendship and loyalty."[7]

While interracial social contacts, if not racially mixed marriages, were hardly remarkable in cosmopolitan New York, they were unthinkable in the society in which Judge Waring had been raised, much more ominous, in fact, than any breakdown of racial bars to voting. But little in the Warings' lives now seemed conventional by Charleston standards. And in the wake of *Brown* v. *Baskin,* the white population pushed the judge's break with his past one step further, leading him to forge enduring social relationships with a number of South Carolina blacks.

The Charleston equal pay case and other civil rights litigation had brought Judge Waring into close contact with the city's black leadership, including NAACP president Arthur Clement and Joe Brown, Clement's successor as chapter president in the mid-1950s. But Mrs. Waring was primarily responsible for the social ties the Warings began to develop with area blacks. Elizabeth may have considered such associations a natural outgrowth of their racial awakening, just as Charleston whites saw them as a cynical ploy to give her and her husband greater credibility in the national civil rights community. A purely social impetus, however, was probably also at work. Elizabeth Waring had always enjoyed an active social life, and their isolation from Charleston's white society was now virtually complete. They were no longer welcome in the homes of her husband's relatives and former friends; and no local white, they repeatedly informed reporters, had paid them a social call since his ruling in *Brown* v. *Baskin.* In the spring of 1949, in fact, they sold the summer home on Sullivan's Island. Under such circumstances, it seemed entirely natural that someone of Mrs. Waring's social bent would attempt to form new friendships. Then, too, as white Charlestonians suspected, and her daughter later conceded, it was an excellent way for Elizabeth to reject the society that had dared to reject her. Whatever her motivation, Elizabeth began to establish friendships with Charleston blacks and persuaded her reluctant husband to purchase an imposing green Cadillac—a symbol of success, she explained, that blacks would expect.[8]

Harry and Corinne Guenveur and their daughter, Mildred Cherry, were apparently the first local blacks entertained at the Warings' Meeting Street home. Harry Guenveur was the Warings' mailman; he and his wife first met the Warings socially through their daughter Mildred, who was married and living with her parents while her husband was in the service. Mildred had studied art at Howard University, and when Mrs. Waring expressed an interest in purchasing handpainted Christmas cards, someone—perhaps Judge Waring's crier John Fleming—had suggested that she contact the Guenveurs' daughter. Elizabeth found Mildred talented and charming, and the two quickly became friends. Soon, the Warings and Mildred's parents became friends as well, and at New Year's in 1950, the Guenveurs hosted a party in the Warings' honor.[9]

Despite the recent changes in his racial thinking, Judge Waring retained traces of ethnocentrism. Talking about his love of New York as late as 1948, for example, he had remarked that he did not "want to go down to China-town or the Italian section," explaining that the people there "may have ver-min on them." But he seemed genuinely to enjoy their new associations; and gradually their circle of black friends grew, expanding beyond Charleston to other communities. Most of their new friends were part of the region's black elite, prominent professionals and businessmen who, like Harry Guenveur, were economically independent of the white establishment. Arthur Clement, for example, managed the Charleston office of a black-owned life insurance company. Frank Veal was pastor of Charleston's Emanuel African Methodist Episcopal church, the largest AME congregation in South Carolina. Mont-gomery P. Kennedy, an outspoken Progressive Democrat, was a Beaufort physician, Roscoe Wilson a Florence dentist. Their wives, who were often closer to the Warings than their husbands, were also educated and articulate. Maude Veal, for example, was a Boston native with two graduate degrees. Before moving to Charleston, she had been dean of women at a black uni-versity. Her great-aunt had helped found the National Association of Colored Women, her grandfather a Charleston hospital for blacks. In 1952, she would overcome local resistance to become the first black member of the Charleston chapter of the League of Women Voters.[10]

Not all their new friends shared a comfortable social background and insulation from the white power structure. In 1916, at age eighteen, Septima Poinsette Clark had begun teaching black children on Johns Island, off the Charleston coast. In 1947, after years of teaching in the Columbia schools, Mrs. Clark moved to Charleston to care for her ailing mother and teach remedial courses to problem students in the city's public schools. She also became active in the city tuberculosis association and black YWCA branch, eventually becoming a member of the city YWCA's interracial governing committee. On one occasion, Mrs. Clark and two white committeewomen had visited Charleston's mayor, seeking police protection from black teen-agers who had been disrupting YWCA activities, as well as the mayor's assis-tance with their efforts to establish a YMCA for the city's black males. The mayor seated the white women, then sat down with his back to Mrs. Clark without offering her a seat. But Mrs. Clark made her point; police protection was provided, and Charleston soon had a black YMCA chapter.[11]

Mrs. Clark's father was a slave, her mother a Haitian immigrant, and she occupied a position in Charleston's black community below that of most of the Warings' other black friends. She was sensitive to her status. "I couldn't play bridge," she remarked matter-of-factly in later years, "with [Arthur Clement's] wife." She also believed that Mrs. Waring expected more regal treatment than she could offer, that the judge's wife "could [not] stoop to a woman whose father was a slave and whose mother was raised in Haiti." After being entertained on several occasions at 61 Meeting Street without Mrs. Waring allowing her to reciprocate, Mrs. Clark insisted that Mrs. War-ing visit her modest home before she would again cross the Warings' thresh-old. "She decided that she would come, and she drank a cup of tea,"

Mrs. Clark later recalled. "But that was okay with me. I just wanted to be sure that she could come and drink something in my house if I could go to her house and eat a meal." She respected Mrs. Waring's courage, though, and adored the judge, whom she found to be a sincere, unassuming friend.[12] Over the years, she proved to be one of the Warings' staunchest defenders.

Among local blacks, however, the Warings' closest, most loyal friend was to be Ruby Cornwell, wife of A. T. Cornwell, a Charleston dentist. Mrs. Cornwell was born in Santee, in coastal Clarendon County. Her father was a Methodist minister, and through her childhood the family lived in many rural charges where schooling provided black children was pitifully poor. But Ruby's parents were determined that she would receive a decent education. During her early youth, they frequently taught her at home or sent her to live with relatives in communities providing reasonably adequate schools for black pupils. Later, she attended Charleston's Avery Institute for a year. Then she had the opportunity to meet the noted black educator Mary McLeod Bethune and soon transferred to the preparatory school Miss Bethune had established in Daytona Beach, Florida. After completing her education at Talladega College in Alabama, she settled in Charleston and married Dr. Cornwell.[13]

As a child, Mrs. Cornwell had developed an intense distrust and dislike of whites, although they had treated her father with the courtesy traditionally accorded black ministers by white southerners and seemed interested in his family. In certain of his charges, in fact, white matrons borrowed books from her mother. But Ruby soon came to realize that most southern blacks lived a slavelike existence and that her parents, because they were black, were denied the social status enjoyed by the lowest whites. "I knew," she would later say, "that they felt that I was not as good as they were, that they were looking down on us. 'Oh, Reverend,' they would say . . . But they still called [my mother] by her first name, and I had to call them 'Miss.' I resented that, and the things they did, not so much to us, but to other blacks. And I resented the fact that the black people were afraid of them." At Daytona, where the Klan rode through the campus during a voter education program for black women, her hatred intensified. "I don't remember being afraid. I was just mad. It made me mad." At Talladega, which, like Avery Institute, was run by the American Missionary Association, she encountered "wonderful," sympathetic white teachers and administrators. But they were northerners, and her hostility for southern whites would persist for years. "I knew intellectually that it was not right for me to think evil things of a person just because he was white any more than it was right for him to think evil things about me because I'm black. But the feeling was there."[14]

In Charleston, Mrs. Cornwell did what she could to challenge the racial indignities that were then a common occurrence of daily life. As a Red Cross volunteer and member of an interracial Urban League task force studying Charleston services to blacks, she insisted that whites address her as "Mrs." And if clothing store clerks refused to extend her the same courtesy or allow her to try on clothes, she carried her trade elsewhere. ("There's soon," her mild-mannered husband joked, "not going to be a store in town where you'll shop—and that will be good for me.")[15]

Mrs. Cornwell first met the Warings casually in the spring of 1949 at the Omega Psi Phi fraternity affair honoring the judge. But she met them socially for the first time at the Guenveurs' party the following New Year's Eve. Shortly thereafter, she went to the Warings for tea, the first of many such visits. Mrs. Cornwell was immediately drawn to both Mrs. Waring and the judge. "They are," she would later say, "just true, sincere people concerned about our welfare." The Warings seemed equally drawn to her. "You, my lovely Ruby," Elizabeth Waring once told her, "you were here all this time. And I was so unaware." Soon they were close friends, and Elizabeth was sharing with Mrs. Cornwell the details of their difficulties with Judge Waring's relatives and former friends. "They know," Mrs. Waring remarked on one occasion, "that I know so much about the dirt that goes on south of Broad Street, and that's why they hate me so." "If the judge and I had been willing to live in sin," she explained on another occasion, "they would have accepted that. Plenty of that goes on. But what they could not tolerate was the fact of the divorce." Tom Waring, she confided, hated his uncle, and the judge had warned his nephew that he would personally horsewhip him if Elizabeth's name ever appeared in the *News and Courier*.[16]

The Warings' relationship with Mrs. Cornwell and their other friends would not be restricted, however, to purely social settings and luncheon gossip. When a black sorority made plans for a debutante ball, Elizabeth and the judge participated in a charm school for the honorees. Often, too, Mrs. Waring visited the YWCA and offered instruction in hygiene and grooming to young black women. "When we hop on these stores for refusing to let you try on dresses," she told them, according to a journalist's account,

> we must never be in the position where they can argue that you are too dirty. I know, I know, if you're white and dirty you still can try on anything in the store, but you can't afford to have them say that about you.

And when Westover, the exclusive Connecticut preparatory school Elizabeth had attended, decided to admit a black student, Mrs. Waring pushed successfully for admission of a student from South Carolina.[17]

In the face of a state interracial commission's inquiries, as well as pressures from other quarters, the Westover School's board of trustees had voted in May 1949, to give "serious consideration" to admitting a "small group" of black students. Protests from alumnae and contributors had momentarily chilled the board's humanitarian zeal. But after a survey revealed that a majority of the school's constituency supported acceptance of a black student and that opponents were unlikely to withdraw their children—or financial support—the trustees announced in May 1950, that future applicants would be considered "without regard to race, creed or colour." At present, they further reported, one application had been received from the West Indies, but no inquiries from "North American Negroes."[18]

To Elizabeth Waring, Miriam deCosta, the bright, pretty daughter of a

State College professor, was the ideal candidate to break Westover's color bar. Miriam initially suspected her sponsor's motives. "I just couldn't believe," she later wrote, "that you were really being completely honest." But Miriam was thrilled at the prospect of attending prestigious Westover, her parents realized the opportunities such an experience would offer, and at Westover, if not in Charleston, the judgment of the wife of J. Waties Waring carried considerable weight. In September 1950, Miriam took the train to Connecticut to start school. "I can never thank you enough for all that you have done for me!" she wrote Mrs. Waring on her arrival. "I am really going to work hard and try to set a fine example for my race, so that you will be proud of me."[19]

Initially, Miriam had difficulty adjusting to Westover's demanding standards. She also learned that bigotry was not unique to South Carolina. The other girls, she wrote Mrs. Waring, were friendly, and the minister of the local Congregational church had delivered a "wonderful sermon" against all forms of segregation. But the first year, she would room alone. "Beth's mother took us out before school closed," she wrote excitedly during the summer before her second year, "and Beth and I are definitely rooming together next year." But she would be disappointed. "By the way," she wrote her sponsor in September,

> I received a letter from Miss Dillingham [the headmistress] about a month ago to inform me that Beth's parents did not want us to room together this year. . . . I know Beth doesn't like it, because she was planning to room with me above her parents' wishes but Miss Dillingham was forced to intercede.

After all, the headmistress explained, she "could not be prejudiced *for* a student just as she couldn't be prejudiced *against* a student." Throughout Miriam's years at Westover, however, Mrs. Waring remained supportive, taking her young friend on shopping trips to New York, impatiently dismissing the scarcity of roommates as the product of pressure from bigoted contributors, and corresponding regularly with Miriam and her parents, offering encouragement and advice.[20]

The Warings also offered their black friends political advice and attempted to persuade them to accept the militant stance they were now embracing. Their closest friends put the judge on a high pedestal, regularly comparing his "conversion" to that of Saul of Tarsus and welcoming his direction as well as Mrs. Waring's. Montgomery Kennedy's wife Jenny, like Mrs. Cornwell and Septima Clark, corresponded regularly with the Warings during their stays in New York, keeping them posted about recent racial developments in South Carolina. "We do not want to become affiliated with any organization," Mrs. Kennedy observed in one letter, "that does not meet Judge Waring's ideals or differs with him." Not all Charleston blacks, however, appreciated the Warings' militancy, or the motives of those blacks with whom they had established their closest ties. At one point, Tom Waring's wife Clelia probed a family servant. "[O]ur Janie," Waring later wrote a friend, said the people who dine with the Warings are regarded by her class of negro (the backbone of the race) as "social climbers," who are not interested in colored people generally but only in their own welfare. She seemed to be familiar with the persons involved and to have no respect for them. The Warings are being patronizing, the negro elite snobbish, which adds to the seamier aspects of the emotions involved while the boobs are taken in with Madame's phony histrionics.[21]

In the manner of prudent domestics, Tom Waring's maid may simply have offered the assessment she suspected her mistress wanted to hear. Clearly, however, certain members of the black community were resentful or envious of those favored with the Warings' association; others feared the impact of this obvious affront to tradition on their future relations with Charleston whites; and still others saw the Warings' militancy as a threat to improved race relations. "I beg to disagree with you on the steps which must be taken against segregation," young Miriam deCosta had written Mrs. Waring during her first year at Westover. "But I think there must be a gradual change, say over 20 years." Miriam was probably echoing not only her parents' views, but those of many other South Carolina blacks as well, as was the Charleston black leader who remarked to a black journalist,

I've been getting things for Charleston Negroes for years. You've got to get it a little at a time. Anyhow, how come it took Judge Waring so long to get religion? Why, he once helped manage the campaign of Sen. E. D. (Cotton Ed) Smith.[22]

The Warings were shocked, hurt, and angered that any South Carolina black could reject their aggressive approach to civil rights reform. Mrs. Waring was a strong-willed woman with little patience for the fainthearted. "Sometimes when it looked like you weren't exactly agreeing with her," NAACP leader Joe Brown would later recall with a smile, "she was ready to flare up." Elizabeth was especially critical of South Carolina's "Uncle Toms." "Since my Judge did what he did," she told black journalist Carl Rowan, "the whites and Uncle Toms have carried on one of the most sickening little games of appeasement you ever saw. They keep the Uncle Toms quiet by dishing up handouts at troubled intervals—sort of be-kind-to-animals week, you know." When blacks told Judge Waring that they were praying for him, Elizabeth would scold, "Don't pray for us. We'll make it. They'll never stop me from showing my face. But for heaven's sake, don't pray for me. Get up off your knees and fight."[23]

The Warings found a number of incidents particularly disillusioning. With their encouragement, local blacks began to press in 1949 for admission of black students to the College of Charleston, which received some $80,000 annually from the city. Soon, however, black leaders had huddled with the mayor and agreed to an arrangement by which the city would provide six scholarships to State College—and efforts to integrate the College of Charleston would be dropped. Judge Waring found the passive demeanor of the State College staff equally offensive. He had initially been optimistic that the college and its new law school could become a center for racial reform. By the spring of 1950, however, his hopes had evaporated. When a law building was dedicated on the campus, he was not invited. When he visited Orangeburg for a court term, only one member of the college staff had approached him, and she was soliciting funds. "I am afraid," he later wrote her,

> that I see [a] pattern of appeasement and conformity to the dominating "white supremacists" who are members of your board of trustees when I was not even accorded the courtesy of a formal invitation to your dedica-tion. Of course, I would not have attended in any event since I would not be willing to be associated with your governor or other members of the board, but, nevertheless, it made me quite sad to realize that your dean and other faculty members who had spoken so bravely of the founding of a fine law school have apparently fallen in step behind their Dixiecrat masters.[24]

Judge Waring's growing distaste for southern moderates was not limited, however, to members of the black community. With rising vehemence, he also attacked prominent white liberals, charging that their gradualist approach to racial reform constituted an even greater threat to southern blacks than the cries of avowed racists. Southern liberals such as Ralph McGill of the Atlanta *Constitution* and Virginius Dabney of the Richmond *Times-Dispatch* regu-larly condemned racial violence, bars to the ballot, and the southern black's deplorable economic status. But they also defended segregation, advocated racial reform through voluntarism rather than federal force, and decried out-side interference in the region's affairs. During Georgia's heated 1946 guber-natorial race, for example, Ralph McGill adamantly declared, "There will be no mixing of the races in the schools. There will be no social equality mea-sures. Now or later." In 1943, moreover, Virginius Dabney, who had won a Pulitzer Prize for his attacks on the poll tax, concluded that a "small group of Negro agitators and another small group of rabble-rousers are pushing this country closer and closer to an interracial explosion." In the 1950s, Dabney would become a leader of his state's massive resistance movement against school integration.[25]

Hodding Carter, editor and publisher of the Greenville, Mississippi, *Delta Democrat-Times,* was the most visible southern liberal of the immediate post-war era and the principal target of Judge Waring's ire. Carter had won a Pulitzer in 1945 for his distinguished editorials on southern racial problems, and Senator Theodore Bilbo, Mississippi's major contribution to the modern ranks of racist demagogues, regularly villified him as a "nigger-loving, Yankee-fied Communist." Like others of his persuasion, however, Carter blamed northern critics for the continued success of the South's Bilbos, embraced the traditional southern resentment of the Reconstruction era, suggested that "the panacea qualities of Federal legislation" were "overestimated," and excori-ated the meddling of uninformed northern "invaders," especially "investigators with books or articles in mind," who assumed that they could acquire com-plete understanding of the region and its problems "in a day and a night."

Carter enjoyed easy access to the national press, and in articles bearing such titles as "Just Leave Us Alone" and "Chip on Our Shoulder Down South," he popularized the major themes and frustrations of southern liberalism, becoming an articulate exponent of the view that the "pressing immediacy for the educational, health, and economic advancement among both races in the South . . . should take precedence over any political or social considerations." Carter left no doubt, moreover, that, in his judgment, the South's salvation lay principally in the hands of enlightened white southerners. In a widely circulated 1949 *Collier's* article, for example, he profiled prominent southerners who were largely responsible, he claimed, for "the flame of purposeful liberalism [then] lighting up dark and tragic corners of a harried region." A cartoon accompanying the article depicted a front line of white educators, journalists, and clerics—but no blacks or judges—driving Klansmen, benighted rednecks, and Black Belt planters into the sea.[26]

Walter White promptly took the *Collier's* piece to task in his syndicated column, applauding certain aspects of Carter's analysis but contending that any reader not familiar with the South might gather from the article that all improvements in conditions for the region's blacks "had come about solely because Mr. Carter and a few other white Southerners had experienced, like Saul of Tarsus, a complete transformation of heart on the race problem." The lobbying of civil rights groups, White contended, had also been influential, as had the rulings of federal judges. In White's judgment, in fact, Judge Waring had struck the "most far-reaching" blows for reform. The Charleston jurist's rulings, White asserted, had "done more to step up the changes Carter writes about than any other events of the last several decades. . . . It is unfortunate," he added,

> that so able a writer as Mr. Carter has subconsciously been guilty of intellectual Jim-Crowism and of regrettable shortsightedness. . . . His contribution would have been many times as important had he been less on the defensive and more frank in telling the full story.[27]

Walter White's published assessment of the *Collier's* article was mild in comparison with Judge Waring's own view of the Carter strain of southern liberalism and its worship of the "false god of gradualism." "There is still some of the Bilbo-Rankin Klan in existence," he wrote an Atlanta University professor in February 1950.

> We have them in our state and they have blossomed into the Dixiecrat movement. But I really do not fear them greatly since they are so unreasonable that the rest of the nation, and even many of the people in the South, repudiate them. . . . [T]he most dangerous people are those represented by . . . Hodding Carter. They preach "leave us alone and we will do good." Unfortunately, a great many well-intentioned people are taken in by all of this and . . . in the North, there are thousands and perhaps hundreds of thousands who want to believe that the Carters are sincere and will solve this situation.

The "old line Dixiecrat intolerance as expressed by Ball of the Charleston News and Courier," he observed on another occasion, "can be beaten down by reasonable exposition. But the Hodding Carter gradualism and appeasement is dangerous. It has so much sweet reason to it." "The really dangerous ones," he asserted, "are those that put on the false cloak of wishing equality for other races but knifing them in the back."[28]

Drawing heavily on the writings of Cash and Myrdal, Waring repeatedly declared in correspondence and speeches that white southerners were suffering from a serious disease requiring drastic treatment, not the palliatives offered by the gradualists. Georgia author Lillian Smith advanced a similar theme in her *Killers of the Dream* and sent Waring a copy. "Cash pointed out unerringly what was the disease," he soon responded,

> but you give a picture of one who has suffered from the disease and has arrived at a clear and healthy viewpoint only after undergoing the throes and tortures of one born in sickness and surrounded by sickness. Having been through the same thing, I have a great sympathy and understanding for your point of view.

Northerners, he added, had largely failed to grasp "the pitiful state of mind of our Southern people." He hoped, however, that Smith's book would be widely read outside the South and that northerners would soon come to "realize that these people here cannot be allowed to continue to take sedatives and claim they are curing themselves." The solution to the "Southern White Problem," he asserted, lay not in the gradualism of the Hodding Carters, but in the federal government insisting "that all forms of segregation by law are un-American and that all people in this country must have an equal opportunity." A few "liberal laws" would not cure the situation, he conceded, but they could go far toward changing southern attitudes.

> When the Jim Crow signs on railroads, buses, waiting rooms, and public conveniences generally, are torn down, many of our people, and particularly the younger ones, will begin to forget that they were there. Now it is enforced because it is the law, but remove that and there may be some hope for improvement. The fact the Whites and Negroes share Pullman cars in interstate commerce creates no disturbance now; and yet when I was a boy, it would have been considered impossible. . . . [I]f we can create a certain status whereby acceptance is enforced in certain respects, the accustomed contacts on a basis of equality will eventually become the practice rather than the exception.[29]

Through correspondence and personal contacts, Judge Waring sought to convince his growing retinue of influential northern friends of the wisdom of his position and the dangers posed by the gradualist persuasion. Mrs. Roosevelt was a major object of his efforts. When the president's widow voiced regret at continued northern prejudice, a *News and Courier* editorial construed her statement as a recommendation that northerners confront their own racial problems before interfering in the South's affairs. The same day the editorial appeared, Waring wrote the former first lady, gently lamenting her "unfortunate" remark and the aid it would give "our enemies." The *News and Courier,* he declared, "is perhaps the worst [newspaper] in the country and makes use of every opportunity to misconstrue and make unfair use of anything that is said. . . . [I]t hates you and your husband for all of the decent things that you both have done and stood for (incidentally, I am greatly complimented that it hates me also)." He was, he assured her, "as impatient with the Northern prejudices as with those of the South—in fact, perhaps more so since the North hasn't the excuse of being born in the foul atmosphere of racial prejudice." But in the North, segregation was not enforced by law and people were not fearful of seeking reform, while in the South "there is such a complete and powerful taboo upon any effort to alleviate the situation that even the few right-thinking people are afraid to come out and do anything." The situation in the North was "disgraceful," he conceded, but the South should not be allowed to "think that it is pure" or to divert attention from its problems with "continuous so-called exposés of Northern prejudice and crime."[30]

For a time following the 1948 elections, Judge Waring was cautiously optimistic that President Truman might launch a postelection assault on the citadels of southern segregation. He was encouraged that the president had given him an audience after the election, and by Truman's remarks during their December 1948 meeting. After the meeting, he wrote the president applauding his "magnificent, single-handed" election victory and urging federal intervention in the South's racial affairs. "The people in this state," he contended "will *not voluntarily* do anything along the lines suggested by you."

> It therefore is necessary for the federal government to firmly and constantly keep pressure. There are many, many people here who are ripe and ready for your program, but they do not include any of our so-called political leaders. The whole trouble is *fear* and it is only when the good people (who . . . unfortunately are timid people) see that strength and force is behind your sound program that they will feel it safe to join with you.

The president, in turn, wrote Waring that he wished "we had more Federal Judges like you on the bench."[31]

Soon, however, Waring would receive a sobering lesson in the realities of practical politics. After a decent interval following the election, the administration began efforts to lure Dixiecrats back into the Democratic fold. In South Carolina, Truman Democrats announced plans for a harmony banquet to be held in Columbia. Strom Thurmond and other prominent Dixiecrats were to be invited. Vice President Alben W. Barkley, a Kentuckian, was to be the principal speaker.

Judge Waring found the prospect of such an affair appalling and quickly made his opposition—and continued distaste for the Charleston newspapers—a matter of public record. The banquet was scheduled for July 1, 1949. In its June 29 issue, the *News and Courier* published the reactions of prominent South Carolinians. "An effort was made," the paper reported,

> to ask J. WATIES WARING, U.S. district judge, (1) whether he would attend, and (2) did he have any statement in regard to the propriety of

making the dinner an all-white affair. The judge's secretary said the judge doesn't give opinions over the telephone. Asked whether he would see a reporter, the secretary replied that there were no appointments open and that the judge was terribly busy.[32]

Late that morning, Waring's secretary telephoned *Courier* reporter S. A. Cothran to arrange an afternoon meeting with the judge. "I appreciate your calling me, judge," Cothran said on entering Waring's chambers. "I don't know whether you do or not," Waring replied. "Sit down." The judge then told the reporter he would grant no more interviews with either Charleston paper and presented Cothran with a prepared statement, "to be printed in full or not at all." The statement read:

> My experience with the lack of fairness and editorial integrity of the Charleston newspaper combination leads me to refuse to furnish any interviews or to authorize any quotation or run the risk of mis-quotation. The newspapers are, of course, privileged, and have the right, to obtain and publish any authorized opinions or statements or any acts of mine. They also, of course, are entirely free to express their opinions of me and of my judicial views, acts, or doings. But I do not feel it is safe to give my personal opinions to be garbled to suit the propaganda purpose of so biased a newspaper. If I should have occasion to give any press release at any time, I shall prefer using some newspaper of higher standards.

The *Courier* carried Waring's complete statement in its next issue but challenged its central premise. An editor's note appended to an article detailing Waring's attack asserted: "The News and Courier has published editorials opposing federal court decisions opening the Democratic party to negroes, but neither in editorials nor in news stories has it attacked or printed anything personally derogatory to Judge Waring."[33]

The judge's reaction to the Barkley banquet was not any more restrained. Although he was no longer talking to local reporters, including Charleston's Associated Press representative, he did respond to inquiries from the AP's Charlotte office. "The Barkley dinner," he wired the Charlotte office, "appears to be solely a political gathering of such a controversial nature that I do not believe it would be suitable for a Federal Judge to attend." It was obvious, however, that his concern was less with the banquet's political character than with the particular political direction it appeared to reflect. "I had supposed when this meeting was first announced," he observed,

> that it would be an endorsement of the National Democratic Party and the Platform on which it based its National Campaign which resulted in the victorious election of President Truman and Vice President Barkley. But now I see no mention of this but only an effort of appeasement and an attempt to invite back into the Party those who bolted and fought it and continue to fight the National Party. This political gathering appears to be an attempt to create a hodge-podge of Dixiecrats and Trumanites. Its purpose seems to be appeasement only. I have no sympathy with, nor do I wish to be a party to, the sacrifice of principles for expediency.[34]

Strom Thurmond boycotted the banquet, as did many other state officials, and Vice President Barkley proved an uncompromising speaker, attacking the Dixiecrats and telling his audience he was not there "to apologize for the Democratic party."[35] But from that point, Judge Waring entertained little hope that President Truman would pursue the militant civil rights agenda he considered critical to the South's salvation. Waring did see promise, however, in the efforts of a small cadre of southern whites who shared his opposition to segregation and distaste for the gradualist philosophy of the region's Hodding Carters and Ralph McGills. And he now had become closely associated with several of the most prominent.

Marion Wright, a South Carolina lawyer then living in the North Carolina mountains, was perhaps the most moderate of Judge Waring's white southern allies. Waring and Wright probably first met at a judicial conference. Like Joseph Fromberg, Wright had been angered when congressmen Rivers and Dorn had polled members of the South Carolina bar in seeking evidence to support Waring's impeachment. "One has come to expect almost anything of a Congressman and, particularly, of a South Carolina Congressman," he had written Rivers after the 1948 senatorial primary. "But your diatribe . . . seems to mark a new low in congressional behavior." Wright's reaction to Dorn's inquiry was no less vehement. Dorn's rejection at the polls, Wright wrote the congressman, "restores confidence in the ability of the average voter to diagnose your appeal for what it was—a cheap and shameful bit of demagogy." Wright mailed Judge Waring copies of the letters and applauded the judge "for the performance of a plain duty." Later, he wrote an article for *The New South,* challenging the traditional southern opposition to "outside interference." Wright and Waring became frequent correspondents.[36]

With Wright as with others, Waring was uncompromising in his growing militancy. When Wright praised Hodding Carter and Ralph McGill in an address to members of the Georgia Academy of Political Science, Waring's response was immediate and predictable. Assailing southern gradualists as "our great menace," Waring championed "the abolition of legal segregation" as "the most important goal to which we should strive." Wright assured his friend that he had classified Carter and those of similar persuasion as "liberal" only as "a diplomatic gesture," taking them "sharply to account" in remarks following the address. But Waring persisted in his efforts to prod Wright toward the aggressive stance he now embraced.[37]

For Waring, Wright's association with the Southern Regional Council was a major concern. The Council was an Atlanta-based interracial body established to promote improvement in the quality of southern life, including conditions for the region's black population. When Waring was first approached in 1949 about becoming active in its work, he had sought Walter White's advice. While labeling the organization "distinctly middle-of-the-road" and adding that it "sometimes [moved] much slower than some people in the South feel is either necessary or effective," White concluded that the Council had "real value" and that Waring's participation might "cure them of their occasional timorousness." In spite of this, however, Waring had been reluctant to become involved. "I do not, in any way, deprecate the work that [it] has done," he wrote a black fund-raiser in May 1950. "[I]t has helped greatly in stirring up interest and has given an opportunity for people of good will in this region to make decided advancements." In his judgment, however, such organizations had largely outlived their usefulness, and the motives of at least some of their members were suspect at best.

> When the nation refused to carry out the great intendments of the Amendments to the Constitution following the Civil War, there was a need and room for an appeasement program which was led and typified by Booker T. Washington. The Negroes, about that time, being denied any "rights," had to ask for "charity." But in my opinion, the Booker T. Washington days have passed. I am not in favor of segregation. And I believe that in the battle for the right, those who really wish to achieve civil rights should take a clear and decided stand. Some of the parties whose names appear on your stationery are appeasers of the first [order]. They play the "Lady Bountiful" role and meet and discuss inter-racial problems. But there are certain ones who definitely will not intermingle with or meet Negroes on an equal basis and who don't dare come out into the open and take an honest stand.

Waring was particularly embittered when the Council endorsed the concept of individual communities deciding on the issue of public school segregation and a regional educational plan under which southern states would provide graduate and professional training to blacks, as the Supreme Court was insisting, but on a segregated basis. Segregationist politicians supported such arrangements, which Judge Waring equated with the status quo.[38]

Marion Wright was an active member of the Council. In November 1951, after Wright condemned segregation in an address to the Council in Columbia, Waring wrote him to inquire whether he had been "able to induce the Regional Council [also] to finally cross the barriers of segregation." He realized, he wrote, that Wright and many other Council leaders had rejected segregation, but noted that a recent Council letter to several southern governors had appeared to support the idea of local option. Such a scheme, Waring declared, would mean that "the complete bar of segregation would continue" in the Deep South. "I am wondering," he added, "whether the organization can be induced to realize that people like the three Governors are never going to willingly do anything to cure this evil."[39]

"I can see," Wright replied, "that you may have some difficulty in understanding the position of the Council on the issue of segregation." The Council's policy, he assured Waring, was one of "strategy" not "timidity." Wright had never heard segregation defended at any of the Council's meetings. "It has been universally admitted to be legally and morally indefensible. We have wanted to end it so soon as it is humanly possible to do so. Our whole effort has been to follow a course which would insure the end of segregation with the greatest dispatch." The members believed, however, that a "dramatic and emotional avowal of our purpose to end segregation" would have been counterproductive, unifying the opposition. Instead, the Council's approach, "whether wise or not," had been "to reduce the outlying forts of segregation one by one with the result that the citadel itself must inevitably fall."[40]

Wright had not actually claimed that every Council member opposed segregation. But Waring promptly pressed him on the point, writing that he was "glad to hear [Wright's] statement that all members are opposed to segregation, per se," adding, "I have heard it suggested, and I am glad if I am wrong, that a number of the members felt that this thing must be worked out in time and that such things as [a] slow approach through regional schools and 'conditioning the Negroes' must first be had." Waring was pleased, he wrote, that Wright's Columbia speech expressed "not only your own views but that of the entire membership."[41]

Soon the lawyer wrote the judge again, conceding that the Council's membership were probably not unanimous in their position, but insisting that most now rejected segregation and that the gradualists were "ashamed to express" their views. At this point, Elizabeth Waring entered the exchange. "So my husband, Judge Waring," she wrote Wright, "does not seem to have been able to get the point over of the crux of his criticism." If a majority of the Council now opposed segregation, Mrs. Waring asked, why had it supported local option? Local option, she asserted, meant continued segregation, "and all you Southerners know that if you face the facts."[42]

While the debate continued, Wright became the Council's president and the organization issued a forceful resolution condemning segregation. At that point, the Warings became members. "I am convinced," the judge wrote Wright, "that the braver members, led by you in particular, have now taken control and that the organization is on the right path and doing fine and militant work." The Warings' doubts about the Council's commitment, however, would linger.[43]

Alabama publisher Aubrey Williams became another of Waring's philosophical allies. A descendant of an Alabama Black Belt family that had lost its wealth and land during the Civil War, Williams was raised on the outskirts of Birmingham, the son of a cabinetmaker. Like Clifford Durr, he was proud of his Alabama heritage but not wedded to its racial mores. During the New Deal, he had served in the Roosevelt administration, first as Harry Hopkins' assistant in the WPA and later as head of the National Youth Administration. He was also active, however, in the controversial Southern Conference for Human Welfare, and when Roosevelt nominated him to a position on the Rural Electrification Administration, the appointment died in the Senate. With financial backing, reportedly from Chicago retail merchant Marshall Field, Williams then returned to Alabama, settling in Montgomery and purchasing the *Southern Farmer,* a near-defunct newspaper. With a format of baking contests, recipes, farm news, and liberal editorials, the *Southern Farmer*'s circulation climbed to more than a million. Williams used the paper as a base for promoting a variety of civil rights causes, including an unsuccessful effort to establish an integrated farmers' union. Like Waring, Williams regularly attacked gradualism and the regional education plan, calling the former a "half-a-loaf" philosophy and contending that adoption of the latter would "deal a body blow to the gains now being made in all parts of the South . . . and . . . set back the fight against segregation many years." Waring and Williams had become friends through Mrs. Roosevelt and other mutual associates. When Williams scored gradualism in a speech to an Atlanta audience and sent Waring a copy, the judge applauded his insight and urged him to write a national magazine article countering Hodding Carter's "illogical but sugar coated" stance. "[Y]ou have touched the most dangerous spot of all," he added, "when you point out that many of the Negro leaders, particularly in the education field, are glad and willing to accept these half-loaves. We have got to do all that we can to show them the true path."[44]

Segregationists regularly branded Williams and other like-minded southerners, especially those connected with civil rights or labor groups, as socialists or Communists. Judge Waring realized that red-baiting was a favorite segregationist tactic. But he was also a staunch anti-Communist, and he generally sought to avoid association with individuals and organizations he believed so tainted. When the New York State Civil Rights Congress asked him to contribute an article to a journal on civil rights violations, for example, he quickly noted that the novelist Dashiell Hammett was the group's chairman and black singer Paul Robeson one of its vice chairmen. Hammet and Robeson were widely considered to be Communists. "That makes me a little suspicious," Waring wrote Walter White. "Can you write me, or better still, send me a wire saying merely, 'Okay' or 'No good'?" Initially, he was perhaps even more dubious of the Southern Conference Educational Fund, a successor to the Southern Conference for Human Welfare, and SCEF's director James Dombrowski. Waring and Dombrowski had first begun corresponding when Dombrowski was director of the Southern Conference for Human Welfare. When Waring issued his ruling in *Elmore* v. *Rice*, Dombrowski wrote him that "Southerners who accept the full implications of the democratic way of life, and I firmly believe that includes the majority of us, will take satisfaction in your decision." The following year, he asked Waring to join other southerners in signing a statement endorsing civil rights, and although Waring declined, the two continued their correspondence. In the spring of 1949, moreover, Dombrowski had helped to organize the meeting at Benjamin Sonnenberg's New York home that Mrs. Roosevelt and the Warings had attended.[45]

When Dombrowski proposed that Waring become a member of the SCEF's board of directors, however, the judge declined because of claims that Dombrowski and his organization were Communist-dominated, charges that probably amounted to little more than red-baiting. In fact, in 1965, the Supreme Court would invoke a rarely used power to enjoin state judicial proceedings to bar Louisiana officials from further prosecution of Dombrowski on numerous criminal charges. The prosecution, the Court held, was part of a scheme to obstruct Dombrowski's civil rights activities rather than a good-faith enforcement of the criminal law. But Waring was sufficiently concerned about Dombrowski's political leanings to seek Walter White's advice again.

White responded that the Southern Conference on Human Welfare, which Dombrowski had directed before formation of the SCEF, had begun as a "magnificent idea"—southerners acting against "inequality, bigotry and sectionalism"—but that it had been permitted by its leadership "to go far beyond its purpose and in some respects to be used by Communists." Waring realized that the NAACP secretary was especially sensitive to Communist influences over civil rights groups, but he, too, concluded that, while "substantially sound," the SCEF "may have been infiltrated by Communists." He continued to endorse the SCEF's work but persisted in his decision to decline membership on its board. Waring's concern with the political ties of his associates proved selective, however. Aubrey Williams was an SCEF official. The judge and Elizabeth also became loyal friends of Myles Horton, director of the controversial Highlander Folk School at Monteagle, Tennessee. Conservatives, including members of the House Un-American Activities Committee, considered Highlander's interracial programs hotbeds of Communism. Yet, in 1950, Waring readily agreed to become one of the school's sponsors. In speeches, moreover, he termed Highlander a "small but bright Beacon" in the cause of human rights.[46]

Throughout 1949 and 1950, Judge Waring continued to broaden his associations with civil rights advocates, garner awards, and rail against the apostles of gradualism, preaching force as the only solution to the South's racial problems. An August 1950 speech at a luncheon given in his honor by San Francisco's Council for Civic Unity best captured, perhaps, the credo he had been steadily evolving since 1945. His topic was "The Menace of White Supremacy." Prejudice was prevalent everywhere in the nation, he told his audience. But in the South, the "false doctrine of white supremacy" was enforced by law and pervaded an entire society, relegating blacks to a "semi-slave" existence. "Everything is separate—and not equal! It can't be done; if it is separate it is not equal." Such conditions constituted a grave threat, he contended, to the nation's international position. The Voice of America could broadcast our democratic principles to the world. But "on the same day and at the same time, the Russian propaganda tells of lynchings in Georgia and outrages in Alabama and South Carolina. And those are facts that speak louder than intentions and words." There was, however, a more fundamental reason for eradicating the evil of white supremacy—the need "to preserve the basic American ideals . . . to cleanse our own hearts and carry out those brave and fine ideals that our founding fathers enunciated." In San Francisco and many other parts of the nation, such a goal could be achieved through local action. "But in my country," he asserted, "that method won't work. In my country we have got to be cured by the other good people of the United States of America . . . by the decent people of America coming in and forcing it."[47]

Those who opposed force—men like Hodding Carter, "the arch-priest of gradualism and 'leave-us-alone'"—were, he added, the "most dangerous" advocates of white supremacy, much more a threat than the Thurmonds, Talmadges, "and other cattle of that kind." For the Carters and McGills were minimizing the South's sickness, offering "sedatives" when what was actually needed was surgery "to cut out this cancer from the body politic." The major reforms to date, Waring asserted, had come through force, not voluntarism. Yet, once southerners had become accustomed to changes enforced through "the strong arm of the law," he assured his audience, "the new practices [would become] a matter of pride even to those who [initially] had vociferously condemned" them, as southern acceptance of black jurors and black participation in party primaries amply demonstrated. "We are a sick people," he concluded, "and only a few of us know it."

> Help us—and help yourselves—to eradicate the great menace of white supremacy, the menace which threatens all of us because it threatens the fundamental ideals and principles upon which the American system (and our religious protestations) are based.

Judge Waring had now completely rejected his past—and the usual inhibitions of the judicial robe as well. But he was not alone. When the Council for Civic Unity honored him, it also honored his wife. By this point, Elizabeth Waring, too, had become a vocal and vehement proponent of equality and complete freedom of choice in racial matters. In fact, to white Charlestonians, she was the "witch of Meeting Street."

Julius Waties Waring, 1880–1968. *Moorland-Spingarn Research Center, Howard University, photo by F. Bachrach*

Waties Waring's parents, Edward Perry and Anna Thomasine Waties Waring. Waring inherited traits from both his handsome, extroverted father and his strong-minded, independent mother. *Photos courtesy of Thomas R. Waring, Jr.*

Annie Gammell Waring, Judge Waring's wife for more than thirty years. In 1945, Waring shocked family and friends when he divorced his devoted "Miss Annie" to marry a younger, twice-divorced northerner. *Photo courtesy of Eleanor Brown*

Elizabeth Avery Waring, Waties Waring's second wife, pictured here with her three children by a first marriage to Detroit lawyer Wilson Mills, whom she divorced to marry wealthy Connecticut manufacturer Henry Hoffman. While wintering in Charleston with Hoffman, Elizabeth met Waties Waring, and, their detractors later remarked with a smirk, it was "springtime for Henry." *Photo courtesy of Ann Mills Hyde*

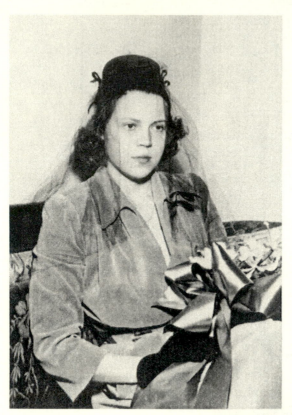

Anne Waring Warren, the only child of Waties and Annie Waring, pictured here on her wedding day.
Photo courtesy of Eleanor Brown

J. Waties and Elizabeth Waring.
Moorland-Spingarn Research Center, Howard University

Senator Ellison D. (Cotton Ed) Smith. Through much of his adult life, Waties Waring was a close associate of South Carolina's low country segregationist politicians, including the colorful and demagogic "Cotton Ed," who played a major role in Waring's appointment to the federal bench. When blacks appeared on the program of the 1936 Democratic national convention, Senator Smith walked out of the hall, returned to his hotel room, and tore his convention credentials to shreds. *AP/Wide World*

Burnet Rhett Maybank, Charleston mayor, South Carolina governor, and U.S. senator. Waring served as Charleston counsel during Maybank's tenure as mayor, and the two were political allies for years. But when Waring outlawed the white primary and issued other civil rights orders, Maybank sought to minimize his role in the judge's appointment to the district court and scorned his former friend, writing one Charleston associate, "Personally I believe . . . that he is crazy and should be in an institution." *AP/ Wide World*

William Jennings Bryan Dorn. In 1948, Congressman Dorn and other contenders for Burnet Maybank's Senate seat sought to make the senator's ties to Judge Waring a major campaign issue. *Photo courtesy of William Jennings Bryan Dorn*

William Watts Ball, reactionary editor of the Charleston *News and Courier*. Ball's paper regularly condemned Judge Waring's decisions but assiduously avoided personal attacks on the judge or his outspoken second wife. *Photo courtesy of the Charleston* News and Courier

Charleston congressman Lucius Mendel Rivers, pictured here early in his long Washington career. Rivers excoriated Judge Waring on the House floor, initiating impeachment efforts and charging that the judge had become a "monster," bent on revenge against a society unwilling to accept his divorce and remarriage. *Photo courtesy of the Library of Congress*

Judge Waring's nephew Thomas R. Waring, Jr., in a comparatively recent photograph. Tom Waring, who succeeded William Watts Ball as *News and Courier* editor and became an articulate spokesman for the segregationist cause in the 1950s, considered his uncle's rulings and attacks on white southerners largely a product of spite against family and former friends. *Photo courtesy of Thomas R. Waring, Jr.*

Although a pariah among white South Carolinians, Judge Waring was honored frequently by black groups and civil liberties organizations throughout the nation. Here, Dr. Benjamin Mays, president of Morehouse College, presents an award to Judge Waring. *Moorland-Spingarn Research Center, Howard University*

Amid the furor following her controversial speech to the black chapter of the Charleston YWCA, in which she termed southern whites "a sick, confused, and decadent people," Elizabeth Waring appeared on "Meet the Press." When asked during the interview whether she favored interracial marriage, she promptly retorted: "I certainly do. My husband is a U.S. Judge and we believe that our state should be part of the U.S. and not have separate laws." *Moorland-Spingarn Research Center, Howard University*

As they became increasingly isolated from South Carolina whites, the Warings established social ties and close friendships with area blacks, further incensing family and former friends. Pictured here at a luncheon for visiting magazine writer Samuel Grafton are, clockwise from Judge Waring, Lillian Wilson, Judge Waring's bailiff John Fleming, Mildred Guenveur Cherry, Grafton (partially hidden), Mrs. Waring, Susan Butler, Septima Clark, Ruby Cornwell, Dr. Roscoe Wilson, and Corinne Guenveur. *Moorland-Spingarn Research Center, Howard University*

Judge Waring and a visitor stand before the Waring home at 61 Meeting Street. Although originally the property of Annie Gammell Waring, Judge Waring and his second wife lived in the house after the divorce while Miss Annie rented the converted kitchen house of a nearby home. Detractors charged that Waring and Elizabeth—the "witch of Meeting Street"—had stolen the house from Annie. *Moorland-Spingarn Research Center, Howard University*

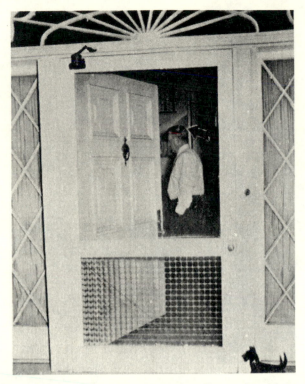

In October 1950, vandals stoned 61 Meeting Street. The Warings charged that shots were also fired and claimed that the Ku Klux Klan was responsible for the attack. In news accounts and photographs such as this one, however, the Charleston newspapers emphasized the minimal damage done the property and dismissed it as the work of youthful pranksters. The federal government placed the Warings under an armed guard, but after an extensive investigation the FBI tentatively concluded that neighborhood teenagers were the culprits. *Photo courtesy of the Charleston* News and Courier

In November following the stoning of 61 Meeting Street, supportive blacks and whites from several southern states made a pilgrimage to the Warings' home. Aubrey Williams, an Alabamian active in numerous civil rights causes, is pictured reading a commendation to Judge Waring. Behind Williams is John Hammond, a member of the NAACP's national board. *Moorland-Spingarn Research Center, Howard University*

Judges Waring, John J. Parker, and George Bell Timmerman, who in 1951 heard the first modern challenge to segregation in the public schools. Parker and Timmerman voted to uphold segregation. Judge Waring vehemently dissented, declaring: *"Segregation is per se inequality." AP/Wide World*

James F. Byrnes, taking the oath of office as South Carolina governor in 1951. Byrnes instituted a program to improve the state's black educational facilities but vowed to close the public schools of South Carolina rather than submit to integration. *Photo courtesy of the Columbia State*

After voting to declare segregated education unconstitutional, Judge Waring retired from the bench and went into "exile" in New York, where he and Mrs. Waring remained active—and combative—in numerous civil rights causes. Here he is pictured receiving an award from the National Committee for Rural Schools. Eleanor Roosevelt is seated on the left. *Moorland-Spingarn Research Center, Howard University*

When Judge Waring died in 1968, his body was returned to his native Charleston for burial. Shortly thereafter, vandals uprooted a magnolia tree his daughter had planted at the gravesite in his memory, and among certain Charlestonians feelings against the judge remain high even today. In 1981, however, Charleston Mayor Joseph Riley readily agreed to have a bronze sculpture honoring Judge Waring placed in the city council chambers, overlooking the federal courthouse in which Waring had served. "It's time," the mayor remarked, "to bring him home." *Photo courtesy of Collection of City Hall, Charleston, S.C.*

6

The Witch of Meeting Street

When Elizabeth Waring was a child, her great hero was Joan of Arc. Standing in her bed and wielding an imaginary sword, Elizabeth would pretend to be St. Joan, symbolically conquering the problems of her parents' troubled marriage and world crises as well. Her flair for the dramatic and desire to give meaning to her life followed her into adulthood. "I think she was always searching," her daughter remarked, "searching for some way to be something, to be recognized. She wanted to help the world, to help make the world better."[1] Charleston and her marriage to Waties Waring had given her both a stage and a cause. Through 1949, Elizabeth had remained largely in the background of the controversy swirling around her husband—a major catalyst for her husband's actions, detractors and supporters alike contended, but a background figure nevertheless. In the winter of 1950, however, that was all to change.

The Speech

Charleston's black YWCA branch held a public meeting each year at its facilities on Coming Street. Miss Rose Huggins, the branch's executive director, had heard Elizabeth Waring speak at a local church and suggested that she be invited to address the branch's upcoming annual meeting. Septima Clark, who was already acquainted with the Warings and was then serving as chairwoman of the branch's committee on management, quickly concurred, and Mrs. Waring was extended an invitation.

Judge Waring had once told an interviewer that he was reluctant to address black groups. He did not "want to be," he said, "on the propaganda end . . . it would be a mistake." But obviously the judge had long since rejected that policy, and it is doubtful whether Elizabeth Waring ever embraced it. During their New York meeting with Eleanor Roosevelt the previous spring, the president's widow had suggested that an improvement in southern racial relations would probably come last to tradition-bound Charleston. Mrs. Waring had agreed, Judge Waring later wrote Aubrey Williams, but remarked that "perhaps this would be the best place to strike a brave blow." The YWCA's annual meeting seemed an excellent opportunity, and Mrs. Waring readily accepted the invitation.[2]

The meeting was scheduled for Monday evening, January 16. On January 11, brief articles announcing the event, identifying Mrs. Waring as the speaker, and inviting the public to attend, appeared in the *News and Courier* and *Evening Post*. Soon, local whites began telephoning the director of the YWCA's white central organization, urging that the invitation be withdrawn or the meeting indefinitely postponed. A number of blacks applied similar pressure. The following afternoon, members of the interracial committee supervising the activities of the central and branch YWCA organizations met and attempted to persuade Mrs. Clark and Miss Huggins to withdraw the invitation. Mrs. Clark found the meeting a strange affair. It began with a prayer for divine guidance and courage, but then the committee members "had professed their desperate fear of having a woman speak to them." Though she hardly needed an explanation, Mrs. Clark asked them to explain their concerns. Whites on the committee began discussing Mrs. Waring's reputation, her marriages and divorces, and the Warings' current status in Charleston society, warning that Mrs. Waring's appearance would seriously jeopardize continued financial support for the branch's activities and maybe those of the central office as well. Mrs. Clark argued that Charleston blacks were hardly likely to be aware of gossip about the Warings' social life, and she and Miss Huggins refused to withdraw the invitation.[3]

Following the meeting, the two women telephoned Mrs. Waring from a pay booth, then visited her home to tell her about the meeting, urge her to resist pressures from whites to withdraw, and ask her to alert them if any blacks tried to dissuade her from speaking. Mrs. Waring listened, assured them she had no intention of withdrawing, and telephoned the YWCA's national organization to protest the local committee's behavior. When Mrs. Clark arrived home that evening, a wire from the national headquarters, inquiring about Mrs. Waring's allegations, was waiting for her. National YWCA officials also contacted the director of Charleston's central organization. The next morning the local committee had another meeting, again attempting to persuade Mrs. Clark to cancel Mrs. Waring's appearance. The director of United Givers, a principal source of YWCA funds, also attended the meeting. He told the group that he had once lived near Mrs. Waring in Connecticut, then launched into a litany of ugly rumors. "You could have lived next door to her," Carl Rowan later reported Mrs. Clark responding, "and she would have been so many miles above you socially that you wouldn't have known which door she used when she left home." Mrs. Clark's own account indicated a slightly more restrained rejoinder, but she obviously made it clear again to the committee that she would neither withdraw Mrs. Waring's invitation nor postpone the meeting. When a prepared statement was placed before Mrs. Clark for her signature, she refused to sign it.[4]

As the night of the speech approached, the Warings sought to secure publicity for the meeting and the controversy it was generating. On Friday, January 13, Judge Waring wrote his daughter and son-in-law to inform them of the pressures to which Mrs. Clark had been subjected, emphasize the importance of accurate publicity, and alert them to the possibility of violence. "Things are getting a good deal stirred up here," he wrote,

> and Negroes, at least some of them, are beginning to pick up a good deal of courage and beginning to insist that they be treated as citizens. The News and Courier is raving every morning and the white political hierarchy is very restless and exhibiting considerable trepidation. There is fear that some of the white politicians will begin to seek Negro votes and there is no telling to what extent they might go to try and break up this meeting, either by suggestions of financial harm or even eventually by physical violence. Neither Elizabeth nor I are greatly concerned by these matters excepting so far as they may be publicized and it is important, if anything out of the way happens, that the truth should be known. For that reason, I thought that I would write and advise you of this since, if anything does happen, it will be advisable to see that true publicity is given, and Stanley has access to sources for that. Of course, no newspaper reporters or radio men in Charleston could be relied on to furnish even a semblance of a true report. If facts are to be obtained, it will have to be by someone coming from the outside. If any further break of any kind occurs, I shall notify you. Perhaps nothing out of the way will occur, however it is advisable to be forewarned in regard to anything in this explosive atmosphere. As a matter of fact, the people here are getting jittery and there is no telling quite which way things may break.[5]

While generally pleased with the coverage given him by the United Press wire service, Judge Waring distrusted the *News and Courier* reporter who served as the Charleston representative of the Associated Press. Accordingly, he had his secretary telephone Paul Hansell, chief of the AP's Charlotte bureau, to suggest that the wire service send a reporter from Charlotte to cover the YWCA speech, implying that the local representative would not provide an unbiased account. Instead, Hansell phoned *Courier* assistant editor Frank B. Gilbreth to make certain that the Charleston paper would send a reporter to the meeting and to indicate that he was planning to ask Judge Waring's secretary to airmail or bus the Charlotte office a copy of the speech. Hansell "said to me," Gilbreth reported to Tom Waring in a memorandum, that "he knew we would give an unbiased account. . . . He said to me that, since Waring seemed to be on the outs with us, AP wanted not to antagonize him, since the judge is news and since UP seems to give him a good play." Gilbreth assured Hansell that the *Courier* would cover the speech. On the morning of the YWCA meeting, moreover, editor Ball cautioned Gilbreth that "if any doubt arises in the interpretation of Mrs. Waring's remarks, to make certain the benefit of the doubt is given to her."

> I don't know what the lady is going to say [wrote Gilbreth in a memorandum to a staffer], but my reaction is not to dignify the talk by giving it too much play. In other words, it seems to me we ought to carry it fairly fully, but inside and under a fairly small head. . . .

Of course if she should say something really sensational, that might be
something else again.[6]

The morning of the meeting, Mrs. Waring walked into the branch building on Coming Street, selected a lectern suitable for her height, and left
money with Septima Clark to be used for purchasing refreshments. Several
white members of the YWCA's central board were also there that morning.
When Mrs. Waring arrived, Mrs. Clark later recalled, they "hid" in a conference room until she left the building. Later, Judge Waring telephoned to
suggest that men be stationed near the light switches of the auditorium in
which his wife was to speak in the event that hoodlums attempted to disrupt
the meeting.[7]

The most volatile element in the atmosphere that evening, however, was
to be Elizabeth Waring's rhetoric. An audience of about 150, including several whites, packed the small meeting room. "My very dear friends," Mrs.
Waring began,

> it was brave of you to invite me to speak here and brave of all of you to
> come to hear me, for the white "powers that be" have done everything in
> their power to keep me from speaking to you Negro people, even to de-
> faming Judge Waring's and my character. But we only feel sorry for them,
> for their stupidity, as it will hurt them, and not us, for it is apparent to
> everyone what their real motive is in not wishing me to speak—fear of the
> judge and me. We to them are like the atom bomb which they are afraid
> we will use to destroy their selfish and savage white supremacy way of life
> and they are quite correct. That is exactly what the judge and I are doing,
> and they know it and see the writing on the wall. But you know and we
> know and they *should* know that there is another use of atomic energy, and
> that is for building and healing and restoring a civilized way of life. That
> is what the judge is trying to do for the good of the white people down
> here as well as the Negro.[8]

The remainder of her speech largely reiterated the tone and themes of
her opening remarks—comprising an intriguing and disturbing mixture of
praise for her husband's "wonderful opinions" and the accomplishments of outstanding blacks, encouragement for southern blacks whose spirits had been
"forged in the furnace of persecution," strident attacks on the "deep and
savage South," and appeals to the revolutionary spirit of the American past.
Southern blacks, she appeared to be saying, were superior to their white
masters. "You are in the springtime of your growth," she told blacks in the
audience, "when great achievements are attained. You Negro people have already picked up the torch of culture and achievement from the whites down
here." Southern whites, on the other hand, were "a sick, confused and decadent people . . . full of pride and complacency, introverted, morally weak,
and low." Spiritually, too, blacks had long surpassed whites. In the past, in
fact, southern blacks had lived "Christ's teaching by the Golden Rule . . .
to the point of . . . weakness and apathy and defeatism too often." Now,
however, the time had arrived for blacks to make a "final push" for equality.

And that effort would require force, just as force had been necessary in 1776. The common man, she exclaimed, had

> always had to secure his rights by force, never by time or the fancy word so often misused, "evolution." . . . This time it is a new type of warfare for you as well as the rest of the world, the modern revolution of a cold war to attain the rights you already legally have, to enforce those rights.

Like most municipal buses, the interiors of Charleston's were bordered with public service and commercial messages. Mrs. Waring found one particularly ironic. "In the Charleston buses, where you Negroes sit in shame, segregated to the rear," she concluded,

> there is a placard saying "respect the rights of others" . . . in the Deep South where no one practices—least of all the bus companies—Christ's command, "to do unto others as you would be done by." On this placard is a picture of some pilgrims in prayer giving thanks for finding the freedom they sought in coming here. Among other things, this placard admonishes, "freedom is everybody's job." Let's follow the bus company's admonition— and right now. Yes, freedom is everybody's job.

Septima Clark's elderly mother, who was sitting in the audience, was probably as traditional in her racial attitudes as Charleston whites were in theirs, and had grown up with a fear of what whites could do. Hearing this speech, she thought that Mrs. Waring and her daughter, seated on the platform with the speaker, would surely be shot. When Elizabeth Waring scorned the "decadence" of southern whites, the elderly black woman became so frightened that she lost the use of her legs and had to be carried from the auditorium. Later that night, when a family dog wagged its tail against a door, she screamed out, certain that the Klan was attacking her home.[9]

Black concern about Mrs. Waring's speech was not limited to Septima Clark's Haitian mother or "Uncle Toms" in Charleston's black community. Mrs. Clark and Miss Huggins wrote Mrs. Waring to thank her for "a successful evening." But Mrs. Clark objected to Mrs. Waring's searing indictment of southern whites. "I want to be very truthful," she would later remark. "I didn't like the idea of her calling them decadent. . . . I have known numbers of whites. They all aren't decadent." She shared her objections with Mrs. Waring. " 'Well, Septima,' " she remembered Elizabeth replying, " 'they *are* decadent! They just don't know how to be humanitarian. . . . She was going to have her way.' "[10]

Mrs. Clark's concerns, of course, paled in comparison with the reactions of many whites. The AP's Charleston representative had attended the meeting, and Judge Waring gave him a copy of his wife's speech. Newspapers throughout South Carolina published lengthy excerpts; the *New York Times, Time,* and other national publications also gave the speech ample coverage; and the Warings mailed copies to friends. Many sympathetic to the couple's stance praised the speech. "When a Northerner goes into Dixie," the Pittsburgh *Courier* editorialized, "and stands up straight in Dixie's front yard and tells Dixie to Dixie's teeth that Dixie is not doing right by almost half of her population just because that half is made up of Negroes, then you can say . . . that there is a Northerner with courage and determination unlimited." Aubrey Williams called the speech "moving and significant . . . one of the finest and most courageous pieces of writing and speaking" he had ever read. A Vanderbilt professor of religion applauded her "courageous stand," and a William and Mary student complained of the "lip service" given equality by "so-called 'Southern leaders.' " Even a number of South Carolina whites praised her stand. An Abbeville man wrote, for example, "Your statement was courageous and clear-thinking, and I long for the day when the people here can deal out justice to the colored man and make friends with him on a more Christian basis than we are now doing." The great-great-granddaughter of South Carolina's last royal governor was equally enthusiastic. "Quite agree," she wired Mrs. Waring, "that any race who refuses an equal chance to their fellow men are certainly a sick, decadent people. They should be banished with Hitler and other destroyers of civilization."[11]

But the overwhelming response of southern whites, and many from outside the region as well, was vehemently negative. For nearly two weeks after the speech, the Warings' phone rang incessantly with abusive, threatening calls. Hate mail—including forty-eight threats turned over to federal authorities—arrived at their home or the judge's chambers in a steady stream. A Camden grandson of a Confederate colonel suggested that Mrs. Waring would be "much more at home in Harlem than in Charleston." A New Yorker expressed hope that she would be *"raped* by a diseased *nigger."* One anonymous correspondent wrote across the top of an editorial critical of the speech: "Too bad you didn't keep quiet! It would have been better to have accepted your *local* snubbing than to be a national joke. And are we laughing!" Another recommended that the Warings read "You have been Used by Jews! Break your Chains!" and other anti-Semitic material available from Gerald L. K. Smith's Christian Nationalist Crusade. Six University of South Carolina students thanked her for her "efforts to incite a revolution by the Negroes of this State. . . . Speeches such as yours," they wrote, "are . . . very conducive to producing better relations between the races, since most white people like very much to be told by people of your eminence that they are inferior to Negroes." A Charlotte matron found Mrs. Waring's remarks "uncouth, rude and undignified"; a South Carolina woman found them "silly, inflammatory nonsense." And a "true Democrate" complained of Judge Waring's abuse of "one of the sweetest ladies you would want to meet," adding, "We have the *Nigger* under our feet and we are going to keep him there, also you and your husband."[12]

A number of letters were thoughtful and diplomatic. A Columbia churchwoman active in the work of the Southern Regional Council wrote that she was "one of many Christian women in South Carolina who are truly interested in the status of the Negro." As a member of a biracial committee, she was trying to use "Christian methods" to improve the conditions of Negroes, particularly women and children. "I was sorry to read of your address," she wrote.

> If you were reported correctly (and I can understand how you may have been reported incorrectly) then I think you have hurt rather than helped our cause. Because your remarks cover South Carolina men and women on the whole, I believe that you owe many men and women in South Carolina an apology. I also believe that our wise Christian Negroes will agree with me that the prejudice which we are trying to erase will be greatly aroused by your caustic remarks.
>
> Many people were sympathetic with and appreciative of Judge Waring's stand. I think now that many people will not feel so kindly towards him.
>
> I trust that you may feel it in your heart to retract the harsh portion of your address.[13]

Most of the critical letters Mrs. Waring received, however, were of the hate mail variety. And South Carolina politicians were highly critical in their discussion of the speech. Strom Thurmond, the *Chicago Defender* reported, was the "first of the Dixiecrats to pout," calling Mrs. Waring's remarks "beneath answering." Greenville congressman Joseph R. Bryson found them "typical of the remarks of the professional uninformed agitator," and predicted that they would "serve to set back the steady course of improvement in race relationships." Another South Carolina congressman condemned her statements as "uncalled for and untrue," while yet another labeled them "sickening," and a member of the Charleston delegation to the South Carolina legislature hurled the ultimate epithet, calling Mrs. Waring a "damn Yankee." Of state politicians, however, Mendel Rivers was her harshest critic. Her harangue was "unfortunate," he told a *News and Courier* reporter, but no more than "what could be expected from an individual completely uninformed on a very complex and trying subject." Her outburst, Rivers added,

> only serves to show what transpires when one whose mental growth occurred in the geographical area of the Detroit race riots and who is so grossly uninformed on local matters, attempts to discuss a situation about which she knows nothing.

The Charleston congressman also hinted at a possible new impeachment inquiry. "Her prophecies of things judically to come," he asserted,

> are so deplorable and so charged with grave implications that I shall await with official interest the next judicial episode, involving the race question, in her husband's court, and I shall be prepared to take whatever appropriate action may be justified.[14]

The southern press also went on the offensive. In an editorial ridiculing Mrs. Waring's "Stupid Attack on the South," the Tallahassee *Democrat* alluded to the Warings' isolation from Charleston society, adding: "Why be angry? She is just the girl who didn't get invited to the party and she had to say something catty about the hostess." Another southern editor agreed, claiming that Mrs. Waring's chief motive was "to vent her spite." But southern gradualist Hodding Carter was to be Mrs. Waring's severest and most effective journalistic critic. In a column carried in the Atlanta *Journal,* Carter accused "the youngish, thrice-married Connecticut wife of elderly" Judge Waring of "a preposterously reverse racism," comparing her to the recently deceased Senator Bilbo and charging that she was

> as guilty of bigotry and deliberate inflammation of racial feeling as ever Bilbo was when she libelled some thirty million white people as being decadent and fanatic and inferior to the nine million Negroes who live beside them. If Bilbo deserved denunciation, so does this woman.

Mrs. Waring's "aberrations," Carter charged, were "neither political nor clinical, but social in the narrow sense of the word." Charlestonians, he explained, could be "and are frequently overbearingly aloof. To pun atrociously, Charleston is a city where many are galled and few are chosen." In the wake of Judge Waring's divorce and remarriage, Charleston society had ostractized the judge and his second wife. "Whatever their inner convictions," Carter charged,

> there can be no doubt that the judge and his wife are also intent upon getting even.
>
> And in a time when so much for good or for ill can come to and out of the South, the judge's wife certainly merits the same condemnation that Bilbo received. I wonder if the press of the nation is responding accordingly.[15]

Two days after the column appeared, Tom Waring wrote Carter a letter, identifying himself as Judge Waring's nephew and asserting that Carter's assessment of the situation in Charleston had "hit the nail squarely on the head." Waring expressed regret that his uncle and Elizabeth had been subjected to abusive letters and telephone calls, "a form of harassment decent people deplore." But he applauded Carter's insight, assuring him that the Warings' "racial 'liberality'" was indeed "largely spite. . . . It would make a good psychological study for somebody," he observed, adding, "It is my guess that most local colored people feel embarrassed by all this hullabaloo."[16]

While Tom Waring welcomed the esteemed Mississippi editor's attack, he assured Carter that he himself was "studiously avoiding entanglement on a personal basis." The *News and Courier* also refrained from editorial comment. In her speech, Mrs. Waring had accused the Charleston papers of suppressing news favorable to blacks. The next morning, the *Courier*'s assistant editor Frank Gilbreth wrote an editorial denying her charge. "If it did not believe that suppressing news is more dangerous than printing news, no matter how distasteful," Gilbreth pointedly wrote, "the News and Courier would have been inclined to suppress and censor her recent speech to a group of negroes. . . . Those are words that should have been suppressed before they were said. . . . Presumably," Gilbreth added, "she speaks for herself, and for herself alone." At an editorial conference later that day, however, it was decided that the editorial would not be run. One editorial did recommend that "discontented blacks . . . escape to Northern cities. . . . The savage South is no place for 'oppressed' colored people." But while urged repeatedly by its subscribers to respond—"You have such a grand chance to score," one wrote—the paper avoided a direct reply. On one occasion, in fact, William Watts Ball editorialized:

> Any person, man or woman, white or colored, has a right to speak in pub-
> lic his or her opinions whether or not they be popular, whether or not they
> be detested by majorities, as long as they fall short of treason and of incit-
> ing immediate riot. Whosoever shall abuse or annoy a person exercising
> that right is not only an enemy of free government but a fool. Whosoever
> shall trespass on the civil rights of a person because of disagreement with
> that person should be arrested and sent to jail.

While rejecting one letter accusing Mrs. Waring of "amateur harlotry," another claiming that "there must be some negro blood in Waring and his wife," and others also considered "too hot to handle," the *Courier,* like the *Evening Post,* did publish a number of vehemently critical letters. Then it refused to publish any more on the subject and persisted in its position despite complaints that, especially in view of the "prominent publicity" given Mrs. Waring's "trash," its decision "showed cowardice and a striking unfairness to its readers."[17]

Mrs. Waring was hardly disturbed by the storm of controversy she had generated. In fact, she appeared to find it invigorating. "[I]f one has a cause," *Time* quoted her as saying, "one has to be willing to suffer for it." The morning after the speech, according to one account, she had strolled into a Charleston hardware store to purchase some mousetraps. "You know," she remarked defiantly to a clerk and other customers, "I'm about ten times as scared of a mouse as I am of the whole Ku Klux Klan." She would not, she vowed to a reporter for a black paper, be intimidated by abuse or demands that she "get out of town."[18]

Mrs. Waring Meets the Press

Now Elizabeth Waring, too, was a national media figure; soon she would have a national forum. In the wake of the YWCA speech, she was invited to appear on the NBC interview program "Meet the Press." In early February, she and Judge Waring took a train to New York for a term of court and, she explained to reporters, "soul refreshment." On Saturday evening, February 11, she went to NBC's studios in Washington, D.C., for the interview. Panelists that night included *American Mercury* editor Lawrence Spivak, the moderator; Louis Lautier, correspondent for the Atlanta *World* and the National Negro Press Association, and the first black to be admitted to the congressional press galleries; Edward Jameson, reporter for the Houston *Chronicle* and other southern papers; and Mae Craig, a Charleston native and Washington correspondent for a group of New England papers. But the "bluntest" questions of the evening, as the *Evening Post* put it, would come from Mary James Cottrell, Washington correspondent for the Charlotte *Ob-*

server and Greenville, South Carolina, *News-Piedmont,* and widow of Jesse
Cottrell, journalist and former U.S. ambassador to Bolivia.[19]

Mrs. Cottrell asked the first question. What had brought Mrs. Waring,
she asked, to the "drastic" conclusion that whites "down here" are a "sick,
confused and decadent people," full of "pride and complacency, introverted,
morally weak and low"? "Living there and observing them," Mrs. Waring
calmly responded. "Any people who enslave the minds and bodies of another people are bound to destroy their own souls." Mrs. Cottrell pressed on.
Critics were charging, she said, that Mrs. Waring favored revolution. "Do
you really advocate revolution?" "If you read my speech," Mrs. Waring answered, "I don't think there's any place in there that could be misconstrued
to mean that. I did say that it was a cold war, but [blacks] would conduct
it in the kindly Christian way in which they have heretofore behaved."

Now it was Mae Craig's turn. "[W]ere you referring," she asked, "only
to Charleston, or South Carolina, or to all of the South?" The "deep South,"
Mrs. Waring replied, which, she said, included every state below North Carolina. North Carolina's university was having a progressive influence there, and
progress was being made in Virginia, too, despite the Byrd machine. "But in
our part," she added, warming to the occasion, "we're an exact replica of
the Russian government. We are just one party with a very powerful Gestapo." "Don't you think it might be better," Mrs. Craig then asked, noting
Mrs. Waring's New England background, "if some . . . forward-looking
Southerners led the movement rather than yourself?" "Wonderful, Mrs.
Craig. Excellent," Mrs. Waring quickly countered.

> That's what I've been waiting for, and so has the Judge. But nobody speaks
> up. And unfortunately it's a little like our government. When nobody speaks
> up in our government, the courts have to do things such as my husband did.

At this point, Louis Lautier got in several sympathetic questions enabling
Mrs. Waring to offer her assessment of the political climate in South Carolina
and the motives underlying the treatment to which she and Judge Waring
had been subjected. Her husband's decisions, she charged, not his divorce
and their marriage, accounted for white South Carolina's hatred of them.

> A very little teeny-weeny group ostracized us because of our divorce. . . .
> But the entire state ostracizes us. No white person has dared to put their
> foot in our front door since the Judge's primary decision, which came two
> years after we were married. Those who would like to are afraid. *Time*
> magazine calls him the man they love to hate. I call him the man they're
> afraid not to hate.

"Southern gentlemen," she added, thought that her husband should have left
invalidation of the white primary to a higher court. "In other words, their
interpretation of the Southern gentleman is a man who double-crosses his
oath of office, double-crosses his government, and certainly betrays his ideals
as a Christian." There was, she agreed, a "better element" of southern whites,
"a little handful of people." But they were unorganized, and in South Caro-

lina's low country, she and her husband were "all alone . . . pitiful and solitary."

> That's why we need the help of the North because in the underground of Europe at least they were organized. The better element we receive letters from. Ministers come up and whisper to us that they're for us, but their congregations would cut their throats if they spoke out.

Lautier raised only a few questions, but Mrs. Cottrell was far from finished. What, she asked, had been Mrs. Waring's reaction to Hodding Carter's charge that her Charleston speech amounted to "Bilboism in reverse?" The southern "parlor liberal," Mrs. Waring rejoined, echoing her husband, was "the most dangerous element we have to face . . . far more dangerous to us than the white supremacist." Carter, Mrs. Cottrell added, had attributed "your trouble" to spite. "Do you feel that you're getting even or do you honestly feel that you're promoting better social relations in the South?" "I think of the suffragists in England in 1914 who were put in jail, each one in a separate cell with a Bible," Mrs. Waring countered.

> It turned out to be perhaps the happiest experience any woman could have in her life, with such a good book as the Bible. To be with my husband alone is, I can assure you, a wonderful experience. I have no desire for revenge. I'm exceedingly happy. But my cause, I can assure you, would not make me any more popular.

Was it not true that Judge Waring had been a major figure in "Cotton Ed" Smith's 1938 campaign in which "the issue was white supremacy?" "I don't know a thing about it. I have never heard that mentioned."

Mae Craig followed Mrs. Cottrell with some pointed queries of her own. "Do you think you can force social relations by a law?" she asked. "If you mean asking Negroes into your house, Mrs. Craig," Mrs. Waring replied, "that is an optional thing entirely." Did she not believe that it was more serious to have discrimination exist in Washington than in the South? "I certainly do. I think Washington is the greatest disgrace there is to this country." But the most heavily baited questions of the evening were yet to come from Mrs. Cottrell. A list of questions apparently prepared for the interview would eventually turn up in the papers of James F. Byrnes. One of the prepared questions read as follows:

> I quote from an interview you granted John H. McCray, editor of the Lighthouse and Informer, South Carolina colored newspaper. After describing how he was received in your home, McCray says—"anchored on a small table (in your drawing room) was a goodsized picture of Mr. and Mrs. Walter White." Since the colored head of the Association for Advancement of Colored People is married to a white woman and you have their picture together in your drawing room does this mean that you favor intermarriage of the races, which is illegal in South Carolina, and furthermore you not only favor outlawing segregation but amalgamation of the races as well?[20]

During the actual interview, however, Mrs. Cottrell used slightly different language to raise the same question, omitting the last clause. "I certainly do," Mrs. Waring quickly retorted. "My husband is a U.S. Judge and we believe that our state should be a part of the U.S. and not have separate laws. I see no reason if they choose to marry why they shouldn't."

Another of the prepared questions referred to John McCray's account of the "favorable reaction from the colored people in Charleston to your speech" and quoted him:

> Foremost among the proud YWCA ladies [McCray had written] is Mrs. Lather Cooper, who presented Mrs. Waring with a huge, lovely bouquet of flowers following her address.
>
> Mrs. Waring in return planted a resounding smack on Mrs. Cooper's jaw, much to her pleasure and surprise.
>
> Afterwards, Mrs. Cooper told friends "I'll cherish that kiss the longest day I live."
>
> Mrs. Waring, do you feel that a Judge's wife going about her husband's home city kissing negroes in public can inculcate anything but ill will for the Judge among the white people of the state and stir up bitter racial strife?[21]

As the interview neared its end, Mrs. Cottrell quoted McCray's description of the "kissing incident, but stopped short of asking the prepared question. Instead, she noted that kissing supporters was a habit of politicians and inquired whether Mrs. Waring planned to run for Congress. "I'm 55 years old and my husband is 70," Mrs. Waring replied. "I very much doubt whether we'd start that now."

Then Mrs. Waring raised a question of her own. "Won't somebody ask me about the outside interference? That's what all the South talks about." Louis Lautier obliged, inquiring whether Mrs. Waring thought the federal government should intervene "if the Southern states do not exercise their rights and correct evils and injustices in matters of civil rights." Mrs. Waring answered with another question. "Aren't you afraid," she asked, "that we're juggling with the rights of the Negro race and the destiny of humanity if you leave them alone?

South Carolina Pariahs

At her suggestion, Judge Waring had not accompanied his wife to Washington. Shortly after the interview concluded, he telephoned the studio from New York to praise her performance. She had indeed made an effective appearance. Her responses had been reasonable, restrained, generally free of the vitriol prominent in her Charleston speech. She had remained, Mary Cottrell herself would later report, "in a good humor all through the broadcast" and chatted pleasantly with the panelists beforehand, remarking, when asked about the judge, that he had given her the orchid she was wearing that evening, then adding, "Don't get me talking about him or I will talk all night, he's so wonderful."[22]

As they had following the YWCA speech, many of the Warings' admirers applauded her stand. Immediately after the interview, for example, John Henry Faulk, a lacturer, humorist, and television personality who would later be blacklisted as a suspected Communist, sat down at a typewriter in his New Jersey apartment and composed a forceful tribute. Mrs. Waring had labeled her Charleston speech "shock treatment" for bigoted southerners. Describing himself as a "nice, safe, white Protestant American [and] Southerner by birth and upbringing," the Texas-born Faulk agreed that racists were "sick, harmful persons who need [a] shock treatment." "The Dixiecrat," he observed,

> sounds the buzzer for all to hear, like the rattlesnake. Hodding Carter and his like, slither in, flick their tongues pleasantly—then strike, like Copperheads. There is not a lot of difference in the effect on the victim of a sting from a rattlesnake or a Copperhead. One is a little easier to detect.

A number of white South Carolinians also rose to Mrs. Waring's defense. "The truth is," a Spartanburg Baptist minister wrote to a local paper, "Mrs. Waring is not mentally or morally sick but rather we who think that she is."[23]

After the television interview, some felt that Elizabeth Waring was not only advocating "war" in behalf of civil rights—she had endorsed interracial marriage as well. The interview had aired only on television, not radio, and relatively few southern homes enjoyed that luxury in 1950. But her remarks were widely quoted in the press, and her appearance precipitated a new round of abusive letters. On one day alone, a Michigan man mailed her numerous vile postcard messages. "If God wanted us to mingle with niggers," he asked, "why did he make them black with such an odor?" Her husband, he concluded, must need "nigger votes." A Charlestonian "who *used* to know you very well, socially," charged that Judge Waring had "never believed in God," speculated that Mrs. Waring had "negro blood," and asked, "have neither of you any pride that you continue to live here? . . . If you continue your practice of breaking up homes, and getting divorces," the letter ended, "it would surprise no one if your next husband would be a negro." Other letters carried similar themes. South Carolina newspapers were also flooded with hostile mail. The *News and Courier* published one lengthy, balanced response, which it considered representative. But many letters that the *Courier* and other papers received were unprintable. One man charged in a letter to the *Courier* that it was "about time that Southern Gentlemen forget their dignity and put on masks," then complained that "there must be some negro blood in Waring and his wife." "I am afraid," Frank Gilbreth responded, "we cannot run your letter . . . without involving you and us in a possible libel suit."[24]

The *News and Courier* again refrained from editorial comment, but certain other southern editors were not so chivalrous. At some point, moreover, the University of South Carolina's student newspaper, the *Gamecock*—and student Charles Waring, Jr., the judge's grandnephew—also joined the attack. One issue of the *Gamecock* carried the following lament:

Got a minute, brother?
Then listen to a tale of misery,
My name's Waring . . . Charles W. Waring, Jr.
That's right, I'm from Charleston. . . . Wait, don't go!
Yes, I go to the university. This is my first year.
No, no . . . he's my great uncle, not my father!
Let's see, I think I saw him in '42 or maybe '43.
Yes, I think my father spoke to him sometime last year.
His wife? No, I never even seen her.
Yes, they say she's from somewhere up north.
Yes, I think so, too.
No, it's just I'm not quite a loving nephew.
That's right.
Well, so long, pal. And say, from now on when you speak
    to me, how about pronouncing it "Warren"?
Thanks, pal.[25]

However, it was the tasteless but clever doggerel of Arthur Stoney that
perhaps provided white South Carolinians the greatest glee. After Mrs.
Waring's YWCA speech, copies of "White Trash" began to appear. Penned
in the Gullah dialect of low country blacks, it read:

Who dis buckra 'omen
What so much talk about?
Been calling white folks names
An' shootin' off he mout'

She ride wit' colored people,
Go calling at deh place
Wit' "Missus dis an' Mistah dat"
An' kiss 'em in duh face.

Now dat ain't natchel bizness
An' make for we to fret
Dis mixin' up lak she done
Gwine mek for trubbel yet.

An know about a lot o' t'ings
An' sure 'nuf ah buhlieves,
When white folks pet up colored
Dere's sumpin up dey sleeve.

An hear a lot o' talkin' 'bout she
And dis is what dey say
W'en white folks pas' 'em on duh street
Dey look de udder way.

Ah goes to see mah w'ite folks
From Battery to de Mall
Ah got to go enn de side gate,
But she can't go at all.

Ah tell dese new young nigger
What's messin' up wit' she:
De trash de w'ite folks trow out
Ain't good enuf for me.

The *News and Courier* refused to publish Stoney's latest effort, but a number of other papers did, and carbon copies of "White Trash" were soon circulating widely through the state. The Warings themselves received several copies in the mail, including one printed on the back of a business card advertising "Bailey's," a Charleston heating and air-conditioning firm. Elizabeth Waring filed the card attached to a sheet of Bible verses, among them Christ's admonition "that ye love one another," as well as this recommendation from St. Luke: "And whosoever will not receive you, when ye go out of that city, shake off the very dust from your feet for a testimony against them."[26]

Again, not surprisingly, South Carolina politicians were also vehemently critical. During her "Meet the Press" interview, Mrs. Waring had included among the "better element" of southern whites Maxie Collins, a Baptist minister and leader in South Carolina's small pro-Truman Democratic contingent. Governor Thurmond promptly dubbed Mrs. Waring the voice of "Trumanites" in South Carolina. Collins in turn threatened to sue Thurmond for libel and sought to distance himself from Mrs. Waring. South Carolina, he told reporters, was not even "ready to discuss the abolition of segregation, much less abolish segregation. . . . I have said repeatedly that segregation must be maintained." No pro-Truman Democrat, he insisted, had ever advocated interracial marriage.[27]

While Collins and Thurmond exchanged charges, South Carolina legislators condemned and ridiculed the Warings on the floor of the state general assembly. In a joint resolution introduced in the state House of Representatives, Greenville legislator Charles Garrett proposed that the state purchase Judge Waring and his "socialite" wife one-way tickets out of the state, "preferably [to] a foreign country." The gift would carry but one stipulation—that the Warings "leave the State of South Carolina and never again set foot on her soil." Cost of the tickets was to be drawn from an $800,000 allocation for an animal science building at Clemson College. "To offset this slight deduction," the resolution provided, "it is suggested that a stall in the mule barn of Clemson College be dedicated to Federal Judge and Mrs. Waring and that an appropriate plaque be erected thereon."[28]

In the state Senate, E. W. Cantwell of Williamsburg County called for an investigation into the circumstances behind Judge Waring's divorce. The previous summer, Senator Cantwell—a lawyer and member of the governor's staff during Olin Johnston's term—had proposed that the judge be deported to North Africa and complained that Waring had once laughed in his face and threatened him with a contempt citation. Now Cantwell contended that Waring's Florida divorce disqualified him from sitting as a judge in South Carolina. "I don't think he is fit to be a judge," Cantwell exclaimed. "Let's send him to New York or New Jersey."[29]

Garrett's resolution attracted many congratulatory letters; the only negative mail, he reported, had come from a North Carolina "socialite." The resolution won easy passage in the state House, with only a single negative vote audible in the press gallery. In the Senate, however, it was quietly buried in the judiciary committee. Senator Cantwell's proposal met the same fate. Though no friend of the Warings, judiciary committee chairman W. B. Harvey of Beaufort County termed Cantwell's proposed inquiry "a useless thing" and successfully resisted his colleague's efforts to have the matter brought to the Senate floor for debate.[30]

As had happened after his unpopular rulings, state politicians with earlier ties to Judge Waring now sought to distance themselves from the couple. Shortly after the YWCA speech, Georgetown attorney Arthur Locke King wrote James F. Byrnes to lament that King had once recommended Waring to Byrnes as a replacement for Judge Myers and that Byrnes' "reply was to the effect that this was in line with your own judgment as to his general fitness and availability." Byrnes, who had recently announced his candidacy for governor, lost no time responding to the disturbing implication that he might bear some responsibility for Waring's appointment. Before his own appointment to the U.S. Supreme Court, as noted in Chapter 1, Byrnes had prepared a list of potential replacements for Judge Myers, and Waties Waring's name was on that list. Now, however, Byrnes hedged about the positiveness of his reply, adding:

> When you say that you proposed that Waties Waring be named to succeed him and I replied that this was in line with my own judgment as to his general fitness and availability, I know it is entirely possible. However, I am sure it was only a general statement such as I would have made as to the availability and fitness of many lawyers, because I had no idea of recommending Mr. Waring.[31]

Potentially, of course, Burnet Maybank was the officeholder most vulnerable to political damage from the current furor, and South Carolina's senior senator attempted once again to minimize his connections with Judge Waring. Shortly after Mrs. Waring's interview on "Meet the Press," elderly Charleston banker C. Norwood Hastie a longtime associate of Maybank, mailed the senator a scrawled note, warning him that Charleston was "seething." Judge Waring, the old man reported, was telling people that he had put Maybank in office "and that all the negroes should get married to whites. . . . If I were you I would come at once," he added. "I tell you, it is going to raise hell next time you run." If Maybank did not get the Warings "out of town," Hastie asserted in a later letter, "you will cause a manslaughter." Nor were Maybank's close friends the only ones to write. "For God's sake," a Columbia constituent wired the senator, "use your influence to impeach" Judge Waring. "The object of the Communist Party world wide is to create class hatred and divide the people. If Earl Browder or William Z. Foster had dictated Mrs. Waring's speech before the Negro YMCA, they could not have improved upon it." " 'Decadent' natives of your state," wrote another constituent, "are wondering why you and Senator Johnston are not using . . . forceful methods to" remove Waring. "It is my information," asserted yet another, "that you are responsible for Old Rosey appointing Waring and [I] am wondering just what you intend doing about this."[32]

Maybank's responses essentially followed the line he had used to answer the allegations of his 1948 primary opponents. No, he had not been Waring's initial sponsor; Senator Smith had recommended him long before Maybank went to the Senate. No, he could not initiate impeachment proceedings; only a member of the House of Representatives could do that. No, he had not even seen Waring "since 1945" (or no, he could recall seeing him only once "since 1933"!). When the Charleston *Evening Post* indicated editorially that the judge had been active in Maybank's first Senate race, however, the senator wrote publisher Edward Manigault a more elaborate rejoinder. Waring, Maybank conceded, had served as Charleston corporation counsel during his tenure as mayor. "In fact, I gave him the position in 1931 upon the request of his old friends (our people) who told me he was hard up and that his law firm had but little business." Waring had also assisted with Maybank's gubernatorial bid, the senator conceded. But, he insisted, "Judge Waring did not support me for the Senate." During that race, Maybank reminded Manigault, Charleston's mayor had opposed Maybank and Waring had told a Maybank campaign manager that "he could not do anything because he depended upon the Mayor and the City administration for his job as City Attorney. These are the cold hard facts." "Of course," the senator added,

> I have not seen Waring in years and no one knows better than you and I the real reason for his change. Personally I believe . . . that he is crazy and should be in an institution. As far as I am concerned, he will go to [blank space] before he ever gets promoted, which is his ambition.[33]

Manigault soon responded, thanking Maybank for alerting him to the *Post*'s "slight misstatement" of fact and promising to update the paper's files. Manigault also relieved himself of his own frustrations regarding the Warings. "It seems amazing," he wrote, "that even the most ignorant and downtrodden should put any faith in the mouthings of a traitorous polecat, but then they have been given the force of the law in the unfortunate circumstances that have come to pass." But the publisher was not without humor. He and a mutual friend, he reported, had recently selected a "city senatorial headquarters residence" for South Carolina's senior senator—"on Meeting Street, below Broad, and you may have the information on application. . . . Please give my best to your guardian Mary Cecil Maybank," Manigault closed. "[C]ome home when you can and let us arrange a turkey hunt on Mr. Cuthbert's preserve."[34]

Not all South Carolina whites were content merely with writing letters. A petition demanding the judge's impeachment began circulating throughout the state, attracting thousands of signatures from "white, adult, voting citizens of South Carolina." The petition charged that Judge Waring "openly, through his wife, [had] advocated both dissension and revolution on the part of the negro citizens against white citizens." Waring's failure to repudiate his wife's "Un-American harangues," the petition continued, had made him "unfit for judicial service, particularly in the event a Court trial must be had between a person of the white race against one of the negro race."[35]

The Warings dismissed the petition as the work of the Klan. In a prepared press release, Judge Waring asserted:

> I understand that the petition attacks my fitness as a Judge because I do not believe in white supremacy. I welcome that explanation. I think that any Judge or other Federal or State official who attempts to pass upon the rights of American Citizens blinded by color prejudice is an unfit public servant. The fact that petitions are being circulated in Colleton County . . . fit unerringly with the two Cross Burnings this weekend in the same area. I welcome the comparison between these views of mine and those of the Pro-Slavery or White Supremacy groups as voiced by their spokesmen of the Ku Klux Klan. The more light shed on this campaign of prejudice, the better.

As a beneficiary of white backlash to President Truman's civil rights program, the Supreme Court decisions chipping away at segregation, and Judge Waring's rulings, the Klan was enjoying something of a rebirth in South Carolina. Although copies of the Waring impeachment petition were being widely distributed at Klan rallies, the petition effort had apparently originated with six Aiken County men with no Klan ties. Their spokesman was J. C. Phillips, a retired merchant mariner who had lived in Charleston nearly twenty years before moving to the Aiken area in the central piedmont. Phillips told newsmen that his committee was "a sort of southern association for the advancement of white people," organized to combat "minority group pressures." With rare exceptions, he claimed, those signing the petition had voiced no criticism of Judge Waring's white primary decisions. "What people do object to is what his wife has been saying and saying that she is speaking for him. . . . Both Judge Waring and his former law partner Mr. Brockinton know me," Phillips added, "and know that I have nothing to do with the Klan."[36]

Frank Gilbreth of the *News and Courier* sought to verify Phillips' assertions with Judge Waring's former partner. Off the record, Brockinton informed Gilbreth that he and Waring had known Phillips for years and that, while he did not know whether Phillips had ever been associated with the Klan, he assumed that the retired merchant mariner was no Klansman. Brockinton adamantly refused to make any comment for publication, telling Gilbreth, "I don't want to get in any newspaper controversy about this. I'm a Southerner. I was born a Southerner, and I'll die one." Gilbreth assured Brockinton that he would not be quoted. "In fact," Gilbreth recalled in a memorandum to Tom Waring, "I assured him of this about twenty times."[37]

By mid-February, Phillips' committee had collected several thousand signatures, and Phillips wrote Senator Maybank, asking that he arrange a meeting for the group with South Carolina's congressional delegation. Maybank gave his usual response, citing the constitutional provision giving the House of Representatives "the sole power of Impeachment" and noting that a senator could only sit as a judge in such cases. "I would not wish to make any statement," he added, "that would disqualify me as a senator sitting in the position of a Judge, and I am sure you and my friends would not wish me to do so." Maybank emphasized, however, that if the House impeached Judge Waring, Phillips could "rest assured that I shall use my efforts on behalf of justice."[38]

Members of South Carolina's House delegation did agree to see Phillips and his group, and a meeting was scheduled for early March in Washington. As the date approached, the committee continued to collect signatures. When a Charleston federal civil servant complained to Mendel Rivers that he and other federal employees had been warned that they might lose their jobs if they signed the petition, the Charleston congressman obtained assurances from Washington civil service officials that government workers had a right to add their names. Judge Waring's later public statements seemed to fuel the petition effort. Speaking in late February to an interracial gathering of some 800 persons at a Harlem church, Waring echoed his wife's Charleston speech, calling southern whites "sick mentally, obsessed with the false doctrine of white supremacy." By the time Phillips' group met with Rivers and other state congressmen, over 20,000 signatures had been gathered, nearly 10,000 from Charleston County alone.[39]

However, this impeachment effort met the fate of earlier ones. An impeachment resolution was prepared, and the South Carolina House approved a $10,000 appropriation to finance an initial investigation. But delegates to the NAACP's southeastern regional conference, meeting in Chattanooga, condemned the "trumped up" allegations against Judge Waring, charging that the effort was "aiding and abetting the enemies of democracy and embarrassing our United Nations delegation before the eyes of the world." Nor were civil rights activists the only critics. Spending $10,000 of the state's money on such an enterprise, the *News and Courier* asserted, "would expose [the] general assembly . . . as composed of a majority of silly creatures. Why make South Carolina ridiculous?" Waring was unfit for office; his courses "disgust[ed]" the paper. But he had committed no impeachable offense. Other state papers generally shared the *Courier's* sentiments. A number of South Carolina congressmen were equally dubious. "I do not think," one warned, that "anybody should go off half cocked." We don't have the evidence against him," a news source in another congressman's office confided to a reporter.

> We certainly can't impeach him for making pro-negro speeches. If we tried to base it on a white supremacy issue, we couldn't muster a handful of votes. We certainly could not succeed if we based it on any court decisions because they're matters for the Supreme Court to correct, if it finds them wrong, and not matters for impeachment proceedings.

The impeachment movement eventually fizzled.[40]

The impeachment threat clearly did not inhibit the Warings or groups bestowing honors on their work in behalf of civil rights. Judge Waring dismissed the effort as "silly." During their New York stay and after their return to Charleston, moreover, they made individual and joint appearances on numerous platforms, espousing the same themes. At an integrated dinner at Washington's Willard Hotel in mid-March, the American Council on Civil Rights, an association of black fraternities, presented them with citations of merit, and Judge Waring told his audience that racial conditions in the nation's capital were "disgraceful . . . even worse . . . than in my part of the country" where "[a]t least . . . a good many of the people don't know any better." At the same gathering, Mrs. Waring told blacks, "Let's all be one. My Negro friends are my best friends; only I don't think of them as Negroes. Will you all help by not calling me white?" Speaking to members of the Foreign Press Association, Judge Waring decried the "insanity" of racial discrimination, attacked southern gradualists, and assured his listeners that South Carolina had "not yet rejoined the Union." In early April, the couple spoke at a meeting of the Richmond Committee for Civil Rights, telling their Virginia audience that southern "hatred of the Negro is an obsession" requiring "shock treatment," that "force, not gradualism, [was] the only way to gain rights for the Negroes of the South," and that the "white supremacist" South was "like Russia," adding, "We do not hate southerners. We just feel very, very sorry for them." At meetings sponsored by the National Lawyers Guild in Washington and Chicago, Judge Waring again urged force, "Not necessarily by bayonets and machine guns," he told his audiences, "but of every court, the Federal Government, the executive power of the President, the force of law enforcement authorities, and the collective force of all right thinking people."[41]

Opposition to such political rhetoric by a sitting judge was not limited to Deep South whites. The Lawyers Guild had mailed all District of Columbia judges invitations to the Washington affair honoring the Warings. None attended. Most had "legitimate" excuses, the black press reported. But former Missouri senator Bennett Champ Clark, a judge of the Court of Appeals for the District of Columbia, was reported to have said "that he did not like Judge Waring, did not approve of what he is doing, and . . . did not care to attend the luncheon." In Chicago, no judge attended a luncheon given in the Warings' honor either, and only three jurists, two of those black, attended an evening banquet. Judge Waring took the "snub" good-naturedly, according to the *Afro-American*. "It's much worse back home. Not a single white neighbor, including relatives, or fellow judges, has visited my home in Charleston since the all-white primary was banned."[42]

"Back home" and throughout the Deep South, resentment of the Warings continued to mount. Seeking to correct the "very many misquotations and grossly garbled accounts" of Mrs. Waring's remarks about interracial marriage, Septima Clark wrote the *News and Courier,* quoting pertinent excerpts from the "Meet the Press" interview. A black veterans organization, moreover, ran an advertisement praising the Warings in the *Evening Post.* But most letters to southern editors were highly critical of the couple, and a number of papers questioned the propriety of Judge Waring's involvement in the political arena. The Savannah *News* lamented the difficulty of mounting a successful impeachment campaign, while the *News and Courier* praised "cloistered servants of the law," in which group it obviously did not place Judge Waring, and the Asheville *Citizen* questioned whether Judge Waring's "usefulness to the Federal bench is not at an end." The Warings' assertions that the NAACP was primarily responsible for any recent improvements in conditions for southern blacks, the Asheville editor added, was "an insult to . . . Southerners of both races [who] were working together in understanding long before the quarrelsome NAACP began to gather strength from extremist elements in the South."[43]

At its annual meeting in Columbia, the South Carolina Sheriffs Association adopted a resolution charging Waring and his "northern born wife" with statements "coldly calculated to wreak a vengeance" upon southern whites. Taken to their "logical conclusion," the sheriffs contended, the Warings' "constant carping" would lead to racial violence and "mongrelization." Earlier, this predicted violence had surfaced in another form. On the evening of March 11, while the Warings were still in New York, a small cross, with the initials "KKK" crudely scratched in its base, was burned in front of their Meeting Street home. The Charleston papers described the flimsy construction of the cross, concluding that the incident was the work of youthful pranksters, as did local police. But Judge Waring scoffed at that theory, blaming the Klan and telling reporters that he knew, "from confidential sources, that there are at least 800 Klan members in Charleston alone." In later speeches, moreover, he assured his audiences that "threats of impeachment, Ku Klux Klan cross burnings, being snubbed, or any other type of intimidation will not change my opinion that segregation and discrimination have no place in a true American democracy."[44]

For a time, there was hope that if Waring could not be impeached, he could at least be transferred out of South Carolina. An official of the Administrative Office of the United States Courts quickly dispelled that notion. The judge's transfer, the office's chief personnel officer informed journalists, would require his resignation from his current position and appointment to a vacancy in another state. No senator, she added, would be likely to give up a patronage opportunity just to accommodate South Carolinians. Senator Maybank did urge Justice Department officials to use their influence in attempting to secure additional temporary assignments for Waring. And in a letter to Ben Scott Whaley, the U.S. attorney in Charleston, the senator claimed to have had some success along that line. On March 8, 1950, Maybank wrote Whaley that he had talked to Peyton Ford, a top Justice Department official, that day, "and my information is that they are going to try and keep the Charleston party out of the state as much as possible because of the enormous complaints they are receiving. . . . I would not hesitate to go the limit . . . when he is in the city," Maybank added, somewhat enigmatically. "After all, you are the 'D.A.' and the people are pretty bitter in the Justice Department. You can expect further assignments for him." On several occasions, the senator also mailed Attorney General J. Howard Mc-

Grath accounts of the Warings' speeches. "I am writing you," Maybank informed McGrath in a letter accompanying one collection of clippings sent the senator by constitutents, "because of the many conversations and protests in writing . . . which I have received." The Warings' remarks, he asserted, were "injuring the cause of Justice. . . . Judging by what I hear, Warings' usefulness as a Judge in South Carolina has ended because of his moral life and his conduct."[45]

As in 1948, however, Mendel Rivers would be the official whose public criticism of Judge Waring after Rivers, then took the floor to emphasize that Waring had urged "force" in the cause of civil rights, Rivers charged on the floor of the House of Representatives that the judge's advocacy "of force against the Government" by "a minority group to obtain its objectives" constituted an impeachable offense. Waring, the Charleston congressman exclaimed, was nothing but a "hypocrite," pretending to advance the cause of civil rights, while actually seeking revenge against the society that had ostracized him and "his wife who runs along with him. . . . His bitterness [had] driven him to the point of seeking martyrdom and a sort of self-imposed crucifixion," said Rivers. More importantly, it had pushed him into the position of "soiling the robes of his office and the dignity of the Federal bench." Rivers did not object, he claimed, to "Waring, the man," expressing his views,

> but the habit of J. Waties Waring, the United States judge, in speaking his mind off the bench and in an incendiary manner is a habit which can and will destroy the faith of the people in the integrity of the United States courts if it is allowed to continue unimpeded.[46]

Joseph Bryson, the South Carolina congressman most outspoken in his criticism of Judge Waring after Rivers, then took the floor to emphasize that South Carolina blacks had voted in the 1948 primary, as Waring had ordered, "without a single act of violence or without suppression or intimidation." "Absolutely," Rivers interrupted. "We have no trouble with them. Of course, they have a right to vote and they are going to vote, but who on earth wants to go out here and tell the people to use force?" Mississippi's John Rankin also joined the attack, advising his colleagues, "I think you are slow about one thing in South Carolina. I am convinced, and have been convinced for some time, that Judge Waring is crazy. They ought to put him in a mental institution and get some sane judge appointed in his place." And on it went.[47]

In a widely quoted press release, Judge Waring dismissed Rivers' latest attack, like those of 1948, as "silly, childish ravings," adding:

> That he, representing the sabotaging, filibustering minority group of white supremacist Dixiecrats, should accuse me of advocating force for a minority Negro group against the government is a malicious lie. I urged that the United States Government enact laws and use the force of laws to protect this Negro minority and save it from oppression by the Southern White Supremacists who deny minorities the equal protection of the law under the Constitution of the United States.

While the Warings' prestige diminished at home, it rose nationally, and they garnered much favorable publicity. The impeachment effort failed, and the Warings continued to amass recognition from civil rights organizations. A Philadelphia group before whom Mrs. Waring spoke pledged $1,000 for Judge Waring's defense in the event of impeachment proceedings. The black press ran lengthy, glowing profiles. In March, for example, the *Chicago Defender* published a two-part article on the "South's Most Courageous Couple." Nor was such publicity limited to black papers. With the Warings' encouragement, Marion Wright had visited Charleston, interviewed the couple, and wrote a tribute to their work and treatment accorded them by the judge's family and former friends. Wright was unable to place his piece with a publisher. During their New York stay, however, Ted Poston, the only black reporter with the *New York Post,* interviewed the Warings and wrote a highly sympathetic profile for his paper. In mid-April, a generally flattering Associated Press profile ran in numerous national papers. "Nobody likes Judge Waring or his missus," the article's author, Sam Sumerlin, reported that one "country storekeeper" had "snorted." "Judge Waring," a bartender had "grimaced." "He's the guy that let the nigger vote."[48]

Outside the black press, however, the most flattering and widely read account of the Warings and the controversy swirling about them was in *Collier's.* In the recent past, writer Samuel Grafton had profiled other civil rights figures for the magazine. In late April, his "Lonesomest Man in Town" appeared. Grafton discussed the bemusement of Charlestonians at the change in their native son's behavior ("Something come over him," one "well-regarded" Charleston attorney was quoted as remarking). He also gave play to their assertions that the couple were now bent on revenge. But Grafton questioned the motives underlying such theories, asserting:

> To shrink this down into a story of a cold man and a divorce is, in an odd way, to make it more socially acceptable. For if Charlestonians were to concede that the judge suffered a sincere revulsion of feeling, they would imply that portents of impending social change have popped up in the heart of their society. By comparison, when they try to reduce it all to a mere social scandal, it is more acceptable.[49]

The balance of the profile was equally sympathetic to the Warings. A loud knock at the Warings' door during Grafton's visit—"Now a white man has knocked on your door at last, you blank-loving blank of a blank"—was recounted, as were offensive phone calls and other abuses and Elizabeth Waring's stock question for all callers—"Is this a nice call?" So, too, were the Warings' version of changes in his racial attitudes, his civil rights decisions, and a dinner party given for Grafton and the Warings' black friends. Accompanying the article, moreover, were numerous photographs, several in color, including one picturing the Warings seated at dinner with Ruby Cornwell, Septima Clark, and other black guests. "It is an unpleasant situation to be in, to stand alone in a community," Grafton quoted Judge Waring remarking.

> But after experiencing it . . . I feel that it is the happiest position I could
> be in. . . . My opponents are the most unhappy people you can find.
> They're all torn apart inside. They try to make you believe that things that
> are not all right are fine, and they sweat as they search for the words to do
> it with. I don't have to engage in those mental acrobatics. I'm almost sev-
> enty, and I've got a cause to live for and a job to do. That's pretty good.
> What can they do to me at seventy that would matter.

When Grafton left the Warings' home, he reported, he had "turned away
with a confused, unexpected feeling that the lonesomest man in town might
very probably also be the happiest."[50]

As on earlier occasions, the Warings received a large number of congratulatory letters in the wake of the Grafton profile. But the Charleston *Evening Post* labeled Grafton another of the "myth-makers," contributing "his
share of bunk" to the portrait of Judge Waring "as a knight in shining armor."
The article also generated a new round of hate mail for the Warings. Was
Mrs. Waring, one anonymous writer asked, "not of the unfortunate mixed
blood." "This is wonderful," a signed note read. "May you remain lonesome
all your life. . . . My wish is that you may not have another guest except
a negro and that no one except negroes ever associate with you." Another
anonymous writer interpreted scripture for the couple, telling them that blacks
"should be a servant all their lives [since] God put the mark on them." A
Texas oil company executive assured Judge Waring that he liked "the Negro
as a human being" but would not have one in his home. "[Y]ou and your
Negro loving wife," he suggested, should "get out of the South."[51]

Tom Waring was also incensed by Grafton's article and by the favorable—
and, in his view, distorted—press publicity his uncle and Elizabeth were attracting. "An especially irritating detail, though a minor one," he wrote another Waring critic shortly after the *Collier's* piece appeared,

> was the quotation of our people as saying, "Something come over him".
> Though no Bostonians, we are not all hicks and this happens not to be a
> local manner of speech. It is something the author . . . brought with him,
> along with his other convictions.

Judge Waring's nephew also "especially" did not agree that his uncle was
the happiest man in Charleston. He hoped that another magazine could be
persuaded "to tell the full and true story," but doubted "whether an editor
of a nationally circulated publication will have the courage to print it. The
Fair Deal version is apparently too popular to buck at the moment."[52]

Tom Waring's reference to an article revealing the "full and true story"
was not merely wishful thinking. On February 1, while Samuel Grafton was
in Charleston interviewing the Warings, he had visited the judge's nephew as
part of his research for the article. Tom Waring refused to be interviewed
for quotation but did agree to provide Grafton with background information.
"I then told him frankly," he later wrote in a memorandum, "the facts I
knew and the opinions I had formed, the latter boiling down to a belief that
the matter now was psychiatric in nature . . . [that] the couple had become

warped with spite." Waring described their marital backgrounds and the attitudes of the community, and he suggested that Grafton ask the couple
"whether Mrs. Waring's [YWCA] speech, which was admittedly made to
shock the public, was intended to provoke civil commotion, specifically riots
and bloodshed."[53]

Concerned about the story Grafton might develop and about the other,
generally favorable, publicity being given the Warings in the national press,
Tom Waring soon approached Ashley Halsey, Jr., a Charleston native on the
staff of the *Saturday Evening Post,* and urged Halsey to write an article on
the Warings. Halsey agreed, and in succeeding weeks he and Tom Waring
corresponded regularly, with Waring providing information about his uncle's
divorce and remarriage, Elizabeth Waring's background and personality, the
property settlement following the judge's divorce, and other details. In an
April 20 letter, Halsey reported that he had completed fifteen manuscript
pages, including a description of the kiss Mrs. Waring had bestowed on a
black woman following the YWCA speech. He was using, he added, "the
colored editor's account of the 'resounding smack on the cheek' episode,
which goes better quoted than in any words I can find." Halsey also reported,
however, that the *Post* apparently would "pass up the subject at least for the
present. Even though the Grafton piece cries out for rectification, my version,
if published soon, might sound like a case of sour-grapes writing on a subject
which a competitor published first."[54]

Halsey continued to work on a manuscript after the *Collier's* article appeared. In early May, he wrote Tom Waring that he planned "to show the
lady in the case as an adventuress who pretty much took over the judge for
her own." Recently, he reported, he had received two letters from Wilson
Mills, Elizabeth Waring's first husband, which "help to build up the case considerably." Elizabeth's daughter, he added, was "only thirteen when this
'model mother' departed to take up with Hoffman." A linguistics expert, he
also noted, had agreed that no native Charlestonian would have used the
phrase, "Something come over him."[55]

Tom Waring encouraged the project, noting at one point that he thought
that adequate details about the judge's property settlement could be obtained
"even if Annie is non compos." The *Courier* editor also provided Halsey
with whatever negative gossip about the Warings he could acquire. Elizabeth,
he reported on one occasion, had ordered a devoted secretary to ride a separate hotel elevator when she traveled with the Warings through the district.
Soon thereafter, the same secretary was fired, even though she denied the
judge's claim that she had "been talking about his affairs." Halsey's manuscript, however, was never published. Nor were efforts of Tom Stoney and
other Charlestonians who apparently considered such projects at various
points during the Warings' years in Charleston.[56]

After their return to Charleston in April, the Warings renewed acquaintances with their growing circle of black friends. In May, Dr. and Mrs. Montgomery P. Kennedy of Beaufort honored them with a reception attended by
about two hundred blacks and several whites. On their return to Charleston

from Beaufort, they stopped briefly at a rural church, where they were greeted by a large group of blacks. "When the negro community heard the Warings were to be feted there," the *News and Courier* reported, "many brought donations ranging from chickens to flowers to assure the success of the occasion."[57]

The Warings had refused, however, to take an active role in a black political effort pushed primarily by *Lighthouse and Informer* editor John McCray. The previous summer, South Carolina Truman loyalist Maxie Collins, whom Mrs. Waring was to include among the "better element" of southern whites during her "Meet the Press" interview, had hinted at a 1950 Senate race against incumbent Olin Johnston. In late January, John McCray had invited the Warings to speak at a Columbia rally. McCray assured them that the event would be nonpartisan, but the Warings suspected an attempt to promote Collins' political aspirations, and especially after Collins' attempt to distance himself from Mrs. Waring following her "Meet the Press" appearance, they wanted no part of such efforts. In March, McCray wrote Mrs. Waring, indicating that Collins now "admits that he had spoken prematurely" and that Mrs. Waring had done "a most excellent job" during the interview. It was "encouraging to know," Judge Waring soon responded, that Collins was making "some progress along racial lines." He insisted, however, that he and his wife would play no role in the upcoming rally. "Mr. Collins," he added,

> would perhaps like to come the whole way, but he is definitely in the political arena and is afraid to stand on principle alone and must follow, to an extent, expediency. It is probably good policy for you to continue to play along with him and his group because they represent a fair advance over the Thurmond-Byrnes group.
>
> However, I would like it very distinctly understood that neither Mrs. Waring or myself are to be, in any way, involved in the political campaign which will soon be entered upon. And for that reason, neither one of us would like to appear at any meeting or rally in Columbia. Whether or not Mr. Collins will be present, it could only be construed from a political angle and we do not wish to be so associated. I am writing this so that our views and position will be crystal clear to you.[58]

Charleston NAACP head Arthur Clement ran a token race against Mendel Rivers in the 1950 Democratic primary, but Maxie Collins chose not to challenge Senator Johnston. As a result, Johnston faced Strom Thurmond in the general election. And in spite of themselves, the Warings become involved in the campaign—as political issues. Repeatedly while campaigning, Governor Thurmond accused Judge Waring of "insulting the people of South Carolina, abusing his office, and demonstrating his unfitness to be a judge." Chiding Johnston for not using his position in the Senate to speak out against "the conduct of the Warings," Thurmond promised that, if elected, he would introduce legislation making it "possible for the people of a state to secure relief from a federal judge who destroys his usefulness on the bench by abus-

ing people over whom he is supposed to preside and by his personal conduct."
The Warings had confided to their black friends that they considered Johnston—who had dominated South Carolina's efforts to preserve the white primary but retained at least nominal ties to the national Democratic party—the
lesser evil in the race. Perhaps privy to such information, Thurmond began
telling his audiences that he thought the Warings were supporting his opponent. Johnston assured voters, on the other hand, that he would do his
"utmost" to get action if Waring's impeachment reached the Senate. He also
engaged in a bit of time-honored race-baiting, telling whites that Thurmond
had appointed a "nigger physician . . . to displace your beloved white physician" on a state medical board, and shouting, when blacks in his audience
objected to his language, "Make those niggers keep quiet!" In the end, Johnston won with 178,000 votes to Thurmond's 154,000. There was "little
doubt," the *News and Courier,* which backed Thurmond, lamented, that most
of the black vote had gone to Johnston, who was closer to the Truman Fair
Deal than Thurmond, "regardless of his epithets."[59]

In the late summer, the Warings left Charleston again, bound for New
York and California. While in California, Judge Waring gave a well-publicized address to San Francisco's Council for Civic Unity, and the couple
spoke before other audiences as well, condemning southern decadence and
preaching racial reform. Judge Waring also held a term of court in San
Francisco, and the circumstances of one criminal prosecution tried before
him quickly aroused his reformer's zeal.

The case in question involved San Francisco attorney Arthur Zamloch,
whose clients included a major West Coast narcotics dealer. Zamloch had
paid hush money to a woman with ties to his client. A jury found him guilty
of conspiracy and bribery, and Judge Waring sentenced him to three years in
prison on the conspiracy charge, two on the bribery count. During the trial,
Waring, like Charles O'Gara, the young government attorney assisting with
Zamloch's prosecution, had become convinced that Zamloch was involved in
a complex web of criminal activities that might reach even into the San Francisco office of the Justice Department's tax division. At Zamloch's sentencing,
Waring praised the prosecution and repudiated as "lower than the criminal"
the lawyer who "prostitutes his skill and dips his hand into ill-gotten gains."
He also asserted that "some of the matters that were aired in this trial . . .
cry aloud for [further] scrutiny and investigation" by the proper authorities.[60]

Judge Waring's term of court was ending that day, and he conceded to
those present for Zamloch's sentencing that his remarks were only suggestions. After the Warings left San Francisco, however, O'Gara and the foreman of the grand jury pursued the case vigorously, ultimately securing additional indictments but also precipitating frequent clashes with the judges of
California's northern district as well as with O'Gara's Justice Department
superiors. While persisting in their efforts, O'Gara and grand jury members
corresponded regularly with Judge Waring, alerting him to new developments
and seeking his advice. "Had it not been for truly American persons like

yourself," a grand juror wrote Waring at one point, "I would have thrown up my hands in disgust and dispair . . . a long time ago. The sense of frustration has been suffocating."[61]

Under Seige

When the Warings returned to Charleston in late September, they found South Carolina embroiled in a crime wave of its own. Ku Klux Klan rallies had become increasingly frequent over the past year; in May, in fact, a Klan motorcade had driven through Charleston for the first time since the 1920s, crossing every major road in the city's black section. At one point, Klansmen had chased an *Evening Post* photographer, but there had been no violence. "Negroes watched . . . silently," the *Post* reported, "but seemed to have no fear." Elsewhere, however, violence had erupted. On August 26, 1950, robed Klansmen clashed with blacks in a black neighborhood of Myrtle Beach. Three hundred shots were fired; when the violence subsided, a Conway policeman, wearing a Klan robe, lay dead. Horry County sheriff C. E. Sasser brought criminal charges against Thomas L. Hamilton, grand dragon of the Association of the Carolina Klans, and four other Klansmen, but a grand jury refused to indict. The beating of three white women in Florence was also attributed to the Klan, as were numerous other acts of violence. Nor were incidents of violence confined to the Klan. In Summerville, a sleepy village a few miles from Charleston, police lieutenant James Adams pumped five bullets into Moses Winn, a black scheduled to testify before a federal grand jury investigating charges of police brutality. The incident had occurred at Winn's home at 2:30 A.M. Winn's wife and daughter were in the yard of the house when the shooting started, and there were no other witnesses. Police investigators said that an unshot pistol was found under a couch in the room where Winn was killed. Adams told a coroner's jury that he had gone to Winn's home to serve a bad check warrant and went at an unusual hour because he had been unable to locate Winn at other times. The coroner's jury decided that Adams had acted in the line of duty.[62]

Following Mrs. Waring's speech to the YWCA, the Warings had become convinced that they, too, were Klan targets. When they first began to receive threatening phone calls and letters following the speech, they had informed Walter White. White had telephoned the FBI in Washington, and bureau director J. Edgar Hoover ordered the FBI's Savannah regional office to make a full investigation. Agents from the Savannah office made several visits to the Warings' home, collecting letters that appeared to contain threats, providing the couple with the telephone numbers of resident agents, and listening to the Warings' assessments of the situation. During one such encounter, Mrs. Waring told the agents that she was "expecting and hoping to raise trouble and that she had in fact expected a possible riot" in the wake of her speech. According to the agents' account, she also said that she intended to make other "inflammatory speeches" and that "the best thing that could happen [for the cause of civil rights] would be for someone to kill her and her husband." She was, she said, "doing everything she could to bring the issue to a head." Both she and Judge Waring told the agents, moreover, that a "series of explosive events" would advance the black cause.[63]

The agents' other contacts with the Warings proved equally provocative. After examining several hate letters that the Warings had given them, the agents decided that they did not appear to constitute violations of the federal extortion statute and turned them over to the local postmaster. When Mrs. Waring learned of this, she charged that the postmaster himself was a Klansman and demanded that the letters be returned. Later, she conceded that she had no evidence that Charleston's postmaster was connected with the Klan, but she and Judge Waring insisted that the city was "controlled" by the group. When the agents offered to have Ben Scott Whaley examine the letters, Judge Waring "indicated his scorn" for the U.S. attorney. When Whaley learned that the Warings had received threatening calls and letters and offered his assistance, Judge Waring had refused to respond except, according to an FBI report, to "grunt."

Shortly after midnight on January 21, however, a "slightly hysterical" Mrs. Waring had telephoned the FBI to report that someone had "jammed" their telephone—a prelude, she feared, to a Klan attack. Judge Waring had then taken over the phone to ask that the telephone company be advised of the problem. The manager of the telephone company was contacted. At 1:10 A.M., Mrs. Waring again telephoned an agent, complaining that the "torture" was continuing. Soon thereafter, the telephone company arranged a second, unlisted number, allowing the Warings to disconnect their listed number at night. But the Warings continued to complain of harassment and charged that the Klan was responsible for the petition demanding Judge Waring's impeachment. At one point, Mrs. Waring told agents in her husband's presence that he was "terribly hurt" that the government "did not think sufficiently highly" of federal judges to provide protection. But neither requested protection, and the FBI agents told them that the Bureau was not authorized to provide a guard.

The Warings' concerns about their safety were apparently sincere. In the ensuing months, they frequently shared their fears with friends, including Ted Poston of the *New York Post*. When they returned to Charleston after the spring court session in New York, Waring wrote Poston a lengthy letter, detailing the "tense" racial situation in South Carolina, Klan activities, the "prevalence" of the Klan "spirit," and the "prejudice" of the Charleston newspapers. "Since we are practically alone, so far as public officials or law enforcement officers are concerned," he observed, "there would be no one on whom to call in the event of an emergency."

> In the event of any trouble arising here, it would be practically impossible to get a true report of the same to the outside world through these [local] sources and any report that was sent would be colored by local prejudice. To be more specific, if harm should come to either of us here, it would almost surely be reported out of Charleston as accidental or perhaps even self-inflicted, and so it seems to me advisable to write you this letter which

you may keep as a permanent record to say that if any injury or death should come to either Mrs. Waring or myself, it would be more than important for those of you who believe in reporting true events to send unprejudiced investigators *immediately* into this locality. Let me assure you that both of us are quite careful in the conduct of our daily lives and that no accidental injury is going to occur if it can be possibly avoided, and if anything does occur, you may rest assured it was caused by intentional attacks. We have often heard reports from similar situations in Germany and in Russia of the purging or disappearance of those whom the oppressors wish to get rid of, that it is a well-known method. Let me assure you that the White Supremacists of South Carolina are not inferior in intent or ingenuity to the Nazis or Soviets.

Waring conceded that his concerns were "wholly or largely speculative. . . . If all goes well, this letter need never come to light, and in fact, it is written to you confidentially. It is suggested, however, that it be sealed and placed in a safe situation where it may be available whenever thought necessary."[64]

Poston soon replied, assuring Judge Waring "that the matter has been disposed of in the manner you suggested." *Post* editor James Weschler, he reported, had promised his "full cooperation in this and all related matters" and was "furious to think that such a situation could even be possible in our country." Poston also thanked Mrs. Waring for clippings from the Charleston papers and asked that she send more for a special file the *Post* had established. "Neither of you will ever know," he added, "what it meant to [Mrs. Poston] and me to meet and know such persons as you two."[65]

During the days following their return to Charleston from California and New York in September, the Warings would later claim, they had again begun to receive annoying telephone calls, Mrs. Waring was jostled on the street by groups of men, and youths taunted her with cries of "witch." While in New York, the Warings had attended a meeting with Eleanor Roosevelt, Nelson Rockefeller, and other civil rights activists and public officials, including Peyton Ford of the Justice Department, at the home of the Walter Whites. On Friday, October 6, Judge Waring wrote White regarding the minutes of that meeting. The meeting had covered a variety of international and national concerns, "too much territory," in Waring's judgment, and he so informed White, adding that "the great problem" facing the country was to convince people of the world

and particularly the Asiatics and others of the dark-skinned race, that the brand of democracy that we are offering is worth having. . . . To my way of thinking, the way to [do] that is not to tell bigger and better lies than the Russians but to do something to cure the evil at home.[66]

Waring's letter made no mention of Klan harassment. Later that day, however, the judge, Elizabeth, or both, may have spoken with White by phone. For the NAACP secretary sent President Truman and Attorney General McGrath a wire that day, which read in part:

We have just been informed by a completely reliable person that attempts to molest Federal Judge J. Waties Waring and his wife may be made in

Charleston, South Carolina, this weekend. We are informed that situation is very tense with crowds milling around streets and that additional crowds are expected to come into Charleston from other parts of South Carolina during [the] weekend. . . . We urge that all necessary and proper precautions be taken to prevent what may be a tragedy both for the Warings and the prestige of America throughout world at this grave period.

When alerted to the situation by Washington authorities, agents of the Savannah FBI office telephoned Charleston agents. The agents there said that Waring had given them no specific information regarding any threats and had requested no protection. The Charleston agents suggested that members of the Savannah office contact Judge Waring directly. Two Savannah agents then went to 61 Meeting Street for an interview. According to their later report, Judge Waring told them that he received threats by telephone and threats on the streets daily, but would furnish no details, saying that such information had been given agents in the past and that no action had been taken. Mrs. Waring told of being jostled by men on the Charleston streets. She also complained that U.S. District Judge Harold Medina and his wife had been provided protection during a recent controversial trial of Communist leaders in New York, and wondered why she and her husband had not been afforded similar assistance. The Warings, the agents would later report, then "entered into a harangue against the Administration and McGrath," and complained of the FBI's failure to deal with Klan violence in the state. It would take, Mrs. Waring had speculated, a "good lynching" or the death of a "prominent white person" to get the "G__ D__ Department to send some good men into South Carolina." Both, according to the agents, said that they "would be willing martyrs for such a cause." Judge Waring claimed that a Klansman had visited his home bearing a copy of the petition demanding his impeachment.

The balance of the weekend was uneventful. In court on Monday, October 9, Judge Waring criticized members of the Alcohol Tax Unit for "adopting" cases from local police for prosecution in federal court. It was time, he said, that local authorities became aware of their own obligations to enforce the law. If the state continued to ask the United States to prosecute its cases, he warned, they soon might find themselves "asking the Federal Government to take over Summerville and Myrtle Beach." He also administered a "tongue-lashing" to a defendant convicted for federal game law violations. Either that afternoon or the previous day, moreover, he had chastised several youths who made insulting remarks to his wife, shouting, "You nasty little wretches! Why don't you go home and have your mother to change your diapers and put clean diapers on your mouths."

That evening, the Warings were at home alone, playing canasta in their living room. The living room windows of the converted carriage house were positioned high off the floor, providing light but no visibility from the house, or to passersby. Suddenly, they heard two or three loud reports which sounded like gunshots, and then they were showered with glass fragments. Crouching near the floor, they rushed into the dining room and telephoned the local FBI, city police, and Judge Waring's bailiff John Fleming. The FBI office was closed for the evening, but Fleming soon arrived and reached the individual agents at home. Herman Berkman, Charleston chief of detectives, also soon arrived.[67]

As Berkman was walking into the Waring's house, he picked up a rock lying on the walk. "See," he said, "it's really nothing but a brick. There's nothing to it." At that point, Mrs. Waring angrily ordered the local police off the property. As they were leaving, four local FBI agents, led by Wilmer Thompson, chief of the Charleston office, arrived. It was then 9:14 P.M. The agents' search revealed that a large object, probably the size of half a brick, had hit the front screen door, puncturing a hole in the screen and damaging the interior door, and that a second object, about the size of an egg, had broken a living room window pane. Two fairly large pieces of mortar were found in the street in front of the house. In the living room, under a sofa, the agents found another, smaller piece of mortar. They found no evidence of gunfire. They suggested that the house had been stoned; Judge Waring, they would later report, appeared to accept their theory. But Mrs. Waring insisted that a machine gun had been fired at the house. While the agents made their search, she phoned Walter White in New York. Before the agents left, she and Judge Waring also phoned the Charlotte office of the Associated Press, a Charleston radio announcer, and other news agencies. Judge Waring told the agents that he was glad the incident had occurred, that now the "outside world" would know what was going on in South Carolina. Mrs. Waring said that "she thought this excitement was 'heavenly' and that while she feared death by fire or water, she would welcome bullets."[68]

The night of the incident, Judge Waring told reporters, "You can expect this sort of thing in South Carolina. It's a state dominated by the Klan—a crime-committing Klan that goes unpunished." The following day, he released a prepared statement. In a note to her husband, Mrs. Waring had offered her assistance. "What do you think of ending your statement to the press with an offensive and strong attack? Here is my suggestion: 'As I represent the United States government in South Carolina, this is just another attack upon the Union by the "white supremacists" of South Carolina.'" Waring's own statement called the incident "an attack upon the union which I represent," as well as "evidence of the stubborn, savage sentiment of this community in fighting the American creed." He also condemned the Dixiecrat movement as "the dying gasp of white supremacy and slavocracy" and vowed to continue his "fight for freedom and democracy."[69]

Judge Waring had appeared "frightened" to FBI agents who visited his home the night of the incident. But he again refused to request the government's protection; when a Charlotte AP reporter asked him whether the assault might force him to change his residence, he "exploded." "Certainly not. My wife and I are staying right here. You can bet on that." He persisted in refusing protection. At 2:00 in the afternoon following the incident, however, the U.S. marshal's office established an around-the-clock guard, with the guards working in pairs on four-hour shifts. When he was at home, the guards sat in an automobile parked in front of his house or stood near his front door.

When he walked to the office, a guard strolled behind him, then took his seat outside the judge's chambers, since Waring would not allow him inside his office. When the Warings went driving, the guards followed.[70]

In its October 11 issue, however, the *News and Courier* reported that "local and federal officials [had] washed their hands of the incident." Noting that only "two small pieces of mortar" had been found, the paper cited a "Savannah FBI spokesman" in reporting that agents had checked the Waring's home and found no federal violation. "We are not doing anything," the spokesman was quoted as remarking, "and at the present time don't plan to do anything." While condemning the "molestation" as "inexcusable and harmful to South Carolina's reputation for law and order," and asserting that the Warings should be given protection, the *Courier* also speculated that the incident had been the work of "misguided pranksters" and dismissed as "farfetched" the Warings' claim that the Klan was responsible.[71]

Angered by the *Courier*'s prankster theory and the statements attributed to the FBI, Judge Waring wrote the Charleston FBI office a letter demanding return of the evidence taken in the agents' search of his home. He sent John Fleming to deliver the letter and retrieve the evidence. "I reported to you," the letter read in part,

> that I heard what I am sure were two or perhaps three sounds of shots, and missiles were hurled against the front of the residence: one which slashed through the wire screen front door nicking the woodwork of the solid front door; one making some bruises on the woodwork near the front door; and another breaking one of the front windows. Your attention was also called to breaks and abrasions running at some length along the side of a mason pillar immediately adjoining the residence.

The agents had removed from the house, he asserted, "a sizeable piece of concrete" that "a member of the Charleston Police Department had said that he picked up off the sidewalk in front of my house," a "very large part of a brick" found outside the house, "a smaller piece of brick" found inside the house, and glass "sweepings." He wanted this evidence returned, he wrote, so that he could contradict the "entirely false" reports of local papers, and because he understood that the FBI was no "longer interested in the incident." Noting that a congressional investigation or inquiry "through private agencies" was "quite likely," he added that he considered it important that the Department of Justice be "relieved of any evidence which may be perhaps used in connection with any investigation wherein it may be a party that is being investigated rather than an investigator." Waring sent copies of the letter to Attorney General McGrath, J. Edgar Hoover, and the agent in charge of the Savannah FBI office, as well as a separate similar letter to the Savannah office. He also sent copies and other material to Walter White and President Truman, informing White that he was "at liberty to show any of this to Ted Poston or anybody else"[72]

But Mrs. Waring had already been talking to Ted Poston. When Elizabeth's daughter Ann Hyde had learned of the stoning incident, she had writ-

ten the Warings, remarking that at times she wished that they would leave
Charleston and "all its insults and attacks." In later years, however, she
would recall that she had never been certain how much of her mother's description of their treatment in Charleston had been fact and how much a
reflection of Elizabeth Waring's penchant for drama. The staff of the *New
York Post* apparently entertained no such qualms. In their accounts of the
stoning incidents, they drew heavily on Mrs. Waring's impressions. "The
stoning of Federal Judge J. Waties Waring's home," the paper reported in its
October 11 issue, "climaxed a week of terror and intimidation during which
Mrs. Waring was jostled on the streets and jeeringly called a 'witch.' " Quoting Mrs. Waring, the *Post* indicated that she "was almost knocked into the
gutter" in one such incident and that "three shots" were fired into the Warings' home. Mrs. Waring had also told the *Post* that she had called Walter
White following the stoning ("If you've lived under what we have been
forced to live under down here since 1947, you'd realize why I wanted some
contact with the outside world—with civilization"), that she had ordered
local police away when they tried to dismiss the assault as a rock-throwing
incident ("We didn't want this covered up, too"), and that Charleston FBI
agent Wilmer Thompson's attitude was similar to that of the Charleston police
("you would have thought that the Judge and I were responsible for what
happened"), though two other agents were "more understanding and thorough" ("they were from Boston"). The *Post* article quoted Judge Waring's
assertion that the Klan was responsible, then concluded with Mrs. Waring's
"one last word for the local hoodlums."

> If they think they can frighten us, they're greatly mistaken. We both believe
> in the dignity and equality of all people and no attacks by race suprema-
> cists—even a fatal one—will ever alter that belief or our determination to
> defend it to the end.[73]

For the *Post*'s next issue, columnist Max Lerner, who had recently met
the Warings, praised "A Judge and His Wife." Lerner was characteristically
provocative:

> In darkest Charleston a drama is being enacted which is one of the most
> arresting in our America. It is the drama of a judge and his wife who are
> keeping a lonely vigil amidst the encircling hostile spears of the city's white
> population.
>   The other day some members of this encircling mob warmed up their
> courage . . . fired three bullet-shots and then sent some bricks and con-
> crete crashing through the windows.
>   Whatever may be true of Southern chivalry, let it not be said that cour-
> age is dead in the hearts of the doughty South Carolinians, who know how
> to defend themselves, their womanhood, and their cherished idols—the in-
> stitution of white supremacy and the precious doctrine of the master race.

The Warings' assailants, wrote Lerner, were "stupid Kluxers and racist
goons"; those who had thrown up "a rigid Iron Curtain around them that no
white dared penetrate" were "Southern Negro-baiting whites, holding the

crumbling citadel of white supremacy." The Warings, on the other hand, were "neither craven victims nor eager martyrs," but "courageous . . . vigorous people with a zest for friendship and conversation and ideas. . . . They may prove expendable," he added, "but in the end their kind will inherit the American earth."[74]

Most of the *Post*'s October 12 treatment of the issue, however, shifted focus from the Warings to the inaction of the FBI and other federal authorities. In an article titled "FBI's Dixie Office Won't Act in Raid on Judge Waring," Ted Poston reported that Savannah regional FBI director Wilson McFarlin had told the paper, "unless something else happens, we are through with the case." Walter White, Poston further observed, had denounced McFarlin's statement as an "open incitement to the Ku Klux Klan and Dixiecrats" and had wired Attorney General McGrath, urging a full investigation. Judge Waring, Poston wrote, had never met McFarlin but "had hoped to hear from him . . . after the cowardly attack on my house." "So far, though," the judge had told Poston, "I have not heard from him." In an editorial entitled "Sleeping G-Men," the paper charged that McFarlin's statement "ought to be interpreted . . . as equivalent to a letter of resignation. . . . Three years ago," the paper recalled for its readers,

> President Truman's Civil Rights Commission found serious evidence that Southern FBI agents frequently wink at the old Southern customs of violating the civil rights statutes. The FBI needs to be reminded once again that it is a unit of the Dept. of Justice, which is an agency of the Federal government.

The *Post*'s staff and "vicious" articles angered J. Edgar Hoover. Ted Poston—identified by one member of the FBI director's staff as "a colored reporter . . . [once] run out of some southern town where he was covering a trial"—was a major irritant. When later *Post* articles relied on unnamed FBI spokesmen, Hoover penned on a Bureau memorandum, "I think it best to accept no calls from Poston so he can't even say he talked to a Bureau representative." Hoover was equally leery of Judge Waring. Charleston agents had given John Fleming the evidence the judge had demanded without seeking a receipt, explaining later that asking for a receipt might "have only inflamed the Judge further." In another penned notation, Hoover called the agents' decision a mistake, adding: "I am not at all concerned about the Judge's sensibilities. His past disregard of truth makes it entirely possible now for him to claim we held out some evidence."

When Attorney General McGrath ordered a thorough investigation of the stoning incident, however, Hoover had Wilson McFarlin pursue the case vigorously, asking him to send the director daily teletypes of his progress. He also sought to make clear that delays in the investigation were the fault of the Department of Justice, not the Bureau. There was probably considerable truth to that assertion. The Warings believed that the Truman administration opposed an investigation that might further offend southern Democrats. No direct evidence apparently exists to support their claim. But when Deputy

Attorney General Peyton Ford informed a Bureau official that the investigation was to be extended, he remarked, according to the Bureau official, that he "did not like to have to go ahead on this case but he could not see any other way out." Whatever the source of the delay, the FBI statement announcing the inquiry to the press was calculated to show "that the delay in making the investigation was occasioned by delays in the Department." The announcement was also timed for initial publication in morning newspapers. "I do not think" a Hoover assistant remarked, that "we should give any aid or comfort to the New York Post," an afternoon paper.

For nearly two weeks after renewal of the investigation was ordered, FBI agents under the direction of Wilson McFarlin collected information, questioning more than a hundred Charlestonians. Those interviewed included the game law violator Judge Waring had admonished in court the day of the incident, several other defendants who had appeared before him, taxi drivers, deliverymen, and other potential sources of information. Recently, however, the general vicinity of the Warings' home had been the target of numerous acts of teenage vandalism and other annoyances, and Judge Waring had told agents the night of the incident that he had chastised several juveniles earlier that day. The agents largely focused their attention, therefore, on neighborhood youths. Judge C. B. Pearce of Charleston's domestic relations court told the officers that the records of his court would be of little help. "Judge Pearce stated," McFarlin would later report, that "his records would not reflect the names of anyone below Broad Street inasmuch as practically all children residing in that section of the city were the sons and daughters of very prominent, wealthy and politically powerful families and as such were not molested by the police but allowed to do much as they pleased unless they became involved in serious crimes." The agents decided, moreover, to question juveniles only with their parents' consent; while many were interrogated, a number of parents, including those of principal suspects, refused to allow their children to be questioned or to respond to potentially incriminating inquiries. When one boy conceded having been with a group of youths who called Mrs. Waring a "witch" and asked her, "Where's your broom?" his father did admonish him not to make such remarks. In the future, he counseled, his son "should merely turn his back on [the Warings]."

Since Judge Waring had mentioned his encounters with Charleston youths, a Hoover assistant instructed McFarlin to reinterview the judge also. But Waring, the teletype stressed, was to be questioned "tactfully" by "two experienced agents" mindful that the judge had claimed that the "stoning was the work of the KKK." On the afternoon of October 17, McFarlin and another agent interviewed Judge Waring. The judge's attitude, McFarlin later reported, was "hostile." He would not describe the people "he alleges are constantly taunting him." He told the agents that he suspected no particular persons other than Charleston's "Klan membership."

Each day that the investigation continued, South Carolina whites grew increasingly resentful. State papers accused the culprits of playing into the Warings' hands. "Judge Waring is not being hurt by this sort of childishness," the Columbia *Record* editorialized. "He even seems to thrive upon it and to enjoy the martyr role in which . . . he has cast himself." The *News and Courier* agreed, calling the vandals the judge's "publicity agents." But the papers devoted most of their attention to lamenting federal interference in a "local" matter, Walter White's "influence" over the Justice Department, and the expense required for the judge's guards. They also challenged the Warings' claim that the Klan was responsible. Several days after the stoning incident, a cross was burned at the home of a black youth who had sought to enroll in South Carolina's all-white medical college. "[E]xcept that cross-burnings have sometimes been associated with the KKK," the *Courier* soon observed in a news article, "there was no indication that the organization was in any way connected with either of the two Charleston incidents of last week." When the city created a no-parking zone in front of 61 Meeting Street to accommodate the guards' automobile, that, too, became an object of press concern.[75]

Letters to newspaper editors echoed such sentiments, at times with a touch of humor. One Charlestonian recommended that two companies of soldiers and a Sherman tank be placed at Judge Waring's immediate disposal, adding: "What are two marshals against the hordes of barbarous and, no doubt, cannibalistic Charlestonians?" A Charleston candidate for alderman sought to turn the investigation to political advantage, writing J. Edgar Hoover and Attorney General McGrath critical letters, and publishing a newspaper advertisement urging parents of children being questioned by the FBI to join him in a protest against the Bureau's conversion into "a gestapo to coerce the South." Yet another Charlestonian, one of the city's few Republicans, wrote the *Courier*, reminding readers that in 1938 the display windows of his store had been shattered repeatedly, and his life threatened, yet Waring, who was then the city's corporation counsel, had "exhibited no interest" in his plight. In fact, Waring had told reporters, when the Illinois native had demanded protection, that "the people of Charleston are tired of being sniped at." Copies of another poem also began to circulate. "It disappoints one in F.B.I.," its last verse read,

> When they frighten kids and make them cry,
> And it simply can't be right.
> It makes one wonder if F.B.I.
> Is what it was in days gone by.
> Are its order from Walter White?[76]

Mendel Rivers soon joined the fray as well. A constituent whose son was called in for questioning had written Rivers, complaining that he had found boys as young as eight at the FBI's office. "I could not help but feel an atmosphere of a foreign country." The constituent could not believe that the FBI "now bows to the demands of a selfish organization, [the] N.A.C.C.P., to investigate throwing of rocks at a citizen's home. This smells like the rule of Hitler or Stalin." Rivers mailed J. Edgar Hoover a copy of the letter, asking for a response. Several days earlier, he had written what the *Evening Post* de-

scribed as a "stinging" letter to Attorney General McGrath, accusing the Justice Department of yielding to NAACP demands and terming the judge "the
most expensive luxury on the federal payroll. . . . It is a peculiar twist of
irony," he added, passionately if inaccurately, "that the man who has run up
and down the landscape of the United States advocating force, now cries for
help when the practical application of his theories is brought to bear on him."
Hoover wrote Rivers and the *Evening Post* letters explaining the legal basis
for the investigation, but the outcry continued.[77]

In an unpublicized, more indirect way, U.S. attorney Ben Scott Whaley
also contributed to the anti-Waring campaign. Judge Waring obviously had a
poor impression of Whaley's work. In 1945, while Whaley was still an assistant U.S. attorney, Judge Waring, according to an FBI report, had vehemently criticized Whaley and other government attorneys for their sloppy
preparation of cases. The agent preparing the report clearly shared the judge's
impression, noting at one point that clerks normally prepared cases and that
the government attorneys knew "very little about any but the most important
matters prior to the time of trial." It is likely that Whaley resented the judge's
remarks, whatever the merits of his complaints.

Over the years, their relations continued to deteriorate. In a 1948 letter,
another FBI agent had reported Waring's off-the-record comment that Whaley
was "too lazy to function properly" as U.S. attorney. More recently, Waring
had instructed his bailiff to tell Whaley's stenographer that she was not to
bring legal papers to the judge's chambers, that Whaley or an assistant government lawyer was to bring them personally. When this same stenographer
later entered the courtroom during a naturalization proceeding, the judge, according to an FBI report, had "entered into a raging tirade," then hailed
Whaley before the court for a reprimand. Waring's attitude toward other
members of Whaley's staff, the report continued, had also grown increasingly
critical. When an assistant government attorney had rested his knee against a
table edge while sitting in the courtroom, for example, Waring's "colored
court crier" had instructed him to put his feet on the floor, indicating that the
lawyer's posture was displeasing to the judge. "[B]ecause of his unpredictable
nature," the agent concluded, "it is difficult to say when some minor act
might send him off into a rampage of criticism." Such reports may not be objective accounts by disinterested parties, but they do reflect the obvious
strains in Judge Waring's relations with Charleston's contingent of Justice
Department lawyers in general, and with Ben Whaley in particular.

Whaley's reaction was thus not surprising when a Justice Department attorney visited Charleston several days after the stoning incident to discuss the
situation with the U.S. attorney and the FBI's resident agents. Whaley took
the occasion to complain of difficulties federal and local officials had encountered in Judge Waring's court. Federal-local cooperation, he contended, was
approaching "a standstill" since local officers did not wish to appear in the
judge's courtroom "to be embarrassed or insulted." Law enforcement, he predicted, "would utterly break down if the situation created by Judge Waring
continued." Charleston FBI agents and J. Edgar Hoover apparently shared

Whaley's impressions. When agents reported the meeting to Hoover, the director sent a memorandum to Attorney General McGrath, summarizing Whaley's remarks and his own concerns at "the grave implications brought about by the conduct of Judge and Mrs. Waring."

Bemused by what they considered gross distortions in national reporting of the stoning incident, Tom Waring and other *News and Courier* staffers undertook a counterattack of sorts, and one going beyond the paper's pages. In responding to queries from other states, assistant editor Frank Gilbreth claimed that "recent exaggerated reports of an attack on the judge's house now seem to have simmered down to two rocks hurled by teen-age youngsters who annoyed various other neighbors, too." In a letter to *New York Post* executive editor Paul Sann, moreover, Gilbreth challenged *Post* versions of the incident, summarized the findings of *Courier* reporters, and took issue with an October 19 *Post* assertion that "a 'full-scale campaign' is under way to 'dismiss' the 'hoodlum attacks' as 'childish pranks.' "

> There is no campaign, full-scale or otherwise, that we know about. The local police think the attack was made by teen-agers. The FBI is questiontioning teen-agers. Many Charlestonians, as we wrote in a news story that you quoted, think it was the crowd of boys that hangs out at [a] drugstore nearby.

Gilbreth believed, he added, that the *Post* "would not deliberately misinform its readers. Neither would we. Perhaps you'd like to straighten things out for your readers, or set us straight so that we can straighten out ours."[78]

Gilbreth's letter had little impact on Sann. The *Post*'s assertion that shots were fired, Sann soon responded, had come from the Warings. "We see no reason to question the word of the Warings," he added. Besides, if shots had been fired into the air, or blank shells used, "then naturally no bullet holes would be in evidence on the structure." Nor did Sann believe that the Warings should be "censured" for ordering local police from their home ("[i]n view of their previous experience . . . when a cross was burned near the house"), or for calling federal officers ("in a case which may well involve a violation of Federal statutes"), or for rebuking juveniles who shouted epithets at Mrs. Waring ("a defense of the honor of his wife"). "As for the theory that teenagers are responsible for the whole thing," Sann concluded,

> it seems to us that it might be in order to look a little deeper. WHY was Judge Waring singled out for attack? Why were no member[s] of the Ku Klux Klan or of the Dixiecrat movement singled out for such treatment at the hands of "teen-agers?" And one might wonder if the action of the teenagers—if indeed any teen-agers were involved in the incident—might possibly have been inspired by the published and spoken opinions of their elders in the community.[79]

Indirectly, and probably without his knowledge, Tom Waring also participated in gubernatorial nominee James F. Byrnes' exchange with a *Post* reporter. Shortly after the stoning of the Warings' home, syndicated columnist Robert S. Allen, the *Post*'s Washington correspondent, had written Byrnes, requesting a statement about "the reported molestation." "Because of my service at the Bar and as a member of the [Supreme] Court," Byrnes refused to comment for publication. But he did write Allen a lengthy letter, advancing the *News and Courier* version of the incident, speculating that "some teenagers out on a lark and possibly taking a drink" were responsible, summarizing the judge's ties to "Cotton Ed" Smith, and recounting details of Judge Waring's divorce and the community resentment it had aroused. "The fact is," Byrnes added, that "before Judge Waring divorced his wife, the women of Charleston had frowned upon the woman who is the present Mrs. Waring."[80]

Later, Byrnes obtained Charleston newspaper tear sheet accounts of the stoning from Tom Waring, along with a letter he had enclosed with the tear sheets. In the letter, Tom Waring had noted national news reports that shots had been fired—accounts contrasting sharply with the findings of the Charleston papers. He also wrote Byrnes that, according to his information, Walter White had telephoned President Truman the evening of the incident. "It looks," he observed, "as though White makes the FBI assignments." Byrnes mailed Robert Allen the tear sheets and Tom Waring's letter. Allen responded that he could "now understand the attitude of the people of Charleston and South Carolina." There was no discernible change, however, in the *Post*'s treatment of the Waring story.[81]

Tom Waring continued to accumulate information relating to his uncle and Elizabeth in an apparent effort to discredit them. The previous winter, he had become concerned that Mrs. Waring's speech to the Charleston YWCA might be a prelude to civil unrest. On the same day that Samuel Grafton had visited his office while conducting research for the *Collier's* profile of Judge Waring, Charleston chief of detectives Herman Berkman had also paid the *Courier* managing editor a visit. Berkman had reported, Waring later noted in a memorandum, that on two occasions since the YWCA speech, blacks had "thrown missiles" at police. Ordinarily, in the past, the detective had added, Charleston had been "quite free from racial disorders of the kind, and most incidents passed off peacefully after a lot of talk."[82]

Like most white Charlestonians, however, Tom Waring considered the stoning of the Warings a minor prank and national press reports a gross exaggeration of the facts. For a time, in fact, he appeared hopeful that the FBI's extensive investigation might be "the reducio ad absurdum" which would provide Ashley Halsey a "peg for 'the other side of the Waring story.' " August Neuse, a crewman on the *Liebenfels,* the German ship that had sunk in the Charleston harbor years before, had settled in Charleston and joined the police force. Neuse was one of the special deputies retained to guard the Warings. On his way home from the office each evening, Tom Waring frequently stopped to chat with the detective in front of his uncle's house. Charleston FBI chief Wilmer Thompson, who had married one of Waring's cousins, was another source of information, as were *Courier* reporters. On October 17, Waring wrote Halsey, enclosing clippings and suggesting that he pursue the story. Waring also poked fun at the FBI's investigation. The inquiry was then focusing on a group of teenagers who frequented one of two neighborhood drugstores operated by a man named Schwettmann. "At present," Waring wrote Halsey,

> G-men are tracking down the Schwettman gang. True to gangland, the members won't talk, but the G-men have orders (from the White House perhaps) to leave no moppet unturned. Most of Charleston has known all along what the G-men are now trying to uncover—that teen-agers rather than Ku Kluxers have been threatening the federal court. Meanwhile one of the new sights of Charleston is the pair of deputy marshals watching 61 Meeting street while madam, like Sister Anne in Bluebeard's castle, watches the marshals from an inside window.[83]

Halsey obviously shared Tom Waring's enthusiasm for the project. His "first intelligence concerning the latest brave stand against South Carolina savagery," he wrote from Philadelphia, came from a black weekly, which report had left him uncertain whether "the judge and wife had been stoned in a spitball variation of the Biblical tradition, shot at with small arms or shelled with heavy artillery." But he had gathered that the couple "survived, undaunted as usual, and that all other white folks in Charleston were nasty-nasty." A *Newsweek* version, he added, had "surpassed even the local Negro press for inaccuracy." He conceded, however, that a full-length article seemed unlikely, since his publisher feared that "a proper debunking" would provoke a libel suit. Halsey did draft a critical editorial for his magazine. But he later informed Waring that the *Saturday Evening Post* "finally and conclusively" would not publish it, adding, "[W]e have fought the good fight here and we have wound up looking like true Confederates." At an Atlanta convention of managing editors, Waring tried to interest representatives of the *New York Times* and several other papers in "the Waring story," "but none would tackle a disagreeable topic." Indeed, when conservative syndicated journalist John Temple Graves referred to Mrs. Waring in one of his columns, William Watts Ball deleted Graves' comments, saying "he didn't want to 'bring in the woman's name.'" "Probably nobody ever will understand the truth about this thing," a resigned Waring wrote Halsey, "but I suppose we'll survive it—if we survive at all."[84]

Wilson McFarlin's investigation supported the theory that the Warings had been the victim of juvenile harassment, but McFarlin's report was never released to the press or to South Carolina officials. McFarlin had told J. Edgar Hoover that he would complete his inquiry by October 21. When that date passed and the FBI's Washington office continued to receive McFarlin's daily progress reports, the director penned on one teletype: "We ought to set a deadline and not go on and on." The following day, October 25, McFarlin informed Washington that he had completed his investigation at 5:30 the previous evening. The Savannah agent's report of the investigation, which ran more than forty pages, speculated that one or more of the youths Judge Waring had rebuked for insulting his wife were responsible for the incident, but concluded that insufficient evidence existed to support any definite findings. Burnet Maybank wrote Deputy Attorney General Peyton Ford and

James M. McInerney, the assistant attorney general in charge of the Justice Department's criminal division, asking them for a copy of the report. "Of course," the senator wrote Ford, "I know all about what happened and I even know who burned the cross in front of the Judge's house. The group consisted of three small children playing a prank, but I would like to have a copy of the report." Neither official would comply, however, Ford writing Maybank, "As you know, investigative reports of the Federal Bureau of Investigation are confidential."[85]

Although the FBI inquiry obviously aggravated local white resentment of the Warings, their closest black friends remained supportive. Despite the Warings' concern for their friends' safety, Ruby Cornwell and Septima Clark insisted on visiting 61 Meeting Street the day after the stoning. The Cornwells also continued to entertain their friends in their home. While the Warings played canasta or bridge on visits to the Cornwells, the judge's guards sat watching from an automobile parked outside. When the Charleston papers complained about the expense of guarding the Warings as they visited friends, Dr. Cornwell would glance at his wife. "You know," he would remark, "who they're talking about, don't you?"[86]

The Walter Whites and other friends outside the South, both black and white, were equally solicitous, as were many persons from various parts of the world who sent letters praising the Warings and condemning their detractors. In an effort to bolster the couple's spirits, Aubrey Williams and Jim Dombrowski arranged a more concrete demonstration of support, organizing a late November "pilgrimage" to Charleston. On a bitterly cold Sunday, some one hundred blacks and twenty-five whites, representing seven southern states and the District of Columbia, met at Charleston's Morris Street Baptist Church, then went to the Warings' home, where Williams presented the judge with a tribute to his "great and good works." Waring in turn welcomed his guests to "darkest South Carolina" and told them that "[t]his day will live long in my memory" and "serve as an incentive to a large group of decent Americans who live up to the ideals of true Americanism."[87]

Charleston was then hosting a meeting of the Southern Governors' Conference, and Alabama Governor James E. Folsom, whose refusal to race-bait would ultimately play a prominent role in his political downfall, sent two aides to pay a courtesy call on Judge Waring. Later, Folsom wrote the judge, applauding his "courageous actions on behalf of the oppressed . . . who for so long have seldom had a spokesman." In his remarks to his fellow governors, however, Governor Thurmond condemned outside "agitators" as the "great tragedy of our day" and expressed hope

> that most southern Negroes will not listen to . . . false leaders and that
> they will realize their best opportunity for progress is a continuation of the
> harmonious cooperation which [has] brought both races so far along the up-
> hill road.[88]

William Watts Ball was apparently optimistic that southern blacks would follow Thurmond's advice. The day after the pilgrimage, the *News and Cou-*

rier observed that racial "agitators" were no longer "dealing with primitive tribes. Years of association with Southern white men have taught the negroes many things." The Charleston paper, like an FBI surveillance report of the pilgrimage, also commented on the political leanings of some of the Warings' guests. Clark Foreman, a former head of the CIO's political action committee, had helped to organize the affair. Foreman, the *Courier* observed, was an "associate of Communist Paul Robeson." He and Dombrowski had been the "moving spirits" behind the Southern Conference for Human Welfare, which the House Un-American Activities Committee had determined to be "Communist-dominated." "Nothing spontaneous about the event," the *Courier* editorialized. "It was planned and organized from headquarters. It had the professional touch."[89]

The Warings had hoped that the pilgrimage would attract considerable national publicity, but they were to be disappointed. Judge Waring had alerted Anne and Stanley Warren and also wrote Jim Dombrowski, emphasizing the need for outside coverage. Charleston's United Press representative was "all right," he informed Dombrowski, but the Associated Press account would come from a *News and Courier* reporter. That "story would be so written and organized," he asserted, "that you would find yourselves a band of Communists; perhaps even Chinese Communists by the time the story broke through the South Carolina Klan Curtain." Shortly after the pilgrimage, a nationally syndicated radio commentator did air a flattering profile, exclaiming that "Americans will long remember Judge Waring of South Carolina as the judge who defied the South in order to live as a true, earnest, and sincere American." But the national press largely ignored the event. *Time* magazine wired *News and Courier* reporter Jack Leland, its Charleston stringer, that the magazine would be interested in a story only if violence erupted, and other national publications generally shared *Time*'s indifference.[90]

When the Warings urged Leland to send *Time* a story about the pilgrimage, he showed them the telegram. The judge, according to Leland, then attacked the Charleston "mentality" and the "twisted and distorted" reporting of local journalists, calling the "head" of the *News and Courier* a "liar and a thief," while Mrs. Waring charged that *Time* publisher Henry Luce obviously feared a drop in his magazine's southern circulation. "Here we have a pilgrimage which is greater than the old Canterbury pilgrimages," she added, her voice filled with indignation, "and they refuse to run it. I know a lot about the Luces."[91]

Nor were local journalists and *Time*'s publisher the only ones to feel the Warings' wrath. On more than one occasion, Marion Wright had warned Judge Waring that South Carolinians were trying to goad him into intemperate remarks. But the stoning and local dismissal of the incident as a misguided but essentially harmless prank had taken their toll. Shortly before the pilgrimage, a rumor had begun circulating that the Warings were planning to purchase a home in Summerville, the nearby town where Moses Winn had been killed. Jack Button, the editor of the Summerville *Scene,* a weekly paper, telephoned Judge Waring for a comment. "Where did you hear such an absurdity, in a Klan meeting?" the judge had reportedly responded, adding that Summerville was a Klan hotbed, that "certain" newspapers "were always telling lies on him," and that Button was welcome to "do the same."[92]

The darker side of the judge's temper also continued to surface in the courtroom. On October 10, the day after the stoning incident, Ernest Southern, of Myrtle Beach, had appeared before Waring, waiving his right to a grand jury and pleading guilty to a violation of the postal laws. Southern had entered his plea without benefit of counsel and apparently with some assurance from a postal inspector that his guilty plea would mete him probation or a light fine. Instead, Judge Waring sentenced Southern to a year in prison. Later, when Southern sought clemency, the judge threatened him with a perjury charge and called his character witnesses "rabble." The defendant, Waring announced in the courtroom, seemed to have the "cozy idea to put a little money in his pocket and drop up here and have a talk with the judge and then go home again." Waring found that "moral or immoral" attitude "astonishing," but noted that the people of Myrtle Beach "seem to think very well of him." At this point, Southern withdrew his guilty plea and petitioned Waring to withdraw from the case. The judge granted the defendant's petition.[93]

Such outbursts obviously provided ammunition for Judge Waring's critics. Summerville editor Button wrote a lengthy column detailing his conversation with the judge. "I submit this summary," he told his readers, "as being worthy of study by those who are interested in human behavior." The *News and Courier* and a number of other papers reprinted Button's column, and Button's journalistic colleagues rushed to the editor's defense. The Chester *Reporter,* a frequent Waring critic, asserted, for example, that Button was a leading opponent of the Klan and that Waring had "acted like an untrained child . . . screaming and babbling into the telephone." Charging that Waring was "a danger to South Carolina and the Nation as a whole," Olin Johnston had the *Reporter* editorial printed in the *Congressional Record.* South Carolina papers gave the Ernest Southern incident equally extensive play.[94]

The couple continued to be the victims of harassment—vicious telephone calls, hate mail, dirt in the gas line of their automobile, and numerous other mechanical problems of suspicious origin. They blamed the Klan, and on more than one occasion they received Klan handbills in the mail as well as threatening letters purporting to have come from the organization. While at the Florence home of Roscoe Wilson, a black physician, and his wife, the Wilsons also received a threatening phone call from a man who identified himself as a Klansman—the third such call that year. The FBI never established a link between the Klan and the Warings' difficulties, and historically members of the clandestine group had rarely been so bold as to attack persons of their prominence. The Klan may well have played some role in the Warings' harassment, however. Through the fall of 1950, the South Carolina Klan experienced a resurgence and was tied to numerous illegal acts. In early November, for example, robed and masked Klansmen broke into the home of a white Horry County farmer recently released from a hospital, whipping him and forcing his two sons to run long distances in their under-clothes. In Anderson, a cross was burned at the home of a white minister who had been critical of the Klan. In the face of growing pressures from the NAACP and other organizations, the FBI launched an investigation. State politicians and South Carolina newspapers also began to speak out against Klan lawlessness. Governor Thurmond vowed to call out the national guard to prevent mob violence, and Governor-elect Byrnes warned Klansmen that their organization had no place in the state.[95]

Even if they had wanted to, however, neither the FBI nor state politicians could eliminate local hatred of the Warings or their pariah status in the judge's native city. Their isolation from white Charleston had long since be-come virtually complete. Now, with guards standing vigil at their home, they appeared to be under seige. During this period, Anne Warren visited Charles-ton. One day, she and her father walked down to the corner of Broad and Meeting streets and stood on the post office steps, watching a parade. When they returned to the house, Anne remarked to her father, he would later recall,

> You know, that was a unique experience. This is my home; I was born and raised here; you were born and raised here. But you and I were there utter strangers to the rest of the people. . . . I felt that you and I were safe and secure and the rest of the people were scared. I never realized before that thousands of people could be scared of two people. And yet they were. They were afraid to look at you. They were afraid to speak to you. They were afraid not to speak to you. They wouldn't see you.[96]

7

"Segregation Is Per Se Inequality"

While Judge Waring was dismantling South Carolina's white primary, urging total racial integration, and in the process becoming something of a southern pariah, the U.S. Supreme Court had been steadily chipping away at segregation in transportation, housing, and higher education. In 1950, the Court decided two extremely significant cases. *McLaurin* v. *Oklahoma* held that a state could not admit a black student to its previously all-white graduate school, then segregate the black student from his white classmates within the institution. On the same day that the *McLaurin* case was decided, the Court handed down an even more important decision in *Sweatt* v. *Painter,* ordering Herman Sweatt admitted to the University of Texas law school even though the state had recently established a law school for blacks. Chief Justice Vinson had observed for the *Sweatt* Court that, in determining whether segregated facilities were equal, trial judges were to consider not only tangible factors, but also intangible factors—"those qualities which are incapable of objective measurement but which make for greatness in a law school."[1]

Judge Waring had followed the line of Supreme Court cases closely, avidly reading the Court's opinions as well as briefs secured from Walter White, Thurgood Marshall, and other sources. He had been particularly impressed with an amicus curiae brief filed by the Federal Council of Churches of Christ in America and the council's assertion that segregation itself "necessarily predicates inferiority rather than equality." The Supreme Court's conclusion in the *Sweatt* case that intangible as well as tangible factors must be considered in segregation cases had convinced him, moreover, that the high Court, too, was now prepared to reject the "separate but equal" "sophistry" of its 1896 decision in *Plessy* v. *Ferguson.* All that was needed, he believed, was a case directly challenging the doctrine of segregation.[2]

For several years, Judge Waring had hoped that such a case would come to his court. In fact, when he addressed members of the Omega Psi Phi fraternity in Charleston in the spring of 1949, he had urged an attack on segregation at the College of Charleston. And he had been deeply disappointed when Charleston's black leadership—after apparently conferring with Walter White and Thurgood Marshall—had accepted the city's offer of scholarships to blacks wishing to attend State College in Orangeburg. Earlier, he had been equally disappointed when John Wrighten and his NAACP counsel had settled for a segregated law school rather than insisting on Wrighten's admission to the University of South Carolina. He had also hoped for a case challenging segregation in the primary and secondary grades. "I had great hopes," he would later say, that NAACP attorneys

> were going to bring cases to crack the educational system—not on the top, but where it ought to start: on the bottom. Prejudice starts when you're a little kid and you go to first grade school and you're told that people have to go through different doors and use different toilets and there's something wrong with the other people.[3]

For a time, it appeared to Judge Waring that he might never get such a case. Certainly, Charleston's black leadership did not appear inclined to file one. In rural Clarendon County, however, events were transpiring which would soon give the judge his case. Clarendon County was in farming and timber country, approximately fifty miles northwest of Charleston. The county was poor and backward, its terrain dominated by disease-breeding swampland. Life was generally hard for its 8,000 whites, often desperate for its 23,000 blacks.

The South Carolina constitution provided that "no child of either race shall ever be permitted to attend a school provided for children of the other race." However, it made no mention of the equality the *Plessy* v. *Ferguson* ruling had assumed, and even the most cursory examination revealed that the state's segregated schools were grossly unequal, especially in rural areas of the South Carolina low country. In the 1948–49 academic year, according to statistics of the U.S. Office of Education, South Carolina spent $148.48 on each white student, $69.95 on each black student; only Mississippi had a poorer record. In Clarendon County, the inequities were glaringly obvious. Clarendon's public schools served 6,531 blacks and 2,375 whites; yet in 1950, the state had spent $395,000 on the county's white schools, exclusive of salaries, and $282,000 on its black schools. Judge Waring often drove through Clarendon County on his way to Florence for court sessions. The white schools he observed in his travels were "fairly respectable looking," he would later recall, but those for blacks were "awful looking little wooden shacks." Black students in the county's District 22 attended two elementary schools, Rambay and Liberty Hill, and Scott's Branch Union, a combination elementary and high school. Unlike the two white schools in the district, Rambay, Liberty Hill, and Scott's Branch had no running water or indoor toilets. At Scott's Branch, for example, two "two-holer" pit privies serviced 694 students. Liberty Hill was a frame building with a tin roof and no underpinning; drinking water was brought in by bucket. Teachers at the black schools taught as many as sixty to seventy-nine pupils in a single class, while the largest white class served thirty-one students. A school lunch program, visual aids and other instructional tools, and auditorium space were provided white students, but not blacks.[4]

Like other blacks in the South, Clarendon's black parents had passively endured such inequities for years. For the past several years, however, a group of blacks led by Joseph Albert DeLaine, a teacher and minister, had been pressing school authorities for modest improvements in the educational opportunities accorded the black children of District 22. DeLaine and his followers were hardly advocating integration; they were merely seeking a school bus and a few other amenities long available to white students. Even so, the group's petitions were greeted with hostility, and its members became frequent targets of reprisal. DeLaine and his family soon left the area, unable, he wrote Mrs. Waring in September 1950, to endure the "sly reign of terror and fear" his efforts had provoked. By that point, however, the movement he had sparked was progressing toward a confrontation in Judge Waring's court. An initial suit seeking only bus transportation for black students was dismissed on technical grounds. But later, twenty black parents, including Harry Briggs, a thirty-four-year-old Navy veteran and service station attendant with five children, had signed a complaint against board chairman Roderick W. Elliott and other members of District 22's board of trustees. On November 17, a little more than a month after his home was stoned, Waring held a pretrial conference in *Briggs* v. *Elliott*. Thurgood Marshall and Harold Boulware represented Briggs and the other plaintiffs at the conference. Although S. Emory Rogers had represented the district school board for decades, Robert McC. Figg was to be the board's principal counsel in the case.[5]

Thurgood Marshall was apparently one of the officials within the NAACP then urging a challenge to the doctrine of segregation. It was difficult to find such a claim, however, in the original complaint filed in the *Briggs* case. The plaintiffs simply attacked the failure of school officials to provide bus transportation for black students and asked Judge Waring to strike down on equal protection grounds the "policy, custom, usage, and practice of the defendants in maintaining public schools for Negro children because of their race and color which are in every respect inferior to those maintained for white children." Marshall and NAACP counsel Robert Carter would later claim that the association was bent on raising the segregation issue in the Clarendon case but were attempting to do so indirectly in an effort to avoid the convening of a special three-judge federal court. Under federal law, a direct assault on state laws requiring public school segregation could be heard only by a three-judge panel convened by the chief judge of the circuit. On such a court, the NAACP would be assured of a favorable vote only from Judge Waring. Marshall's apparent tactic, therefore, was to file an equal-facilities complaint that would be heard by Judge Waring alone, then somehow raise the segregation issue in that context.[6]

At the pretrial conference, however, Judge Waring quickly made it clear that he would be no party to such a ploy. During the conference, Marshall indicated that the plaintiffs were challenging the constitutionality of South

Carolina's segregation statutes. "Well, I pointed out to him right there from the bench," Judge Waring later recalled,

> that in my opinion the pleadings didn't raise the issue. I said, "You've partially raised the issue, but of course can and may do what has been done so very, very often heretofore: decide a case on equal facilities—if you can prove what you say you can prove, that the schools aren't at all equal. It's very easy to decide this case on that issue, and not touch the constitutional issue at all, but it's general policy of American courts not to decide a constitutional issue if it can be decided on some other issue."

Marshall first attempted to argue that the complaint did include a challenge to segregation. When Judge Waring remained unconvinced, however, the NAACP counsel asked permission to amend the complaint. Waring suggested that instead the plaintiffs ask for a dismissal of the case, then "bring a brand new suit, alleging that the schools of Clarendon County, under the South Carolina constitution and statutes, are segregated, and that those statutes are unconstitutional, and that'll raise the issue for all time as to whether a state can segregate by race in its schools." Marshall, Waring later remembered, "looked rather astonished." "He was as surprised as I was," Bob Figg also recalled. But Marshall agreed to the proposition. The original suit was withdrawn, and on December 22, 1950, a new complaint was filed with the court.[7]

A number of factors probably explain Judge Waring's reaction to the original suit. He surely must have realized that a three-judge panel of southerners was unlikely to reject the *Plessy* doctrine, especially in the sensitive field of public school segregation. But he did not share the pragmatism that years of "shufflin' through Dixie," as the NAACP's chief counsel often put it, had nurtured in Thurgood Marshall. Win or lose, Waring wanted the "false doctrine" of segregation attacked, attacked now, and in his court. Correspondence between Waring and New York domestic relations court judge Hubert Delany, an NAACP board member, indicates, moreover, that neither jurist considered Marshall—or Walter White either, for that matter—sufficiently "militant" on the issue. Waring may have sensed a need, therefore, to prod the NAACP's legal staff into a stance he believed them too timid to embrace. He may have thought, too, that it was time for the association's attorneys to share the heat. As Robert Carter would later remark, "his behind was on the block, and I guess he wanted ours to be, too." In any event, the new complaint petitioned, among other things, for a ruling that South Carolina's policy of "separate and segregated schools" was unconstitutional. Accordingly, Judge Parker organized a three-judge panel and scheduled a hearing in the case for late May. The panel was to consist of Parker, Waring, and Judge Timmerman.[8]

In the months before the three-judge hearing, Judge Waring made a belated attempt to maintain a low profile. In January, he and Mrs. Waring granted Carl Rowan, then a reporter for the Minneapolis *Tribune,* a seven-hour interview. With tears often streaming down his face, Waring spoke to the black journalist of his commitment to civil rights, their treatment by Charleston whites, and betrayal by "Uncle Toms" in the black community. "I admit I miss the shop talk," he told Rowan. "I miss chatting about this Supreme Court ruling or such and such a case." But he had no regrets for the social isolation he claimed his decisions had caused. "Socially, I miss no one. I lost small brains and found larger ones. I have met southern Negroes and northerners of both races whom I would not have known except for this." He could understand his fellow townspeople's commitment to the past, "to rice and recollections," he often called it. "White supremacy is a way of life. You grow up in it and the moss gets in your eyes. You learn to rationalize away the evil and filth and you see magnolias instead." But he had escaped that "web of prejudice and hatred," and he had no regrets. When he and Mrs. Waring walked or drove through Charleston, black children would wave and smile, whispering to each other. "Then I know that, though their parents are afraid to cry out, I do not walk alone. Then I know the gain I have made. I am not living a phony life. I can look myself in the face, confident that I am meting out justice." Nor did he appear concerned about his safety. His guard, he said, was a "nuisance." "Perhaps," he added, "there could be nothing better than that the white supremacists should kill me. No, I am not foolish. I don't want to die. But it is time some white dies to wake up America. They kill Negroes like flies and, as a white Georgian put it after a lynching, 'It's just another nigger. It didn't stop a checker game.' "9

Following the interview, Rowan wrote the Warings that he considered Charleston "the desert of democracy" and the couple "a fountain of hope . . . that has emerged from this land I thought so barren of morality." Like Samuel Grafton, Rowan had been surprised at what he discovered when he visited 61 Meeting Street. He had expected to find "two lonely old people, bent under the terrible weight of social ostracism. Instead I saw how tiny are the people of Charleston. I know that white Charlestonians are the lonely people, lonely in a society laid desolate by their own narrow minds and souls. You two are the conquerors, standing above the ruins." Rowan's paper soon published his tribute to the couple as part of a series recounting the journalist's travels through the South; the series later appeared in book form. While the *Briggs* case was pending, however, the Warings generally avoided public statements.10

Perhaps in part for that reason, the number of annoying telephone calls and the amount of hate mail dwindled significantly. The judge told a Justice Department representative retention of the guard was entirely up to the department. But in early December, federal officials decided against lifting the guard detail on Judge Waring, following the recommendations of Charleston's U.S. attorney, marshal, and chief deputy marshal. Ben Whaley, a Justice Department official reported, "in particular considers it advisable to continue maintenance of the guard as local feeling is very bad and he fears that publication of the removal of the guard at this time might incite trouble."

However, in early February, the Warings began a six-week stay in New York; when they returned to Charleston, the guard detail was not renewed.

Mendel Rivers attempted to secure a seat on the House Un-American Activities Committee so that, he announced to reporters, he could investigate the backgrounds of Waring associates. But his bid was widely criticized by civil rights leaders. Walter White wrote the committee chairman, for example, that permitting the Charleston congressman "to gain the vantage point of [committee] membership . . . as a means of further indecent attacks would fully arouse the indignation not only of American Negroes but all decent American white people." On January 18, White wrote Judge Waring that the efforts of "your friend, Rivers," to "carry on his one-man lynching bee" via a HUAC seat had failed. "I quite agree with you," White added, that "he is an ass as well as a knave." From then until the May hearing, Rivers and other South Carolina politicians offered little public comment about the Warings. Apparently unaware that white South Carolinians preferred to have the couple out of state as much as possible, a Georgia congressman criticized the judge's frequent temporary assignments to courts remote from his native state—assignments, he charged, that were really more an opportunity for Waring "to advance his theory of social reform" than to conduct judicial business. Nothing came, however, of the congressman's proposal to restrict such trips.[11]

While Judge Waring maintained a low profile, South Carolina officials reacted to the approaching hearing. Initially, Governor Byrnes seemed uncharacteristically combative. At his inauguration in mid-January, the governor told his fellow citizens that the abolition of segregation would "endanger the public school system in many states." A week later, he told members of the general assembly that the "overwhelming majority of colored people" did not want "forced" integration, adding, "The politicians in Washington and the Negro agitators in South Carolina who today seek to abolish segregation in all schools will learn that what a carpetbag government could not do in the Reconstruction period, cannot be done in this period." His remarks at a March meeting of the state education association were even more pointed. "If the court changes what is now the law of the land," he observed,

> we will, if it is possible, live within the law, preserve the public school system, and at the same time maintain segregation. If that is not possible, reluctantly, we will abandon the public school system.

When Dr. Ralph Bunche attacked Byrnes as an "anti-Negro bitter-ender," South Carolina newspapers rushed to the governor's defense. Even the Florence *Morning News,* a model of moderation by *News and Courier* standards, scorned Bunche for "incorrectly reason[ing] that segregation is an injustice to the Negro." Bunche, the paper advised, "should survey the testimony of Southern Negroes that segregation is [their] salvation. . . . [S]egregation," it editorialized, "must remain. It is socially imperative that it be so; it is morally sound and proper."[12]

Governor Byrnes and other state politicians persisted in their defense of segregation. But they also realized the obvious—that there were glaring inequities in the educational opportunities afforded black and white children in South Carolina's public schools, disparities they must at least begin to reduce if they hoped to preserve their segregated institutions. With an eye on the May hearing, the general assembly levied a 3 percent sales tax, the first in the state's history. Proceeds from the tax were to be used to finance a bond issue providing up to $75 million in additional educational funds and $7.5 million for the acquisition of school buses. The legislature also responded to the recent rise in Ku Klux Klan activity. South Carolina politicians had been attacking the Klan with growing frequency. Now, the legislature made the wearing of masks a criminal offense.

Such developments, of course, were hardly a harbinger of any fundamental change in the racial attitudes of South Carolina whites, and certainly not in Judge Waring's native city. In the early spring of each year, students at the College of Charleston participated in a campus oratorical contest, with the winner receiving a medal, the Bingham Award. Francis Sturcken had won the contest for three consecutive years. In his 1951 essay, "The Liquid South," young Sturcken made the remarkable assertion—remarkable given the setting, at least—that segregation laws were "based upon the lie that the Negro can be segregated and not discriminated against. . . . In a complex society such as ours," he contended, "this is, of course, impossible. You can have no segregation without discrimination." Sturcken had recently polled his fellow students. Of 153 interviewed, he reported, ninety-one had agreed that blacks had "the moral or ethical right to attend" the College of Charleston; 126 had said that they would not be "antagonized" by the presence of blacks in the student body. "Why don't Southern educators wake up and stop listening to 'ballyhooing' political demagogues?" Sturcken concluded. "The segregated educational system is doomed."[13]

Judge Waring was heartened to learn of such thinking among students at his alma mater—and surprised that the College of Charleston would award a prize for an essay essentially following his own views. He invited Sturcken to visit his chambers for a lengthy conversation, found the student "completely liberalized and civilized," and mailed mimeographed copies of "The Liquid South" to associates throughout the country. John McCray reprinted the essay, as did the New York *Herald Tribune,* among other papers. And Benjamin Mays devoted a newspaper column to Sturcken's "boldly stated" theme. But white Charlestonians obviously did not share the enthusiasm. In the past, the winner of the Bingham Award had recited his oration during chapel exercises, recordings had been broadcast over a local radio station, and the Charleston papers had carried summaries or lengthy excerpts. On this occasion, however, Sturcken was informed that chapel time normally given the contest winner was to be devoted instead to a speech on an "important" subject. "The Liquid South" apparently got no mention, moreover, in the local press.[14]

The *Briggs* hearing was scheduled to begin on Monday, May 28. On Sunday morning, John Hammond, an NAACP board member and record company executive who had recently become a reporter for the New York *Compass,* telephoned the Warings from North Carolina to tell them he was making better progress than expected motoring down from New York to cover the trial for his paper. He would arrive, he told Elizabeth, in time for dinner. "[O]ur maid eager to get her precious Sunday afternoon and evening off," Mrs. Waring wrote in a diary she was keeping of events surrounding the Clarendon case, "we sat down to a tough roast of veal but merry hearts." Hammond, a white from a privileged background, was among the more militant members of the NAACP's executive board, and a favorite of the Warings. They listened eagerly as he related what he knew of the strategy Thurgood Marshall planned to pursue at the hearing. The Warings had planned for Hammond to stay at their home during the trial, but Marshall and the reporter's editor had advised against it. Following dinner with his friends, Hammond borrowed Mrs. Waring's typewriter and went to a local hotel for lodging, while the Warings prepared for the next day.[15]

"The day dreamed and prayed would arrive has come," Mrs. Waring's May 28 diary entry began. The region's blacks shared her enthusiasm. Early that morning, Ruby Cornwell had taken a bus downtown, determined to be among the first spectators to enter Charleston's small federal courtroom. "None of us realized," she later said, that "we were right in the midst of a revolution." But she knew she wanted reform, and she had been furious with those blacks "who wanted to go slowly. I wanted it to happen . . . now while I could participate." On that day, at least, she was not alone. When Judge Waring arrived at 9:00 A.M., the courthouse steps and corridors were jammed with hundreds of blacks, and the marshal had erected rope barriers to allow a passageway for the judges, attorneys, and court personnel. "They had come there on a pilgrimage," Judge Waring would later recall. "There were battered looking automobiles parked all around the courthouse. People showed a great desire [for] a little whiff of freedom. They had never known before that anybody'd stand up for them, and they came there because they believed the United States district court was a free court, and believed in freedom and liberty." Their presence bolstered Judge Waring's spirits. "To me it was a heartening thing . . . it's awfully heartening when you get poor, ignorant, illiterate people who suddenly sniff a little breath of freedom, and they want more of it. And they get thirsty for it."[16]

When the marshals finally opened the doors to the courtroom, Mrs. Cornwell was the first to enter. She took a seat on the first row, and other spectators filed in after her. The press was well represented also. Joining John Hammond in the press section were Ted Poston of the *New York Post,* journalists from numerous black papers, and representatives from the major wire services, the *New York Times,* and the Chicago *Sun-Times.* A Swedish exchange student then attending South Carolina's Winthrop College was there, too, covering the trial for two Swedish papers. The small, second-floor courtroom was not nearly large enough to accommodate the crowd, and those unable to gain entry sat or stood in clusters on the courthouse steps and in its corridors, talking in hushed tones. At 10:00 A.M., the judges filed in.

Judge Waring spotted Mrs. Cornwell sitting on the front row. A flicker of mild surprise played across his face.[17]

During dinner the previous evening, John Hammond had told his hosts that Thurgood Marshall anticipated a lengthy hearing, running perhaps as long as two weeks. Marshall was planning, Hammond had added, to spring a string of surprise witnesses, Mrs. Waring had written in her diary, on "that diabolically clever demon Figg." Soon after the hearing began, however, Figg was to make a surprise move of his own.[18]

Several days earlier, Bob Figg had gone to Clarendon County to examine the school system he would be defending and to confer with school board attorney Emory Rogers about what claims to equal facilities the defense might be able to make at the hearing. "I found," he would later say, "that the facilities were not only not equal . . . they were very embarrassingly unequal." Figg knew that Judge Timmerman would side with the defendants. Timmerman was a tall, strong-faced man who reminded Figg of General Claire Chenault, the World War II hero. When Winston Churchill had been introduced to Chenault, he had turned to an aide and remarked, "Thank God, he's on our side." Several days after the *Briggs* hearing, Figg would tell Timmerman of Churchill's observation. "Every time I felt real down during the Clarendon hearing," he added, "I'd look up at you and think, 'Thank God, he's on our side.' " Figg knew, too, that Judge Waring would vote against segregation, whatever the status of the Clarendon schools. Though not a member of Waring's social circle, Figg and his wife had attended the New Year's parties Waties and Annie Gammell had given. As lawyers, he and Waring had also tried a number of cases together, often on the same side. Figg considered Waring "a good lawyer and a good judge except when he got in these race matters. And then something took charge of his emotions." Figg realized, therefore, that "we had to try [the case] to Judge Parker." And he doubted that Parker would buy an equal-facilities claim where the schools at issue were in fact hopelessly unequal. After talking with Emory Rogers, Figg returned to his Charleston law office and telephoned Governor Byrnes. "I said, 'This is going to be a very embarrassing situation. The other side is just going to have a field day. They're going to make us look ridiculous.' " Figg suggested that the defendants go into court, admit the inequities, and ask for time to rectify conditions. Byrnes agreed, and Figg typed a statement to present to the three-judge panel.[19]

Although the plaintiffs were now challenging the policy of segregation, Thurgood Marshall had planned to devote the first portion of his clients' case to the gross disparities in educational opportunities afforded the black and white children of District 22. In fact, some of the expert witnesses to be used in supporting the plaintiffs' contention that segregated schooling was inherently unequal had not yet reached Charleston. Judge Parker had hardly called the hearing to order, however, when Robert McC. Figg rose to concede substantial inequities and to describe the $75 million bond issue and other steps being taken to equalize the school facilities. "The defendants," Figg asserted, reading from his prepared statement, do not oppose an order finding that inequalities in respect to buildings, equipment, facilities, curricula and other aspects of schools provided for white and colored children now exist, and enjoining any discrimination in respect thereto.

They urge the court in its discretion to give them a reasonable time to formulate a plan for ending such inequalities and for bringing about equality of educational opportunity in the schools of the districts, so that they may present such a plan . . . for the court's consideration, the court retaining jurisdiction of the cause in the meantime so that it may be enabled to grant such relief as may be proper in the event the defendants fail to comply with . . . constitutional standards.

Figg's move caught the plaintiffs' counsel off balance. Complaining that the state was attempting to "choke off" some of his witnesses, Thurgood Marshall decided against calling the plaintiffs and other witnesses he had intended to use in establishing what the defendants were now admitting. Marshall found Judge Parker to be an impatient presiding judge; when he began asking L. B. McCord, Clarendon's school superintendent, questions designed to establish that segregation was required by law in South Carolina, Judge Parker interrupted. "You are asking questions where there is no dispute," he told Marshall. "Let's get to the disputed matter." When Marshall called District 22 board chairman Roderick W. Elliott and began asking Elliott about the number of black and white schools in the district, Parker again interrupted, observing that "counsel can agree" on such matters.

Once he got to several expert witnesses, Marshall's line of questioning began to move more smoothly. Matthew J. Whitehead, an assistant professor of education at Howard University, had made two surveys of District 22's schools, one the previous November and one in April. Under Marshall's questioning, Whitehead provided detailed testimony regarding the physical facilities provided the district's students. Blacks, he reported, had no visual aids except run-down blackboards, teaching loads were heavier, and cracked tables and broken chairs used instead of desks. No black school, he added, had a lunchroom, auditorium, or gymnasium—facilities available to white students. The white schools had indoor flush toilets, three each for boys and girls, while Scott's Branch school had outdoor toilets with wooden seats— "one seat and no urinal for 300 boys and one seat for 304 girls." Students at the two other black schools also had outdoor toilets. Under cross-examination by Robert Figg, moreover, Whitehead refused to concede that facilities for black students could be made adequate through repairs to existing structures.

Marshall's interrogation of Whitehead focused on tangible inequities. During examination of other expert witnesses, however, the plaintiffs' counsel raised what, for Judge Waring, was the crucial question before the court. Harold J. McNally, associate professor of education at Columbia University, followed Professor Whitehead to the witness stand. Marshall questioned McNally briefly, then turned the witness over to Robert Carter. Assuming only "the fact of segregation," Carter asked McNally, could white and black children ever receive an equal educational opportunity in a segregated system? "White children as well as Negroes," McNally responded, "are being short-changed where segregation is practiced. So far as Negroes are concerned, segregation itself implies a difference, a stigma, and relegates the segregated group more or less to second class." Other witnesses for the plaintiffs agreed. "Segregation cannot exist without discrimination," Ellis Knox, a black professor of education at Howard University, testified. "It is detrimental to the minority group and does not prepare children to be members of the human race." Dr. Kenneth Clark, an assistant professor of psychology at the City College of New York, who, with his wife, was director of a center for children with emotional problems, concurred. Clark told of a "doll test" he had been administering to young children. When some 400 children had been asked to choose between brown and white-skinned dolls, those of both races had generally preferred the white doll. When Clark had administered the test to sixteen black Clarendon County students, he had obtained the same responses. The children's preference for the white doll was evidence, he said, that segregation began to generate attitudes of inferiority at an early age. Clark also cited results of a recent survey indicating that most of the nation's psychologists considered segregation detrimental to children of both races. "[T]he Negro children of Clarendon County," he concluded, "have been subjected to an obviously inferior status and have been definitely harmed, with the kind of injury that will endure as long as the situation endures."

While Kenneth Clark was testifying, Judge Parker declared a lunch recess. Mrs. Waring had decided not to attend the hearing—for several reasons, she wrote in her diary, but principally because her presence "might cause a riot I am so hated here." Persha Singer, a nonsoutherner who had become the judge's secretary in 1949 and shared the Warings' commitment to civil rights, had telephoned her frequently during the morning, however, and during the recess Mrs. Waring joined her husband for lunch to hear his account of the morning's events. The first session, he reported, had not gone well. Bob Figg's concession of inequities had caught Marshall badly off guard, and the hearing was proceeding slowly, too slowly apparently, for Judge Parker, who seemed testy and impatient.[20]

By this point, Judge Waring was becoming convinced that he would be alone in his decision to reject segregation. He was familiar with rumors that Judge Timmerman had led a movement to fire the minister at his Batesburg church for merely suggesting that segregation might be unChristian, and he had long ago dismissed his colleague as a thoroughgoing Confederate. But Waring had long admired Judge Parker, who, after all, had written a forceful opinion affirming his white primary ruling. In an unpublished 1948 interview, moreover, Mrs. Waring had said of Parker, "He's good; he is benevolent. You just feel his goodness and impartiality." Now, however, Judge Waring doubted whether Parker would ever agree to reject segregation, and Mrs. Waring's impression of the circuit chief judge was strongly negative. "All pretense by Judge Parker of recent years," she would record in her diary entry for the first day of the *Briggs* hearing, had "now dropped." He was seething, she wrote, with "hatred and jealousy of my great Judge and [our] stand and speeches for Negro rights. . . . All this," she added, "has hurt and disillusioned Waties more than any of the rest of the ostracism." While she and Judge Waring lunched, Parker and Timmerman sat at a table nearby. Neither jurist invited the couple to join them nor acknowledged their presence.[21]

Whether by accident or design, a Charleston street repair crew had begun work outside the courthouse as the hearing was getting under way, and the noise of the equipment filled the courtroom. To eliminate that problem, Judge Parker and the crew leader worked out an arrangement whereby the crew would work only during recesses of the court. For a time after the lunch recess, the press of the crowd in the corridor outside the courtrom also threatened to prevent resumption of the hearing. Following the recess, a marshal had attempted to open the doors to the courtroom so that journalists and spectators could return to their seats, but the pressure of the crowd against the doors obstructed his efforts. For many minutes, the crowd pushed and shoved, the "shrill cries of women," the *News and Courier* later reported, rising "above the tumult." The marshal suggested to the judges that the spectators be excluded from the courtroom for the remainder of the hearing. Judge Waring objected. "Open those doors," he shouted, "and let the people in." At Judge Parker's request, Thurgood Marshall attempted to calm the crowd. His pleas were ignored, but eventually the courtroom was again filled and the hearing resumed. Just as she had that morning, Mrs. Cornwell was the first person admitted. When Judge Parker had recessed the proceedings for lunch, she had backed out of the courtroom and stood just outside its doors, munching on two prunes and a sandwich while she waited for the hearing to continue.[22]

After the recess, Thurgood Marshall paraded several more expert witnesses before the panel. A dean of students and professor of education and psychology at West Virginia Wesleyan College, which had begun to admit black students for the first time two years earlier, testified, for example, that integration had caused "no emotional tensions" at his institution. "The Negro students," he said, "have been accepted with open arms." As he had with the previous witnesses for the plaintiffs, Robert McC. Figg challenged the basis for much of the witnesses' testimony. He also took issue with the credentials of one of the plaintiffs' experts. When Robert Carter asked Louis Kesselman, a political scientist at the University of Louisville, to assess the adverse effects of segregation, Figg objected. "Do you seriously contend that he is qualified to testify as an educational expert?" Judge Parker asked Carter. "What do you say about that, Mr. Marshall?"

> MR. MARSHALL: May it please the Court, what we have been trying to do is to present as many experts in the field with as many different reasons why we consider that segregation in and of itself is injurious to the child who is segregated.
>
> JUDGE PARKER: Are you going to offer any more witnesses along this line?

MR. MARSHALL: No, sir. The other witnesses are *real* scientists.
JUDGE PARKER: Well, I'll take it for what it's worth. Go ahead.

But the most effective examination of the day was Thurgood Marshall's questioning of a hostile witness. Because of the state's surprise concession that District 22's segregated schools were unequal, Marshall did not have enough witnesses available for the plaintiffs' attack on segregation to fill the afternoon session. Accordingly, Robert Figg called as a witness for the defendants E. R. Crow, a former county school superintendent then serving as director of the state Educational Finance Commission, an agency recently created to supervise South Carolina's school equalization efforts. Under Figg's questioning, Crow explained how additional funds were to be allotted individual districts under the state's new funding program. Figg also questioned Crow about the probable consequences of "mixed" schools. "In my opinion," the witness testified, "it would eliminate public schools in most if not all of the counties." "Would there be," Figg then asked, "community acceptance or the possibility of violent emotional reaction?" "There would be a violent reaction, I am sure," Crow responded.

Then it was Marshall's turn. After getting Crow to concede that there were no blacks on the finance commission, and attempting to get the witness to agree that, under the new equalization program, it was "possible . . . for Negro schools not to get a nickel of" the funds, Marshall turned to Crow's assertion that South Carolina would abandon the public schools rather than submit to integration. "Do you mean to say," Marshall asked, "that the white people of South Carolina would deprive their own children of an education because of this?" "I didn't say that, " Crow retorted. "But I don't believe the legislature would appropriate money, or that communities would levy taxes, to support mixed schools." Why, Marshall then wanted to know, did Crow believe that integration would lead to violence? He had drawn his conclusion, the witness responded, "mostly from what people say." "Mostly which people?" Marshall asked. "White people?" "Mostly," Crow replied, but also from "Negro school administrators." Could Crow name those administrators? No, he could not "recall their names."

Marshall then asked Crow whether he considered South Carolinians "a law-abiding people." "Is it your testimony," he asked, "that if this court issues an injunction, the people of South Carolina would not obey it?" Robert Figg objected, protesting that no injunction issued by the court would be directed at the people generally. "This court is going to assume," Judge Parker interjected, "that any injunction issued will be obeyed." But Marshall was not finished. When Crow again stated that "the elimination of segregation would bring undesirable results," Marshall countered, "Isn't it a fact that the only basis of your reasoning is that you have all your life believed in segregation?" "That is part of it, I suppose," Crow answered, "but not all." "Thurgood is merciless," Kenneth Clark whispered to a friend at this point, "simply merciless."[23]

Marshall's grilling of Crow had bolstered the spirits of black spectators, and the hapless former school superintendent—whose name alone offered many possibilities—became the target of numerous jokes. "His name ain't Jim," one spectator was overheard remarking, "but it might as well be." "Thurgood Marshall," another jested, "sure loves to eat crow." Nor was Robert Figg ignored. "Mr. Figg," smiled yet another black, "got his law degree when he finished school, but he just got his baccalaureate address from Thurgood Marshall."[24]

Judge Waring also considered the afternoon session an improvement over the morning proceedings, but he was generally disappointed with Marshall's performance. Ordinarily, the traditions of judicial propriety inhibit judges from discussing pending cases, especially with the press or partisans of either side. But Judge Waring was not so restrained. When John Hammond visited the Waring home after the afternoon session, the judge and Elizabeth criticized Marshall for failing to anticipate the defendants' trial strategy. Especially in light of the state's concessions, Elizabeth advised, Marshall would do well to focus all his energies on the doctrine of segregation rather than build evidence of tangible inequities, which could be corrected and were irrelevant to the central issue. At that point, Mrs. Waring later wrote in her diary, Hammond became "furious at me, as he gets periodically [since we] both feel so strongly on this subject close to our hearts as well as [our] minds." Hammond had been a strong critic of the NAACP, its "caution and fear and bickering." But he knew how much "hard work" the association's counsel had devoted to preparing the case, and he considered the Warings' criticism unfair. He "stormed" from the house. Later that night, however, he was back "for a quick game of Canasta. . . . Waties and I retired for the night," Mrs. Waring recorded in her diary, "smiling together . . . over our John and his attractive ways."[25]

The next morning, Thurgood Marshall and Robert Carter examined two additional expert witnesses regarding the effects of segregation on young children. Under questioning by Carter, David Krech, a visiting professor of social psychology at Harvard, termed "legal segregation . . . probably the most important factor in exciting harmful effects on the mental, emotional, physical and financial development of a Negro child," and claimed that state-enforced segregation was "also injurious to white children."

> Legal segregation involves a legal definition of an individual as inferior. Because it is legal and obvious, it gives environmental support to the belief that Negroes are in some way different from white people. Segregation arises from racial prejudice and also causes racial prejudice. Legal separation starts the process of differentiation at a crucial age, and—except in rare cases—if it is continued for 10 or 12 years the child never recovers.

Helen Trager, a Vassar lecturer and participant in a Yale University research project studying the exposure of black children to segregation, followed Krech to the stand. Mrs. Trager testified that children were aware of racial differences by age five; that white children in that age group "talked freely about race, while Negroes showed obvious discomfort or avoidance"; and that children of both races saw "being a Negro as a disadvantage. . . . [A] child who expects his group to be rejected," she asserted, "is not going [to be] a well-developed human"; the feelings of self-doubt that segregation instilled in children at an early age, she added, were a major obstacle to learning. As she testified, Bob Figg turned to another of the state's lawyers. "Damn," he remarked, "she's having fun." Under cross-examination by Figg, however, Mrs. Trager conceded that her only experience in the South had come during World War II, when her husband was stationed in Charleston. Earlier, David Krech also admitted to Figg that he had never conducted experiments in states in which segregation was required by law, that his opinions were drawn entirely from "reading and research."[26]

When questioning of Krech and Trager was completed, an again embarrassed Thurgood Marshall informed the judges that his next witness, University of Chicago anthropologist Robert Redfield, was not expected to reach Charleston until that afternoon. Judge Parker was obviously annoyed. He reminded Marshall that both sides had been warned to proceed in a timely fashion. "The best thing a man can do with a case in court," he pointedly added, "is to attend to it. Both sides should have paid more attention." Redfield had also testified for the NAACP in the Texas law school case, *Sweatt* v. *Painter,* contending essentially, as Marshall put it, that black children given equal educational opportunities "do about as well as anybody." Marshall considered Redfield's testimony vital to the Clarendon County case. Sensing Parker's displeasure, however, he agreed that the professor's testimony in the *Sweatt* case could simply be incorporated into the *Briggs* record. He and Figg also told the court that they had no more witnesses to call. At shortly after 11:30 A.M., therefore, counsel began their closing arguments.

In his summation to the panel, Thurgood Marshall argued his clients' case on both particular and broad grounds. Citing *Sweatt* and other recent cases, he contended that the Supreme Court had gradually "developed the idea that even when facilities are equal, segregation itself is detrimental." Legal segregation, "with its halo of respectability," he asserted, branded the black child as inferior "in his own mind," setting up a "road block in his mind which prevents his ever feeling he is equal." But even if the judges were unable to accept the proposition that segregated education is inherently unequal, the plaintiffs were still deserving of immediate relief. The defendants, after all, had admitted that the black schools of Clarendon County were inferior to those afforded white children, and the Supreme Court had repeatedly held that "human rights are now." Yet the state had offered nothing but a promise "to borrow some money after July 1, and build some schools later. . . . Even assuming good faith," said Marshall, "it would be impossible to carry through this program in the next few weeks or months. There is no relief for the Negro children of Clarendon County except to be permitted to attend existing and superior white schools." When black students had been admitted to previously segregated schools, he added, referring to graduate and professional education, "nothing has happened" and "everything has been fine."

Robert McC. Figg naturally disagreed with Marshall's assessment. The very Congress that had proposed the Fourteenth Amendment and its equal protection guarantee, he told the panel, had established segregated schools for the District of Columbia. Since the amendment's adoption, moreover, segregation has become a well-established legal doctrine, "a normal and not an abnormal procedure." Racially mixed schools had not worked in South Carolina during Reconstruction, he asserted, and they would not work now. "We have been making great progress in race relations," he observed, "and there will come a time . . . when the problem we are discussing here today will no longer exist in the United States." To throw "the races into mixed schools" now, however, would produce "utter confusion." Figg had recently discussed the issue, he told the court, with Howard Odum, a University of North Carolina professor and distinguished southern student of race relations. Forced mixing of the races, Dr. Odum had assured Figg, "would destroy 23 years of my work in that field." Arguing that "[y]ou can't pass laws against the 'mores' of peoples, against their heritage," Figg quoted Odum extensively. He also brought to the court's attention the recent remarks of Dr. Frank Graham, former president of the University of North Carolina and perhaps the leading southern liberal of the day. "To our good Northern friends," Dr. Graham had recently remarked to members of the North Carolina general assembly, "I emphasize the unwisdom of using federal legislation and force at educational levels beyond the levels of acceptance by the people in the States. Such unwise compulsions cause bitter setbacks, not enduring progress."

At one point during Figg's closing arguments, Judge Parker asked him what sort of decree he would suggest that the panel impose. Figg responded that the defendants wanted "a reasonable time to formulate a plan for ending the inequalities."

JUDGE PARKER: Well, I'm not much impressed with that. You have come here and admitted that facilities are not equal, and the evidence shows it beyond all peradventure. Now, it seems to me that it's not for the Court to wetnurse the schools. Assuming that segregation is not abolished by the decree, it would be proper for this Court to direct an equalization of educational facilities. And we wouldn't tell you how to do it. We wouldn't attempt to supervise the administration of the schools; all we can do is to tell you to do what the Constitution enjoins upon you. Now what I'm asking you is, what sort of decree ought to be entered with that end in view.

MR. FIGG: I think, if your Honor please, that the decree should take into account the fact that school buildings cannot be built overnight. . . . [If] we didn't measure up,—if there was any derailing of this program, the Court would have the same jurisdiction that it would have today to guarantee immediate and proper relief.

JUDGE PARKER: Well, the Court would have that anyhow. The Court, in the exercise of its contempt powers would deal with failure to comply with its decree. But that's a different sort of thing from holding the case back here and changing the decree from time to time. And that's what you seem to suggest, and I'm not certain that that's what you want us to do.

Parker then cited a Virginia case in which a district judge had ordered equalization of facilities within a given period.

Judge Waring had remained silent through most of the hearing, raising only a few perfunctory questions. But Judge Parker's reference to the Virginia case as a possible guide concerned him. "Wasn't the Virginia case," he asked, "brought on the distinct plea of separate but equal facilities and asking that they be equalized? As I understand it, this Court has got to face the issue of whether segregation is inequality per se or not." "Well, that is unquestionably true," Parker responded, "but he's making his argument on the theory that segregation would not be abolished, and I'm asking him what decree he suggests if the Court takes his view of the segregation issue."

Judge Parker's queries to Figg and response to Judge Waring suggested his likely position in the case. When the attorneys had finished their closing arguments, however, Parker asked whether they planned to file briefs in the case. On learning that neither side intended to file a brief, Parker reminded Thurgood Marshall that, in his view, the Supreme Court had made it clear in *Sweatt* that it would not "disturb" the *Plessy* decision. "It seems odd," he added, "that you ask us to disturb this case without filing a supporting brief." Marshall assured the court that the plaintiffs would file a brief within a week, and Bob Figg was allowed an additional week within which to submit a reply. The plaintiffs' counsel and Judge Waring could hope, therefore, that Parker's stance in the case was still undecided.

As the hearing's second and final day was coming to a close, Mrs. Waring strolled down Meeting Street to the courthouse, her "head down," she would write in her diary, "except to the few Negroes I wished to have see me." After inviting several to her home for a social, she mailed some letters. Then she, Ted Poston, and one of the plaintiffs' witnesses walked back to 61 Meeting. As word of the gathering spread, the doorbell began to ring continually, "admitting more Negro friends or would-be friends." Soon, the downstairs rooms were filled with talk of the hearing and civil rights. Mrs. M. E. Tilley, an Atlanta churchwoman who had served on President Truman's civil rights committee and was active in the Southern Regional Council, expressed confidence that the church would eventually move the South toward racial reform. "The church!" Ted Poston or another journalist snorted as Mrs. Waring passed through the room with a tray of ginger ale. "The church has been the worst enemy of Negro rights and the worst hypocrite of all." Elizabeth agreed. Mrs. Tilley, Elizabeth wrote later in her diary, was "too religious to suit me," a "Pollyanna" who thinks "that there is good in everyone, even the savage southerner." But she found Ted Poston's "other extreme of cynicism" equally distasteful.[27]

After most of the guests had left, Judge Waring returned from an hour-and-a-half conference with the other members of the three-judge panel. Ruby Cornwell and two North Carolinians who had come to Charleston to observe the trial were still at the house, talking with Elizabeth. The North Carolina visitors asked for the Warings' "autographs which gave us memories of up-North audiences, [since] down here familiarity breeds contempt." Mrs. Cornwell was disappointed with the hearing. "I feel so let down," she moaned. "It must be the beast in me for I expected more to come and [for the hearing] to go on for days and then it all broke down. Why? I am so ignorant of courts and law; explain, please, to me why it all stopped so suddenly. Why didn't Marshall bring more witnesses? Why didn't he speak out more strongly?" The North Carolina observers defended Marshall and praised his restraint, pointing out that *Briggs* was not a jury case and did not call for emotional appeals. While they were talking, Mrs. Waring later recorded in her diary, "my poor Judge had to sit there silent and contained." Finally, her diary records, Elizabeth "squeaked out, 'Ruby, your ingenue role of ignorance isn't getting by with me. You rogue, you know perfectly well that you are correct.' The Judge scowled at me. Then they left and the Judge dropped down dejectedly into his chair."[28]

Alone now with his wife, Judge Waring described his conference with Parker and Timmerman. "With complete disillusionment and utter contempt," Elizabeth would write in a rambling diary account of the conversation,

> he told me of Judge Parker's throwing aside all the testimony and [the] issue of Segregation and just reasoning, . . . "Jim Byrnes will equalize the schools; just give him time. Jim found this State in an awful condition—you know South Carolina was in dreadful shape when he took over—did this at great personal sacrifice to pull this State up and we must help him—he is taxing the people to raise the money and we can't hinder him by interfering with State affairs." My Judge with disgust told him Byrnes was no better and even worse than Thurmond because a hypocrite and that Byrnes was a White Supremacist just holding on to Segregation, etc. But to no avail. Judge Timmerman [was] just a dummy throughout . . . the only "happy warrior" of the three judges because completely sold on and the tool of White Supremacy. Parker knows better and was miserable in rationalizing with his conscience and his eyes on [a] Supreme Court [seat] . . . and 1952 close at hand and an assured Republican victory . . . [and] Parker a Republican. . . . Parker tried to get my Judge to make it unanimous by saying smoothly, "You know we try in our court to all agree," etc. Waties told him firmly he was going to write a strong dissenting opinion. Parker was furious.[29]

Judge Waring's own account of the conference, recalled several years later, would differ in detail and tone. Judge Timmerman, Waring would observe, was a "rigid segregationist. I was and am an equally rigid anti-segregationist. And Judge Parker is an extremely able judge who knows the law, and follows the law, but quite unwillingly in the Southern country. He just set his feet on Plessy against Ferguson and said, 'We can't overrule Plessy.'" Waring tried to convince Parker that a decision for the plaintiffs would not require a direct rejection of *Plessy,* a Louisiana precedent involving segregation on railroad cars. He also argued that the *Sweatt* case and *McLaurin* v. *Oklahoma,* the companion case to *Sweatt,* had "in effect" overruled *Plessy'*s underlying assumptions. But his colleagues remained unmoved, with Timmerman committed to "states' rights" and Parker to precedent. What-

ever their differences, however, the two versions made the conference's out-
come clear—Parker and Timmerman would side with the defendants, and
Judge Waring would file a vigorous dissent. The briefs filed by the parties
after the hearing had no effect on that division.[30]

While no doubt virtually unanimous in their commitment to segregation,
South Carolina politicians were hardly of one mind regarding the best way
to respond to the *Briggs* suit. After passage of the $75 million school bond
issue, several politicians brought an unsuccessful state court suit to enjoin the
program, charging that under provisions of the South Carolina constitution
the bond issue should have been submitted to a referendum of the electorate.
Governor Byrnes and most other politicians seemed convinced, however, that
the equalization effort was imperative if segregation were to be preserved.
Pointing out that the state supreme court had upheld a 1929 highway bond
issue that had not been submitted to the voters, Attorney General T. C. Calli-
son defended the program, asserting that the state must either allow the funding scheme to take effect or face a revolution against its most fundamental
traditions. State senator Edgar Brown agreed. Calling its opponents "meddlers," Brown argued that the bond issue would "give us the opportunity" to
equalize the state's schools and preserve segregation. A number of state officials were even more outspoken, condemning the current state of South
Carolina's segregated schools. Speaking to members of a Charleston civic
club, Ernest F. Hollings, who was then speaker pro tempore of the South
Carolina House, scorned the "miserable" condition of the public schools in
his state. Sixty percent of recent South Carolina draftees, he told his audience,
were rejected because of illiteracy—the highest rejection rate in the nation.
"We used to be able to say 'Thank God for Mississippi,' " he added, "but we
can't say that anymore." In Charleston County alone, Hollings asserted, there
were sixty-five one- or two-room, pit privy, pump handle schools. He had
recently visited a school on Johns Island in which a single room housed
two classes of forty-three and forty-seven children—all taught by one teacher.
"There were three little colored children in every desk, and on the walls were
the U.S. and South Carolina Constitutions guaranteeing every child, white
or black, equal chance. The name of that school was Promised Land. I don't
think you are proud of things like that. I know I'm not. . . . High illiteracy," he concluded, "means low per capita income. We have got to educate
our youth regardless of court decisions." The equalization program, he asserted, could take the state a long way in that direction.[31]

The editorial positions of state newspapers varied, too, but were generally sympathetic with the equalization program. On January 1, 1951, William Watts Ball had surrendered editorship of the *News and Courier* to Tom
Waring. But the old man continued to contribute editorials and other material to the paper, and he was as irascible as ever. Two days after the *Briggs*
hearing ended, the *Courier* published the last installment of a Ball series recounting "amusing incidents" connected with South Carolina lynchings. After a white man was hanged in Spartanburg, Ball had reported, a white on-
looker observed one of the "colored folk" present muttering to himself.

"What the devil are you mumbling about?" the white spectator angrily demanded. Did the old man regret that scoundrel's fate? "No suh, I ain't sorry," came the hasty reply. "I think Marse John got off mighty light." Ball, Tom Waring, and other contributors to the *Courier*'s editorial and news pages harangued regularly on the segregation issue. If South Carolinians were ordered to integrate their schools, the paper was convinced, "98 to 99 percent of the white people in the state would withdraw their children" from the public schools and educate them privately. It was thus "difficult" for the *Courier* "to see what, except confusion," the NAACP hoped to achieve. Nor was the paper enthusiastic about the equalization program—an attempt, as it saw it, to improve educational opportunities for black children through the imposition of enormous financial burdens on the backs of white taxpayers. Had the state's whites taxed themselves to give blacks equal schools and colleges in the past, it editorialized, South Carolina would be a "negro state" with few whites. In fact, the current costs were one factor that kept South Carolina "in poverty," relative to states with "no negro burden to carry." A number of other papers were equally intransigent. Many, however, defended the equalization program and questioned the wisdom of threats to close the public schools. In a June 13 editorial, for example, the Florence *Morning News* complained that "[f]orced mixing of the races in the public schools would prove disastrous to inter-racial good will . . . create dangerous and explosive social tensions . . . [and] be socially and economically unfair to Negro children and Negro teachers." But the paper vigorously supported equalization, calling the effort "a challenge to the good sense, to the levelheaded judgment of Southern men and women."[32]

For Judge Waring, of course, the equalization program was at best a contradiction in terms and at worst a cynical attempt to divert attention from the inherent evils of segregation. In the days after the hearing, he and Elizabeth had grown increasingly despondent. The brief Thurgood Marshall had filed with the court following the hearing had been a great disappointment—a lackluster document which, in Waring's judgment, largely skirted the central issues. Malicious gossip about Marshall's out-of-court behavior during the trial—including stories of drunkenness and sexual misconduct—was also rampant in the black community, providing fuel for blacks supportive of equalization and fearful of integration and for white reaction to "forced" mixing. John Hammond's reports from the NAACP's New York headquarters about the immediate future of the association's assault on segregation had been equally discouraging. "Let down depressing since the trial," Mrs. Waring wrote in a June 12 diary entry. The "enemies" of integration, both white and black, were "rising up again, crawling out of their holes and spewing their venom. . . . The Negro variety [are] usually politicians, doctors and dentists, preachers and worst and most vociferous of all, school teachers. . . . My beloved Waties," she added, "has been even more disgusted and hopeless than John [Hammond] and last week became so angry and upset that I had to talk and reason and soothe him . . . until after midnight . . . to get him back to his . . . normal self which is really more hopeful than I am. . . . I try to hide my compleat defeatism." "When one breaks one pane of glass in their prison window," the judge had complained of black "traitors" in their midst, "they cry out with terror that it will hurt them."[33]

The day after that difficult evening, however, a letter of praise had arrived from an unlikely source—a man who had served on a jury that tried a civil case in Judge Waring's court the previous week. He congratulated Waring on his conduct during those proceedings. All the jurors, he wrote, had been favorably impressed. That evening, a black man had telephoned from Philadelphia to say that he had read a profile of the Warings in a local paper and admired what they were doing. "This lifted up my poor dear husband's spirits more than anything I could say to him," Mrs. Waring wrote in her diary. "Waties' eyes were filled with tears when he came to tell me of this. . . . He was greatly cheered all evening as I read to him and we played Canasta." On Friday, June 15, John Hammond flew down to Charleston for a visit with the couple. The conversation was essentially pessimistic, but the occasion a happy one—the celebration of the Warings' sixth wedding anniversary.[34]

On June 16, Judge Parker mailed Waring and Timmerman a draft of his opinion and decree in the *Briggs* case. "If Judge Waring wishes to dissent, as he indicated that he might," Parker noted in an accompanying letter, "I suggest that he note that fact on the copy of the decree and return it to me together with any dissenting opinion that he wishes to file." When the Warings walked to the post office to check their mail the next morning, they found the Parker draft—"a disgusting appeasement to the South's White Supremacy," Mrs. Waring would later record in her diary, by a judge "who knows better and must have done a job of self deceit . . . and rationalizing to get around his conscience and usually excellent common sense reasoning." By this point, Judge Waring had drafted his dissent. Now that Parker had completed the majority opinion and decree, Waring read his draft to Elizabeth and called his secretary to his chambers to type the final version. While this was happening, the parishioners at St. Michael's church across the street were celebrating the venerable institution's second century, and the pealing of its bells could be heard through Charleston. "Little do the bell-ringers know," Elizabeth would later recall thinking, "that they are celebrating the final writing of" her husband's dissent. "Peal away old church bells," she said to herself, "for right here a South Carolinian whose ancestors were here when your church . . . was built two hundred years ago is striking a blow for freedom of all people."[35]

When Parker and Timmerman learned that Judge Waring was filing a dissent, Parker requested an opportunity to see the dissent before filing his majority opinion. Judge Waring sent both jurists a copy. When Mrs. Waring received a threatening telephone call, she urged the judge to place a sealed copy of his dissent in the clerk's office to await filing of the Parker opinion and the court's decree. Judge Waring agreed, placed his dissent in a legal-sized manila envelope, and gave it to his clerk, Ernest Allen. On the outside of the envelope, he wrote: "The Clerk will file same if Judge Waring be prevented from attending to usual duties of office by death or physical or mental incapacity. Otherwise, to be held until an opinion or opinions are filed by Judges Parker and Timmerman." By the next day, rumors were circulating through Charleston that a decision was imminent. On June 21, Mrs. Waring wrote in her diary that Judge Parker, then holding court in Asheville, North Carolina, must be feeling "rage and resentment" over the Waring dissent. She had wagered her husband, she also wrote, that Parker would yet attempt to pressure his colleague into withdrawing the dissenting opinion. On Saturday morning, June 23, Ernest Allen told reporters that he "may have something of interest for you at 11:00 a.m." At that hour, he passed out copies of the opinions and decree. Earlier that day, Judge Waring had given Elizabeth an autographed copy of his dissent. "To my precious Elizabeth," it was inscribed. "This could not have been done without her *love* and *encouragement* and *support*."[36]

Judge Parker's majority opinion in the *Briggs* case essentially tracked the arguments he had made in conference. Citing *Plessy* and other relevant precedents, Parker and Timmerman rejected the plaintiffs' challenge to segregation, observing: "It is . . . well settled that there is no denial of the equal protection of the laws in segregating children in the schools for purposes of education, if the children of the different races are given equal facilities and opportunities." The defendants had conceded that the segregated schools at issue were unequal; they were thus required to "equalize" South Carolina's educational facilities. Within six months, moreover, they were to file a progress report with the court. The plaintiffs' counsel had argued that *Sweatt* v. *Painter* and *McLaurin* v. *Oklahoma* supported their claim. But in *Sweatt,* Parker asserted, the Supreme Court had "expressly refused" to overturn *Plessy,* and the segregation within an institution at issue in *McLaurin* "involved humiliating and embarrassing treatment of a Negro graduate student to which no one should have been required to submit. Nothing of the sort is involved here." Both cases, moreover, concerned graduate and professional education in which integration posed problems "essentially different from [those] involved in education at the lower levels."

> In the graduate and professional schools the problem is one of affording equal educational facilities to persons sui juris and of mature personality. Because of the great expense of such education and the importance of the professional contacts established while carrying on the educational process, it is difficult for the state to maintain segregated schools for Negroes in this field which will afford them opportunities for education and professional advancement equal to those afforded by the graduate and professional schools maintained for white persons. What the courts have said, and all they have said in the cases upon which plaintiffs rely is that, notwithstanding these difficulties, the opportunity afforded the Negro student must be equal to that afforded the white student and that the schools established for

furnishing this instruction to white persons must be opened to Negroes if this is necessary to give them the equal opportunity which the Constitution requires.

The problem of segregation at the common school level is a very different one. At this level, as good education can be afforded in Negro schools as in white schools and the thought of establishing professional contacts does not enter into the picture. Moreover, segregation at this level is not a matter of voluntary choice on the part of the student but of compulsion by the state. The student is taken from the control of the family during school hours by compulsion of law and placed in control of the school, where he must associate with his fellow students. The law thus provides that the school shall supplement the work of the parent in the training of the child and in doing so it is entering a delicate field and one fraught with tensions and difficulties. In formulating educational policy at the common school level, therefore, the law must take account, not merely of the matter of affording instruction to the student, but also of the wishes of the parent as to the upbringing of the child and his associates in the formative period of childhood and adolescence. If public education is to have the support of the people through their legislature, it must not go contrary to what they deem for the best interests of their children.[37]

Nor, wrote Parker, could the widespread practice of segregation in other jurisdictions be ignored. Seventeen states required segregation by law; Congress provided for it in the schools of the District of Columbia. Earlier cases upholding segregation were thus "not . . . dealing with hypothetical situations or mere theory, but with situations which have actually developed in the relatioinship of the races throughout the country." Certain witnesses had testified "that mixed schools will give better education and a better understanding of the community in which the child is to live than segregated schools." Other testimony had supported the view "that mixed schools will result in racial friction and tension" and that segregated schools were "the only practical way of conducting public education in South Carolina." To the majority, such questions "were not questions of constitutional right but of legislative policy, which must be formulated, not in vacuo or with doctrinaire disregard of existing conditions, but in realistic approach to the situations to which it is to be applied." Parker and Timmerman were not about to enter that legislative domain.

> [W]hen seventeen states and the Congress of the United States have for more than three-quarters of a century required segregation of the races in the public schools, and when this has received the approval of the leading appellate courts of the country including the unanimous approval of the Supreme Court of the United States at a time when that court included Chief Justice Taft and Justices Stone, Holmes and Brandeis, it is a late day to say that such segregation is violative of fundamental constitutional rights. It is hardly reasonable to suppose that legislative bodies over so wide a territory, including the Congress of the United States, and great judges of high courts have knowingly defied the Constitution for so long a period or that they have acted in ignorance of the meaning of its provisions. The constitutional principle is the same now that it has been throughout this period, and if

conditions have changed so that segregation is no longer wise, this is a matter for the legislatures and not for the courts. The members of the judiciary have no more right to read their ideas of sociology into the Constitution than their ideas of economics.[38]

Judge Waring often remarked that he wanted to "preach a sermon," not deliver a "dry-as-dust" legal discourse in his civil rights opinions, adding: "I had hopes that decent people could be aroused." Perhaps more than any of his other opinions, his *Briggs* dissent conformed to that standard. By admitting tangible inequalities and promising to make improvements, he asserted, the defendants were attempting "to avoid the primary purpose of the" plaintiffs' suit. "If a case of this magnitude can be turned aside and a court [refuse] to hear these basic issues," he contended,

> by the mere device of admission that some buildings, blackboards, lighting fixtures and toilet facilities are unequal but that they may be remedied by the spending of a few dollars, then, indeed people in the plight in which these plaintiffs are, have no adequate remedy or forum in which to air their wrongs. If this method of judicial evasion be adopted, these very infant plaintiffs now pupils in Clarendon County will probably be bringing suits for their children and grandchildren decades or rather generations hence in an effort to get for their descendants what are today denied to them. . . . If this be the measure of justice to be meted out to them, then, indeed, hundreds, nay thousands, of cases will have to be brought and in each case thousands of dollars will have to be spent for the employment of legal talent and scientific testimony and then the cases will be turned aside, postponed or eliminated by devices such as this.

The only question before the court, Waring contended, was the doctrine of segregation, and that issue should be faced "simply and factually and without fear, sophistry and evasion," or resort to the "false doctrine" of "separate but equal."[39]

The majority, of course, had faced that issue and had elected to side with the state and the force of precedent. For Judge Waring, however, segregation was nothing more than a remnant of slavery, a product of "unreasonable, unscientific and . . . unadulterated prejudice" forbidden by the Constitution. The "results of all this warped thinking," he asserted, were clearly evident in the attitudes of "poor under-privileged and frightened . . . Negroes in the southern states; and in the sadistic insistence of the 'White supremacists' in declaring that their will must be imposed irrespective of rights of other citizens." The Fourteenth Amendment was intended to eradicate this "stigma" and confer upon blacks "full rights as citizens." The amendment remained a promise unfulfilled. But in the *Sweatt* and *McLaurin* cases, the Supreme Court had come close to giving it full meaning, concluding in *Sweatt*, for example, that intangible, and not merely tangible, factors were to be the measure of equality. Now the *Briggs* court had the opportunity to take the final step.[40]

The defendants had produced but two witnesses, Waring asserted, neither of them an educational expert. Both had testified that schools provided black children needed improvement. One, "significantly named Crow," had "stated flatly that he believed in separation of the races and that he [had] heard a number of other people say so, including some Negroes, but he was unable to mention any of their names." Numerous witnesses for the plaintiffs, "some of them of national reputation," had testified, on the other hand, that "the mere fact of segregation, itself, had a deleterious and warping effect upon the minds of children," that "the humiliation and disgrace of being set aside and segregated as unfit to associate with others of different color had an evil and irradicable effect upon the mental processes of our young which would remain with them and deform their view of life until and throughout their maturity." From "actual study and tests in various parts of the country," they had shown "beyond a doubt" that segregation has an adverse effect on white as well as black children and that the feelings of prejudice derived from segregation were acquired in very early childhood.

> When do we get our first ideas of religion, nationality and other basic ideologies? The vast number of individuals follow religious and political groups because of their childhood training. And it is difficult and nearly impossible to change and eradicate these early prejudices, however strong may be the appeal to reason. There is absolutely no reasonable explanation for racial prejudice. It is all caused by unreasoning emotional reactions and these are gained in early childhood. Let the little child's mind be poisoned by prejudice of this kind and it is practically impossible to ever remove [it].

To Waring, the conclusion mandated by such testimony and by "all of the legal guideposts, . . . common sense and reason" was clear:

> [S]egregation in education can never produce equality . . . it is an evil that must be eradicated . . . [and] the system of segregation in education adopted and practiced in the State of South Carolina must go and must go now.
>   *Segregation is per se inequality.*[41]

The press gave the *Briggs* opinions extensive coverage, and grateful southerners were soon sending Judge Parker congratulatory letters. One friend, a North Carolina attorney writing to request a copy of the majority opinion, assured the Fourth Circuit's chief judge that "[t]his one blood concept in the end result would be a mongrel race possessing but little, if any, of the good of either race. . . . I guess," he added, "that I will do some 'cussing' aplenty when I read the dissent." An Alexandria, Virginia, lawyer, a self-described "progressive southerner," thanked Parker for "the respite which your decision may give the South" and promised him "that a great many of our fellow men will make good use of the time you have afforded us." A Birmingham friend wrote to "congratulate you that you found a way to uphold segregation."[42]

South Carolina politicians echoed the sentiments of many of those writing Judge Parker. In replying to those who wrote to praise his decision, Parker studiously avoided expressing his personal feelings, writing one admiring associate only that the case "was presented with a good deal of feeling on both sides, but it seemed to me that the law had been pretty clearly settled by the Supreme Court." When Robert Figg discussed the segregation issue with Professor Howard Odum, the University of North Carolina professor, a close friend of Parker's, assured Figg that Parker opposed integration as much as Odum did. Until the decision was announced, however, the defendants and their counsel could not be absolutely certain of Parker's vote. Now they knew. Governor Byrnes praised Parker's rationale as "unanswerable," ranking the *Briggs* panel's presiding judge with Stone, Holmes, and Brandeis. Other state politicians and newspapers followed suit. The Columbia *Record,* although claiming that segregation was "on the way out," argued that "the process cannot be speeded by the resort to force. Folkways are the product of education and are not susceptible to Federal injunction."[43]

Bolstered by the *Briggs* decision and hopeful that the Supreme Court might also uphold segregation, Governor Byrnes and most other state political figures attempted to project a positive image, dropping for the time being their threats to close the public schools if ordered to integrate. The day before the *Briggs* ruling was announced, Tom Waring wrote Byrnes, requesting an interview when the governor next visited his summer home near Charleston, and raising two pointed questions. "Would South Carolina," the judge's nephew wanted to know, "really close up the public schools," as Byrnes had earlier promised, "rather than accept racial mixture?" And had Byrnes "line[d] up in advance some of the other governors who have expressed similar views to present a united front?" The governor's views, "as relayed by a Southern editor," Waring asserted, "would present the South Carolina position more clearly than the straight press accounts have been able to do." Should the district court or Supreme Court rule against segregation and "drastic action" become necessary, Waring added, "it might be well to prepare outsiders' minds for the cold fact that we are not bluffing." But Governor Byrnes was not in a fighting mood, especially after the three-judge panel's favorable ruling. "[A]t this time," the governor wrote Waring, "I do not want to make for publication any additional statement on the subject of whether South Carolina would close the public schools rather than providing for mixing the races." In his *Briggs* dissent, Judge Waring had termed Byrnes' earlier statements about closing the schools a "threat." In his letter to Tom Waring, the governor disputed the judge's assessment. "I stated my views," Byrnes wrote, "because I realized the danger of an adverse decision and I found that few people in the State were giving consideration to what course should be followed in the event of such decision."[44]

While South Carolina politicians were praising Judge Parker's reasoning and taking comfort in his defense of tradition, others were expressing their views on segregation in stronger terms. While the case was pending before them, an Atlanta woman had sent each of the judges a letter proclaiming that racial integration was part of a Vatican plot to overthrow the United States. After the decision was announced, Judge Waring had received in the mail a newspaper clipping discussing Governor Byrnes' support of segregation. Across the top of the clipping was typed a message, which read in part: "Regardless of what you [or] any NEGRO COMMUNIST agitator says, our Honorable Governor WILL KEEP THE STATE OF SOUTH CAROLINA WHITE. You should be in Russia where you belong, not here trying to wreck this good state." But others applauded Judge Waring's position. Two Charleston whites, one an attorney who regularly visited the judge's chambers at Christmas to pay his respects, came by to offer their congratulations. Myles Horton wrote Waring immediately, asserting that "Some day your dissent will become the law of the land." Nathan B. Kogan, a New York attorney who had been active in the National Lawyers Guild, agreed, writing, "Do not be disheartened—the dissenting opinion will stand as a beacon lighting the path toward tearing down the false barriers between the races." James Dombrowski and Aubrey Williams also sent their congratulations, and Williams expressed cautious optimism that thoughtful southerners were beginning "to face the ugly truth of this evil, this canker in the body of the South, and to disassociate themselves from its forces." In an editorial applauding the dissent, moreover, the *Herald Tribune* found Governor Byrnes' assessment of the rationale behind the *Briggs* majority subject to "serious difference of mind," adding, "In our opinion, there is no justice in compulsory separation of the races." Quoting Waring's dissent, the paper concluded that "any system based on the color of a man's skin is un-American and wrong." Other national papers and the black press also praised the dissent.[45]

Judge Waring had been as deeply disappointed with his *Briggs* colleagues as Governor Byrnes had been pleased with their ruling. But the expressions of support his dissent attracted bolstered his spirits. "Your . . . letter covering my dissent," he wrote Judge Hubert Delany, for example, "comes to me as a most heartening tonic. It is really quite wonderful to receive the support of a tru[ly] fine thinking legal mind." In an interview with a black reporter, he asserted that the battle against segregation could not be "fought by a few brave people here in the South. It must have the support of everyone throughout this land." He expressed confidence, however, that with continuing pressure, the citadels of segregation would eventually crumble.[46]

Decisions of three-judge district courts are appealable directly to the Supreme Court, and immediately following the decision, Waring began to lobby NAACP officials to file an immediate and uncompromising appeal. In a June 28 letter to Judge Delany, he restated his firm belief "that the courts of this land have got to accept the Fourteenth Amendment as a true declaration of full rights of citizenship to *all* citizens and they really must drop the veil of sophistry and evasion that has so often been used." *Sweatt* and other recent cases, he added,

> almost cross the threshold, but do not quite do so. I have great hopes that the Briggs case may shove them across and I believe they certainly have an opportunity (and God knows I have done my best to give it to them) to finally declare that segregation is per se inequality. I took occasion to underscore that statement as a separate paragraph. This was not done in an attempt for a dramatic flourish but in the hopes that it might catch the eye

of the readers and particularly that it might put squarely before our highest court an issue that must and should be decided.

He now hoped that the NAACP's legal department would file an appeal and motion for an early hearing, as well as seek supporting briefs from numerous organizations. The solicitor general of the United States, he reminded Delany, had filed a brief and participated in oral argument in *Sweatt* and other recent cases, and "the Association should bring strong pressure to bear to have this done again," and to bring religious organizations and labor unions into the fray.[47]

Then, Waring turned his attention to the NAACP's legal staff. He was not certain that the "present staff [was] sufficiently equipped" to handle an effective appeal and suggested that special counsel be retained. "Between you and me," he observed, *Briggs* "was not very well presented in the court here. You may recollect that no briefs were filed until after the court asked for them and then the one that came was one of those colorless routine affairs reciting the various decisions which we all know." Any appeal carried to the Supreme Court, he insisted,

> must be handled in a *militant* manner and not in routine pedestrian fashion. The National Board should see to it that some real enthusiasm and fire and imagination is put into the appeal if there is to be an appeal. This case is one that will not be won by sitting down and casually mentioning some authorities. It has got to be won by an enthusiastic attack upon the citadel of "white supremacy" and it has got to be won by a determined fight by determined lawyers calling for a reversal and not apologizing for appealing.

He had "great faith," he wrote, in the commitment of Delany, John Hammond, and a number of other NAACP board members. He believed, too, "that Walter White is now fired with enthusiasm." He urged Delany, however, "to use eternal viligance . . . in order that the matter be carried forward in a militant fashion and carried forward NOW without delaying for conferences, consultation, advice or reconsideration and perhaps presentation in other or better atmospheres. . . . [T]his," he was convinced, was "the opportunity to achieve a great victory."[48]

Judge Delany was hardly in need of conversion. Through him and other like-minded NAACP board members, Judge Waring hoped to push the association's counsel, especially Thurgood Marshall, into a more aggressive posture than he thought they had been pursuing. Waring also approached Marshall directly. Although in later years, Marshall wrote that his memory of the *Briggs* litigation had grown "dimmer" over the years, he did state, "One thing I am positive about is that Judge Waring had *absolutely nothing* to do with our legal strategies." Be that as it may, Marshall and Waring corresponded and talked about the *Briggs* case on several occasions in the days following the district court's ruling. On the day that the decision was filed, the NAACP began its annual convention in Atlanta. Marshall distributed mimeographed copies of Judge Waring's dissent to the delegates and also extended the judge his personal appreciation. On June 25, Waring wrote Marshall, citing a number of pertinent cases that "seemed to me inappropriate in an opinion although they might be useful in a brief." On July 6, Marshall responded, indicating that he would "look into the matters suggested in" Waring's letter and was "sure they will be most helpful." He also noted that he planned to file a *Briggs* appeal by July 20 and asked for Waring's travel plans "so that I can arrange to present the petition and other papers to you wherever you are." After a brief visit to New York in the middle of the month, the Warings planned to spend the balance of July and August at a resort in Rhode Island. Judge Waring notified Marshall of his itinerary and suggested that the NAACP counsel file the appeal with Judge Parker rather than with him since "you are not appealing from my decision." While the Warings were in New York, Marshall and the judge spoke briefly by phone. Then, on July 24, Marshall wrote Waring that an appeal had been filed on July 20. He regretted, he added, that he and the judge had not been able to talk at greater length when the Warings were in New York. There were "many things," he wrote, that he wanted "to talk to [Waring] about, most of which cannot be put in a letter."[49]

Attached to Marshall's letter was a copy of the jurisdictional statement he had filed in the plaintiffs' behalf. The statement had been hurriedly prepared, Marshall conceded, at a time when half of the legal staff was on vacation. But it clearly set forth the only issue of contention between the parties—"the question of the constitutionality of the laws requiring segregation of the races in public education." The trial testimony of expert witnesses for the plaintiffs, the statement asserted, had "established the fact that the segregation of Negro pupils in these schools would *in and of itself* preclude an equality of education offered to white pupils or pupils in a non-segregated school." The defendants' two witnesses had not rebutted that testimony, and the plaintiffs were entitled to relief.[50]

In the jurisdictional statement, Marshall had contended that the district court erred in predicating its decision upon the *Plessy* precedent and disregarding principles recognized in *McLaurin, Sweatt,* and other more recent cases—principles "in conflict with the rationale of the *Plessy* case." In two letters to Judge Waring, Judge Delany questioned the wisdom of basing the plaintiffs' case on a rejection of *Plessy.* Waring had conceded in his *Briggs* dissent that the Supreme Court had refused to overturn *Plessy* in the *Sweatt* case. He had argued, however, that *Plessy* had involved segregation in transportation and that a decision outlawing segregation in the public schools thus did not require a direct repudiation of *Plessy.* Judge Delany agreed. "It may be that I am super critical," he wrote Waring in one letter, "but I do not believe that we need to go to the Supreme Court with hat in hand asking them whether or not it is . . . time to overrule *Plessy* v. *Ferguson.* As you so clearly pointed out in your decision, *Plessy* . . . is not controlling and should not be controlling." "[W]e should by-pass the Plessy case," he asserted in the second letter, "and use the arguments that were outlined in your decision. . . . The basic principle that we should hammer at constantly is 'Seg-

regation is per se inequality.' " Delany also attacked the tone of the NAACP legal department's press release announcing the appeal, calling it "so negative and so apologetic that I hoped you would not even see it." In his judgment, the only proper approach was "to take the aggressive, militant position backed up by righteous indignation which so constantly permeated" Waring's opinion. "With that approach," he observed, "I do not see how we can lose. After all if the person arguing the appeal has the good sense to follow the line of reasoning so magnificently outlined in your opinion that is all that is needed."[51]

At least in his correspondence with Marshall, however, Judge Waring's assessment of the jurisdictional statement was more sanguine. He agreed with Marshall that it was "somewhat lengthy and that it and the argument show signs of hurry." But he also concluded that it made the "necessary points" and that the Supreme Court would also read the two district court opinions. "I do not see how the Court," he observed, "can possibly fail to realize the importance of the questions involved and that this is at last a frontal attack on Segregation." What was now critical, in his judgment, was preparation of an appellate brief that would "cover the case adequately and block all efforts by the opposition to induce the Supreme Court to evade this basic question. May I suggest the use of the phrase 'Segregation is per se inequality.' " The time to begin that brief, he contended, was now. Delay might result in "another emergency or rushed job. . . . We do not want *this* Brief," he added, "to be a rush job."[52]

Judge Waring's strident attacks on traditions and personalities likely to be the subject of litigation in his court no doubt had raised some eyebrows, even among those sympathetic with his position. Even so, such statements could perhaps be defended as an exercise of free speech, just as the judge's courtroom outbursts could be blamed on the hostile atmosphere in which he worked. By the usual standards of judicial conduct, however, his attempts to influence the tenor of NAACP appeal efforts in the *Briggs* case seemed indefensible. Judges are simply not expected to play an active part in the preparation of cases with which they are directly involved. By this point in his career, though, it was clear that Judge Waring was no longer concerned with proper judicial behavior. Instead, he was like a disciple with a mission, and one essentially religious in its intensity. He had persuaded the *Briggs* plaintiffs to make a formal assault on the "false doctrine" of segregation. He had drafted the first modern judicial "sermon" repudiating that doctrine. And he now could not bring himself simply to sit idly by while *his* cause moved through the appellate process.

Had Judge Waring's critics become aware of his lobbying campaign, the revelation undoubtedly would have sparked another round of impeachment threats. That his efforts were not made public, however, did not prevent Tom Waring from once again seeking to secure what he considered to be a true account of his uncle's role, and the motivations underlying that role, in South Carolina's civil rights struggles. While the Warings were in Rhode Island escaping the sultry Charleston summer and the chill of its white populace,

Julian Krawcheck, a reporter for the *Cleveland Press* with family roots in South Carolina, began writing a profile of Judge Waring. While researching the piece, he contacted Tom Waring, an old friend, seeking the *Courier* editor's general impressions and response to a number of specific questions. The memorandum Waring prepared in reply to Krawcheck's inquiries was prompt and by now predictable. The judge "and his wife," Waring wrote, "do not speak to me; they cut me, and not the other way. The same applied to many (almost all, I should say) white people in this community. In all the instances I know of the Warings did the cutting." Because of their family relationship, Tom Waring had "refrained from writing about them in outside publications." But he had "burned to correct the libelous and slanderous remarks they and others have made about us in writings and speeches." He had suggested to newspaper and magazine writers connected with national publications that "they tell the true story, but none is willing to buck the 'Liberal' line. They prefer the lies because they follow the party line."[53]

Although not willing to comment for attribution, the judge's nephew also responded to Krawcheck's list of questions. A "surprising number" of Charlestonians agreed with his white primary decisions, "though political parties are not mentioned in the U.S. Constitution so far as I am aware." What people objected to was "the provocative language of his decision and his subsequent outbursts. . . . Nobody likes to be called 'savages,' especially by one of their own who till June of 1945 also was a 'savage.'" After their "unsavory and brutal double divorce," several of their "erstwhile bridge companions were cool, as inevitably happens in a circle when there is a domestic bustup." But "[t]he real ostracism was done by the Warings." Over the years since their marriage, there had been numerous embarrassing scenes involving the couple, "too numerous to mention but good tea-party gossip." Yes, a foul ball was knocked through a window of a room in which Mrs. Waring was present by a Citadel cadet playing baseball. "I don't believe it was intentional." Yes, for most of his life, Judge Waring had been a leader of South Carolina's white Democratic party and "local contact man for Cotton Ed Smith, the old white supremacist, and never a breath was uttered on admitting the Negro." The judge now ties his civil rights stance to "injustices" he observed from the bench.

> Others say his wife, in pique at supposed social slights, deliberately dreamed up the worst revenge she could take on Charlestonians,—namely, racial mixture. Their only social connections with local people now are Negro—and they swap parties with the Negro uppercrust.

Was the judge "embarrassed by Negro effusions? Not so anyone can notice." Black and white supporters "led a pilgrimage to his house some months ago for Judge Waring day. Nobody was ejected." Is their any "unexpressed" public support for his position? "Many Southerners," Tom Waring responded,

> believe that the advancement of the Negro (through years of fostering by and association with Southern white people) has reached the stage when further concessions can be made. There is considerable sentiment in favor

of letting Negroes vote in the Democratic primary, as well as considerable opposition. The mixing of races in schools is generally opposed by virtually all white people and, in my opinion, most Negroes, but the latter are terrorized by the NAACP and dare not say so out loud. (Most Negro teachers would lose their jobs for lack of qualification [were schools integrated].)

It is doubtful whether Tom Waring expected Krawcheck to produce the sort of profile he believed should be written about his uncle. If he entertained any such hope, however, Krawcheck's response to the material Waring had furnished must have had a sobering effect. Krawcheck wrote the Charleston editor that his own "emotions" about Judge Waring were mixed. As a member of an "oft-persecuted" minority group, he confessed, he was "more inclined than most Southerners to sympathize with efforts to aid *any* minority group." He agreed that Judge Waring apparently had "been intemperate in his conduct, however basically right he might be in his beliefs," and that he might have been motivated by a "desire for revenge." He also observed, however, that the judge "might be capable of deeper emotion than most of us, and his provocations greater."[54]

Tom Waring could understand Krawcheck's "emotional pushes and pulls," but he hoped the journalist would "not allow them to sway a trained newspaper reporter's ability to sift through to the FACTS." He also questioned "all this talk about 'liberalism' [and] 'minority persecution.' . . . The hard core fact," he wrote Krawcheck, "is that nowhere in the world has there been LESS persecution than in America under our present system . . . ever in history. . . . The destruction of that system now going on," he added,

> inevitably will lead to the historic cycle of democracy to dictatorship. Then there will be persecution again. We thinking people should do our part to prevent COMPULSIONS from doing the very things we try to prevent. By compulsions I mean central government regulation of folk customs, personal and private concerns, and destruction of home rule.[55]

In his memorandum, Waring had advised Krawcheck that a "decent piece" on his uncle would require more extensive research "than a few clippings or some blowing off of steam from me," adding, "In my opinion this is one of the most sensational stories in America today." Krawcheck had interviewed other South Carolinians, and he also reached Judge Waring by phone in Rhode Island. In the profile he produced, Krawcheck quoted the usual complaints of South Carolina whites, including several from Tom Waring, attributed to a "fellow Charlestonian." In the main, though, it was a sympathetic treatment. "I've got a cause to live for and a job to do," he quoted the judge at one point. "That's pretty good. What can they do to me, at 71, that would matter? I'm happier than they are." Tom Waring wrote Krawcheck to thank the journalist for a copy of the profile. "It follows the line of most of what has been published," he observed. "In my opinion the facts still have not been thoroughly understood and published. The same words are just being tossed round in various combinations. But then I'm a reactionary."[56]

Tom Waring might have been unable to secure truly critical scrutiny of his uncle by an "outsider," and unwilling to launch his own public assault. But he and his newspaper staff could do their part to defend the racial mores Judge Waring was challenging. Shortly after the *Briggs* decision was announced, W. D. Workman, the *News and Courier*'s Columbia correspondent, spoke to a Charleston civic club about the state's options in the event the Supreme Court ordered desegregation. Given the "recent fear" of the courts, he told his audience, it was unlikely that state officials would attempt to nullify or ignore such a decision. At the same time, "submission" seemed unthinkable. In some upstate metropolitan areas, said Workman, officials might be able to avoid race mixing by gerrymandering school districts; but, given housing patterns, that tactic would not be feasible in Charleston and other cities of the low country, or in rural areas. It might also be possible to limit black attendance by relaxing attendance regulations and tightening academic requirements, and separation of students by gender could be used to "minimize consorting of the sexes among the races." But Workman also suggested another alternative—abandonment of the public schools. He warned blacks, too, that integration would mean job losses for about 7,000 black teachers and administrators since school boards would naturally be unwilling to have black teachers instruct or supervise white children.[57]

The *Courier* gave Workman's speech, including his warning about the likely impact of integration on black school personnel, extensive coverage. In the fall, moreover, the paper editorially endorsed the findings of another of its reporters. In a series of articles on Clarendon County developments since the spring court hearing, reporter Bryan Collier concluded that citizens of both races, among them several of the *Briggs* plaintiffs, preferred segregated schools. Collier's assertions, the *Courier* observed, "accurately reflect the general feeling among colored people as well as white, despite the attempts of the National Association for the Advancement of Colored People to prove otherwise." *Lighthouse and Informer* editor John McCray found "nothing alarming in Mr. Collier's conclusion that Negroes in [Clarendon] county want better facilities . . . , not necessarily the end of segregation itself." However, he insisted that the NAACP had made it clear to all the *Briggs* plaintiffs that it was segregation that was being attacked in the suit. Noting that the issue was "greater than the limits of one school district," he asserted, too, that the governing bodies of the 6,000-member black state teachers association, 125,000-member African Methodist Episcopal Church, 350,000-member black Baptist congregations, the Methodist, and the AME Zion churches, as well as numerous other black groups had "all gone on record as opposing continuation of segregation." The *News and Courier* and other state papers would continue to argue, though, that South Carolina's blacks, like its whites, wanted the schools to remain segregated.[58]

The *Courier,* of course, was not merely opposed to integration; it also doubted the wisdom of the additional expenses to be incurred in upgrading black schools. "Education for what?" an October editorial asked. "For relief rolls? Will the South, the country, be willing to support hordes of colored farm folk OUTSIDE the school-houses in the style to which the pupils will be accustomed?" When a *Courier* editorial claimed that racial conditions were "generally satisfactory," a Catholic priest at the Charleston Naval Base responded, "Our segregated pattern of life is the evil not the ideal of the South. The sin of us Southerners is that we are too proud to admit our wrong, too selfish to live our beliefs, too blind to see that things are not 'generally satisfactory.'" Presumably, however, many whites shared the *Courier*'s intransigence.[59]

Governor Byrnes continued to defend the equalization program. By fall, however, voters were beginning to complain about the 3 percent sales tax being used to fund the project, and the governor began to hedge on what the money would be used for. Speaking to members of the South Carolina Association of School Trustees in October, he said that South Carolina was "in the cellar of illiteracy" and that the funding program was designed to improve education for all students, not merely black children. He emphasized, moreover, that the state was attempting to equalize its schools "because it is right and because it is wise." Resuming a more aggressive stance on segregation, he also announced that the state had retained West Virginia native John W. Davis, a former solicitor general of the United States and one of the nation's most distinguished lawyers, who maintained a winter residence near Charleston, to argue the *Briggs* case before the Supreme Court. He assured his audience, too, that the funding program would be carried out and segregation maintained whatever the courts decided. The equal protection guarantee applied only to state schools. If integration were ordered, he promised, public schools would simply be replaced with "private" institutions beyond the reach of modern judicial constructions of the Constitution. "Whether we have public or private schools," he added, "we are going to need school buildings."[60] When he addressed the general assembly in January 1952, the governor continued on this theme, calling for abolition of the state constitutional guarantee of free public schools for South Carolina's children.

Judge Waring was not surprised that Governor Byrnes would call for an end to public education. "[A] few years ago," he wrote his daughter and son-in-law, "a person would have been called insane who would have forecast that the Governor of any state of these United States would advocate the abolition of public education." Now, on the other hand, such a proposal was just another reflection of "the extent to which . . . the die-hard white supremacists are willing to wreck everything for their obsession." He was mildly surprised, however, that John W. Davis had been induced to join the defendants' cause. He realized, he wrote John Hammond, that Davis had "gone completely reactionary," but thought "that decency would have restrained him from accepting representation of the southern 'slaveocracy'." He was also amazed, frustrated, angered, and deeply disappointed at the reaction of law faculty at the University of North Carolina to a book review he wrote for that reputed citadel of southern progressivism.[61]

In August, while the Warings were still vacationing in Rhode Island, M. H. Ross, the associate editor of the *North Carolina Law Review,* wrote Judge Waring, indicating that he was seeking "stimulating and thought-provoking" book reviews, and inviting the judge to contribute a review of a recently published civil liberties text. In a separate letter, and "[w]ithout in any way representing the views of the Review or its other editors," Ross expressed "personal appreciation and admiration" for Waring's "courageous" *Briggs* dissent. Waring's opinion, wrote Ross, was

> in the finest American and Southern historical tradition as well as vocalizing the dreams and aspirations of a majority of all the people in our "Silent South." Let the loud handful of disbelievers in American freedom and democracy rave on. The common people of our nation and of the world will remember your earnest exposition long after the spiritual heirs of the Dred Scott position are forgotten.[62]

In November, Judge Waring would decline an opportunity to speak before a Chicago civil rights group, explaining that he was "refusing any invitation to make public addresses on racial questions" while the *Briggs* case was before the Supreme Court. He readily accepted the law review's invitation, however, writing its associate editor from Rhode Island.

> It is you fine young men coming through our institutions of learning who must see to it that this America of ours is reserved from the evil blight of racial prejudice. Your University has always been reputed to be advanced and liberal in its teaching and because it is a Southern institution it can have great influence in helping to eliminate the prevailing wrong thinking in our part of the Country.

On returning to Charleston, he wrote the review and mailed it to Ross. The review did analyze its purported subject, but was mostly an exposition of Judge Waring's racial views. "It will be interesting to see the reaction," he wrote Ross, "in your community. It may not be popular but my views and I believe yours are not very popular in the solid south. It is time, however, for the benighted to get some enlightenment and if we can do a little along these lines, it will be helpful."[63]

Ross thought the judge's review was "an excellent contribution in the field," offering only "minor, Editorial suggestions." He soon wrote Waring, however, that "others here are presenting graver objections." He was, he assured the judge, "presently engaged in discussions which I hope will iron out these difficulties," and would appreciate Judge Waring's patience. But the judge was not a patient man. "Do I gather from this," he had soon responded,

> that your board of editors or faculty or other officials have any objection to my being invited to contribute to the Review? If this be so, of course, I wish to be advised. If anybody in official position in the University of North Carolina has such an objection, I should like to have the reason stated and if it is because of my having presented my views quite clearly as to the American creed and voice[d] serious objections to the doctrine of the white supremacists, then, of course, I do not wish to have my name appear in a publication which is controlled by such an ideology. . . . Of course, I understand that this is probably personally embarrassing to you, but you will

realize that it was at your invitation and solicitation that I offered this article and I am in no sense requesting the North Carolina Law Review to publish it.[64]

On December 6, more than a month after Judge Waring had submitted
the review, Paul A. Johnston, the law review editor-in-chief, mailed the judge
a three-page list of suggested revisions. A student board of editors had offered
some "technical" suggestions. Another editorial board, composed of students
and faculty, recommended more substantive revisions. The suggestions, Johnston stressed, were in no way intended "to alter in any way the meaning of
the book review, but merely to suggest what we think would be a more accurate and less controversial method of presentation." Judge Waring saw the
suggestions in a different light. "[I]t is quite apparent," he wrote Johnston,
"that your boards do not like my method of treatment . . . and wish to re-
write the article so as to be more pleasant and conform to the pattern of
'white supremacy' that dominates the community," to, in short, "substitute
weasel words for plain factual statements." For that sort of review, he added,
the editors should have approached the governor of South Carolina or
Georgia, a North Carolina federal judge (one of whom had recently ruled
against integration of the University of North Carolina law school until reversed by the Fourth Circuit), or "North Carolina's own native son who is
so well known throughout the nation, T. Lamar Caudle." (In November,
amid growing evidence of his involvement in influence peddling and related
conduct, President Truman had demanded Caudle's immediate resignation as
assistant attorney general in charge of the Justice Department's tax division.)
His only reason for accepting the invitation to write a book review, he added,
had been "that it came from your University."

> I had . . . felt that the University of North Carolina occupied a unique
> position. It seemed to be about the only place of light in the deep South. In
> great part, I was led to this through the fine stand that Frank Graham had
> taken when President of the University and his sharing, and efforts, in the
> Civil Rights Program. Of course, I should have been warned that these
> indicia did not truly represent the basic thought of your State. *Senator*
> Graham, like Galileo, recanted *President* Graham's brave statements. And
> the University, itself, refuse[d] to follow the Supreme Court's opinions in
> the Sweatt and McLaurin cases.[65]

The "palpable reason" for the "suggestions," wrote Waring, was clear:
"you are afraid to publish an article signed by me in view of my outright
civil rights stand and you are worried that it may offend your governing
bodies and perhaps be offensive to some of the legal and industrial supporters
of your University who wish to continue the south in the pattern of segregation whereby the ruling class creates a secondary citizenry and benefits by the
exploitation of cheap labor." The editors were not to "edit or change" his
review "in any way." Nor was the review to be published, "even if your
boards should again meet in conference and come to a realization of what a
stupid move this is and how you have laid yourself open to exposure. . . .

[N]one of this," he concluded, was "of a confidential nature"; in the future he would not "hesitate to discuss the matter . . . pointing out that the boasted liberalism of the University of North Carolina is not even skin deep and really differs in no material way from South Carolina, Georgia and the other citadels of prejudice and 'white supremacy'." Waring mailed a copy of the letter to M. H. Ross. "What a pathetic situation this is at your University," he also wrote Ross. "[Y]ou have my deepest sympathy."[66]

When the defendants filed their six-month report on December 20, Judge Waring proved no more flexible with his colleagues on the three-judge *Briggs* panel. The report largely summarized the state's plans for the Clarendon County schools, including a promise to have spent over $500,000 for new black facilities by the 1952–53 school year. When the report had been on file for ten days and the plaintiffs raised no objections, Judge Parker recommended to Waring and Timmerman that the panel simply issue an order indicating that it had been received and that the defendants were to file further reports at later dates. Judge Waring quickly responded that, given his *Briggs* dissent, he could not join such an order—an order which, in his view, seemed to carry out fully the views of the *Briggs* majority by continuing "the present system of running schools in South Carolina and apparently contemplat[ing] court supervision over the progress of the years." Instead, he would file a memorandum in which he would contend that the panel had no jurisdiction in the case while Supreme Court review of its ruling was pending. He would also argue again that the panel was "not meeting or deciding the real issues in the case." Parker then suggested that the panel merely permit formal filing of the report, send a copy to the Supreme Court, and withhold further action while the appeal was pending. "I imagine that Judge Waring will have no objection to this order and will sign it," Parker added, "since it is a mere formal order. If, however, he desires to dissent from it, he can note his dissent thereon." Waring did dissent, contending that the report and the panel's latest order had "no place in this case."[67]

Two members of the Supreme Court agreed with Judge Waring. Justices Hugo L. Black and William O. Douglas argued that the additional facts the defendants' report contained were "wholly irrelevant" to the broad constitutional challenge to segregation that the *Briggs* plaintiffs had mounted. In a brief, unsigned opinion issued on January 28, 1952, however, a majority of the Court vacated the district court's original decision and remanded the case for further proceedings in South Carolina. The remand, the Court noted, would give the three-judge panel an opportunity to act on the report, and the high Court the benefit of the panel's views.[68]

While disappointed with the Supreme Court's action, Judge Waring was hopeful that the Court had "merely sidestepped the decision temporarily," sending the case back to South Carolina "for a 'breather.'" State politicians considered the remand a heartening sign, a possible indication that their segregated schools might be left alone if the high Court could be convinced that the state was making a good-faith equalization effort. And if state officials were pleased by the Supreme Court's action, news from Judge Waring's chambers must have made most of them ecstatic. By January 26, 1952, Waring had served ten years on the federal bench and, given his age, was eligible for retirement at full salary. On that date, he sent letters to President Truman and Judge Parker, informing them of his intention to retire on February 15.[69]

Soon, too, he made it clear to Judge Parker that he would no longer serve on the *Briggs* panel. On February 9, Parker wrote Judge Waring and Judge Timmerman that a hearing in the *Briggs* case was tentatively scheduled for Columbia on February 29. But Waring informed his chief judge that he would not participate. "As the matters to be submitted to this proposed hearing," he asserted, "are entirely under the separate but equal theory and seem to be entirely irrelevant to the basis of the case which is the matter of whether Racial Segregation is Constitutional, I would not be willing to accept a designation to sit with you in the case or take any part in it." Conceding that he had "no power, of course," to require a retired judge "to render judicial service unless he is willing to do so," Judge Parker then designated Armistead M. Dobie of the court of appeals to replace Waring on the panel.[70]

In an admiring editorial, the *New York Times* praised the retiring jurist's "good and faithful service," terming him "A Judge Worthy of Honor." In recent years, the *Times* observed, "many of his friends [had] ostracized themselves out of his excellent company. . . . The reason for this development," it added, "was that Judge Waring had taken seriously two documents which had had the backing of some other distinguished Southerners—the Declaration of Independence and the Constitution of the United States." Other national papers and the black press published similar editorials, and Maude Veal wrote the *News and Courier* that she considered herself "a better Christian and a better American for having known this noble couple." A small number of white South Carolinians also offered private praise. For example, R. K. Wise, a Columbia attorney, wrote Waring that while "some of the politicians are delighted that you are leaving the bench," Wise was not. He had never "appeared before a Judge who was fairer in his rulings and who knew how to handle the Court as well as you did." To Wise, Waring was "one of the greatest District Judges" ever to have served in South Carolina. The Charleston newspapers obviously did not share such assessments. But they greeted the announcement of Judge Waring's retirement, as the judge himself later conceded, with "tasteful" restraint. While presenting its own version of the reasons underlying the Warings' local difficulties, the *News and Courier* concluded simply that the judge's decision to retire and move to New York "seems the best solution of an uncomfortable situation."[71]

Later, the *Courier* would editorialize that "aside from 'crusading' on the Negro question," which it "believes was a basic mistake, Judge Waring made an excellent record on the bench. He possesses judicial dignity, intelligence and ability as a lawyer, all qualities that should be present in a judge." When Septima Clark asked that the paper reprint the *Times* editorial, Tom Waring obliged. Other state papers generally followed the *Courier*'s approach, and several were almost complimentary. The Rock Hill paper observed, for example:

We disagree with many of his "liberal" views and some of his court decisions. But we chose not to sit in the seat of judgment. Maybe we are behind
and beside of the times, which is worse even than being ahead.[72]

The Warings had leased a New York apartment. On the day that Judge
Waring's clerk announced the January 28 retirement of the judge to the press,
Mrs. Waring telephoned Samuel B. Lewis, the local Atlantic Coast Line passenger agent, requesting February 16 accommodations to New York. Did she
want the usual round-trip tickets? Lewis asked. "No," Mrs. Waring responded, "it will be one-way. We aren't coming back. It will all be in the
papers today." Lewis had been considering buying a home in Charleston
since selling a family farm several years earlier. He wondered whether the
Warings were interested in selling their Meeting Street home. While he was
debating calling them, his phone rang again. Mrs. Waring had decided to
change their reservations to Monday, February 18. Lewis inquired whether
the Warings wanted to sell their home, and by that evening a deal had been
struck. Judge Waring's price had been $20,000, and, Lewis told reporters,
"[h]e didn't budge a dollar."[73]

While awaiting their departure, the Warings made arrangements to dis-
pose of their car and some of their furniture and to ship the rest to New
York. The judge also completed as much pending judicial business as possible, and when a Greenville churchwoman wrote to indicate that she accepted "the gradualist approach," and thought it "well that so many of
us are . . . moderate," he found time to fire yet another volley at such
thinking. "If a Negro, a Chinese, or an Indian is an American citizen," he
wrote, "he is entitled to all the rights of an American citizen, not to be
given to him as a matter of favor in the future by some sniveling gradualist,
but now, today and this hour." Then, on Monday, John Fleming, Joe Brown,
and Brown's uncle accompanied the couple to the Charleston railroad station
and watched as they boarded the train for New York. As long as segregation
remained the law of the land, they had told Ruby Cornwell and their other
black friends, they would not return.[74]

The close proximity of the retirement announcement to the Supreme
Court's remand of the *Briggs* case had led at least one of the judge's friends
to suggest that the latter had been the catalyst for the former. In a letter to
John Hammond, Waring did suggest that his retirement would focus "the
eyes of the country on the sidestepping issue in the Supreme Court." The
decision to retire, however, apparently had been made long before the high
Court's action. On the day that Judge Waring gave his *Briggs* dissent to his
clerk for filing, Mrs. Waring had written in her diary, "I feel now that it is
done that this is our last act. . . . Our period of usefulness is over in the
South at least." On January 9, moreover, the judge had written Anne and
Stanley Warren regarding their efforts to find the Warings a New York apartment. "[W]e have no inhibitions as to living anywhere just so it is in New
York," he wrote. "You can cover Manhattan from the Battery upward but
don't go across the river into the Bronx and, for God's sake, don't put us in
Brooklyn."[75]

Judge Waring's decision to retire probably reflected a complex of factors. As a retired judge, he wrote Benjamin Mays, he would be completely free to speak out on civil rights issues, "no longer muzzled by cases pending or expected to be brought before me." He also had no desire to continue to participate in the *Briggs* litigation. "If I had sat on such a court," he wrote John Hammond, "and gone into the matter of passing upon drawings and discussing the size of black boards and lighting facilities, I would have descended into the separate-but-equal arena . . . [and] I could not convince other members to [reject] the separate-but-equal theory. I hope that my refusal to sit may have some influence upon the Supreme Court and the mind of the country." The attitudes of South Carolina whites also apparently had an influence. "Life was getting more and more burdensome down South," he would later say. "If one is very unhappy in his own home, where he goes through all the insults . . . and the complete ostracism, it hurts, it pains, and it runs you rather miserable. . . . You hate to be in a foreign land where you're hated all the time. . . . [A]lmost anything I did would be colored by the ill-will of those people. They would feel that I'd done it from wrong motives." If the Supreme Court ordered an end to segregation, and he was called upon to implement such a ruling, such hostility would have been particularly unfortunate. "I thought that," he would recall, "had better be done by someone else who was not as objectionable to the people of the district as I was." If, on the other hand, the high Court affirmed Parker and Timmerman, "the whole matter would be utterly hopeless for many years to come." He wanted no part of that process.[76]

Judge Waring hoped, too, that his retirement would put Charleston blacks "on their mettle," prodding them to show "courage and come out on their own fighting basis." He had been disappointed that few civil rights cases had been filed in his court. In a letter written to John Hammond the day his retirement became effective, he lamented the NAACP's failure to bring many cases to his court; asserted that Hammond, not the association's legal staff, had been "mostly responsible for the fact that there ever was a Clarendon School case"; and complained that while *Briggs* had given him an opportunity to attack segregation, he had worked "without the benefit of briefs or serious preparation or presentation by the NAACP legal department." On the drive to the railroad station the following Monday, he raised the same concerns with Charleston NAACP leader Joe Brown. "You know," Brown would later recall Waring remarking, "I was a little disappointed. You knew almost the way I was going to rule. Why didn't you bring more cases?" He and Mrs. Waring had been disheartened, too, John McCray would later report, that some blacks "began to turn tail and run" after the cross-burning and stoning incidents, that their circle of black friends had steadily dwindled, and that a number of prominent blacks were defending equalization or even the status quo. And when black children who traditionally serenaded prominent white families at Christmas passed them by and sang instead before the home of a Waring enemy in the same neighborhood, they were deeply saddened. Privately, they told McCray that the "turntails" had hurt them more than anything else and were perhaps the decisive factor in their decision to leave Charleston. In an interview following his retirement, Judge Waring told a reporter for a black paper that the "only people I fear in this fight are the weak-kneed colored people of our state." The "poorer" blacks, he added, were "the brave ones,"

> but they need stronger and surer support from the people who should be in the position of leadership . . . the Negro ministers, the Negro school teachers, the Negro professional people . . . many [who] benefit directly from this system of discrimination are the ones who should be in the lead in the fight . . . but many of them are terrified.

His retirement, he hoped, would put them on notice that they must be the instruments of their own salvation.[77]

Whatever their motivations for leaving, Judge Waring would tell reporters after his retirement that they had left Charleston "with no regrets whatever." Nor had they, he added, any regrets about the record he had forged. "I have tried, to the best of my ability," he remarked to another journalist, "to administer simple justice. . . . I have been decried and despised and hated. But I shall be satisfied if it can be said of me, as it was said of Grover Cleveland: 'We love him for the enemies he made.' " At some point, moreover, he had drafted a memorandum itemizing the losses and gains of his "break with South Carolina and Charleston." The gains heavily outnumbered the losses. When he had talked with a *New York Times* reporter about the beauty of Charleston, however, nostalgia had crept into his voice, and in his memorandum he had conceded that "[t]o have an entirely different ideology and conception of civil rights, duties, and responsibilities from the community in which you live [was] . . . unfortunate." The Warings' friend Myles Horton understood. In a letter to the judge, Horton quoted the words of nineteenth-century Charleston novelist and poet William Gilmore Sims. The passage read:

> . . . simple change of place is seldom exile
> . . . there's a truer banishment.
>   'Tis to be
> An exile on the spot where you were born;
> A stranger on the hearth which saw your youth,
> Banished from the hearts to which your heart is turned.[78]

8

The New York Years

Soon after the Warings' arrival in New York, John J. Parker wrote the judge, asking him to hold a term of court in Wheeling, West Virginia. Retired federal judges are frequently called upon for such duties, but Judge Waring quickly made it clear that he had no interest in returning to southern or border states for judicial duty. Earlier, he had informed his circuit chief judge that he and Mrs. Waring hoped that they could "do more effective work in breaking down the evils of racial prejudice from . . . outside the curtain of White Supremacy." Now, he indicated that some of the judges in New York's southern district had been urging him to assist in relieving congested dockets there, but that he had not yet fixed a definite time for taking on such duties. "If and when I do take on assignment for Court work," he pointedly added, "I think I would prefer working here in a much more comfortable and congenial surrounding which I have come to appreciate and enjoy." He remained firm in this resolve. When, in 1955, Parker again invited him to attend a session of the Fourth Circuit judicial conference and to hold a term of court in West Virginia, he declined both invitations.[1]

Their first months in New York were busy and essentially happy ones for the Warings. As an admiring *New York Post* profile published shortly after their arrival indicated, "personal messages of affection and esteem" came to their 952 Fifth Avenue apartment virtually every day. Some simply thanked them for their sacrifices. "I want you to know how sorry I am," one black woman wrote, "that you had to give up your home in the South because you have tried to help my people. I do hope that you will have a good life here. May God bless you . . . [and have] pity on those who ostracized you, for they suffer more than they have caused you to suffer." Others sought to honor them or solicit their aid. "They beg him," *Post* reporter Henry Beckett observed, "to found and lead some organization to further the cause of civil rights. They express pride because the Warings have become fellow citizens here. They wish to honor them with dinners. They want the judge and his wife to speak to them and to attend their churches."[2]

During the spring and summer of 1952, the Warings were extremely ac-

213

tive. In March, he was guest speaker at the annual banquet of the Harvard Law Review Association and at an NAACP meeting in Philadelphia, telling the latter gathering that the Christmas bombing murder of a Florida NAACP leader and his wife was simply a "good, old-fashioned white supremacy lynching," and adding, "every time some fellow begins to step up for his rights, a policeman finds him troublesome and ends up shooting him." In April, the New York chapter of the American Civil Liberties Union gave a luncheon in their honor and heard the judge urge people to pressure Congress and presidential candidates in behalf of racial reform. In May, he spoke at the thirty-fifth anniversary dinner of the National Urban League; the *Chicago Defender* again honored his significant contributions to democracy; and an interdenominational organization of ministers presented him with its annual Roosevelt brotherhood medal at a Harlem church. During June commencement ceremonies at which President Truman spoke, Howard University awarded the judge a doctor of laws degree. The same month, in Chicago, he and Mrs. Waring were given what *Nation* magazine termed "a tumultous reception" at the general conference of the AME church. Speaking to the conference's more than 10,000 delegates, he urged each of the two major political parties to adopt strong civil rights planks, scorned all forms of racial discrimination, and insisted that Congress safeguard voting rights, provide equal employment opportunity, and protect the "security of person and property." He also called on the president to integrate immediately all armed forces and forbid discrimination in government contracts. In numerous other forums, he and Mrs. Waring voiced similar themes. He made it clear, too, that his opposition to those who espoused "gradualism" in racial change extended to northern black leaders as well as southern liberals, condemning "Uncle Toms" within civil rights groups. And he refused to appear before any black organization that excluded whites from its membership.[3]

Waring also tried to influence national political leaders. The judge had long been disenchanted with the Truman administration. When he retired from the bench, however, the president told a South Carolina reporter that he thought Waring had been "a very great federal judge," adding, "I'll say that for your benefit." Shortly before the Howard commencement exercises, Waring wrote Truman a lengthy letter, praising the president's most recent statements in behalf of civil rights and warning Democrats not to trust Byrnes, Talmadge, and other "Dixiecrat" leaders "whose talk of support of our party is merely a desire to retain their own selfish power through the un-American doctrine of 'White Supremacy.'" Nor was he patient with the party's efforts to keep its southern wing in the fold. When the party's 1952 presidential nominee Adlai Stevenson picked Alabama senator John Sparkman as his running mate, and Sparkman appeared to repudiate the Democrats' civil rights plank during a national interview program, Waring wrote Stevenson a strong letter of protest. "[U]nless clearly repudiated by you, Governor," he asserted, Sparkman's statements "will and should definitely drive away from supporting you those of us who believe that the time has come for America to cleanse itself of this evil disease of racial prejudice which is gnawing at the vitals of our body politic and is making a sham of our loud but hypocritical show of democracy."[4]

Governor Stevenson did not answer Judge Waring's letter. The Warings were soon to learn, moreover, that their strident, no-compromise stance had limited appeal among political leaders, certain segments of the black press, and the leadership of the major civil rights organizations, although they remained heroic figures among blacks and whites favoring their militant approach to civil rights. Following Judge Waring's speech to the NAACP in Philadelphia, for example, Sadie Alexander, a prominent black attorney who, with her husband, was a close friend and supporter, wrote Elizabeth Waring a letter. While in Philadelphia, the Warings had visited the couple's home and met their young daughter. "You and I," Mrs. Alexander wrote Elizabeth, "cannot estimate what it means to a child, in her adolescent years, to listen, see, and talk with, as a friend, a Federal judge and his wife, who have sacrificed position, economic and personal security for a principle which involves the child's security and freedom."[5] But others found the Warings' militancy politically naive, or resented their verbal assaults on blacks who favored a gradual approach to racial reform.

On one occasion shortly after their arrival in New York, such concerns led to a rare attack on the Warings in the black press. For one thing, there was much less coverage generally of the Warings after they moved to New York. In the wake of his uncle's retirement, Tom Waring had printed the *News and Courier*'s version of the couple's Charleston experiences, then distributed copies to the Associated Press and other publishing conduits in yet another effort "to prevent further libeling of this community." Several days later, he sent his staff a memorandum indicating that his uncle's departure from Charleston had "greatly diminished" his news value. Future stories regarding events involving Judge Waring were to be treated according to normal news standards. The judge's statements, on the other hand, were to be considered "propaganda rather than news." Stories based on the judge's remarks were to either be dropped or run "briefly with a small headline." The Warings would continue to receive generally favorable coverage in the national press and black papers. But it was not to be as extensive as that given their activities before his retirement. Following their appearance at the Chicago AME conference, for example, there had been, with few exceptions Mrs. Waring wrote a journalist friend, an "amazing silence." And in mid-June, the *New York Times* had refused to publish a letter the judge had written to the *Times* editor, citing its exceptional length. Earlier, moreover, the *Pittsburgh Courier*, one of the more conservative of the black papers, criticized Judge Waring for his attacks on "so-called gradualists and appeasers within our group." The *Courier* would yield to no one in its "admiration" of the judge. Nor did it know a single prominent black who did not want an end to racial segregation "in every form." But opponents of segregation "who are active and not retired must be realistic and reasonable," the paper asserted. As long as segregation was the law in sixteen states, people must be gradualists "or face prison and ruin, in which event they would be of no service to themselves nor

to their group." Judge Waring, the paper contended, was "unfair and certainly unrealistic to expect them to sacrifice themselves and their families in
order to avoid the 'smear' of gradualism when they have no alternative." Judicial action itself, it added, was "an example of gradualism at its best, and
scarcely a revolutionary process." Judge Waring knew that and should remember it before further attacking black leaders. "While we are awaiting the
arrival of Utopia," the paper concluded, "we have to live, and a live gradualist is better than a dead revolutionist."[6]

In a *Lighthouse and Informer* editorial, John McCray challenged the
Pittsburgh paper's assertions.[7] But segments of the national black leadership
no doubt shared its sentiments. Even so, the Warings would remain adamant
in their position. And this intransigence—combined with their temperamental
personalities—was to lead to frequent clashes with various figures in the civil
rights movement, especially during their early years in New York.

In fact the first such incident began to develop even before the Warings'
departure from Charleston. Shortly after Judge Waring's retirement was announced, Walter White suggested that the NAACP give a dinner in their
honor once they were settled in their New York apartment. The Warings
were "honored and pleased" by the invitation. To their growing irritation,
however, planning for the affair became embroiled in numerous delays. When
Anne Warren told NAACP board member John Hammond of an apparent
News and Courier report that her father was being asked to continue serving
on the Clarendon County school case, White became concerned that the
NAACP dinner might force the judge to withdraw from the litigation. Waring
quickly dismissed the rumor as a "complete lie," insisting that no such article
had appeared in the Charleston papers and that he had no intention of sitting
"in any rehearing or pass[ing] upon any separate-but-equal matter." When
he arrived in New York, he wrote White, he would be retired and there would
"be no embarrassment for me to speak to you as any other American citizen."[8]

The choice of a moderator for the event proved a more protracted and
sensitive problem. The Warings considered White the logical selection to host
the affair, but White thought it more appropriate, given his status as an
NAACP official, to select someone else. White's first choice was Judge Learned
Hand, the distinguished federal appeals court jurist, but he also suggested
New York's Nelson Rockefeller and Missouri senator Stuart Symington. Judge
Waring was not enthusiastic about any of his friend's suggestions. Not surprisingly, given Judge Hand's status as a leading advocate of judicial self-
restraint, Waring did not "think too much" of that choice. "I don't think he
is sufficiently liberal," he wrote White, "and doubt whether he would do it
anyhow. I am not sure that his heart is entirely in matters of this kind." He
agreed that Rockefeller and Symington were "important people and it might
be advantageous to have them tied in with the cause." But it appeared to
Waring that "even better ones might be obtained," including Senator Herbert
Lehman of New York and Minnesota's Hubert Humphrey, both of whom were
"able and militant."[9]

Judge Waring correctly predicted Judge Hand's reaction. In what White termed a "frank" letter, the appeals court judge declined involvement in any affair honoring his outspoken and controversial fellow jurist. White wrote Hand, thanking him for considering the invitation. "Judge Waring's controversiality," he added,

> is due to the fact that as a native-born Southerner, son of a Confederate veteran, he believed so strongly and courageously in the Federal Constitution that he dared advocate compliance with the Constitution in a section of the country where such compliance so far as Negroes are concerned is an anathema to the bigots.
>
> We want to honor him because in risking and incurring contumely, ostracism and even mob violence, he dared to stand without equivocation for the principles of justice laid down in our laws and traditions.

White was thus "not shocked but a little puzzled" at Hand's refusal to participate. Judge Waring was not. Nor was he surprised when White continued to have difficulty securing a political or judicial moderate to serve as toastmaster.[10]

But he was increasingly irritated by it. Early on in their correspondence about the dinner, White had raised a "somewhat embarrassing" subject—use of the affair as an occasion for announcing an NAACP fund-raising effort. Judge Waring initially had no objection to White's proposal. Soon, though, he became convinced that the NAACP director was primarily interested in the Warings' fund-raising value—and in finding a dinner chairman sufficiently bland in his political image to promote, not impede, that effort. The decision of the NAACP's Legal Defense and Educational Fund to extend an invitation to a Naval admiral was "the last straw." In late March, Waring wrote White that "it would be quite undignified for [him] to continue to shop around the country to find a presiding officer." The time had long passed for the event to be considered a gesture of welcome; now, it "would be only another fund raising event. . . . [I]n addition to all of this," Waring pointedly added, "I have accepted several invitations to address different organizations which did not have to overcome this fear complex. . . . I cannot tell you how deeply I appreciate your suggestion and efforts and how much I value our friendship. But I must ask that you drop the Dinner."[11]

To no avail, White and other association officials continued to encourage the dinner. White reminded Waring, for example, that he and others of like mind must attempt to expand the ranks of those committed to the cause of civil rights. "There is some value," he wrote the judge, "in keeping the converted converted; there is equal importance in converting the unconverted." Waring was not impressed. "[S]urely you must know by this time," he wrote White,

> that big business and politicians are not going to stick their necks out and openly defy the patterns of White Supremacy. And where is there a Church leader who would so commit himself?
>
> No, the only people who would want to take part are those decent Americans who are not afraid of their business, political or social existence.

A business executive might be asked how his corporation meets the impact of the segregation laws of the South. A politician might have to be counted on the matter of the filibuster in Congress. And a poor snivelling minister would have to be reminded of the forgotten and out-moded theory of Brotherhood.

No, Walter you cannot convert the people who are not with us by asking them to commit themselves on such dangerous ground and to give money for something that they as yet do not favor. I represent the cult of complete abrogation of all racial distinction. And while I would have enjoyed this proposed honor, I realize that I am of absolutely no use as a bait to get the opposition into the fold.[12]

In late April, the NAACP's executive board met and voted to invite Dr. Ralph Bunche to chair a dinner in Waring's honor, and Thurgood Marshall telephoned the judge to inform him that Bunche had agreed to serve—Waring's first communication with the NAACP's chief counsel, the judge later wrote Bunche, since the Warings' arrival in New York. But Waring then contacted Dr. Bunche, outlining the project's history, complaining of the association's "inter-office bickering and solicitation of people outside of our realm of opinion," and asserting that, in his judgment, he and Bunche "should not be put on show." When the NAACP's national president Arthur B. Spingarn sought to intervene, suggesting that Waring meet with an association committee to discuss the matter, the judge was courteous but firm; plans for the dinner were dropped.[13]

Tensions between Judge Waring and NAACP officials that spring did not end with the decision to cancel the dinner. As a member of the association's national board, Judge Hubert Delany had recommended that Waring be invited to give the major address at the NAACP's annual convention in Oklahoma City. The judge apparently agreed, and his name was included on the convention program. But ultimately he refused to appear. He had become increasingly concerned that the association's officials were too closely aligned with the Democratic party, so much so that their ties with the party, he feared, might force them into compromises on civil rights. In late May, he had written Walter White, asserting that the Democrats and "White House Palace Guard" were attempting "to appease *all*" the party's branches and charging that there could be "no compromise with the Dixiecrats." He had always been a Democrat, but he now believed that those committed to racial reform "should not be any longer tied up so that we are not free to go to those who will really give us Civil Rights, not only by word but by deed. However bad the Republicans with Taft or Eisenhower may be they would be preferable to a Democratic party allied with the Dixiecrats." When Waring became convinced that White and other members of the association staff would be committed to the Democratic ticket in the fall elections, he decided to withdraw from the convention program. "If I were to appear," he informed Louis T. Wright, chairman of the association's executive board, "I would have to be frank in stating my views relative to alliances and commitments of the staff to one political party; and also I would criticize the lack of activities of the legal staff in attacking (without continuous delay and evasion) what I consider the basic evil . . . segregation." In a letter to Judge Delany, moreover, he insisted that he was "not going to make any appearances under the 'management' of the staff. That Dinner disgrace taught me never to be caught again." Enclosed with the letter was a *Lighthouse and Informer* editorial critical of the NAACP's legal staff. "You see," he wrote, "what the simple folk think of the legal staff." According to reports in the black press, a delegation of association officials, led by publicity director Henry Lee Moon, visited the Warings' apartment in an effort to resolve the judge's concerns. But they had no success. On the third day of the late June convention, it was announced that he would not appear.[14]

The abrupt removal of Judge Waring's name from the convention program was itself an embarrassment to Walter White and other NAACP officials. The publicity given the incident in the black press must have been equally disturbing. The *Chicago Defender* claimed, for example, that Walter White's off-the-record remarks about the incident were "inconsistent with the actual facts" and recommended a re-examination of NAACP policies to determine whether "the association has veered from its announced intention of fighting for full integration of Negroes into American life." The assessment of *Afro-American* reporter James Hicks was even harsher. Judge Waring's "unconditional surrender" approach to racial reform, wrote Hicks, had won "the hearts and admiration of millions of minority group members and these supporters range from board members of the NAACP to grass roots supporters in small NAACP branches scattered over the country." Waring, Hicks asserted, believed that segregation should be attacked now, in all its forms, and that any individual opposed to complete desegregation should himself be opposed. Walter White, Thurgood Marshall, Roy Wilkins, and other association staff members, on the other hand, could not embrace that stance. Instead, they sometimes were willing to look the other way. "Thus," concluded Hicks,

> we find the unusual situation of a prominent Southern-born white man, who has given up most of the things he holds dear in life, charging a group of colored men with not having the courage to go as far and fight as hard as he is willing to fight for the things which are most dear to them.[15]

Following the NAACP controversy, civil rights leaders continued to praise Judge Waring's courage and sacrifice, but his relations with Thurgood Marshall and a number of other major figures in the movement were to remain strained at best. Nor were the NAACP incidents to be the judge's only public conflicts with civil rights groups. In 1954, he was elected to the board of the National Urban League, but only after an abrasive fight within the organization. The most moderate of the nation's civil rights groups, the Urban League and its white president, prominent New York realtor Robert W. Dowling, had come under increasing attack in the black press and within the league's membership for failing to take an aggressive stand against discriminatory housing practices. The league's militant faction circulated a petition urging Judge Waring's addition to the organization's executive board. When the nominating committee omitted his name from the list of nominees, his supporters sought to add his name to the list. President Dowling protested that such an action would amount to a vote of no-confidence in the nominating committee. But after bitter debate, some of it centering on Judge Waring's militancy, the delegates approved a motion of Kenneth Clark, the psychologist who had testified for the *Briggs* plaintiffs, to nominate Waring from the floor. Shortly thereafter, he was elected to membership.[16]

Despite resistance to his selection, Judge Waring agreed, "after long consideration" and "great hesitation," to serve on the league's board, writing a friend that he hoped to "be of some use in joining with the more militant thinking members" and did not believe he should "be influenced by any feeling of resentment at the difficulty my friends had in getting me elected." Partly in protest against the judge's treatment, however, two board members did resign. The nominating committee's "actual turning down of the candidacy of one of America's great jurists," wrote one to President Dowling, "clearly implied that he was evidently too radical because he has proven beyond doubt his belief in true equality." Later, Judge Waring himself resigned from the Manhattan-Westchester County board of the National Conference of Christians and Jews, scoring the national organization's failure to adopt a nonsegregation policy for all its local chapters.[17]

Judge Waring's impatience with the fainthearted also extended to those in the movement who were targets of Communist smear campaigns. The judge himself would remain a staunch anti-Communist. In 1953, he refused to participate in a Carnegie Hall meeting supporting clemency for convicted spies Julius and Ethel Rosenberg. The meeting's organizer emphasized that it would focus "exclusively upon" the clemency issue, not on the Rosenbergs' guilt or innocence. But Waring declined to participate, wiring sponsors that "The Rosenberg case is one for decision [by] the Courts and the President." The same year, he and Mrs. Waring resigned from Southerners for Civil Rights. "We have had to fight," he informed the group's president, "to get the organization to protect itself from Communist infiltration by the by-laws begrudgingly inserted on the subject at our insistence and we feel that our general attitude will keep us constantly critical of the board which is not a good thing for cooperation. When not in full sympathy, much less confidence, with the policies of an organization it is best to resign." At the same time, he was a frequent critic of the House Committee on Un-American Activities and signed petitions seeking its abolition. He also recognized, of course, that redbaiting was a favorite tactic of the segregationists. And he remained loyal to Myles Horton, Horton's wife, Aubrey Williams, and James Dombrowski, despite charges that Horton's Highlander School and the Southern Conference Educational Fund, with which Williams and Dombrowski were connected, were hotbeds of communism. In fact, when Marion Wright expressed shock that a Methodist publication in Georgia had charged the Southern Regional Council, which Wright headed, with fomenting "Communist" doctrine, Waring was amazed that his friend could be "surprised at this attack." "The term

'Communism,' " he wrote Wright, "is just the usual curse word . . . [of] the prejudiced and vicious." In the same letter, moreover, he expressed pleasure that the Council was planning to work with the Highlander School. "What wonderful people they are," he wrote of the Hortons, "brave and entirely without evasions or sophistries. They too have been subjected to the Communist smear."[18]

Waring was disappointed and perplexed, however, when Horton chose silence rather than outspoken indignation as a defense against a southern senator's investigation into alleged Communist infiltration of the civil rights movement. As the Supreme Court moved toward a decision in *Brown, Briggs,* and the other school segregation cases in early 1954, Mississippi senator James Eastland journeyed to New Orleans for a one-man subcommittee hearing of the Senate Internal Security Committee. Other subcommittee members boycotted the hearing, but Eastland had a field day, calling to the witness stand Myles Horton, James Dombrowski, and Virginia Durr, as well as assorted former Communists brought in to challenge the other witnesses' loyalty. Though refusing to furnish Eastland with the names of donors, Dombrowski testified extensively about the activities of the Southern Conference Educational Fund. But the other witnesses were decidedly uncooperative. While Eastland questioned Mrs. Durr, Justice Black's sister-in-law—who considered the Mississippi senator "common as pig tracks"—powdered her nose. Myles Horton refused to discuss the beliefs and affiliations of other persons, including Dombrowski; when Eastland interrupted his attempt to explain the constitutional grounds on which he based his refusal to testify, ordering him ejected from the hearing room, Horton resisted, shouting: "They're treating me like a criminal. You're just putting on a show here—that's all."[19]

Judge Waring was "unalterably opposed" to one-man hearings and considered the spectacle of a white-supremacist senator investigating groups advocating racial justice a mockery of due process. Pleading insufficient knowledge of the "charges and countercharges" at issue, however, he refused to join Eleanor Roosevelt, Mary Bethune, and others in a protest against Eastland's tactics. He was convinced, moreover, that the conduct of Horton and the other witnesses had "done our cause of freedom great harm," playing "directly into the hands of those who wish to smear the fight for racial equality with the *brand* of communism." When "faced with such an inquiry, however stacked the cards appear to be," he wrote James Dombrowski,

> I think it a grievous mistake to set up legal objections to the inquiry itself. The organization if its record is right (and it is fighting for a fine cause) should be willing to open its books and records to any scrutiny. It should be proud to show to this Dixiecrat Senator that it is above suspicion. But now the picture is otherwise. I know nothing of these witnesses who told of the organization's origin. If they were lying why not take the stand and cram their lies down their throats? Why refuse to produce the names of the organizers and supporters? And what useful purpose could be attained by Myles Horton refusing to say if he knew James Dombrowski as one who had

taught at Highlander. In a fine clean cause such as the abolition of racial segregation we should not be ashamed of our motives, our acts or our associates.[20]

If the conduct of the witnesses at Senator Eastland's March 1954, hearing was a source of concern to Judge Waring, however, the action of the Supreme Court some weeks later was to be more than adequate compensation. After the Court had vacated the district court's original judgment in the *Briggs* case, Judges Parker, Timmerman, and Dobie, Waring's replacement on the three-judge panel, had reviewed the defendants' initial compliance report and reaffirmed the original decision to reject the plaintiffs' challenge to segregation, but required South Carolina to equalize its educational facilities. The plaintiffs then filed another appeal with the Supreme Court. In the interim, however, *Brown* v. *Board of Education,* a challenge to segregation in the schools of Topeka, Kansas, had arrived at the Court and was placed at the top of its segregation docket. By the fall of 1952, cases challenging segregation in Virginia, Delaware, and the District of Columbia were also before the Court. In December 1952, the Court heard oral argument in the cases. In September 1953, Chief Justice Vinson died, replaced by Earl Warren. That December, the Court heard further argument in the cases. Already, however, the new chief justice was beginning to move his brethren toward a unanimous decision, to be embodied in a single opinion.[21]

As the high Court slowly progressed toward a decision, South Carolina officials continued with their equalization efforts, with state papers defending segregation and condemning the burdens "forced mixing" would inflict on citizens of both races. Characteristically, the *News and Courier* was the most vociferous keeper of the faith. "Would it be Christian," one of its editorials asked, "to load the white man's burden on the frail shoulders of a grade school child—on YOUR child?" If the Supreme Court rejected segregated education, another asserted, the trend toward segregated housing patterns might be "intensified. . . . Sections where Negroes now predominate would be left increasingly to the Negroes, where they could form their own school districts and levy taxes to support their own schools." The paper was not "recommending" such a development, "merely forecast[ing] what may happen, in the event of an unfavorable Court decision." A *Courier* news article concluded, as had others before it, that many Clarendon County blacks disliked the "notion of 'mixed' classrooms." And when John W. Davis argued South Carolina's position before the Supreme Court, Tom Waring termed his performance "masterful," the arguments of the plaintiffs' counsel "vague and legalistic."[22]

Letters to the editor, including a number from local blacks, also generally defended the status quo. When the *Courier* published photographs of the school facilities being constructed for Clarendon County's black children, facilities it would later claim "far surpass[ed]" any offered white students, Charleston NAACP head Arthur Clement wrote the editor that "[n]o matter what South Carolina may do, as commendable as it may be . . . there has already taken place a conditioning of mind, spirit and body that will never be corrected in present generations." But a black minister contended that members of his race, through their desegregation efforts, were "saying to ourselves in stronger words than the white man has ever said that we are an inferior race of people." A black woman asserted, moreover, that "we can own businesses, properties or anything else and we are free to go wherever we want to go among our own race, so until we make up our minds to leave well enough alone there will be some kind of confusion." In their letters to the *Courier,* white opponents of integration were more direct. "Regardless of what the so-called Supreme Court does," wrote one, "let South Carolina quit public schools altogether." But the paper's editor was, as usual, bluntest of all. The South, he insisted, "will evade any ruling to mix the races in schools."[23]

At one point, the *Courier* turned its attention once again to Judge Waring. In a late February address at a New York church, Waring praised J. A. De-Laine, saying of the Clarendon minister, "It is because of that one man's tenacity" that the segregation cases were in the Supreme Court. For his efforts, the judge claimed, DeLaine's home had been burned, the county fire department had refused to fight the blaze, his insurance company had refused to pay for the damages, and a former black school official had sued him for libel, winning a judgment from an all-white jury. The *Courier* soon took issue with a number of Waring's allegations, arguing, among other things, that DeLaine was no longer living in the house when it burned, the house was outside the fire department's jurisdiction, and DeLaine's insurance company had eventually honored his claim. DeLaine then prepared a lengthy rejoinder to the *Courier's* contentions and attempted to persuade members of the Clarendon NAACP to sign his statement. But he had no success. "They . . . seem to fear," he wrote Judge Waring, "that unpleasantness will be renewed against them."[24]

But Earl Warren's appointment to the Supreme Court bolstered Waring's confidence that his cause would ultimately prevail. In an exclusive January interview with the Montgomery, Alabama, *Advertiser,* Thurgood Marshall had expressed confidence that blacks would follow a line of "complete cooperation, not upheaval," if segregation were outlawed and speculated that such a ruling would have no "effect for thirty years" in certain areas of the South's Black Belt. Any change, he added, "must be gradual and it must be through cooperation at the local level." While Waring was hardly likely to approve of such rhetoric, he apparently had been satisfied with the NAACP's major presentation of the segregation cases before the Supreme Court. Marshall had provided him with copies of the briefs the association filed with the Court. "Please accept my hearty congratulations and thanks for the admirable presentation," the judge wrote Marshall on receiving the Defense Fund's principal effort.

> The brief shows a vast amount of difficult and diligent research work and gives a clear and convincing picture of the whole matter. And I especially like the clear cut attack on Plessy . . . which is indeed the bedrock of all the confused and tangled thinking of many years. If we can only get that

repudiated we will have a much easier path. I do not see how the Court can any longer tolerate the 'separate but equal' theory. They themselves have chiselled away all of its foundations and I do believe that they will overturn it in its mistaken entirety.

As the Court moved toward an announcement of its decision, his confidence grew. "I'm just damn fool enough to believe," he told friends, that "we've got to win."[25]

On Monday morning, May 17, Elizabeth Waring found her husband sitting in their apartment, jotting notes to himself on a sheet of paper. He had thought that the Supreme Court would probably announce its decision in late June, near the end of its term, as it frequently did in important cases. Now, he told his wife, he had a vague hunch that a decision might come down that day, and he wanted to be prepared in case reporters asked him for his reaction. During the night, Elizabeth told her husband, she had had the same feeling.[26]

Shortly after noon, a secretary in the office of NAACP publicity director Henry Moon telephoned the Warings' apartment. The Supreme Court, she reported, was planning to announce its ruling that day. She was unaware what its decision would be. Soon, however, the airwaves were filled with the news—the Court had unanimously held that segregation had "no place" in the field of public education, that "[s]eparate educational facilities are inherently unequal"—an echo of Judge Waring's dissent three years earlier. The Warings were jubilant. They had expected vindication, but not a unanimous decision. Elizabeth began telephoning their friends, inviting them to a celebration party that evening.[27]

Chief Justice Warren's opinion largely embraced the rationale of Judge Waring's *Briggs* dissent. "To separate [children] from others of similar age and qualifications solely because of their race," he had written,

> generates a feeling of inferiority as to their status in the community that may affect their hearts and minds in a way unlikely ever to be undone. . . . "Segregation of whites and colored children in public schools has a detrimental effect upon the colored children. The impact is greater when it has the sanction of the law; for the policy of separating the races is usually interpreted as denoting the inferiority of the negro group. A sense of inferiority affects the motivation of a child to learn. Segregation with the sanction of law, therefore, has a tendency to [retard] the educational and mental development of negro children and to deprive them of some of the benefits they would receive in a racial[ly] integrated school system." Whatever may have been the extent of psychological knowledge at the time of *Plessy* v. *Ferguson,* this finding is amply supported by modern authority. Any language in *Plessy* v. *Ferguson* contrary to this finding is rejected.[28]

As Robert McC. Figg would point out with smug satisfaction thirty years later, however, Warren made no mention of the Waring dissent. Instead, the chief justice had quoted from the opinion of the trial court in the *Brown* case—an opinion which agreed that segregation had a damaging effect on minority children, yet upheld segregated schooling on the authority of *Plessy.*

In an amicus curiae brief filed in the petitioners' behalf, counsel for the Congress of Industrial Organizations (CIO) had contended that "segregation *per se*" was inequality, as Waring had argued. But the CIO brief had not cited Waring, nor had any of the other briefs or counsel during oral arguments before the Court.[29]

Waring regretted the omission but praised the Court's decision, telling a reporter:

> This decision will make history and will erase the shame of the Dred Scott and Plessy against Ferguson cases. The Court has affirmed our belief in the Declaration of Independence and the Constitution and has finally killed the hypocrisy of those who practice a vicious form of racial bias under the sophistry of the so-called separate but equal doctrine. For a long time we have suffered under the taunts of foreign enemies who have proclaimed that we did not live up to our protestations of true democracy. We are now freed from that charge, and democracy and decency prevail.

He also admired Chief Justice Warren's handiwork. "It's clear-cut. It's simple," he would later remark. "The great beauty of the Warren opinion is that it's not a learned opinion . . . you can summarize [it] by saying that segregation isn't fair, that's all." He realized, too, that, whatever its language, the Court was essentially concluding, as he had, that "segregation is *per se* inequality." "That was Warren's opinion," he would later say. "I think that summarizes the whole thing. It comes to that." He was only surprised, he told friends who gathered in their apartment that momentous evening, that it had taken "so long to discover that the Constitution meant what it said."[30]

If the Court and counsel publicly ignored Judge Waring's role in the segregation debate, his supporters did not. The party at their apartment that evening quickly became as much a homage to the hosts as a celebration of the judicial victory. Soon after the decision was announced, moreover, the Warings' telephone had begun ringing with congratulatory messages, and letters and telegrams soon followed. "When the news broke," Maude and Frank Veal wired the Warings, "we pictured you two on the platform [at the AME convention] in Chicago singing the Battle Hymn of the Republic." "In the midst of all the jubilation," wrote Ralph Bunche, "I cannot forget your courage, foresight and statesmanship." When Waring's name was mentioned at a black Virginia church the day after the decision, another admirer reported, there was "thunderous applause." The black press was equally enthusiastic, the *Chicago Defender* proclaiming Waring "the first federal jurist" to oppose "segregation in all phases of American life," and other journalists offering similar assessments. For the balance of the year, there was to be steady praise. And on the decision's first anniversary, a CIO-sponsored radio commentator analyzed the Supreme Court's ruling, but devoted most of his attention to Judge Waring. "[M]ost important perhaps of all," John W. Vandercook told his listeners, "there loomed over that Court judgment the action, the quiet courage, the figure, of a single man . . . Judge J. Waties Waring." Waring's *Briggs* dissent, said Vandercook, was "a classic in the history of

American jurisprudence. . . . If the . . . Supreme Court decision has an immediate ancestor, that is it."[31]

As soon as he heard the news of the Court's decision, Marion Wright, too, had written his friends, asserting that "No one more than you is entitled to take pride and satisfaction in the result." In his role as self-described "gadfly to the state," Wright also wrote Dean Samuel Prince of the law school at the University of South Carolina, offering a suggestion "without for a moment deluding [himself] into feeling that it will be warmly received." He proposed that the law school, or the state bar association (which Prince also headed), or the two acting jointly, arrange a dinner in Judge Waring's honor and present South Carolina's native son with a suitable award. Waring, Wright asserted, was the "one South Carolina jurist of national reputation." A dinner in his honor would reflect the state bar's willingness "to accept without reservation what the Court has directed." It would also help to atone for the "sordid" treatment accorded the judge and enable the state's lawyers to "lift our heads in pride at the man's remarkable judicial achievements and at the strength of his character." Of course, Wright added, "all Negro members of the bar should be invited and there should be no segregation at any point in the proceedings"; otherwise, "the whole idea would be hollow and spurious." The university's law students, he concluded, were now forming their impressions of their chosen profession. "Too often it has its vulgar overtones. But in the one act I have proposed you could do more good than by a thousand lectures to convince those whose training is in your hands that the profession has its noble aspects."[32]

As Wright had predicted, his suggestion was not "warmly received." By the end of 1954, however, he was to participate in a South Carolina ceremony honoring the Warings. When they had left Charleston, the Warings had vowed not to return as long as segregation was the law of the land, and they persisted in that position. In 1952, when James Dombrowski had invited Judge Waring to be the guest of honor at an academic conference on youth and racial discrimination to be held on the campus of a black university in Columbia, Waring declined. He and Mrs. Waring had been "greatly touched," he had written Dombrowski, by the 1950 pilgrimage he, Aubrey Williams, and others had arranged to their Meeting Street home. He reminded Dombrowski, however, "that it was not a movement that received any popular support. The Southern Whites did not join in the movement and the Negroes did not dare to be seen . . . it showed how pitifully few people in the South are willing to stand up and be counted." A conference of professors at a segregated college would be "different. It does not require much courage to go there." But he wanted no part of it.

> I believe that we have got to break the back of the present legal sanction of segregation before we can accomplish any good by talking or conferences in the South; this must come from the people of the whole nation awaking to the necessity of action through national legislation and court action. We cannot "educate" Byrnes or Sparkman or the other Southern politicians. But

if and when the Federal Government honestly and sincerely (if ever) takes appropriate action the little people of the South will accept and indeed in time come to like [the] clearing up of their backward part of the Country.

In the wake of the *Brown* decision, however, their black South Carolina friends urged the couple to return to Charleston for a ceremony honoring the judge's role in the attack on segregation, and the Warings reluctantly agreed to accept. Marion Wright, other Waring loyalists, Thurgood Marshall, and NAACP board member John Hammond were also invited to attend.[33]

Seemingly, no event involving the Warings could be free of controversy. Thurgood Marshall was unable to attend because of illness, the same reason given for his failure to attend an NAACP fund-raising testimonial held in the Warings' honor in New York a month after the Supreme Court's ruling. But even the faithful John Hammond showed signs of defection. He at first agreed to attend, then declined, angered over the Warings' failure to include his wife in a number of recent social engagements. He had assumed, he wrote the judge, that the Charleston affair was intended "to pay tribute to the courage of the South Carolinians who brought the suit and stood up in the face of terror and abuse. I did not realize that this was a dinner primarily for you and Elizabeth." Waring responded in kind, insisting that Hammond "knew definitely" the event's purpose. "The great cause of humanity and idealism will go onward," he added, "and we cannot stop to mourn a casualty. But you were fine for a period."[34]

Whatever the impact of Hammond's defection, the Warings would find their Charleston visit a moving experience. When they arrived at the city's old North Station on the afternoon of November 6, they were met by several hundred cheering blacks, then taken by motorcade to the Cornwell home, where they were to stay during their visit. That evening, an audience of 300 attended ceremonies at a black elementary school, where Marion Wright presented the judge with a bronze plaque and termed Waring's "conversion no less miraculous than the blinding flash of light which fell upon Saul as he journeyed down to Damascus." Filling in for Thurgood Marshall, Robert Carter praised Waring for cutting through the "legal sophistry" of the separate-but-equal doctrine, while state NAACP president James Hinton claimed that Waring had "done more for us than Abe Lincoln," and other speakers offered like tributes to "Our Judge." In accepting the plaque, Judge Waring reminded his audience of Victor Hugo's injunction "that a man should so live that he will be cursed by the past and blessed by the future." His dissent in the Clarendon County case, he recalled, had run twenty printed pages. "Maybe," he added, "I should have said, 'It's all nonsense,' and signed my name." The next afternoon, Septima Clark entertained the Warings at her home, and that evening, the Cornwells hosted a reception in their honor. "A great tribute," Judge Waring later wrote Marion Wright. "Elizabeth and I were overjoyed at the love and affection shown by our people."[35]

Most white South Carolinians, of course, did not share the feelings of those who gathered in Charleston to praise the Warings. Another of Arthur Stoney's doggerel efforts had begun circulating through Charleston. "You ax me what he cum for den," one stanza read,

> If he got no fambily or fren?
> Seems like some coloreds acting smarty,
> Is giving him a nigger party.

Ridiculing Marion Wright's conferral of "saintship," the *Evening Post* reminded its readers that the judge had not given up the salary the "white" Democratic party gave him. Moreover, as Marion Wright was planning to journey to Charleston for the ceremony, Beverley Herbert, an elderly Columbia lawyer and longtime acquaintance of Wright and the judge, had written the Southern Regional Council president, urging him to stay away and attributing South Carolina's ill-feeling toward Judge Waring to his personal life rather than his civil rights rulings. Herbert's plea had no influence on Wright. "[T]o my mind," he had responded, "Judge Waring should stand or fall upon the merit or demerit of his judicial opinions and not upon matters connected with his personal life." Chief Justice Warren had not been involved in a divorce, he reminded Herbert, nor had President Eisenhower's attorney general Herbert Brownell. Yet southern officials had recently hurled "childish" insults at both men. "Unfortunately," Wright asserted, "there seems to be something in the mentality of the segregationist which inspires him to give an exhibition of bad manners. My theory is that he is well aware that he cannot use logic or reason . . . so he must resort to insult." The Warings' treatment by Charlestonians had stemmed not from their personal lives, but from his decisions and their "compulsion to be decent to all men, whether they be white or black." His fellow townspeople simply could not forgive that trait. But then, Wright concluded, "the state of public opinion in Charleston in recent years would have made it a chilling, if not hazardous, experience for Jesus Christ or Gandhi to have lived in that community."[36]

By South Carolina standards, Herbert had once been relatively liberal, a state representative for the American Civil Liberties Union who had supported Judge Waring's initial white primary ruling. His letter to Wright, however, was no surprise to Waring, though it did make him "a little sick at the stomach." When South Carolina had begun to close ranks against racial reform, the judge wrote Wright, Herbert had become a "rabid White Supremacist," writing the ACLU's New York office that he was no longer a member and demanding that his name be removed from the organization's membership files. Now, in Waring's eyes, he was "just a querulous old man feeling sorry that he once had some glimmering of progressive thinking."[37]

For a time after the Supreme Court announced its decision in the segregation cases, Judge Waring had been naively optimistic that compliance would be relatively speedy. "There will be resistance in some benighted quarters of course," he wrote a black Charleston friend in June, "but the great body of right thinking people in the country will accept the decision with approval and breathe a sigh of relief that America has found its soul. And this applies to the good people of the South who have not heretofore dared to come out in the open because of the segregation laws and the blatant demagogues." When he and Mrs. Waring visited Charleston in November, he was still confident. "I sensed a feeling of conscious strength in the colored leaders of the community," he wrote Marion Wright. "The walls of segregation are falling fast and the Negroes as well as the right thinking whites of the South know it. The law is now on our side and the segregationists are to be classed with the lawbreakers."[38]

Even by that point, however, the intensity of southern opposition to the Supreme Court's decision was becoming increasingly evident, especially in the Deep South states. In South Carolina, Governor Byrnes expressed "shock" at the Court's action and halted further work under the equalization program. In January, Judge Timmerman administered the oath of office to his son, George Bell Timmerman, Jr., who, as Byrnes' successor, vowed to preserve South Carolina's "way of life." As a candidate, Timmerman had accused the NAACP of following the "Communist line" and asserted, "Nowhere in my Bible does forcing little children in their formative years to mix with other races seem to me to be an application of the Golden Rule." In February, following his inauguration, he presented South Carolina's congressional delegation with two bills to limit the jurisdiction of federal courts over state and local education. One called for removing jurisdiction from all federal courts; the other, drafted, according to press reports, by Robert McC. Figg, proposed denying the Supreme Court and circuit appeals courts jurisdiction, while preserving the authority of district judges, such as Judge Timmerman. South Carolina's general assembly also began digging the trenches. In July, its special school segregation committee urged continued operation of the public schools under current regulations. In its January report, the committee proposed eliminating compulsory school attendance, authorizing attendance officers to "influence" and "persuade" attendance, empowering school boards to transfer students from county to county, and vesting the boards with powers to lease as well as sell school property.[39]

Some southern whites initially reacted calmly to the news of desegregation. For example, the day the *Brown* decision came down, members of a white Savannah civic club took the news calmly, some even applauding the announcement. A number of southerners, including Professor Howard Odum of the University of North Carolina, had predicted a relatively speedy public acceptance and smooth transition. Soon, however, the news, editorial, and letters columns of southern papers were bristling with defiance. In Charleston, the *Evening Post* accused the Supreme Court of amending the Constitution "by fiat," while the *News and Courier* charged that the "decision drove another nail into the coffin of states' rights." Although the Court had rejected segregation, it delayed issuing a decree to enforce its decision pending further oral argument. At least until the Court acted, the *Courier* asserted, school boards should resist NAACP pressures to change their placement policies.

By holding fast now, the school boards have nothing to lose and they may have something to gain. If worse comes to worst, they can dump the whole problem into the Supreme Court's lap and leave public education of Negroes to the federal government. It would save enough local taxes to permit the white people to buy a better brand of schooling than they now enjoy.[40]

In its May 30, 1954, issue, the *Courier* published the sermon of a Charleston clergyman who had called *Brown* the most "unrealistic and unfortunate" decision in the Supreme Court's history. Earlier, *Courier* columnist W. D. Workman contended that South Carolina's equalization program and other evidence of the South's "good will" toward blacks had contributed to "the undoing of the Southern position. Instead of manifesting any gratitude for the obvious change in attitude and even more obvious change in school facilities, the hard core of the National Association for the Advancement of Colored People has continued to demand the elimination of separate schools, demanding education not so much as integration." The federal government, added Workman, seemed concerned only with black children. "Nothing has been said about the potential psychological effect of enforced comingling . . . on the personalities of white children." Letters to the *Courier* were often more vehement than its editorial and news columns. "Just look at the nations that have become a boiling pot for different races," asserted one, "and see what they have now: sickness, disease, cancer, leprosy, famine, revolts, uprisings, murders, and the like, so we pray that God forbid that we ever integrate." Nor were integration, the Court, and the NAACP the only targets. In the wake of *Brown,* the ranks of the Ku Klux Klan swelled dramatically; for more sedate opponents of racial change chapters of the Citizens' Council, a group formed specifically to combat integration, sprang up throughout the South. In Mississippi, Hodding Carter expressed his "moral" opposition to segregation, but contended that the Court's action had hampered the "gradual process" of desegregation, forcing supporters and opponents to "extremes." When Carter attacked the Citizens' Councils, however, the Mississippi House of Representatives adopted a resolution accusing him of lying, slandering his state, and betraying the South.[41]

While opposition to *Brown* I, as the Supreme Court's first ruling came to be known, continued to fester, the Court moved toward a second decision in the school segregation cases. For several days in mid-April 1955, the Court heard oral argument regarding the sort of implementation decree it should issue. John W. Davis had died in March, and Robert McC. Figg now assumed principal responsibility for arguing South Carolina's position before the Court. Counsel for the petitioners contended that their clients' constitutional rights were "present and personal," but Figg urged the justices to remand the cases to the trial courts for a gradual implementation process and to impose no time limit for compliance. Requiring integration by the beginning of the 1955 school year, he warned, "would mean the end of the public school system in the district" he represented. Ultimately, the Court opted for the approach Figg advanced. On May 31, 1955, the justices unanimously remanded the cases to the trial courts for implementation of the principle announced in its

1954 decision. Those courts and school boards were to act in "good faith" and move with "all deliberate speed." But reasonable delay would be tolerated.[42]

Brown II was as comforting to segregationists as *Brown* I had been disturbing, bolstering their hopes that integration might now be delayed indefinitely. In an editorial entitled "For the 'Gradual' Approach," the *News and Courier* applauded the Court's rejection of deadlines and accurately predicted "a long-range campaign that will stretch over many years."

> When it comes to patience, is the white man inferior to the Negro? Once it is shown that Southern white people are determined neither to yield to the mixiecrats nor to give up their public schools, adjustments can and will be made. Someday, we hope, the Northern press will grow weary of waving the bloody shirt at the South and look to problems closer home.

Governor Timmerman was more direct. "[I]f you let one . . . come in," he asserted, "you've opened the door. There can't be any compromise—you can't compromise right with wrong."[43]

The governor's father and other members of the three-judge panel to which the Supreme Court had relegated the fate of the *Briggs* plaintiffs was to be of no help to those favoring integration. On July 15, the panel, in a brief, unsigned opinion, enjoined the defendants from refusing to admit children to schools on account of their race, "from and after such time as they may have made the necessary arrangements." But the district court imposed no time limit for compliance. In its opinion, moreover, the panel provided the rhetorical ammunition that became a staple of the massive resistance movement to integrate. "It is important," the panel observed,

> that we point out exactly what the Supreme Court has decided and what it has not decided in this case. It has not decided that the federal courts are to take over or regulate the public schools of the states. It has not decided that the states must mix persons of different races in the schools or must require them to attend schools or must deprive them of the right of choosing the schools they attend. What it has decided, and all that it has decided, is that a state may not deny to any person on account of race the right to attend any school that it maintains. This, under the decision of the Supreme Court, the state may not do directly or indirectly; but if the schools which it maintains are open to children of all races, no violation of the Constitution is involved even though the children of different races voluntarily attend different schools, as they attend different churches. Nothing in the Constitution or in the decision of the Supreme Court takes away from the people freedom to choose the schools they attend. The Constitution, in other words, does not require integration. It merely forbids discrimination. It does not forbid such segregation as occurs as the result of voluntary action. It merely forbids the use of governmental power to enforce segregation. The Fourteenth Amendment is a limitation upon the exercise of power by the state or state agencies, not a limitation upon the freedom of individuals.[44]

Nor was Judge Waring's replacement on the Charleston bench much cause for optimism among civil rights advocates. For a time, Mendel Rivers had campaigned for the position, meeting at one point with President Truman at the White House. But the prospect of the Charleston congressman's appointment had aroused an immediate and intense outcry within the nation's civil rights leadership. Walter White wired the president that Rivers "had persistently and blatantly advocated treatment of American Negroes but little different from that of the days of slavery," adding, "We could conceive of no person less fit than he is to administer even-handed justice and to uphold obedience to the federal Constitution." Eventually, the nod went to Ashton Williams. Judge Waring considered the Lake City lawyer a "decent man," and Williams had been one of the few South Carolina Democrats to remain loyal to the national party in the 1948 election. But Williams did not have the passion for racial equality of Judge Waring. While hearing a 1955 challenge to segregation in South Carolina state parks, he lumped the NAACP and Ku Klux Klan together, asserting "that no progress can be made unless and until both . . . are wholly eliminated from the picture in South Carolina."[45]

While raising the spirits of segregationists, *Brown* II had been a bitter disappointment to those favoring a concrete and speedy end to the inequities of a segregated society. "I'm tired," *Afro-American* columnist James Hicks lamented, echoing the frustrations of many other blacks, "tired of fighting and bickering for something which I know belongs to me." When Elizabeth Waring brought Hicks' "poignant and heartbreaking" words to her husband's attention, he admonished her to "remember Arthur Garfield Hays' wise axiom, 'We may not always win in our fight for Civil Rights but we NEVER LOSE.' " Later, Elizabeth wrote a lengthy letter to the *Afro-American,* attempting to cast the current state of the movement in a generally favorable light.[46] But the Court's decree had disheartened the judge. When it appeared that the NAACP might relax its pressures for racial reform in South Carolina, moreover, he again lashed out at the association's chief counsel.

In its August 30, 1955, issue, the Columbia, South Carolina, *Record* reported that Thurgood Marshall had informed Clarendon County school officials of the NAACP's plans to leave that system alone and concentrate its efforts on other areas, "in view of the acute problems to be solved in desegregating the schools there." In a letter to the *Record,* Marshall charged that the story was "completely inaccurate." Following the July 15 hearing at which the *Briggs* panel had imposed no deadline for compliance, Marshall had spoken, he conceded, with the defendants' counsel. But he had told them only that he would not present black children for admission to white schools at the opening of the school year. "I made it clear," he insisted, "that we would not give up any of our rights."[47]

The newspaper's report came at a discouraging time for militant low country blacks. Many blacks who had earlier signed petitions supporting integration were now repudiating their signatures. "I was not too surprised when some of the colored people began" to weaken, a dejected Ruby Cornwell wrote the Warings, "but I was not prepared for the wholesale back-sliding in some of the communities. It is most discouraging and depressing. Of

course, that is the work of the Citizens' Councils! What can be done to coun-
teract it?" Judge Waring found a number of Marshall's recent press statements disturbing. When he learned of the *Record* story, he complained to
Roy Wilkins, and Marshall sent him a copy of his rejoinder to the paper. "I
had supposed," the judge soon replied,

> that you would have known that it is very dangerous to make any so-called
> private statements to the lawyers representing the Clarendon County School
> officials. I know them and I had supposed you did also. . . . But you [ap-
> parently] still believe in the sincerity of the Dixiecrat lawyers. Perhaps a
> few more "legal lynchings" will enlighten you.[48]

Whatever the NAACP's resolve, however, it became increasingly clear
that the pace of desegregation might be even more protracted than the movement to dismantle the *Plessy* doctrine. Any hope for quick compliance was
now yielding to the realities of massive resistance; in South Carolina, the
judge's nephew Tom Waring was becoming a leading spokesman for the anti-
integration movement. Citing the requirements of editorial freedom, Tom
Waring resisted the urgings of "Cotton Ed" Smith's son Farley to become a
leader in the Citizens' Council movement. But Waring and his paper regularly attacked the NAACP, the Supreme Court, and other threats to southern
tradition. In a variety of settings, he also accused the national press of erecting a "paper curtain" round the South, shutting "out the Southern side of
race relations from the rest of the country," and deluging the nation with
"anti-Southern" propaganda unequaled since the 1851 appearance of *Uncle
Tom's Cabin*.[49]

Soon, Tom Waring would carry his cause to a national audience. After
Brown I was decided, Herbert Ravenel Sass, a former *Courier* staffer who
had written free-lance articles for a variety of major publications, urged Waring to write a pro-South piece for a national magazine. Sass also wrote the
editor of *Harper's,* indicating that his friend wanted "to be heard." When
Harper's expressed interest, Waring sent them a manuscript. "I knocked off
what I thought was a very reasonable piece," he later recalled, "very moderate, toned down, no rabble-rousing stuff." But his first effort was promptly
rejected. "So I took all the venom, all the poison, out of it, and made it just
sweetness and light." That effort, too, was returned. Finally, Waring attached
a disclaimer, absolving *Harper's* of any agreement with his position; that tactic succeeded. Waring's "The Southern Case Against Desegregation" appeared in the magazine's January 1956, issue. "The point of view expressed,"
Harper's assured its readers, "is far removed from that of the Editors." But
southerners like Waring believed, "with some reason," that they had been
denied a fair hearing in the national press, and the magazine wanted to give
the *Courier* editor—"a conservative, and a gentleman [with] instincts of decency and good will"—a chance to defend the segregationist cause.[50]

"The Southern Case Against Desegregation" was to be the prototype for
future briefs in behalf of segregation, including Richmond editor James Jackson Kilpatrick's controversial 1962 book with an almost identical title.[51]

The "vast majority" of southern whites, Waring argued, were persons of "good will" who favored "uplift of the Negro." But change was "being forced at too fast a pace" and with no regard for state sovereignty. Southerners were "willing and eager to have the Negro earn greater acceptance on many levels—especially economic." But they are better equipped than northerners to oversee the process of black advancement, and they realized that mixed schooling was not a proper avenue to that goal, "certainly not at this stage of affairs." Cultural differences separating blacks and whites were simply too great—the incidence of crime, venereal disease, and illegitimacy among blacks too high; the level of intellectual development too low. Integration, as its advocates contended, might help to reduce the cultural differences separating the races, but "a single generation of white children [would] bear the brunt of the load." At present, southern parents were no more willing to make that "sacrifice" of their children than the nation had been willing to honor Prohibition. The Supreme Court might have outlawed official segregation, but the "bootleg" variety would remain. Eventually, Waring concluded, the problem might largely disappear.

> If the North continues to appeal to Negroes as a land of integration and the South continues to attract white settlers, the racial proportions may grow more nearly equal. Then the North may become more tolerant of the Southerners' view of race problems, and the South better able to handle its dwindling Negro problem. Southerners will glady share the load.

When the *Harper's* article appeared, Mendel Rivers had it reprinted in the *Congressional Record*. Was its author related to Judge Waring? a Georgia congressman asked Rivers on the floor of the House. "Yes," Rivers responded.

> He is a nephew of that degenerate who has found that he cannot live in my part of the world. . . . He has gone to that haven, that refuge, New York, where peace, law, and order are the order of the day. . . . And may God have mercy on his miserable soul.

Later, Tom Waring proposed that copies of the article and Rivers' remarks be mailed to Citizens' Council members and other like-minded souls. Rivers readily agreed, sending out numerous copies at government expense, but deleting, at the *Courier* editor's suggestion, the Charleston congressman's references to Judge Waring. The article garnered Tom Waring 800 letters, all complimentary—and *Harper's* editor an almost equal number of negative reactions. It also briefly gave Waring something approaching the celebrity status his uncle had long enjoyed. For the better part of a year, he traveled about the country and into Canada, spreading the segregationist gospel at Columbia, Brandeis, and other campuses; before civil groups; on radio interview programs; and in other settings. "I was doing it," he later recalled, "with the full knowledge and expectation of being licked. But I felt that I had a duty to the southern white people . . . the ordinary, run-of-the-mill white people, to present their case; and if we got licked, we didn't get licked by default . . .

I didn't realize," he added, "that I was going to get beaten as quickly and as bad as we got licked. When we got licked, we really got licked in a hurry, and it was bad. I thought it was going along longer."[52]

In terms of public acceptance of their positions, Tom Waring, James Kilpatrick, and other defenders of segregation may have been defeated quickly. But Clarendon County's schools would not begin to be integrated until 1965, and extensive desegregation was not to take place in South Carolina or elsewhere in the South for well more than a decade after *Brown* II—and then only after Congress authorized federal officials to withdraw funds from school systems failing to develop effective desegregation plans. For that period, the twilight years of his life, Judge Waring continued to work in behalf of civil rights and to urge aggressive federal intervention in the cause of racial reform. He became a member of the board of the American Civil Liberties Union and chairman of its due process committee. He also served as president of the National Committee for Rural Schools, an organization which, under his leadership, attempted to provide food, clothing, and agricultural supplies for blacks in the rural South. And he lectured widely and participated in numerous civil rights forums.

Nor did he lose his zeal or impatience with the fainthearted. In a television interview program on the life of Booker T. Washington, for example, he praised Washington as a "very great humanitarian" but concluded that he had ministered only to the immediate needs of his people while endorsing segregation, encouraging blacks to be "good, second-class citizens," and leaving them "in chains." Lester Grainger, director of the National Urban League, called Waring's allegations "a bit unjust. . . . You're charging him for being a nineteenth century leader in the nineteenth century." But Waring was unmoved. Washington, he insisted, had become the "darling" of the white supremacists by persuading blacks to "be sheep and obey your masters . . . always begging, not demanding," when he should have taught them to be "dignified human beings."[53]

Waring's ire extended to the feeble efforts of the Eisenhower administration and congressional Democrats in behalf of civil rights. The administration-sponsored Civil Rights Act of 1957, the first federal civil rights legislation since Reconstruction, was more loophole than law. While it was pending in Congress, *New York Times* columnist James Reston endorsed its enactment, concluding that "a slice of bread" was better than nothing. Judge Waring disagreed. "The people of this Country," he wrote the editor of the *Times,* "have waited for almost eighty years for its representatives in Washington to implement" the Reconstruction amendments. To date, though, the executive branch had given them "mostly lip service" and Congress had done nothing. The Senate had reduced the current civil rights bill to one dealing only with the right to vote. And while that was a "slice" in the right direction, Lyndon Johnson, John Kennedy, and other Senate Democrats had recently added an amendment that guaranteed a jury trial for voter registrars charged with contempt for failing to obey the bill's anti-discrimination provisions. The amendment thus placed enforcement of the law "in the hands of juries made up of people dedicated to opposition to the Civil Rights Amendments" and crippled the ability of federal judges to enforce voting rights decrees. Judge Waring could not accept such "oily manipulation of an honest attempt into a dishonest result." If the amendment could not be rejected, Congress should kill the entire bill "and wait . . . more years for the American people to awake to what is being done to their ideals and principles. . . . Yes, Mr. Reston," he bitterly concluded, "I'll settle for a slice of bread however thin, provided it is still bread. But I'll not settle for a slice that is infested with dead mice and cockroaches. That's what you ask us to take."[54]

The *Times* did not publish Waring's letter, but James Reston did reply, lamenting the judge's "pessimism" and disillusionment "about the results of your long fight for equal rights in the South." Given the absence of any national legislation for over three-quarters of a century, Reston could not understand "why people are not prepared to accept what little progress they can get." In a rejoinder to Reston, the judge indicated that he was disappointed that the *Times* had chosen not to publish his letter, but assumed "it wishes to shield its correspondents and especially wishes to avoid controversy." Reston was wrong, he added, in accusing him of pessimism. He had faith in the "essential and eventual decency" of Americans. And while he was impatient with delay, he was willing to wait for progress. He was simply unwilling "to swap principle for expediency" and disappointed "that the Democratic party (of which I have been a lifelong member) should go along with candidates Lyndon Johnson and John Kennedy. They want to pass this bad bill in the hope that its narcotic effects will give them the 1960 nominations. Perhaps it will, but I predict that our people will awaken and not fall for Texas gas and oil mixed with Massachusetts cowardice."[55]

As his response to the Reston column indicated, however, Judge Waring reserved most of his fire for the Democratic party. The efforts of Adlai Stevenson to keep disgruntled southerners in the party were a constant irritant, and in 1955, he and Mrs. Waring resigned from a New York Democratic club after it endorsed Stevenson's renomination. "I trust," he wrote club officials, "that the party may yet be saved from this surrender and that Democrats can still be liberals; but there is danger of our being forced to accept Republicans in this appeasement of Dixiecrats." When a rumor circulated after the 1960 elections that John Kennedy might select J. William Fulbright as his secretary of state, he wrote the president-elect a passionate letter of protest, charging that the Arkansas senator had signed the Southern Manifesto and that his appointment would be an affront to "decent thinking Americans" and to "the many colored citizens who voted for you," as well as the nations of Asia and Africa. While Kennedy's campaign and inaugural address had temporarily allayed the judge's concerns about the young president's commitment to civil rights, Kennedy's early civil rights record had caused him "much disappointment." "We can never be able to advance materially in Civil Rights," he wrote Mrs. Roosevelt, "until the Federal Government moves into the field, not in token announcements, speeches and platforms, but in *honest sincere* acts." He considered Kennedy's proposed constitutional amendment to ban the poll tax a particularly "callous, cruel, dishonest and cynical act." The poll tax, he contended, was "the least of our worries," and the administration's resort to the "extraordinary rememdy" of a constitutional amendment

> to cure a very minor trouble a brazen attempt to hood wink the American people. . . . This Administration must be shown that votes cannot be garnered every time by fooling the people, and that brave acts must accompany brave words. In the long [run] we have to win. But it is getting very very long.[56]

On one occasion, Judge Waring's activities again attracted the animosity of the South Carolina press. In early 1956, the National Committee for Rural Schools was collecting money and food to be distributed to poor blacks in the rural South. In March, a "food caravan" arrived in Columbia, enroute to Summerton, site of the Clarendon County school desegregation suit. The Charleston papers apparently ignored the event, but the Columbia *State* heaped scorn on the project and the motives of its organizers. Previously, three truckloads of foodstuffs had been shipped to Clarendon County from New York and Philadelphia, but the March caravan consisted of only three automobiles, their passengers, and supplies, and one of the passengers was a cameraman for a documentary film company. If there was "any need" in Summerton, *The State* editorialized, the food being transported there "would not be a handful." The project, it charged, was one of "agitation," not "charity." Summerton's mayor had "heard of no starving Negroes" in his community; in the paper's judgment, the whole affair was simply a publicity stunt. But Judge Waring, who had been the project's "inspiration," was the paper's principal target. "Behind the movement," it informed its readers, "is that old hand at trouble making, Judge J. Waties Waring, formerly of Charleston but now, thank goodness, residing in another state." Waring, *The State* charged, still harbored ill will against his native city and state and was using this "so-called food and clothing caravan carrying more people than supplies" to vent his hatred and promote "anti-South propaganda." South Carolina NAACP president James Hinton repudiated *The State*'s attacks and asserted that Waring needed "no defense from me or any other citizen who sees straight." But the paper, like Summerton's mayor, dismissed the caravan as nothing more than "political bunk."[57]

Others, of course, still continued to honor the judge's service to civil rights. In 1956, the Buffalo, New York, church where J. A. DeLaine now served as pastor renamed itself the DeLaine-Waring AME Church. In 1957, the American Jewish Congress cited his "contributions to civil rights and liberties," prompting the Charleston *Evening Post* to remind its readers that the judge was still clinging to "one cherished relic of old times"—the salary "the white Democratic party and segregation brought him." In 1959, a troupe of actors performed a play, "The Man on Meeting Street," during an evening in his honor at New York's Roosevelt Hotel. When President Kennedy appointed Thurgood Marshall to a federal appeals court seat, moreover, the NAACP lawyer acknowledged the "debts" civil rights advocates owed the judge and a number of other southern jurists. And when President and Mrs. Kennedy hosted a White House reception celebrating the Emancipation Proclamation's hundredth anniversary, the Warings were invited, though neither apparently attended. But such events and the judge's later activities attracted little press notice, and the rigors of age steadily reduced the pace of his work. His contacts with Martin Luther King, Jr., and other civil rights leaders of King's era were to be largely pro forma.[58]

He did not, however, lose his fire. In the summer of 1963, the Associated Press ran a flattering profile, summarizing his judicial career, his "ostracism" by his fellow Charlestonians, and his determination to live out his life "in exile." The *News and Courier* carried the story. But in an editor's note, the *Courier* claimed again that the Warings were responsible for their social isolation in his native city. The Associated Press asked the judge for comment. "As usual," he remarked, "the News and Courier perverts the truth." When Judge Timmerman died, a reporter asked Waring for comment. "That's very interesting," he replied. "Thank you for telling me. I do not think it would be seemly of me to comment at all."[59]

Like her husband, Elizabeth remained a person of strong will until the end. In 1956, Septima Clark was fired from her Charleston teaching position under a South Carolina law forbidding NAACP members to hold state jobs. But Mrs. Clark was just beginning her efforts in behalf of civil rights. At sixty-two, she left Charleston, working first at the Highlander School, then as a member of Dr. King's Southern Christian Leadership Conference in Atlanta. In 1962, E. P. Dutton published an autobiographical account of her role in the civil rights movement. Mrs. Clark's book praised the Warings but was mildly critical of Mrs. Waring's 1950 speech at the Charleston YWCA and her assault on "decadent" southern whites. Mrs. Waring was offended and wrote her friend a harsh letter; Mrs. Clark's reply was gentle and complimentary. But Mrs. Waring remained unmoved. When Mrs. Clark visited New York, Elizabeth refused to see her.[60]

By 1960, Mrs. Waring had become a virtual recluse to all but their closest friends. Elizabeth had always been a handsome woman of impressive bearing. By the late 1950s, however, she had become overweight. Largely as a consequence of a hiatus hernia, which forced her to sleep sitting on a sofa, she had also become increasingly stooped. "She suddenly changed," her daughter would later recall, "from being what I had always thought was my very striking, gorgeous mother into something rather different." She continued to be a prolific correspondent and to maintain massive collections of clippings on the civil rights movement. But whether out of vanity or for some other reason, Mrs. Waring began to spend her days in lounging gowns, never venturing out of their apartment. "She was an invalid, but she was also a very strong, athletic person," her daughter would later remark. "I thought it was very queer."[61]

As the years passed, Judge Waring also became increasingly deaf and blind; these afflictions curtailed many of his pleasures, including the theater, bridge, dinner parties, and baseball games. "Elizabeth devotedly read aloud to him," Anne Warren later wrote Tom Waring's sister Rosamond Salmons regarding her father's last years.

> He also had radio and television, of course, though he was most selective and interested almost entirely in programs of public affairs (he felt the great threats to the nation were the war in Vietnam, Black Power, Richard Nixon, and Bobby Kennedy [in, roughly, that order]). . . . He never outgrew his loathing of snow and ice and was constantly devising utopian schemes for better street cleaning methods.[62]

Anne Warren's marriage had ended in divorce in 1955. In the years immediately before her father's death, she and the judge talked frequently by phone and had lunch together once or twice each month. In late 1967, he confided to her that he had been suffering from indigestion. A physician recommended an operation to remove a growing intestinal obstruction. But Elizabeth Waring had a healthy skepticism about the medical profession, and following what Anne termed "frank conversations" with his wife, the judge decided to forego surgery. For a time, he seemed better and decided that he had merely been suffering from a virus.[63]

Some years before, the Warings had moved from their Fifth Avenue apartment to a small apartment at the Hyde Park Hotel on 77th Street. On Christmas day, 1967, Anne met her father at the apartment and walked with him over to the Carlisle Hotel where they had taken Christmas dinner together the past several years. Explaining that he had experienced some discomfort from indigestion that morning, the judge had only an omelet. But he seemed in excellent spirits, enthusiastically discussing the moral and legal implications of heart transplant operations then being performed in South Africa. In one case, the heart of a black man had been transplanted into a white. "If I were in politics in South Africa and that man *was not on my side,*" he joked, "I would challenge his right to vote as a white man."[64]

The following day Anne phoned her father's physician and learned that the judge's tumor was almost certainly malignant and in a short time would cause a complete intestinal blockage and "horrendous" pain. Morphine in increasingly greater doses would provide the only relief, and even that would by no means be complete. The doctor assured Anne that the Warings knew the prospects but had continued to decline surgery. From that point on, Waring's condition continued to deteriorate. "And what do you think about going to the hospital?" Anne asked her father one day. "I think it is inevitable," he replied, "and that it means death."[65]

On January 19, he was taken by ambulance to St. Luke's Hospital. Before leaving the apartment, and although obviously experiencing considerable pain, he gave his wife and daughter specific instructions for managing in his absence. At the hospital, a considerate ambulance driver rolled him to his room. The judge thanked him for his kindness. "I certainly would have had a terrible time walking all this way through the hospital." He paused, his eyes twinkling. "But I know how to walk into a courtroom."[66]

Anne remained at the hospital until 8:30 that evening, talking with her

father between tests and the questions of physicians. He was delighted that
the supervisory nurse was a Jamaican black and pleased that their house-
keeper had been able to stay with Elizabeth during his absence. "We telephoned Elizabeth," Anne later wrote Rosamond Salmons, "to assure her that
he had a nice room and was being looked out for. There is absolutely no
question that he and Elizabeth were deeply in love until the end." The next
morning, his physician telephoned Anne to report that her father's condition
had worsened during the night. He had been in a coma for several hours. At
9:10 a.m., he died. "I was, and am, very proud of him," Anne wrote Mrs.
Salmons.[67]

Others were also proud of this son of a Confederate veteran. "He was a
valiant figure of high principle and courage, with a historic mission to perform," Roger Baldwin of the American Civil Liberties Union wrote Mrs.
Waring. "I know that you are proud," added Carl Rowan, "that the Judge's
indestructible monument is the army of Americans who walk a bit more
proudly because of the courage he had in interpreting the rules of justice."
During a memorial service at a midtown Manhattan church where the judge
had participated in many civil rights forums over the years, Kenneth Clark
described Waring's "respect for the dignity of man unqualified by the ir-
relevancies of color" and his belief in "the responsibility of certain human
beings to assume the obligations of leadership in helping their fellow human
beings control their tendencies toward cruelty and in increasing their potential for good." Many others, famous and obscure, expressed similar sentiments. "Your father died," a Charleston woman wrote Anne, "and a part
of me went with him. . . . I was so *very* proud of him. Proud of his courage—he did what I felt needed to be done." The woman's eldest son had
been a member of the judge's fraternity at the College of Charleston. "I can
only hope," she wrote, that "he will be the type of man your father was."
She had been "fortunate" enough to escape Charleston's "provincialism" for
many years. Recently, however, she had returned " 'home again.' . . . [I]t
really hasn't changed much," she wrote, "since your father went 'into exile.' "[68]

Now, Judge Waring, too, was going home again. On January 17, grave-
side services were held at Charleston's Magnolia Cemetery. Though intending
"no disrespect" for the dead, the Columbia *State* expressed hope that "the
fabrication of his 'social ostracism' " would be buried with him. The Charleston papers, however, treated the judge's death with restraint. The *News and
Courier* called him a man "of intelligence and force" and a judge of "uncommon ability." "Though many former associates . . . questioned Judge
Waring's judgment and some even doubted his sanity," the *Evening Post* observed, "no one challenged his courage. . . . Historians," the *Post* added,

will record that Mr. Waring, as a federal judge, had unusual perception into
the future. The rulings he handed down two decades ago stunned a whole
region of white people. The same decisions today would hardly cause a rip-
ple of surprise among the same people.[69]

But few Charleston whites could truly forgive or forget. St. Michael's rector and his assistant performed the funeral service. Rosamond Salmons and her husband, Judge Waring's nephew Charles, and another family member sat with Anne Warren and Elizabeth's daughter Ann Hyde during the service. But Tom Waring did not attend. When Anne arrived in Charleston, he had telephoned her to offer his assistance and agreed to attend his uncle's funeral if she wanted him to come. Anne left the decision to him, and he decided that he "neither needed nor wanted to be present." The morning of the funeral, D. A. Brockinton, Jr., asked his father whether he planned to be present for his former law partner's burial. "No," the elder Brockinton replied. "That was just a chapter in my life that's over and done with . . . like a bad dream." Gus Tamsberg, who had served as city council clerk during Waring's years as Charleston corporation counsel, felt a "sense of loss" at the judge's passing, and he debated attending the funeral. Ultimately, though, he, too, stayed away. In fact, fewer than a dozen whites were present. But Anne Warren understood. When an admirer of Judge Waring condemned Charlestonians for betraying "their great heritage of . . . nobility," she responded, "Why is it considered desirable to respect a man in death when respect was withheld during his lifetime? My own feeling is that white Charleston had the insight to know that Judge Waring would have rejected such a belated homage."[70]

The judge would have been moved, however, by the tribute given him by South Carolina blacks. In a letter to the *News and Courier*, Ruby Cornwell wrote, "The judge comes home. We welcome you, our judge. We love you. We are honored to have you rest here in our midst." Elsewhere in the world, she added, reference to Charleston was "quite apt to produce a response—'Oh yes, Charleston—you had a judge there!' " When Mrs. Cornwell telephoned Joe Brown with news of Waring's death, the Charleston NAACP leader began calling association leaders throughout the state. On the day of the funeral, more than 200 blacks gathered in a church near the cemetery. When the hearse carrying the judge's body passed by, a motorcade of blacks filed in behind, following the hearse into the cemetery, where they paid their last respects to "Our Judge." In late Janury, the state NAACP conducted a memorial service in the judge's honor at Allen University in Columbia.[71]

Elizabeth Waring was unable to attend her husband's funeral. Following the judge's death, she entered a nursing home in Weston, Massachusetts, near her daughter's home. (Ann Hyde's husband was then on the staff of Andover Academy.) On a trip through New England, Mrs. Cornwall visited her friend at Weston. "It was clear," Mrs. Cornwell would recall, "that, with the judge gone, she wanted to die." On October 30, 1968, she passed away. Her daughter, her son, her daughter's husband, and Elizabeth's nurse attended the funeral in Charleston. Septima Clark, who had been unable to attend Judge Waring's funeral, was also there, as was Mrs. Cornwell. "Weren't but nine" in all, Mrs. Clark later said, sadness in her voice.[72]

In South Carolina, feelings against the Warings and the image they—

and the judge's native city—had been given in the national press did not disappear with their deaths. The uprooting of the magnolia sapling Anne Warren had planted at the gravesite was only one reflection of the continued hostility. Local reaction to television coverage of the judge's funeral was another. Charles Kuralt reported Judge Waring's funeral for CBS News, quoting Joe Brown—"the only Charlestonian we could find who would speak of him"—and concluding, "There are few white mourners here today. Many people, have paid a price for their civil rights advocacy, a United States District Court judge among them." While preparing his report, Kuralt had enjoyed "generous quantities of conversation and Rebel Yell" with Tom Waring. In a letter to the network reporter, the *Courier* editor lamented Kuralt's "perpetuation" of the impression "that Charlestonians ostracized Judge Waring on account of his judicial decisions," adding, "Of course you had the correct information that this story is a myth." A Charleston matron was less diplomatic. Kuralt's "impassioned and soulful dissertation," she wrote the reporter, "left me—for one—slightly nauseated." Kuralt, she charged, could have gotten the true story from the "most illiterate man on the street," or from the judge's "honored and brilliant" nephew. Instead, he had interviewed "the NAACP god of Charleston." The answer to Judge Waring's becoming a civil rights "crusader," she claimed, rested in one sentence—"Hell hath no fury like a woman scorned."[73]

Later that year, Charleston writer Gordon Langley Hall, adopted son of British actress Dame Margaret Rutherford, shocked Charleston when he underwent a sex-change operation, then, as Dawn Hall, married her black servant. Hall's British relatives apparently approved the marriage. Only an aunt expressed any reservation, remarking, "I do wish Dawn wasn't marrying a Baptist." Before the wedding, however, three elderly Charleston matrons—bearing an apple pie for Hall and a watermelon for her intended—visited Hall's Society Street mansion, urging her to cancel the marriage plans. One of the visitors called Hall "a traitor like Judge Waring" and asked whether she wanted "to be exiled, too." When the church where the wedding was to be performed received bomb threats, the ceremony was moved to the drawing room of Hall's home; detectives were called in to search the cellar for explosives.[74]

In 1976, CBS broadcast "With All Deliberate Speed," a dramatization of the roles of J. A. DeLaine and Judge Waring in the demise of state-imposed segregation. The same year, *Charleston Magazine* published a profile that came close to accepting the local version of the Waring story. But in the years after his death, his place in the civil rights movement received little attention. In South Carolina, anti-Waring feelings have remained intense in certain quarters, just as the Warings' black friends would continue to revere their sacrifices.

But time—and changing political realities—can heal many wounds and blur many memories. In the spring of 1985, blacks held 310 elective offices in South Carolina. Strom Thurmond and other white politicians now vie for black votes. In Charleston, Septima Clark and Ruby Cornwell have long been involved in a variety of biracial civic activities. Arthur Clement, the Progressive Democrat and NAACP leader of the 1940s and 1950s, became a Republican. He also wrote an occasional column for the *News and Courier* and became the first black member of the Charleston Rotary Club. His sponsor was Tom Waring.[75]

Feelings about the Warings have also mellowed. For many years, the College of Charleston has awarded promising black students scholarships endowed by Ann Hyde in the Warings' memory. When it was proposed that a sculpture honoring Judge Waring be placed in the city council chamber, Charleston Mayor Joseph Riley readily agreed, telling a sympathetic Waring cousin, "it's time to bring him home." In 1979, the NAACP's national organization dedicated a bronze sculpture, its third annual Walter White Award, to Judge Waring's memory, applauding his "unswerving" efforts to uphold the law and "passionate . . . pursuit of justice," despite "continuing personal and public harassment." During ceremonies in the Charleston city council chamber, April 14, 1981, Mayor Riley placed the sculpture in the southwest corner of the chamber, overlooking the federal courthouse. The mayor termed Judge Waring a man of "uncommon achievement." But Joe Brown was the principal speaker on that occasion. Brown traced Judge Waring's judicial record and praised his courage. Then, he contrasted Waring with another judge. "[I]f Pontius Pilate had had the backbone of J. Waties Waring," he told those gathered that day, "there would be no Easter because Jesus would not have been crucified."[76]

Epilogue

At Christmas in 1951, shortly before Judge Waring's retirement, Anne and Stanley Warren visited her father and Elizabeth in Charleston. While there, they also enjoyed the hospitality of other family members and friends. These contacts offended both the judge and Elizabeth. On a drive through the plantation country along the Ashley River Road, the Warings voiced their disappointment that Anne and Stanley had not been more supportive of them. When the couple returned to New York, Stanley wrote his father-in-law and Elizabeth a lengthy letter, apologizing for having "somehow fallen quite unconsciously and thoughtlessly into a laissez-faire attitude that cried out for a swift jolt" and assuring them of the Warrens' loyalty.

> As with me, the sudden realization of what we were doing to you and Elizabeth was a terrible, frightening blow to Anne. In some unfathomable manner we overlooked the fact that the lines have been drawn and . . . it is time to stand up and be counted. Don't worry about us—ever. No matter what happens, should we never see you two again, we are standing up and being counted on your side of the barricades, come what may. And thanks for hitting me between the eyes as you did on that drive. I got straightened out and Anne will let you know in her own words how much she learned was wrong. When I pointed out the telling fact that, should the position be reversed and she become the object of senseless vilification, just where you and Elizabeth would stand, she burst into tears. This is not a plea for sympathy, nor an excuse, nor even an apology, but a sudden realization of our abject stupidity. I am ashamed of myself, thoroughly and so is Anne.[1]

Whether Anne ever wrote or discussed the matter with her father is not known. Within months of the Warings' arrival in New York, however, the judge had virtually disowned his daughter. Apparently, the Warrens' attitude toward Elizabeth was a major source of his concern. "When the Warings retired to New York," Tom Waring would later say, recalling conversations with Anne, "the Warrens were living in Brooklyn. And Elizabeth, in that take-charge manner of hers, had come to Anne's home with such frequency that her husband Stanley said, finally, that he wanted relief. Anne took it up with her father. He was immediately resentful, as he was of any criticism involving his wife. I'm sure he would have accepted criticism of himself much more gracefully. But he had this fetish, finally, about acceptance of his wife." Elizabeth's daughter offered a similar assessment. "I think the tension may have been—I'm sorry to have to say this—over my mother. I know [Anne] adored her father. . . . My mother was very strong; 'you're either for me or against me.' . . . And she may have felt at times that Anne was not attentive enough to Waties. She may have wanted Anne to take a more active role in helping them in New York."[2]

Whatever the catalyst, Judge Waring's relationship with his daughter continued to deteriorate during the Warings' first summer in New York. Their contacts that summer were limited largely to letters, and those purely formal, pertaining chiefly to investments made of the proceeds from the sale of the family home at 61 Meeting. Anne's letters, as her father later noted, were now to him alone, though previously she had addressed her correspondence to Elizabeth as well. At one point, Elizabeth visited Anne without Judge Waring's knowledge, urging her to speak with him, and as he later put it, "try to establish some clear understanding of our affairs." Anne did visit her father; but, again according to his account, only chatted briefly about current events, then "left for some more important engagement."[3]

In early October, and perhaps as a gesture of reconciliation, Anne mailed the judge a magazine clipping and note. In response, her father wrote his daughter a devastating, emotional, five-page letter. Elizabeth, he wrote, had "labored unceasingly to try to bring you and me together," using "every conceivable method to cure what I have long believed to be . . . incurable." For a time, an automobile, dresses, house furnishings, and other gifts had "seemed to help." But Elizabeth now realized that Anne had never shown him any "gratitude or affection."

> If you will hark back over the course of the years you will recall that you have never really given me any true love or affection. For years I tried to shut my eyes to your real attitude. In my lonely desire to have someone love me unselfishly I turned to the only one who might be that one—my only child. As a child in Charleston you gave some intellectual interest but never affection. . . . And now let's be really frank; you have never been interested in me or my work. Oh, occasionally you are aroused to accept an award for me and meet [prominent personalities] or go to Ben Sonnenberg's house and meet Eleanor Roosevelt. Those things have kept you and Stanley alerted to the possible advantage of having me as your father. But you were not interested enough to go to Harlem to hear me speak. And I do not believe you ever read my dissenting opinion in the Clarendon School case; or at least if you did you never joined many thousands of people who took the trouble to call or write to me. They were really interested in human rights and strange to say they were interested in me. How different my daughter.[4]

And on it went, as he attacked his daughter's "disgraceful lack of interest and ghastly failures" in school, her "sloppy" employment habits and career record, her "hobnobbing" in Charleston "with those who were vilifying me," and her opposition to his decision to retire, a decision reached only "after most careful consideration and . . . calculated as most beneficial to the cause of civil rights." She should review, he asserted, "the many, many disappointments" she had caused him. But now, he concluded, his "sorrow" was no longer for himself.

> I used to be terribly lonely craving a warm affection and understanding and mutual love. And for years I struggled to get some substitute from a daughter who, I hoped, might come to give these to me. That I now know is hopeless. But I have found in Elizabeth my heart's desire and she gives me everything I could ask for. . . . People say that it is never a waste to have loved some one even though it eventually is killed and comes to an end. I did at one time love you as the only thing I had. But you have chosen to kill that. So be it. And I am fortunate that I now have entered into another life where you cannot hurt me and where I have the fullness of a perfect love. How I wish you had this also.[5]

At Christmas that year, Anne penned her father a brief note. She had not attempted to answer his letter, she wrote, first, because it was "unanswerable," and second, because if she had, he would "undoubtedly think of other complaints. Still," she added, "in spite of your feelings for me, which must be extremely painful for you, there is one thing you cannot put a stop to—and that is my love for you, which continues and will continue." Gradually, after that, Anne and her father resumed reasonably cordial relations. "She stayed an outcast . . . for about eighteen months," Tom Waring later recalled. "Then, he began to take her to the theater and out to dinner, and finally, . . . she restored civil relations with Elizabeth, too." In his last years, Anne and her father were apparently quite close. But there was always to be a certain distance between them. In the summer of 1960, Anne wrote a series of articles on Charleston for the *New York Post*. Some of her Charleston friends and relatives thought that she had been unduly harsh on her native city. One of her friends wrote her that the people there were "most unhappy." If they had not written to tell her so, the friend added, she suspected it was because "they do not know how to. Perhaps they do not want to hurt you, and yet the youth we know here socially speaking . . . do not always object to crushing people." Some suggested that Anne, who by then had been divorced for several years, needed the money; others decided that she was "trying to get back in her father's graces and she thinks this is the way." Anne did need the money, but she was amused at the notion she was attempting to please her father. "[H]e thought I had been rather too gentle with Charleston," she wrote a friend there. "He has got over his resentments now—but there was a week or so there when the pieces may well have caused a complete end to whatever good graces exist."[6]

In 1957, Anne purchased a weekend cottage in Blairstown, New Jersey. The year after her father's death, she moved there permanently, becoming publications consultant to Blair Academy. The years following Judge Waring's death were lonely and illness-plagued for her. By 1979, she was suffering from severely crippling arthritis. Her pain had become intolerable, and the prospects for successful surgery seemed bleak. On November 29, a friend later wrote, "she solved the dilemma by suicide."[7]

Anne remained proud of her father to the end. Perhaps more than any-one else, however, she also recognized the complexities of his personality. When Judge Waring died, his cousin Dorothy wrote Anne a sympathetic letter of condolence. When Dorothy Waring was a young girl, she and her mother had often visited the judge and Annie Waring; and she was a favorite of the judge. After the divorce, however, she had sided with Annie. In her letter to Anne, Dorothy insisted that she considered the judge's rulings a duty, that she had simply been unable to condone his treatment of Anne's mother. "It was a tragedy," Anne responded,

> that my father's personality made it impossible for him to accept anything but the absolute. I am sure that many people felt with you that his judicial decisions were his duty. Unfortunately, he insisted always on complete ac-ceptance, which included approval of his divorce and remarriage. He never was an easy man. I fully realize that the choice many Charlestonians were offered was all or nothing. No one can be blamed for answering "nothing."[8]

Anne's assessment and her relationship with her father reflect the darker, tormented side of Judge Waring's personality. It is not difficult to accept that such a person could reject those who condemned his private life or official conduct. Nor is the notion that such a person's regard for his own judgment, feelings for his wife, and resentment of his society's treatment of her could affect his courtroom behavior as well as the tone of his opinions and off-the-bench statements. This man, whose "smartness bordered on insolence," could be coldly contemptuous of any one, friend or enemy, who did not embrace his stance—or share his zeal.

Not so easily accepted, however, are the claims of critics that Elizabeth Waring exerted a Svengali-like influence over her husband and that his efforts in behalf of civil rights were acts of revenge against his native city and state rather than a reflection of sincere commitment. Even the Warings' most en-thusiastic partisans agreed that Elizabeth had an influence on her husband's thinking. "She was," Arthur Clement remembered,

> a very beautiful woman and a very articulate woman. . . . She would domi-nate a conversation, and she was always an activist. . . . I think it was in-escapable that she opened up his eyes to a whole lot of things. . . . Under her influence, he became very humane. And I suspect that there was no way he could escape her influence, no way.[9]

Especially as Judge Waring became increasingly isolated from his family and friends, Elizabeth undoubtedly did exert a considerable influence over his thinking, just as she very likely fed his resentments. But Judge Waring was a strong-willed, dominating figure throughout his life; the image of him as a compliant old man mesmerized by a younger wife whom he adored ultimately strains credibility. In the Waring Papers, which the judge characteristically left to Howard University, there is an audio recording of an interview, apparently conducted in 1948, with Judge Waring. Mrs. Waring participated in portions of the interview. The image reflected is of an absolutely devoted and loyal wife whose respect for her husband and his place in history bordered on adoration. Her affection and total loyalty probably best explain the enduring quality of their relationship. They also suggest that, in that relationship, she was arguably as much influenced as influential.

The theory that Judge Waring's civil rights stance was inspired largely by a desire for revenge is even more difficult to accept. The Warings were obviously contemptuous of southern whites; those feelings undoubtedly affected the tenor of his behavior and statements. But Waties Waring the religious skeptic and United Nations supporter had hardly been a typical Confederate even before his complete break with his past. His equal pay rulings, moreover, preceded his divorce; his efforts in behalf of civil rights continued long after his retirement from the bench; and his harsh attacks on those who did not share his militancy were no respecter of region or race. In light of such factors, it is unfair to dismiss his struggle for racial justice as an exercise in spite. His militancy may have been politically naive—though probably no more so, in the long term, than Chief Justice Warren's appeal to the heart. But the revolution in his thinking was sincere—even if the darker side of his personality served as a catalyst.

Whatever the actual motivations underlying Judge Waring's role in the modern civil rights movement, he evokes extreme images in the eyes of supporters and critics alike. "Possibly he deserves a better place in history than I would give him," Tom Waring recently remarked of his uncle. "On the other hand, I think he may not deserve quite as good a place as he's been given. . . . I suspect that they said to each other, 'What can we do to get back at these people? What will hurt the most?' And what would hurt the most was to turn topsy-turvey the racial pattern of life [southerners revered]." Charleston blacks and others with fond memories of "Our Judge," on the other hand, would probably share the assessment of columnist Edwin Yoder. When Judge Waring died, Yoder was associate editor of the Greensboro, North Carolina, *Daily News*. "Tom Waring, for all his knowledge of the south," Yoder wrote Charles Kuralt on learning of the judge's death, "has forgotten that we were Americans before we were Southerners. Waties Waring's crime was that he did not forget."[10]

Notes

Preface

1. 347 U.S. 483 (1954).

2. *Afro-American*, May 29, 1954.

3. For accounts of the party, see *Afro-American*, May 29, 1954; *New York Post*, May 18, 1954; *Amsterdam News*, May 22, 1954; Poppy Cannon, *A Gentle Knight: My Husband Walter White* (New York: Rinehart & Co., Inc., 1956), pp. 249–55.

4. Briggs v. Elliott, 98 F. Supp. 529, 548 (E.D.S.C., 1951).

5. *New York Post,* May 18, 1954.

6. Briggs v. Elliott, 98 F. Supp. at 547.

7. Harold Burton Papers, Library of Congress, Washington, D.C.

8. Robert McC. Figg interview, Columbia, S.C., June 17, 1985.

9. For the fullest account of the development of that strategy, see Richard Kluger, *Simple Justice* (New York: Vintage Books ed., 1975), chs. 25–26.

10. Briggs v. Elliott, 98 F. Supp. at 541, 542, 548.

11. Judge Waring apparently first made the statement in public during a newspaper interview. *New York Post*, November 2, 1948.

12. Thomas J. Jones to Anne Waring Warren, January 29, 1969, Magnolia Cemetery files, Charleston, S.C.

13. Ruby Cornwell interview, Charleston, S.C., June 11, 1985.

Chapter 1

1. The genealogies of both families are found in "Waring Family" (compiled by Joseph Ivor Waring), *South Carolina Historical and Genealogical Magazine* 24 (1923): 81–101; and "The Waties Family of South Carolina" (compiled by J. D. Bull), *South Carolina Historical and Genealogical Magazine* 45 (1944): 12–22.

2. This discussion is drawn from Arthur Mazyck (1883) and Gene Waddell (1938), *Charleston in 1883* (Easley, S.C.: Southern Historical Press, 1883 and 1938). Robert Rosen, *A Short History of Charleston* (San Francisco: Lexikos, 1982), is a very readable, generally excellent account of the city's social and political history. John Joseph Duffy is perhaps the best student of Charleston's political history since the Civil War. See his "Charleston Politics in the Progressive Era" (Ph.D. dissertation, University of South Carolina, 1963).

3. *The Reminiscences of J. Waties Waring* (hereinafter cited as *Reminiscences*) (New York: Columbia University, Oral History Research Office, 1972, microfiche), pp. 1–3; *News and Courier* (Charleston, S.C.), March 21, 1916. The *Reminiscences* are interviews conducted 1955–57 as part of Columbia University's oral history project. Harlan B. Phillips and Louis M. Starr conducted the interviews with Judge Waring.

4. *Reminiscences*, pp. 5–6.

5. Ibid., p. 6.

6. Ibid., pp. 6–7.

7. Ibid., p. 4.

8. Ibid., pp. 12, 15.

9. Ibid., pp. 12–13.

10. Ibid., pp. 18–23.

11. Ibid., p. 26.

12. Ibid., pp. 26–42.

13. Ibid., pp. 43–49.

14. Ibid., p. 50.

15. Ibid., pp. 51–53.

16. Ibid., pp. 53–54, 61–64, 67–72.

17. Unless otherwise indicated, the discussion of the *Liebenfels* case is drawn from *Reminiscences*, pp. 55–60; *News and Courier*, March 9, 1917, March 10, 1917, October 11, 1917, October 12, 1917.

18. For a profile of Grace and his tenure as mayor, see Rosen, *A Short History of Charleston*, pp. 123–33.

19. *Reminiscences*, pp. 65–66, 73.

20. D. A. Brockinton, Jr., interview, Charleston, S.C., June 13, 15, 1985. Brockinton is the son of Waring's law partner. When these interviews were conducted, the elder Brockinton was ninety-five, the dean of the Charleston bar. In preparing for the second interview with me, Brockinton's son discussed Waties Waring with his father, including questions raised in the first interview.

21. Ibid.

22. *Reminiscences*, pp. 92–93.

23. Thomas R. Waring, Jr., interview, Charleston, S.C., June 10, 1985.

24. Ibid.; *Reminiscences*, p. 93.

25. Brockinton interview; T. R. Waring interview; August J. Tamsberg interview, Charleston, S.C., June 13, 1985; Figg interview.

26. Tamsberg interview.

27. For a profile of his administration as mayor, see Rosen, pp. 133–34.

28. The discussion of Charleston's financial recovery from the Depression is drawn from *Reminiscences*, 93–109; Tamsberg interview.

29. Journal of City Council, Charleston, S.C., 1931–43.

30. Waring to Henry W. Lockwood, October 14, 1941; Waring to August J. Tamsberg, September 17, 1940, personal files of August J. Tamsberg.

31. Journal of City Council.

32. *Reminiscences*, pp. 10–12.

33. Brockinton interview; Tamsberg interview.

34. John M. Fray to Dwight M. Green, September 16, 1941; Dwight M. Green to Waring, September 22, 1941, personal files of Thomas R. Waring, Jr. (hereinafter cited as T. R. Waring files).

35. J. Waties Waring to Dwight M. Green, October 14, 1941; Waring to Henry W. Lockwood, November 3, 1941, T. R. Waring files.

36. Tamsberg files; *News and Courier*, July 21, 1948.

37. *The State* (Columbia, S.C.), September 14, 1938.

38. *The State,* September 16, 1938; September 18, 1938; September 21, 1938.

39. Ibid.

40. Figg interview; Tamsberg interview.

41. *The State,* September 19, 1938.

42. *The State,* September 20, 1938; September 21, 1938.

43. *The State,* September 21, 1938.

44. Ibid.

45. Ibid.

46. Ibid. For a study of the most significant years of Smith's career, see Selden K. Smith, "Ellison DuRant Smith: A Southern Progressive, 1909–1929" (Ph.D. dissertation, University of South Carolina, 1970).

47. *News and Courier,* November 18, 1944.

48. Figg interview.

49. *Reminiscences,* p. 130a; Brockinton interview; Figg interview; T. R. Waring interview.

50. *News and Courier,* November 18, 1944.

51. *Reminiscences,* pp. 130a–131a.

52. Ibid., pp. 130a–132a; Figg interview; J. Waties Waring file, U.S. Department of Justice.

53. *News and Courier,* January 16, 1939.

54. Brockinton interview.

55. *Reminiscences,* pp. 135a–136a.

56. *News and Courier,* October 2, 1941; Figg interview.

57. *News and Courier,* October 2, 1941. The list is on file in the Burnet R. Maybank Papers, College of Charleston.

58. The letters are reprinted in U.S., Congress, *Congressional Record* 94: 9788–89.

59. Ibid.

60. *Reminiscences,* pp. 173a–178a.

61. Maybank Papers.

62. Figg interview; *Reminiscences,* p. 137a.

63. Francis Biddle to Frederick Van Nuys, January 9, 1942, reprinted in U.S., Congress, *Congressional Record* 94: 9789.

64. Ernest W. McFarland to Burnet R. Maybank, August 3, 1948, Maybank Papers. McFarland was the subcommittee chairman.

65. *News and Courier,* January 13, 1942.

66. McFarland to Maybank, August 3, 1948, Maybank Papers.

67. *Evening Post* (Charleston, S.C.), December 19, 1941; *News and Courier,* December 19, 1941.

68. Ibid.

69. The text of Waring's acceptance speech is on file in the J. Waties Waring Papers, Moorland-Spingarn Research Center, Howard University, Washington, D.C. The Waring Papers are in excellent collection but contain virtually no material dated earlier than 1945.

Chapter 2

1. *New York Times,* February 15, 1920.

2. *Reminiscences,* pp. 151a–152a. A summary of his appellate review record is included in the Waring Papers.

3. Ibid., pp. 152a–153a.

4. Ibid., pp. 142a–143a.

5. Ibid., pp. 143a–144a. Waring to Tom Clark, June 10, 1946, October 8, 1946, Waring Papers. On October 18, Clark wrote Judge Waring, indicating that a special department representative would soon call on the judge to receive his suggestions for expediting such cases, Waring Papers.

6. Ibid., pp. 153a–154a; *Evening News* (Newark, N.J.), September 30, 1944.

7. Ibid., pp. 147a–148a.

8. Unidentified clippings, Waring Papers. Judge Waring discussed his nonracial cases in *Reminiscences,* pp. 128a–171a, 128–195.

9. Ibid.

10. *Reminiscences,* pp. 159a–166a.

11. Estep v. United States, Smith v. United States, 327 U.S. 114 (1946).

12. Trial transcript, United States v. Smith. A copy is on file in the Waring Papers.

13. Unidentified clipping, Waring Papers.

14. Miller v. Long, 71 F. Supp. 603, 605 (E.D.S.C., 1945); *Reminiscences,* p. 165.

15. Beasley v. United States, 81 F. Supp. 518, 524–525 (E.D.S.C., 1948). The English precedent on which Waring relied was Scott v. Shepherd, 2 W.Bl. 892 (1773).

16. *Reminiscences,* p. 170; Todd Atlantic Shipyards Corp. v. *The Southport,* 95 F. Supp. 331 (E.D.S.C., 1951); South Carolina Highway Dept. v. United States, 78 F. Supp. 598 (E.D.S.C., 1948).

17. *News and Courier,* March 27, 1945.

18. Brockinton interview.

19. This discussion of Annie Gammell's association with Sarah Bernhardt is drawn from an undated United Press profile published in the *News and Courier,* personal files of Anne Waring Warren.

20. T. R. Waring interview.

21. Brockinton interview.

22. Ibid.

23. After his death, some of Stoney's friends published a collection of his work, *A Miscellany of Doggerel Rhymes* (privately published, 1964).

24. Tamsberg interview.

25. Ann Mills Hyde interview, Corrales, N.M., August 16, 1985; David Mills interview, Detroit, Mich., October 17, 1985.

26. Information regarding Elizabeth Waring's background is included in her obituary in the *New York Times,* November 1, 1968, and a profile in the *Chicago Defender,* March 11, 1950, among other sources.

27. Hyde interview.

28. Mills interview.

29. Ibid.; Hyde interview.

30. Ibid.

31. Mills interview.

32. Ibid.; Hyde interview.

33. Hyde interview; T. R. Waring interview; *Chicago Defender,* March 11, 1950.

34. Brockinton interview; Hyde interview; T. R. Waring interview.

35. Mazyck and Waddell, *Charleston in 1883.*

36. T. R. Waring interview.

37. Unless otherwise indicated, this discussion of the Waring divorce is based on the record of Waring v. Waring, No. 62096-E, Circuit Court, Duval County, Fla.

38. T. R. Waring interview.

39. *News and Courier,* June 9, 1945, June 18, 1945; T. R. Waring interview; Hyde interview.

40. T. R. Waring interview; Margareta Childs interview, Charleston, S.C., June 14, 1985; Brockinton interview.

41. Brockinton interview; T. R. Waring interview.

42. Ibid.; Joseph Young interview, Charleston, S.C., June 12, 1985.

43. T. R. Waring interview.

44. Ibid.; *News and Courier,* March 15, 1945; Waring to T. R. Waring, Jr., November 6, 1946, T. R. Waring files.

45. T. R. Waring, Jr., to Waring, November 7, 1945, T. R. Waring files.

46. T. R. Waring interview.

47. Waring to Charles W. Waring, November 15, 1945, T. R. Waring files; Dorothy Waring interview, Summerville, S.C., June 11, 1985; Charles W. Waring to Waring et al., June 18, 1948, Waring Papers.

48. United States v. A. H. Fischer Lumber Co., 162 F. 2d 872 (4th Cir., 1947).

49. Brockinton interview; T. R. Waring interview; T. R. Waring files.

50. Ibid.

51. Brockinton interview.

52. Ibid.; Young interview.

53. Figg interview; Young interview.

54. T. R. Waring interview; Young interview. Correspondence between Elizabeth's first and third husbands is on file in the Waring Papers.

55. T. R. Waring interview; Dorothy Waring interview.

56. *News and Courier,* December 13, 1954, December 16, 1954.

Chapter 3

1. Brockinton interview; Tamsberg interview.

2. Joseph Arthur Brown interview, Charleston, S.C., June 15, 1985; Duvall v. Seignous, Civil Action No. 1083, unpublished consent decree, Waring Papers.

3. *Amsterdam News,* June 9, 1951.

4. *Reminiscences,* p. 225; *Duvall* v. *Seignous,* unpublished consent decree.

5. The state's action is summarized in Thompson v. Gibbes, 60 F. Supp. 872, 874–75 (E.D.S.C., 1945).

6. *The State,* May 10, 1945, May 27, 1945; *News and Courier,* May 10, 1945; *Reminiscences,* pp. 226–227.

7. Ibid.

8. Thompson v. Gibbes, 60 F. Supp. at 874–75.

9. Ibid., 875–76, 878.

10. *Reminiscences,* p. 225; A. G. Flora to Waring, March 6, 1946, Waring Papers; J. Heyward Gibbes to Waring, June 7, 1945, Waring Papers.

11. Edgar Brown to Waring, June 6, 1945, Waring Papers; Waring to Brown, June 12, 1945, Waring Papers; Waring to J. Heyward Gibbes, June 12, 1945, Waring Papers.

12. *Reminiscences,* pp. 196–198; *New York Times,* December 4, 1947; *Herald Tribune* (New York), December 4, 1947.

13. Ibid.

14. *Reminiscences,* p. 202.

15. Ibid., pp. 205–213.

16. Unless otherwise indicated, this discussion is drawn from *Christian Science Monitor,* November 7, 1946; *New York Times,* November 6, 1946; *The State,* November 6, 1946; *News and Courier,* November 6, 1946.

17. *New York Times,* August 18, 19, 1946.

18. *Reminiscences,* pp. 215–229.

19. Quoted in *United States* v. *Shull,* draft of unfiled memorandum order, Waring Papers; *New York Times,* September 27, 1946, September 29, 1946.

20. *New York Times,* October 10, 1946.

21. *Reminiscences,* pp. 215–224.

22. Ibid.

23. The draft is on file in the Waring Papers.

24. Ibid.

25. *Reminiscences,* p. 222.

26. *The State,* November 7, 1946.

27. *Reminiscences,* pp. 222–223.

28. Ibid., pp. 223–224; *The State,* undated clipping in Waring Papers.

29. *Lighthouse and Informer* (Columbia, S.C.), February 9, 1952; Samuel Grafton, "Lonesomest Man in Town," *Collier's,* April 29, 1950, p. 49.

30. *Reminiscences,* pp. 234–240.

31. Ibid., pp. 240–245. The December 12, 1948, issue of the *News and Courier* published a profile of Samuel Fleming as part of a series on "successful South Carolina negroes."

32. Ibid., pp. 245–246; *News and Courier,* October 26, 1948.

33. Ibid., p. 244.

34. *News and Courier,* February 14, 1942.

35. Unless otherwise indicated, this discussion is drawn from *Times-Dispatch* (Richmond, Va.), April 26, 1947, January 22, 1948, January 23, 1948, January 31, 1948.

36. *Times* (Roanoke, Va.), April 27, 1947; unpublished and undated interview with Judge and Mrs. Waring, Waring Papers (hereinafter cited as unpublished interview).

37. Ibid.; *News Leader* (Richmond, Va.), April 26, 1947; John J. Parker to Waring, April 29, 1947, John J. Parker Papers, Southern Historical Collection, University of North Carolina at Chapel Hill.

38. T. R. Waring interview; Figg interview; Leon M. Bazile to Waring, April 20, 1947, Waring Papers; Waring to Bazile, April 22, 1947, Waring Papers; George R. Humrickhouse to Waring, April 23, 1947, Waring Papers; Waring to Humrickhouse, April 23, 1947. Brazile was the state circuit judge in whom the juror confided.

39. United States v. Gardner, Criminal No. 4517, affidavit of Joseph E. Proffit, September 26, 1947, Waring Papers.

40. United States v. Gardner, Criminal No. 4517, unpublished Memorandum Opinion, October 10, 1947, Waring Papers.

41. This profile is drawn from William Peters, "A Southern Success Story," *Redbook,* June 1960, pp. 40–41ff.

42. Missouri *ex rel.* Gaines v. Canada, 305 U.S. 337 (1938).

43. Quoted in Wrighten v. Board of Trustees, 72 F. Supp. 948, 951 (E.D.S.C., 1947).

44. Robert L. Carter to Waring, May 22, 1947, Waring Papers; Waring to Carter, May 26, 1947, Waring Papers; *Wrighten* v. *Board of Trustees,* Plaintiff's Memorandum of Law, Waring Papers.

45. Wrighten v. Board of Trustees, 72 F. Supp. at 953.

46. *Wrighten* v. *Board of Trustees,* unpublished Memorandum Opinion, July 12, 1948, Waring Papers. "It seemed like an absurdity to start a new law school there," Waring later remarked. "As I said to some of my friends afterwards, 'It would have been a lot cheaper for the state of South Carolina to buy three more chairs [for] the Law School in Columbia than to build a $200,000 building and put an initial appropriation of $30,000 for a law library, and hire seven professors for these three would-be lawyers.' " *Reminiscences,* p. 258.

47. *Reminiscences,* pp. 256–258.

48. Ibid., pp. 247–248.

49. Newberry v. United States, 256 U.S. 232 (1921); Nixon v. Herndon, 273 U.S. 536 (1927); Nixon v. Condon, 286 U.S. 73 (1932); Grovey v. Townsend, 295 U.S. 45 (1935).

50. Classic v. United States, 313 U.S. 299, 318 (1941); Smith v. Allwright, 321 U.S. 649 (1944).

51. Elmore v. Rice, 72 F. Supp. 516 (E.D.S.C., 1947); *Reminiscences,* pp. 251–254; V. O. Key, Jr., *Southern Politics in State and Nation* (New York: Vintage Books edition, 1949), pp. 626–629.

52. *News and Courier,* September 23, 1946; Quoted in Key, *Southern Politics,* p. 627.

53. *Elmore* v. *Rice,* Plaintiffs' Memorandum of Law, June 3, 1947, Waring Papers.

54. United States v. Classic, 313 U.S. at 318–19 (emphasis added); *Elmore* v. *Rice,* Arguments for Defendants on Motion to Dismiss, June 3, 1947, Waring Papers.

55. *Reminiscences,* p. 263.

56. Walter J. Suthon to Waring, May 7, 1947, Waring Papers; Waring to Suthon, November 11, 1947, Waring Papers; Note, "Negro Disenfranchisement— A Challenge to the Constitution," *Columbia Law Review* 47 (January 1947): 97.

57. Elmore v. Rice, 72 F. Supp. at 526, 527; *New York Times,* July 13, 1947.

58. Elmore v. Rice, 72 F. Supp. at 528.

59. T. R. Waring interview.

60. *Evening Post,* July 15, 1947; W. W. Ball to T. R. Waring, August 3, 1947, Thomas R. Waring, Jr., Papers, South Carolina Historical Society, Charleston, S.C.

61. *News and Courier,* August 20, 1947; Rice v. Elmore, 165 F. 2d 387 (4th Cir., 1947).

62. *New York Times,* July 14, 1947; Benjamin Mays to Waring, July 29, 1947,

Waring Papers; Waring to Charleston Chapter of the NAACP, July 28, 1947, Waring Papers; Waring to Colored Interdenominational Ministers Union, July 21, 1947, Waring Papers; Seth C. Taft, *Yale Law Journal,* to Waring, July 21, 1947, Waring Papers; Victor G. Rosenbloom, Columbia University law student, to Waring, September 11, 1947, Waring Papers.

63. Stephen Nettles to Waring, October 8, 1947, Waring Papers; Waring to Dr. Robert B. Burrows, July 24, 1947, Waring Papers; Waring to S. M. Atkinson, Methodist cleric, July 17, 1947, Waring Papers; Waring to Mrs. Philip Clark, July 17, 1947, Waring Papers; Waring to Joseph A. McElroy, Episcopalian cleric, July 17, 1947, Waring Papers; Waring to Mrs. George Howe, July 15, 1947, Waring Papers.

64. Waring to Stephen Nettles, October 10, 1947, Waring Papers; Waring to Burrows; Waring to Mrs. S. B. Alexander, July 15, 1947, Waring Papers.

65. Waring to George F. Zook, December 22, 1947, Waring Papers.

Chapter 4

1. Anne Waring Warren to Dorothy Waring, April 17, 1968, T. R. Waring files.
2. Ibid.; Waring to Anne and Stanley Warren, June 21, 1946, Waring Papers.
3. Ibid; Waring to Anne and Stanley Warren, January 19, 1948, Waring Papers.
4. Stanley Warren to Warings, April 20, 1948, Waring Papers.
5. The full oath is quoted in Brown v. Baskin, 78 F. Supp. 933 (E.D.S.C., 1948).
6. *Southern Patriot,* June 1948, p. 1; William P. Baskin telegram to Waring, July 10, 1948, Waring Papers; Waring telegram to Baskin, July 11, 1948, Waring Papers; *Reminiscences,* pp. 277–289, 291–294.
7. Transcript of Brown v. Baskin, Civil Action No. 1964, a copy of which is on file in the Waring Papers.
8. *News and Courier,* July 29, 1948; *Reminiscences,* p. 287; Rowena W. Tobias, "Lost Cause, 1948," *Nation,* August 14, 1948, p. 187.
9. Unless otherwise indicated, this discussion is drawn from the trial transcript.
10. J. Arthur Clement interview, Charleston, S.C., June 11, 1985.
11. Brown v. Baskin, 78 F. Supp. at 939.
12. *Evening Post,* July 22, 1948.
13. William M. Ashby to Waring, July 20, 1948, Waring Papers; *News and Courier,* July 17, 1948; *Pittsburgh Courier,* July 24, 1948; Edgar S. Fraley to Waring, August 16, 1948, Waring Papers; Juliette Morgan to Waring, August 1948, Waring Papers; Robert H. Ayers to Waring, December 9, 1948, Waring Papers.
14. *Greenville News,* undated, Waring Papers; *Florence News,* July 10, 1948, July 17, 1948.
15. *Reminiscences,* pp. 305–306.
16. Arthur M. Wilcox memorandum to T. R. Waring, February 3, 1948, T. R. Waring files; unpublished interview, Waring Papers.
17. T. R. Waring interview. John D. Stark, *Damned Up-Countryman: William Watts Ball, A Study in American Conservatism* (Durham, N.C.: Duke University, 1968), is an excellent biography of Ball.
18. Ibid.
19. *News and Courier,* July 2, 1948, July 23, 1948.
20. *News and Courier,* July 20, 1948, July 23, 1948, July 18, 1948.

21. *News and Courier,* July 22, 1948, July 29, 1948.

22. *News and Courier,* July 22, 1948, July 20, 1948, July 29, 1948, July 21, 1948, July 28, 1948.

23. *News and Courier,* July 21, 1948, July 27, 1948, July 18, 1948, July 19, 1948, July 23, 1948.

24. *News and Courier,* July 25, 1948.

25. *News and Courier,* July 17, 1948, July 21, 1948.

26. Ibid.

27. *News and Courier,* July 1, 1948; *The State,* June 22, 1948.

28. *Brown* v. *Baskin* trial transcript.

29. Ibid.

30. *Reminiscences,* pp. 291–293.

31. *News and Courier,* July 17, 1948, July 22, 1948.

32. *News and Courier,* July 22, 1948; William Jennings Bryan Dorn interview, Greenwood, S. C., June 18, 1985.

33. William Jennings Bryan Dorn to Frank E. Cope, April 28, 1948, William Jennings Bryan Dorn Papers, South Caroliniana Collection, University of South Carolina, Columbia, S.C.; John D. Britton to Dorn, April 30, 1948, Dorn Papers; Dorn to Britton, May 4, 1948, Dorn Papers; Dorn to C. E. Jones, May 4, 1948, Dorn Papers.

34. Dorn interview.

35. *News and Courier,* July 1, 1948, July 29, 1948; Dorn interview.

36. A copy of H. Res. 704 is on file in the Waring Papers; Dorn interview.

37. U.S., Congress, *Congressional Record* 94: A4654–55.

38. Ibid.

39. *News and Courier,* July 29, 1948, July 22, 1948.

40. *News and Courier,* July 1, 1948.

41. Waring to Burnet Maybank, January 7, 1942, Maybank Papers; Waring to Maybank, September 13, 1945, Maybank Papers; Maybank to Waring, September 21, 1945, Maybank Papers; Waring to Maybank, February 6, 1947, Waring Papers; Waring to Maybank, February 12, 1947.

42. *News and Courier,* July 22, 1948, July 26, 1948, July 29, 1948, July 31, 1948.

43. U.S., Congress, *Congressional Record* 94: 9456.

44. *News and Courier,* August 3, 1948.

45. U.S., Congress, *Congressional Record* 94: 9788–89; Ernest W. McFarland to Burnet Maybank, August 3, 1948, Maybank Papers.

46. *News and Courier,* August 8, 1948.

47. L. Mendel Rivers to Waring, May 4, 1946, Waring Papers; Rivers to Waring, April 10, 1946, Waring Papers; Rivers to Waring, April 18, 1946, Waring Papers; Rivers to Waring, October 4, 1946, Waring Papers.

48. U.S., Congress, *Congressional Record* 94: 9752–53.

49. Ibid.

50. *Evening Post,* August 7, 1948, August 5, 1948.

51. *Evening Post,* August 5, 1948; tear sheet of Walter White column, "Congressional Reforms Overdue," Waring Papers; *Evening Post,* August 6, 1948.

52. Waring to John J. Parker, August 5, 1948, Waring Papers.

53. John J. Parker to Waring, August 6, 1948, Waring Papers; *Evening Post,* August 5, 1948.

54. *News and Courier,* August 12, 1948, undated clipping, Waring Papers.

55. Clement interview; *Evening Post,* August 12, 1948; Waring to John J. Parker, August 11, 1948, Waring Papers; Waring to Simeon Hyde, Jr., August 11, 1948, Waring Papers.

56. Figg interview; *Herald Tribune,* August 10, 1948.

57. Tobias, "Lost Cause, 1948," p. 187; "The Man They Love to Hate," *Time,* August 23, 1948, p. 17.

58. *Sunday Herald* (New Britain, Conn.), August 29, 1948.

59. Stanley Warren to Warings, undated, Waring Papers.

60. Ann Hyde to Waring, July 17, 1947, Waring Papers; Waring to Simeon Hyde, Jr., Waring Papers.

61. *Daily Press* (Santa Barbara, Calif.), undated, reprinted in *Evening Post,* August 27, 1948.

62. *New York Times,* October 12, 1948.

63. *Evening Post,* August 27, 1948; *News and Courier,* October 14, 1948, October 15, 1948.

64. *Evening Post,* October 20, 1948.

65. *News and Courier,* October 19, 1948, October 15, 1948.

66. A copy of the hearing transcript is on file in the Waring Papers.

67. The letter is on file in the Waring Papers.

68. Waring to Stanley Warren, October 22, 1948, Waring Papers.

69. This discussion is drawn from Tom Peck memorandum to T. R. Waring, October 23, 1948, T. R. Waring files.

70. *News and Courier,* October 23, 1948; Waring to Stanley Warren, October 27, 1948, Waring Papers.

71. *News and Courier,* October 23, 1948.

72. J. V. Nielsen, Jr., memorandum to T. R. Waring, T. R. Waring files.

73. *New York Post,* November 2, 1948.

74. Ibid.

75. Ibid.; Brown v. Baskin, 80 F. Supp. 1017 (E.D.S.C., 1948); *Evening Post,* December 2, 1948.

76. *Evening Post,* December 4, 1948.

77. *New York Times,* December 3, 1948; *Reminiscences,* pp. 223, 271–272.

78. *New York Times,* December 3, 1948; "Tribute to Judge Waring," *Lawyers Guild Review* 9 (1949): 5–7.

79. See generally Hollinger F. Barnard (ed.), *Outside the Magic Circle: The Autobiography of Virginia Foster Durr* (University, Ala.: University of Alabama Press, 1985).

80. "Tribute to Judge Waring," pp. 5–6.

81. *News and Courier,* August 9, 1948; Lewis W. West to Waring, August 11, 1948, Waring Papers.

82. Joseph Fromberg to William Jennings Bryan Dorn, August 10, 1948, Waring Papers; *News and Courier,* August 12, 1948.

83. Joseph Fromberg to Waring, August 19, 1948, Waring Papers.

84. Waring to John J. Parker, August 5, 1948, Waring Papers; Parker to Waring, August 6, 1948, Waring Papers; Waring to Parker, August 9, 1948, Waring Papers; Parker to Waring, August 18, 1948, Waring Papers.

85. T. R. Waring files.

Chapter 5

1. *New York Times,* January 2, 1949, February 21, 1949, February 27, 1949; *Lighthouse and Informer,* April 16, 1949; *Pittsburgh Courier,* May 21, 1949.

2. Anne Warren to Waring, undated, Waring Papers.

3. *World Telegram* (New York), June 3, 1949; Waring to Eleanor Roosevelt, June 13, 1949, Waring Papers.

4. Waring to Thurgood Marshall, December 4, 1948, Waring Papers; Marshall to Waring, December 8, 1948, Waring Papers; Waring to Marshall, December 11, 1948, Waring Papers; Waring to Marshall, November 14, 1949, Waring Papers.

5. Thurgood Marshall to John H. McCray, December 12, 1949, Waring Papers; Waring to Marshall, February 8, 1949, Waring Papers; Marshall to John Wrighten, February 21, 1949, Waring Papers.

6. Walter White to Waring, April 19, 1949, Waring Papers; Poppy Cannon, "The Eleanor Roosevelt of the Caribbean," *Negro Digest,* October, 1950, pp. 52–59; Elizabeth Waring to Jack Thompson, December 29, 1949, Waring Papers.

7. *Chicago Defender,* March 11, 1950; *Pittsburgh Courier,* March 11, 1950; *New York Age,* March 18, 1950.

8. Hyde interview; *News and Courier,* June 22, 1949.

9. Cornwell interview.

10. Unpublished interview, Waring Papers; Ruby Cornwell interview, Charleston, S.C., June 11, 1985; Brown interview; Clement interview; *Pittsburgh Courier,* August 30, 1952.

11. Septima P. Clark interview, Charleston, S.C., June 11, 1985; Septima P. Clark, *Echo in My Soul* (New York: E. P. Dutton, 1962), pp. 3–7.

12. Clark interview.

13. Clement interview; Cornwell interview.

14. Cornwell interview.

15. Ibid.

16. Ibid.

17. Ibid.; reprint of Carl T. Rowan, "How Far From Slavery: A Negro's Report on Revisiting the South," series originally published in 1951 in the Minneapolis *Tribune;* Carl T. Rowan, *South of Freedom* (New York: Alfred A. Knopf, 1952), pp. 83–100.

18. Edwin C. Northrop and Louise Bulkley Dillingham to alumnae, parents, and friends of Westover School, May 1, 1950, Waring Papers.

19. Miriam deCosta to Elizabeth Waring, September 19, 1950, Waring Papers; Beautine deCosta to Elizabeth Waring, October 22, 1950, Waring Papers.

20. Miriam deCosta to Elizabeth Waring, April 19, 1951, Waring Papers; deCosta to Elizabeth Waring, June 24, 1951, Waring Papers; deCosta to Elizabeth Waring, September 11, 1951, Waring Papers; deCosta to Elizabeth Waring, September 30, 1951, Waring Papers; deCosta to Elizabeth Waring, November 22, 1951, Waring Papers.

21. Cornwell interview; Mrs. M. P. Kennedy to Warings, undated, Waring Papers; T. R. Waring to Ashley Halsey, Jr., April 26, 1950, T. R. Waring files.

22. Miriam deCosta to Elizabeth Waring, April 19, 1951, Waring Papers; Rowan, "How Far From Slavery," Waring Papers.

23. Brown interview; Rowan, *South of Freedom,* p. 96.

24. *Lighthouse and Informer,* May 7, 1949; Waring to Cassandra Maxwell, May 10, 1950, Waring Papers.

25. *Constitution* (Atlanta, Ga.), April 9, 1946; Virginius Dabney, "Nearer and Nearer the Precipice," *Atlantic Monthly*, January 1943, p. 171. Major studies of "Jim Crow Liberalism" include Morton Sosna, *In Search of the Silent South: Southern Liberals and the Race Issue* (New York: Columbia University Press, 1977); Bruce Clayton, *The Savage Ideal: Intolerance and Intellectual Leadership in the South, 1890–1914* (Baltimore: Johns Hopkins University Press, 1972); and Jack Temple Kirby, *Darkness at Dawning: Race and Reform in the Progressive South* (Philadelphia: Lippincott, 1972). David W. Southern, "Beyond Jim Crow Liberalism: Judge Waring's Fight Against Segregation in South Carolina, 1942–52," *Journal of Negro History* 65 (Fall 1981): 209–227, one of the few scholarly studies of Judge Waring's career published to date, focuses on this aspect of Waring's philosophy.

26. Hodding Carter, "Chip on Our Shoulder Down South," *Saturday Evening Post*, November 9, 1946, pp. 18–19, 145–148; Hodding Carter, "Just Leave Us Alone," *Saturday Evening Post*, January 14, 1950, pp. 30, 90–92; Hodding Carter, "The Civil Rights Issue As Seen in the South," *New York Times Magazine*, March 21, 1948, pp. 15, 52–55; Hodding Carter, "A Southern Liberal Looks at Civil Rights," *New York Times Magazine*, August 8, 1948, pp. 10, 20, 25; Hodding Carter, "New Rebel Yell in Dixie," *Collier's*, July 9, 1949, pp. 13–15, 63–65.

27. Walter White column, undated, Waring Papers.

28. *Christian Science Monitor*, April 20, 1950; Waring to J. Max Bond, February 21, 1950, Waring Papers; Waring to Marion Wright, February 9, 1950, Waring Papers.

29. Lillian Smith, *Killers of the Dream* (New York: Norton, 1949); Waring to Lillian Smith, December 9, 1949, Waring Papers.

30. *News and Courier*, October 24, 1949; Waring to Eleanor Roosevelt, October 24, 1949, Waring Papers; Eleanor Roosevelt to Waring, October 28, 1949, Waring Papers.

31. Waring to Harry S. Truman, December 6, 1948, Waring Papers; Truman to Waring, December 10, 1948, Waring Papers.

32. *News and Courier*, June 29, 1949.

33. S. A. Cothran memorandum, undated, T. R. Waring files; *News and Courier*, June 30, 1949.

34. A copy of the telegram is on file in the Waring Papers. It also appeared in *Evening Post*, June 30, 1949.

35. *Charlotte Observer*, July 2, 1949; *News and Courier*, July 2, 1949.

36. Marion Wright to L. Mendel Rivers, August 12, 1948, Waring Papers; Wright to W. J. Bryan Dorn, August 12, 1948, Waring Papers; Wright to Waring, July 31, 1948, Waring Papers; Waring to Wright, April 18, 1949, Waring Papers.

37. Waring to Marion Wright, February 9, 1950, Waring Papers; Wright to Waring, February 10, 1950, Waring Papers.

38. Walter White to Waring, April 19, 1949, Waring Papers; Waring to Cassandra Maxwell, May 10, 1950, Waring Papers.

39. Waring to Marion Wright, November 16, 1951, Waring Papers.

40. Marion Wright to Waring, November 21, 1951, Waring Papers.

41. Waring to Marion Wright, November 23, 1951, Waring Papers.

42. Marion Wright to Waring, December 4, 1951, Waring Papers; Elizabeth Waring to Wright, December 6, 1951, Marion Allen Wright Papers, Southern Historical Collection, University of North Carolina at Chapel Hill.

43. Waring to Marion Wright, December 17, 1951, Waring Papers.

44. Barnard, *Outside the Magic Circle*, pp. 99, 117, 124, 246–247, 249; Waring to Aubrey Williams, February 9, 1950, Waring Papers. A copy of the address, "The Failure of Gradualism," is on file in the Waring Papers.

45. Waring to Walter White, January 31, 1950, Waring Papers; James Dombrowski to Waring, July 17, 1947, Waring Papers; Waring to Dombrowski, October 29, 1948, Waring Papers; Dombrowski to Waring, April 12, 1949, Waring Papers.

46. James Dombrowski to Waring, December 6, 1948, Waring Papers; Waring to Dombrowski, December 11, 1948, Waring Papers; Dombrowski v. Pfister, 380 U.S. 479 (1965); Waring to Walter White, April 7, 1949, Waring Papers; White to Waring, April 19, 1949, Waring Papers; Waring to White, April 22, 1949, Waring Papers; Dombrowski to Waring, June 13, 1949, Waring Papers; Waring to Myles Horton, February 21, 1950, Waring Papers; drafts of speeches on file in the Waring Papers.

47. *Sun-Reporter* (San Francisco), August 26, 1950; an unidentified newspaper reprint of the address on file in the Waring Papers.

Chapter 6

1. Hyde interview.

2. Clark, *Echo in My Soul*, pp. 95–97; Clark interview; unpublished interview, Waring Papers; Waring to Aubrey Williams, January 25, 1950, Waring Papers. This discussion is also drawn from a typed report prepared by Septima P. Clark, on file in the Waring Papers, and from an oral history in the Septima P. Clark Papers, College of Charleston.

3. Clark, *Echo in My Soul*, pp. 96–97.

4. Ibid.; Clark interview; Rowan, *South of Freedom*, p. 90.

5. Waring to Anne and Stanley Warren, January 13, 1950, Waring Papers.

6. Frank B. Gilbreth memorandum to T. R. Waring, January 16, 1950, T. R. Waring files; Gilbreth memorandum, January 16, 1950, T. R. Waring files.

7. Clark interview.

8. A copy of the manuscript from which Mrs. Waring spoke is on file in the Waring Papers.

9. Clark interview.

10. Septima P. Clark and Rose E. Huggins to Elizabeth Waring, January 24, 1950, Waring Papers; Clark interview.

11. *The State*, January 17, 1950; *New York Times*, January 18, 1950; "South Carolina: Marching through Charleston," *Time*, January 30, 1950, p. 18; *Pittsburgh Courier*, undated, Waring Papers; Aubrey Williams to Waring, January 23, 1950, Waring Papers; Thomas H. Button to Elizabeth Waring, January 24, 1950, Waring Papers; Randall Brooks to Elizabeth Waring, January 29, 1950, Waring Papers; Maisis Armytage-Moore telegram to Elizabeth Waring, undated, Waring Papers.

12. *Reminiscences*, pp. 305–306. The hate mail is on file in the Waring Papers.

13. Mrs. J. Ashby Turner to Elizabeth Waring, January 19, 1950, Waring Papers.

14. *Chicago Defender*, January 28, 1950; *News and Courier*, January 18, 1950.

15. *Tallahassee Democrat*, undated, Waring Papers; *Hendersonville Times-News*, February 18, 1950; *Atlanta Journal*, January 29, 1950.

16. T. R. Waring to Hodding Carter, January 31, 1950, T. R. Waring files.

17. Ibid.; Frank B. Gilbreth draft editorial, T. R. Waring files; *News and Courier,* January 23, 1950, February 3, 1950; hate mail in T. R. Waring files.

18. "South Carolina: Marching through Charleston," p. 18; Rowan, *South of Freedom,* p. 93.

19. *World Telegram and Sun* (New York), February 22, 1950; *Evening Post,* February 13, 1950. For a slightly edited transcript of the interview, see "Mrs. Waring Meets the Press," *American Mercury,* May 1950, pp. 562–569.

20. A copy of the list of questions is on file in the James F. Byrnes Papers, Clemson University.

21. Ibid.

22. *Greenville News,* February 19, 1950.

23. John Henry Faulk to the Warings, February 11, 1950, Waring Papers; *Spartanburg Herald,* February 24, 1950.

24. Hate mail on file in Waring Papers and T. R. Waring files; *News and Courier,* February 16, 1950; Frank B. Gilbreth to Ira Calvin White, February 8, 1950, T. R. Waring files.

25. T. R. Waring files.

26. The business card and verses of scripture are on file in the Waring Papers. The *Myrtle Beach News,* March 10, 1950, was one of the papers printing "White Trash."

27. *News and Courier,* February 14, 1950.

28. *Evening Post,* February 15, 1950. A copy of the resolution is on file in the Wright Papers.

29. *Lighthouse and Informer,* June 11, 1949; *News and Courier,* February 23, 1950.

30. *News and Courier,* February 23, 1950; unidentified clipping, Waring Papers.

31. Arthur Locke King to James F. Byrnes, January 21, 1950, Byrnes Papers; Byrnes to King, January 25, 1950, Byrnes Papers.

32. C. N. Hastie to Burnet Maybank, two undated letters, Maybank Papers; H. G. Willingham telegram to Maybank, February 15, 1950, Maybank Papers; R. S. Lee to Maybank, February 14, 1950, Maybank Papers; J. L. Kennedy to Maybank, February 24, 1950, Maybank Papers.

33. Burnet Maybank to C. N. Hastie, February 17, 1950, Maybank Papers; Maybank to H. G. Willingham, February 15, 1950, Maybank Papers; Maybank to Edward Manigault, February 17, 1950, Maybank Papers.

34. Edward Manigault to Burnet Maybank, February 20, 1950, Maybank Papers.

35. Copies of the petition are on file in the Waring Papers and the Maybank Papers.

36. *News and Courier,* February 9, 1950; unidentified clipping, Waring Papers. A copy of the Waring press release is on file in the Waring Papers.

37. Frank B. Gilbreth memorandum to T. R. Waring, February 9, 1950, T. R. Waring files.

38. J. C. Phillips to Burnet Maybank, February 18, 1950, Maybank Papers; Maybank to Phillips, February 22, 1950, Maybank Papers.

39. *Evening Post,* March 3, 1950; *Evening Star* (Washington, D.C.), February 27, 1950; unidentified clipping, Waring Papers.

40. *New York Times,* March 19, 1950; *News and Courier,* March 18, 1950, March 19, 1950; unidentified clipping, Waring Papers. A copy of the funding resolution, which died in the state Senate, is on file in the Wright Papers.

41. *News and Courier,* March 10, 1950, April 3, 1950; *Washington Post,* March 18, 1950; *New York Times,* March 17, 1950; *Afro-American,* April 8, 1950.

42. Ibid.

43. *News and Courier,* March 2, 1950, April 22, 1950; *Evening Post,* March 18, 1950; *Savannah News,* April 8, 1950; *Asheville Citizen,* April 4, 1950.

44. *News and Courier,* March 12, 1950, undated clipping, Waring Papers; *Mirror* (New York), undated, Waring Papers; *New York Post,* March 12, 1950.

45. Unidentified clipping, Waring Papers; Burnet Maybank to Ben Scott Whaley, March 8, 1950, Maybank Papers; Maybank to J. Howard McGrath, March 20, 1950, Maybank Papers.

46. U.S., Congress, *Congressional Record* 96: 4930–31.

47. Ibid.

48. Waring to Raymond Pace Alexander, May 4, 1950, Waring Papers; *Chicago Defender,* March 11, 1950, March 18, 1950; Marion Wright to Waring, April 28, 1950, Waring Papers; Wright to Waring, November 16, 1950; *New York Post,* March 4, 1950; *Christian Science Monitor,* April 20, 1950; *News and Courier,* April 29, 1950. A copy of the press release is on file in the Waring Papers.

49. Samuel Grafton, "Lonesomest Man in Town," *Collier's,* April 29, 1950, pp. 20–21 ff.

50. Ibid.

51. *Evening Post,* April 25, 1950. Mail sent to the Warings following appearance of the Grafton profile is on file in the Waring Papers.

52. T. R. Waring to N. G. Sherouse, April 29, 1950, T. R. Waring files.

53. T. R. Waring memorandum, February 2, 1950, T. R. Waring files.

54. T. R. Waring to Ashley Halsey, Jr., April 12, 1950, T. R. Waring files; Halsey to T. R. Waring, April 14, 1950, T. R. Waring files; Halsey to T. R. Waring, April 29, 1950, T. R. Waring files; T. R. Waring to Halsey, April 26, 1950, T. R. Waring files.

55. Ashley Halsey, Jr., to T. R. Waring, May 4, 1950, T. R. Waring files.

56. T. R. Waring to Ashley Halsey, Jr., April 26, 1950, T. R. Waring files.

57. *News and Courier,* May 13, 1950.

58. Unidentified clipping, August 29, 1949, Waring Papers; John McCray to Warings, January 28, 1950, Waring Papers; McCray to Elizabeth Waring, March 13, 1950, Waring Papers; Waring to McCray, March 16, 1950, Waring Papers.

59. Clement interview; *Evening Post,* June 3, 1950; *News and Courier,* June 3, 1950; Waring to Anne and Stanley Warren, July 5, 1950, Waring Papers; *The State,* May 24, 1950; "Fielder's Choice," *Time,* July 24, 1950, pp. 17–18.

60. *San Francisco Examiner,* August 30, 1950; *San Francisco News,* August 29, 1950. The transcript of the sentencing proceeding is on file in the Waring Papers.

61. *San Francisco Chronicle,* January 11, 1951; Frederic Nerney to Waring, July 20, 1951, Waring Papers.

62. *Evening Post,* May 13, 1950; *The State,* October 1, 1950, October 3, 1950, October 6, 1950, October 11, 1950; *Florence News,* September 30, 1950; *News and Courier,* October 3, 1950.

63. Except where otherwise noted, the discussion in the remainder of this chapter is drawn from correspondence, memoranda, and reports in the J. Waties Waring file, U.S. Department of Justice.

64. Waring to Theodore Poston, April 4, 1950, Waring Papers.

65. Theodore Poston to Waring, April 13, 1950, Waring Papers.

66. Waring to Walter White, October 6, 1950, Waring Papers.

67. *Reminiscences,* pp. 307–308; *New York Post,* October 11, 1950.

68. Ibid.; Justice Department file.

69. *New York Times,* 10 October 1950. Mrs. Waring's note and a copy of the press release are on file in the Waring Papers.

70. *The State,* October 10, 1950, October 12, 1950; *New York Times,* October 12, 1950.

71. *News and Courier,* October 11, 1950.

72. Waring to agent in charge, Charleston FBI office, October 12, 1950, Waring Papers; Waring to agent in charge, Savannah FBI office, October 12, 1950, Waring Papers; Waring to Walter White, October 12, 1950, Waring Papers; Waring to Harry S Truman, October 13, 1950, Waring Papers.

73. Ann Hyde to Warings, October 14, 1950, Waring Papers; Hyde interview; *New York Post,* October 11, 1950.

74. *New York Post,* October 12, 1950.

75. *Evening Post,* October 10, 1950, October 13, 1950; *News and Courier,* October 11, 1950, October 17, 1950; *The Record,* October 12, 1950.

76. *News and Courier,* October 17, 1950, October 18, 1950, October 21, 1950. A copy of the poem is in the T. R. Waring files.

77. *Evening Post,* October 17, 1950, October 30, 1950.

78. Frank G. Gilbreth to John S. Williams, October 21, 1950, T. R. Waring files; Gilbreth to Paul Sann, October 25, 1950, T. R. Waring files.

79. Paul Sann to Frank B. Gilbreth, October 26, 1950, T. R. Waring files.

80. Robert S. Allen to James F. Byrnes, October 17, 1950, Byrnes Papers; Byrnes to Allen, October 28, 1950, Byrnes Papers.

81. T. R. Waring to James F. Byrnes, November 1, 1950, Byrnes Papers; Robert S. Allen to Byrnes, October 30, 1950, Byrnes Papers.

82. T. R. Waring memorandum, February 2, 1950, T. R. Waring files.

83. T. R. Waring to Ashley Halsey, Jr., October 17, 1950, T. R. Waring files; T. R. Waring interview.

84. Ashley Halsey, Jr., to T. R. Waring, October 23, 1950, T. R. Waring files; Halsey to T. R. Waring, November 24, 1950, T. R. Waring files; T. R. Waring to Halsey, November 30, 1950, T. R. Waring files. A copy of Halsey's draft editorial is in the T. R. Waring files.

85. Burnet Maybank to Peyton Ford, November 30, 1950, Maybank Papers; Ford to Maybank, November 29, 1950, Maybank Papers.

86. Clark interview; Cornwell interview.

87. *The State,* November 27, 1950; *New York Post,* November 27, 1950.

88. James E. Folsom to Waring, December 5, 1950, Waring Papers; *The State,* November 28, 1950.

89. *News and Courier,* November 27, 1950.

90. Waring to James Dombrowski, November 7, 1950, Waring Papers; Jack Leland memorandum to T. R. Waring, undated, T. R. Waring files. A transcript of the radio broadcast is on file in the Waring Papers.

91. Jack Leland memorandum to T. R. Waring, undated, T. R. Waring files.

92. *News and Courier,* November 25, 1950.

93. *News and Courier,* December 7, 1950.

94. *News and Courier,* November 25, 1950; U.S., Congress, *Congressional Record* 96: A7382–83.

95. *Reminiscences,* p. 316; *Florence Morning News,* December 16, 1950; *The State,* November 9, 1950, November 10, 1950, November 19, 1950.

96. *Reminiscences,* p. 310.

Chapter 7

1. Sweatt v. Painter, 339 U.S. 629, 634 (1950); McLaurin v. Oklahoma, 339 U.S. 637 (1950); *Reminiscences,* p. 340.

2. Waring to Thurgood Marshall, November 14, 1949, Waring Papers; Waring to Walter White, January 6, 1950, Waring Papers. A copy of the Council brief is in the Waring Papers.

3. *Lighthouse and Informer,* February 2, 1952; *Reminiscences,* p. 340.

4. The statistics are drawn largely from the record of *Briggs* v. *Elliott,* a copy of which is in the Waring Papers; *Reminiscences,* p. 341.

5. J. A. DeLaine to Elizabeth Waring, September 23, 1950, Waring Papers; Figg interview. J. A. DeLaine's efforts are well told in Kluger, *Simple Justice,* ch. 1.

6. Kluger, *Simple Justice,* ch. 1.

7. *Reminiscences,* p. 345; Figg interview; *The State,* November 18, 1950.

8. Waring to Hubert T. Delany, June 28, 1951, Waring Papers; Delany to Waring, July 24, 1951, Waring Papers; Delany to Waring, July 30, 1951, Waring Papers.

9. Tear sheets of the newspaper column drawn from the interview are in the Waring Papers.

10. Carl T. Rowan to Warings, January 22, 1951, Waring Papers; Rowan, *South of Freedom,* pp. 83–100.

11. J. Waties Waring file, U.S. Department of Justice; *News and Courier,* January 11, 1951; Walter White to Francis E. Walter, January 12, 1951, Waring Papers; White to Waring, January 18, 1951, Waring Papers; unidentified clipping, Waring Papers.

12. The texts of Governor Byrnes' inaugural address and address to the general assembly are part of the *Briggs* record, Waring Papers; *News and Courier,* May 20, 1951, April 1, 1951; *Florence Morning News,* April 3, 1951.

13. A copy of Sturcken's oration is reprinted in the New York *Herald Tribune,* June 12, 1951.

14. Waring to James Dombrowski, May 10, 1951, Waring Papers; *Herald Tribune,* June 12, 1951; *Lighthouse and Informer,* undated clipping, Waring Papers; *Pittsburgh Courier,* June 9, 1951.

15. Mrs. Waring's diary (hereinafter cited as Elizabeth Waring diary) is in the Waring Papers.

16. Ibid.; Cornwell interview; *Reminiscences,* p. 358.

17. Cornwell interview. Unless otherwise indicated, the discussion of the hearing which follows is drawn from the *Briggs* record, a copy of which is in the Waring Papers, and from *News and Courier,* May 29, 1951, May 30, 1951, and *The State,* May 29, 1951, May 30, 1951. See also, for example, *Afro-American,* June 6, 1951; "Races: Segregation's Day in Court," *Newsweek,* June 11, 1951, p. 30.

18. Elizabeth Waring diary.

19. Figg interview.

20. Elizabeth Waring diary.

21. Ibid.; *Reminiscences,* pp. 336–337; unpublished interview, Waring Papers.

22. *Reminiscences,* p. 355; *News and Courier,* May 29, 1951; Cornwell interview.

23. *Lighthouse and Informer,* June 2, 1951; Cornwell interview.

24. *Lighthouse and Informer,* June 2, 1951; *New York Post,* May 29, 1951.

25. Elizabeth Waring diary.

26. Cornwell interview.

27. Elizabeth Waring diary.

28. Ibid.

29. Ibid.

30. *Reminiscences,* pp. 358–360.

31. *News and Courier,* June 2, 1951, June 15, 1951, undated clipping, Waring Papers.

32. T. R. Waring interview; *News and Courier,* June 1, 1951, May 30, 1951, undated clipping, Waring Papers; *Florence Morning News,* June 13, 1951, June 7, 1951.

33. Waring to Hubert T. Delany, June 28, 1951, Waring Papers; Elizabeth Waring diary.

34. Elizabeth Waring diary.

35. John J. Parker to Waring, June 16, 1951, Waring Papers; Elizabeth Waring diary.

36. Waring to John J. Parker, June 18, 1951, Waring Papers; Waring to Parker, June 19, 1951, Waring Papers; captioned envelope, Waring Papers; *Evening Post,* June 23, 1951; inscribed copy of *Briggs* dissent, Waring Papers.

37. Briggs v. Elliott, 98 F. Supp. 532, 535 (E.D.S.C., 1951).

38. Ibid., p. 537.

39. *Cleveland Press,* August 14, 1951; 98 F. Supp. at 540.

40. 98 F. Supp. 542.

41. Ibid., pp. 546–48.

42. John W. Hester to John J. Parker, June 25, 1951, John J. Parker Papers; Hester to Parker, June 29, 1951, Parker Papers; Armistead L. Boothe to Parker, June 26, 1951, Parker Papers; Henry Upson Sims to Parker, June 28, 1951, Parker Papers.

43. John J. Parker to Henry Upson Sims, July 2, 1951, Parker Papers; Figg interview; *Herald Tribune,* June 28, 1951, quoting Columbia *Record* editorial.

44. T. R. Waring to James F. Byrnes, June 22, 1951, T. R. Waring files; Byrnes to Waring, June 27, 1951, T. R. Waring files.

45. Elizabeth M. Ford to Waring, May 29, 1951, Waring Papers; undated captioned clipping from Columbia *Record,* Waring Papers; Elizabeth Waring diary; Myles Horton to Waring, June 26, 1951, Waring Papers; Nathan B. Kogan to Waring, June 27, 1951, Waring Papers; Waring to James Dombrowski, June 26, 1951, Waring Papers; Aubrey Williams to Waring, June 29, 1951, Waring Papers; *Herald Tribune,* June 28, 1951.

46. Waring to Hubert T. Delany, June 28, 1951, Waring Papers; *Pittsburgh Courier,* July 7, 1951.

47. Waring to Hubert T. Delany, June 28, 1951, Waring Papers.

48. Ibid.

49. Thurgood Marshall to author, July 8, 1985; Marshall to Waring, July 24, 1951, Waring Papers; Waring to Marshall, June 25, 1951, Waring Papers; Marshall to Waring, July 6, 1951, Waring Papers; Waring to Marshall, July 9, 1951, Waring Papers.

50. Thurgood Marshall to Waring, July 24, 1951, Waring Papers. A copy of the *Briggs* jurisdictional statement is in the Waring Papers.

51. Hubert T. Delany to Waring, July 24, 1951, Waring Papers; Delany to Waring, July 30, 1951, Waring Papers.

52. Waring to Thurgood Marshall, July 26, 1951, Waring Papers.

53. T. R. Waring memorandum, undated, T. R. Waring files.

54. Julian Krawcheck to T. R. Waring, August 4, 1951, T. R. Waring files.

55. T. R. Waring to Julian Krawcheck, August 6, 1951, T. R. Waring files.

56. *Cleveland Press,* August 14, 1951; T. R. Waring to Julian Krawcheck, August 20, 1951, T. R. Waring files.

57. *News and Courier,* July 3, 1951.

58. *News and Courier,* October 11, 1951; *Lighthouse and Informer,* October 13, 1951.

59. *News and Courier,* October 10, 1951, September 21, 1951.

60. *Evening Post,* October 16, 1951. Davis' role in the litigation is discussed in William H. Harbaugh, *Lawyer's Lawyer: The Life of John W. Davis* (New York: Oxford, 1973), ch. 28.

61. Waring to Anne and Stanley Warren, January 9, 1951, Waring Papers; Waring to John Hammond, October 17, 1951, Waring Papers.

62. M. H. Ross to Waring, August 13, 1951, two letters, Waring Papers.

63. Waring to Waitstill H. Sharp, November 8, 1951, Waring Papers; Waring to M. H. Ross, August 17, 1951, Waring Papers; Waring to Ross, October 30, 1951, Waring Papers.

64. M. H. Ross to Waring, November 10, 1951, Waring Papers; Waring to Ross, November 14, 1951, Waring Papers.

65. Paul A. Johnston to Waring, December 6, 1951, Waring Papers; Waring to Johnston, December 10, 1951, Waring Papers.

66. Waring to M. H. Ross, December 10, 1951, Waring Papers.

67. John J. Parker to Waring, January 2, 1952, Waring Papers; Waring to Parker, January 3, 1952, Waring Papers; Parker to Waring, January 5, 1952, Waring Papers; Waring to Parker, January 8, 1952, Waring Papers.

68. Briggs v. Elliott, 342 U.S. 350–52 (1952).

69. Waring to Nathan B. Kogan, February 6, 1952, Waring Papers; Waring to Harry S Truman, January 26, 1952, Waring Papers; Waring to John J. Parker, undated, Waring Papers.

70. Waring to John J. Parker, February 11, 1952, Waring Papers; Parker to Waring, February 13, 1952, Waring Papers.

71. *New York Times,* February 4, 1952; *Amsterdam News,* February 22, 1952; *Pittsburgh Courier,* March 22, 1952; *News and Courier,* January 29, 1952, February 8, 1952; R. K. Wise to Waring, February 4, 1952, Waring Papers.

72. *News and Courier,* undated clipping, Waring Papers, February 6, 1952, February 22, 1952; *Evening Record* (Rock Hill, S.C.), quoted in ibid., February 22, 1952.

73. *News and Courier,* February 22, 1952.

74. Mrs. E. C. Thomas to Waring, January 5, 1952, Waring Papers; Waring to Thomas, February 8, 1952, Waring Papers; Brown interview; Cornwell interview.

75. Waring to John Hammond, February 15, 1952, Waring Papers; Elizabeth Waring diary; Waring to Anne and Stanley Warren, January 9, 1952, Waring Papers.

76. Waring to Benjamin Mays, March 29, 1952, Waring Papers; Waring to John Hammond, February 15, 1952, Waring Papers; *Reminiscences,* pp. 375–376.

77. Waring to John Hammond, February 15, 1952, Waring Papers; Brown interview; *Afro-American,* November 29, 1954; *Pittsburgh Courier,* undated clipping, Waring Papers.

78. *New York Times,* February 24, 1952; unidentified clipping, Waring Papers; memorandum on file in Waring Papers, Myles Horton to Waring, undated, Waring Papers.

Chapter 8

1. John J. Parker to Waring, April 22, 1952, Waring Papers; Waring to Parker, April 25, 1952, Waring Papers; Waring to Parker, February 14, 1955, Waring Papers.

2. *New York Post,* March 9, 1952.

3. Waring to L. Harrison Thayer, February 28, 1952, Waring Papers; *Philadelphia Tribune,* March 11, 1952; *New York Times,* April 17, 1952, May 11, 1952, May 20, 1952, June 14, 1952; *Afro-American,* May 24, 1952; "Judge Waring on the Civil Rights Issue," *Nation,* June 7, 1952, pp. 540–542; Waring to Wilfred H. Kerr, March 11, 1952, Waring Papers.

4. Unidentified clipping, Waring Papers; Waring to Harry S Truman, June 9, 1952, Waring Papers; Waring to Adlai Stevenson, August 12, 1952, Waring Papers.

5. Sadie Alexander to Elizabeth Waring, March 13, 1952, Waring Papers.

6. *News and Courier,* February 25, 1952; T. R. Waring to Frank J. Sterzel, February 25, 1952, T. R. Waring files; T. R. Waring memorandum to staff, T. R. Waring files; Elizabeth Waring to Ethel Payne, June 4, 1952, Waring Papers; *Pittsburgh Courier,* May 30, 1952. A copy of Judge Waring's letter to the *Times* is in the Waring Papers.

7. *Lighthouse and Informer,* May 30, 1952.

8. Waring to Walter White, February 4, 1952, Waring Papers; White to Waring, February 7, 1952, Waring Papers; Waring to White, February 9, 1952, Waring Papers.

9. Walter White to Waring, February 7, 1952, Waring Papers; Waring to White, February 9, 1952, Waring Papers.

10. Walter White to Learned Hand, February 15, 1952, Waring Papers; Waring to White, March 26, 1952, Waring Papers.

11. Walter White to Waring, February 7, 1952, Waring Papers; Waring to White, February 9, 1952, Waring Papers.

12. Walter White to Waring, April 1, 1952, Waring Papers; Waring to White, April 7, 1952, Waring Papers.

13. Arthur B. Spingarn to Waring, April 30, 1952, Waring Papers; Waring to Ralph Bunche, April 29, 1952, Waring Papers; Waring to Spingarn, May 2, 1952, Waring Papers; Bunche to Waring, May 8, 1952, Waring Papers.

14. Hubert T. Delany to Waring, June 19, 1952, Waring Papers; Waring to Walter White, May 29, 1952, Waring Papers; *News and Courier,* July 8, 1952; Waring to Delany, June 18, 1952, Waring Papers; *Chicago Defender,* July 5, 1952.

15. *Chicago Defender,* July 5, 1952; *Afro-American,* July 26, 1952.

16. *Amsterdam News,* June 19, 1954; *Afro-American,* June 19, 1954.

17. Waring to George D. Cannon, June 25, 1954, Waring Papers; *Herald Tribune,* June 27, 1954; *Amsterdam News,* July 3, 1954; George D. Cannon to Robert Dowling, June 21, 1954, Waring Papers; *Afro-American,* undated clipping, Waring Papers.

18. Waring telegram to Henry Pratt Fairchild, March 12, 1953, Waring Papers; Waring to Emma Gelder Sterne, June 3, 1953, Waring Papers; *New York Times,* February 9, 1961; Waring to Marion Wright, May 16, 1953, Waring Papers.

19. *New York Times,* March 21, 1954; James Dombrowski to Waring, April 9, 1954, Waring Papers. For Mrs. Durr's colorful account of the hearing, see *Outside the Magic Circle,* pp. 254–273.

20. Waring to James Dombrowski, March 31, 1954, Waring Papers.

21. Briggs v. Elliott, 103 F. Supp. 920 (E.D.S.C., 1952). Kluger, *Simple Justice,* chs. 25–26, provides the most thorough account of the Supreme Court's involvement with the segregation cases.

22. *News and Courier,* November 20, 1953, October 31, 1953, December 20, 1953, December 8, 1953.

23. *News and Courier,* June 12, 1953, December 21, 1953, December 7, 1953; undated clipping, Waring Papers; December 14, 1953, December 3, 1953.

24. *New York Times,* March 1, 1954; *News and Courier,* March 7, 1954; J. A. DeLaine to Waring, March 25, 1954, Waring Papers. A copy of DeLaine's statement is in the Waring Papers.

25. *Reminiscences,* pp. 367, 377–378; *New York Times,* January 24, 1954, summarizing the Marshall interview; Waring to Thurgood Marshall, November 27, 1953, Waring Papers.

26. *Reminiscences,* pp. 368–379.

27. Ibid., pp. 367, 369; Brown v. Board of Education, 347 U.S. 483, 495 (1954).

28. Brown v. Board of Education, 347 U.S. at 494–95.

29. Figg interview. The briefs and arguments presented to the Supreme Court in the school cases are available in *Landmark Briefs and Arguments of the Supreme Court of the United States: Constitutional Law,* ed. Philip B. Kurland and Gerhard Casper (Arlington, Va.: University Publications of America), vols. 49–49A.

30. *News and Courier,* May 18, 1954; *Reminiscences,* p. 367. A play, "The Man on Meeting Street," performed at the Roosevelt Hotel, November 15, 1959, as part of ceremonies honoring Judge Waring, quoted extensively from an audio recording made at the Waring apartment the evening of the Supreme Court's decision. A script of the play is in the Waring Papers.

31. Maude and Frank Veal telegram to Warings, May 17, 1955, Waring Papers; Ralph Bunche to Waring, May 20, 1954, Waring Papers; Walter Offutt to Waring, June 1, 1954, Waring Papers; *Chicago Defender,* undated clipping, Waring Papers. A transcript of the Vandercook broadcast is on file in the Waring Papers.

32. Marion Wright to Warings, May 17, 1954, Waring Papers; Wright to Samuel Prince, August 2, 1954, Waring Papers.

33. Waring to James Dombrowski, November 6, 1952, Waring Papers; Cornwell interview; Brown interview.

34. *Herald Tribune,* June 17, 1954; John Hammond to Waring, November 2, 1954, Waring Papers; Waring to Hammond, November 4, 1954, Waring Papers.

35. *Afro-American,* November 20, 1954; *New York Times,* November 8, 1954;

News and Courier, November 7, 1954; Waring to Marion Wright, November 12, 1954, Waring Papers.

36. *Evening Post,* November 9, 1954; Marion Wright to Beverley Herbert, December 13, 1954, Waring Papers.

37. Waring to Marion Wright, October 19, 1954, Waring Papers; Waring to Wright, January 12, 1955, Waring Papers.

38. Waring to John McFall, June 8, 1954, Waring Papers; Waring to Marion Wright, November 12, 1954, Waring Papers.

39. *News and Courier,* June 14, 1954, January 19, 1955, July 16, 1954, February 15, 1955, July 29, 1954, January 12, 1955.

40. *New York Times,* May 15, 1954; *Evening Post,* May 17, 1954; *News and Courier,* May 29, 1954.

41. *News and Courier,* May 30, 1954, May 28, 1954, September 13, 1954; "The No. 1 Story," *Time,* January 17, 1955, p. 67; Hodding Carter, "The South and I," *Look,* June 28, 1955, pp. 74–80.

42. Brown v. Board of Education, 349 U.S. 294 (1955). A transcript of the oral argument is in *Landmark Briefs and Arguments.*

43. *News and Courier,* June 11, 1955, July 29, 1955.

44. Briggs v. Elliott, 132 F. Supp. 776, 777 (E.D.S.C., 1955).

45. *News and Courier,* March 26, 1952, August 24, 1955; Walter White telegram to Harry S Truman, March 28, 1952, Waring Papers; *Reminiscences,* p. 380; *Evening Post,* June 17, 1952.

46. *Afro-American,* June 21, 1955.

47. *Record,* August 30, 1955; Thurgood Marshall to editor, Columbia *Record,* September 9, 1955, Waring Papers.

48. Ruby Cornwell to Warings, September 13, 1955, Waring Papers; Waring to Thurgood Marshall, September 17, 1955, Waring Papers.

49. T. R. Waring to Farley Smith, June 11, 1955, T. R. Waring files; W. D. Workman, *The Case for the South* (New York: Devin-Adair Co., 1960), p. 68.

50. T. R. Waring interview; editorial note and "The Southern Case Against Desegregation," *Harper's,* January 1956, pp. 22–24, 39–45.

51. James Jackson Kilpatrick, *The Southern Case for School Segregation* (New York: Crowell-Collier, 1962).

52. U.S., Congress, *Congressional Record* (daily ed.), January 5, 1956, p. 165; T. R. Waring to Mendel Rivers, January 26, 1956, T. R. Waring files; Rivers to T. R. Waring, January 31, 1956, T. R. Waring files; T. R. Waring interview.

53. An audio recording of the program is in the Waring Papers.

54. *New York Times,* August 4, 1957; Waring to editor, *New York Times,* August 5, 1957, Waring Papers.

55. James Reston to Waring, August 8, 1957, Waring Papers; Reston to Waring, August 19, 1957, Waring Papers; Waring to Reston, August 10, 1957, Waring Papers.

56. Waring to Lexington Democratic Club, November 23, 1955, Waring Papers; Waring to John F. Kennedy, November 20, 1960, Waring Papers; Waring to Eleanor Roosevelt, March 29, 1962, Waring Papers.

57. *The State,* March 18, 1956, March 19, 1956, March 20, 1956, March 21, 1956.

58. *News and Courier,* July 19, 1956; *Evening Post,* April 20, 1957; *New York Post,* October 7, 1962. The invitation to the White House reception and admission card are in the Waring Papers.

59. *News and Courier,* August 30, 1963; unidentified clipping, Waring Papers.

60. Clark, *Echo in My Soul,* pp. 95–99; Septima Clark to Elizabeth Waring, October 12, 1962, Waring Papers; Clark interview.

61. Hyde interview.

62. Anne Warren to Rosamond Salmons, January 23, 1968. Mrs. Salmons furnished the author with a copy of the letter.

63. Ibid.

64. Ibid.

65. Ibid.

66. Ibid.

67. Ibid.

68. Roger Baldwin to Elizabeth Waring, January 25, 1968; Carl Rowan to Elizabeth Waring, January 25, 1968; Jane T. Hammes to Anne Warren, January 12, 1968. Ann Hyde furnished the author copies of these and other condolence letters. A copy of Kenneth Clark's eulogy is in the Waring Papers. The judge's *New York Times* obituary appeared in the paper's January 12, 1968, issue.

69. *The State,* January 14, 1968; *News and Courier,* January 13, 1968; *Evening Post,* January 13, 1968.

70. Anne Warren to Rosamond Salmons, January 23, 1968; T. R. Waring interview; Brockinton interview; Tamsberg interview; Gordon Moss to Anne Warren, January 19, 1968, Waring Papers; Warren to Moss, February 8, 1968, Waring Papers.

71. *News and Courier,* January 23, 1968; Brown interview. Joe Brown furnished the author with a copy of the program for the Allen University memorial service.

72. Hyde interview; Cornwell interview; Clark interview. Mrs. Waring's *New York Times* obituary appeared in the paper's November 1, 1968, issue.

73. Charles Kuralt to T. R. Waring, January 17, 1968, T. R. Waring files; T. R. Waring to Kuralt, January 19, 1968, T. R. Waring files; Natalie Towler to Charles Kuralt, undated, Waring Papers. A transcript of the Kuralt broadcast is in the Waring Papers.

74. *New York Times,* November 21, 1968; "Dawn's New Day," *Newsweek,* December 2, 1968, p. 34; Dawn Langley Simmons to author, June 20, 1986.

75. *Charleston Magazine,* April 1976, pp. 8–11; Clark interview; Cornwell interview; Clement interview.

76. Mary Frances Derfner to author, June 16, 1986. Proceedings of City Council, Charleston, S.C., April 14, 1981.

Epilogue

1. Stanley Warren to Warings, December 27, 1951, Waring Papers.

2. T. R. Waring interview; Hyde interview.

3. Waring to Anne Warren, August 8, 1952, Waring Papers; Waring to Anne Warren, October 3, 1952, Waring Papers.

4. Waring to Anne Warren, October 3, 1952, Waring Papers.

5. Ibid.

6. Anne Warren to Waring, undated, Waring Papers; T. R. Waring interview. Informal notes exchanged between Anne Warren and Charleston friends are in the Waring Papers. One of those writing was a cousin, Sarah Toomer, who at the time was working in Mendel Rivers' Charleston office.

7. Eleanor Brown to author, July 12, 1985.

8. T. R. Waring interview; Dorothy Waring interview; Anne Warren to Dorothy Waring, April 17, 1968, T. R. Waring files. Dorothy Waring was for many years secretary to Robert McC. Figg.

9. Clement interview.

10. T. R. Waring interview; Charles Kuralt to Anne Warren, February 29, 1968, Waring Papers.

Bibliographical Note

The J. Waties Waring Papers in the Moorland-Spingarn Research Center at Howard University were the principal source of research for this biography. Judge Waring donated his papers to Howard before his death. As though part of a conscious decision to blot out all record of his life before his marriage to Elizabeth Avery Waring and his earliest civil rights decisions, the papers contain little dating earlier than 1945. The materials that are included in the collection, however, are voluminous and superbly indexed. They include extensive correspondence, transcripts and records of Judge Waring's civil rights cases, transcripts of speeches and addresses, and nearly twenty cartons of newspaper and magazine clippings pertaining to the judge's career and related aspects of the civil rights movement. Particularly since Judge Waring was no more inhibited in private letters than in judicial opinions and public statements, his correspondence, as well as that of the Warings' associates, is a rich source of insight into feelings and attitudes as well as events. The collection of newspaper clippings, moreover, includes a wealth of editorials and articles from the black press, material otherwise difficult, in many instances, to obtain.

Other archival sources also proved valuable. The Citadel papers of Charleston congressman L. Mendel Rivers contained no relevant material; nor did the gubernatorial papers of Senator Strom Thurmond and the Olin Johnston papers in the South Carolina state archives, or the papers of Charleston *News and Courier* editor William Watts Ball at Duke University. The journals of the Charleston city council, however, provided important information regarding Judge Waring's years as city attorney. Senator Burnet Rhett Maybank's papers at the College of Charleston contained interesting material regarding the senator's relationship with Judge Waring—and his later attempts to distance himself from the controversial jurist. The papers of Congressman William Jennings Bryan Dorn in the South Caroliniana collection at the University of South Carolina were an excellent source of material regarding attempts by Dorn and other candidates to use Judge Waring—and his ties to Senator Maybank—as an issue in their 1948 campaign for Maybank's Senate seat. The papers of Judge John J. Parker and Southern Regional Council president Marion A. Wright in the Southern Historical Collection at the University of North Carolina at Chapel Hill were also helpful, as were those of Septima P. Clark at the College of Charleston. Of great value, moreover, was the J. Waties Waring file in the archives of the U.S. Department of Justice, which contains, among other material, reports, memoranda, and correspondence relative to his appointment to the federal bench and FBI investigations of incidents of harass-ment during the Warings' later years in Charleston. As important as any of this archival material, however, was a file that Thomas R. Waring, Jr., had developed on his uncle over many years. The longtime *News and Courier* editor's papers in the archives of the South Carolina Historical Society in Charleston were also fruit-ful. But Tom Waring's private file proved an invaluable source of memoranda and correspondence not otherwise available. Finally, the Waring divorce record in the circuit court of Duval County, Florida, furnished important information regarding that critical episode in the judge's life.

While such sources were essential to my research, a number of recorded inter-views helped to complement the archival material. Ruby Cornwell, Septima Clark, Arthur Clement, and Joseph Arthur Brown were among the Warings' most loyal black friends during the couple's stormy years in Charleston. They provided valu-able impressions and insights regarding the Warings' association with Charleston blacks, the work of local civil rights groups, South Carolina's political climate dur-ing Judge Waring's last years in Charleston, civil rights litigation, and the Warings' treatment by members of the white community. Although from a different perspec-tive, Tom Waring spoke frankly about Judge Waring's family, early life, and ca-reer; the judge's divorce and remarriage; his own relations with his uncle; and the Warings' growing isolation from his relatives and former friends. The judge's cousin Dorothy Waring also shared her impressions, as did Charleston attorneys August Tamsberg and Joseph Young. D. A. Brockinton, Jr., the son of Judge Waring's longtime law partner, also discussed such matters, as well as his father's relationship with the judge and their law practice. The younger Brockinton also spoke with his elderly father about Judge Waring, then shared those recollections and impressions. Robert McC. Figg, who practiced law for years in Charleston and was chief counsel for state officials in the South Carolina counterpart to *Brown v. Board of Education,* discussed the state's strategy for defending segregated schooling before Judge Waring and other members of a three-judge court, as well as the judge's Democratic party activities and appointment to the federal bench. William Jennings Bryan Dorn candidly recalled use of Judge Waring as a political campaign issue, while Elizabeth Waring's daughter Ann Hyde and son David Mills provided a useful perspective regarding their mother's life before her marriage to Judge Waring, as well as insights into her personality. Others interviewed were also helpful. For chronology as well as a flavor of the times, newspaper and maga-zine articles were another important primary source. Of South Carolina papers, the Charleston *News and Courier* and Columbia *State* were most systematically ex-amined. But the clipping files in the Waring Papers, the papers of Waring con-temporaries, and the Justice Department were invaluable as well.

Despite the wealth of primary material available, Judge Waring has been the subject of little scholarly research. The few published articles are indicated in the notes to this book. The most extensive study to date is Terry Robert Lewis' unpub-lished 1970 Ph.D. dissertation, "J. Waties Waring, Spokesman for Racial Justice in the New South" (University of Utah). While drawing little on the Waring Pa-pers, Lewis' study is a competent work.

Index

275